The Heart
of the Order

Also by Thomas Boswell

WHY TIME BEGINS ON OPENING DAY
HOW LIFE IMITATES THE WORLD SERIES
STROKES OF GENIUS

THOMAS BOSWELL

The Heart
of the Order

DOUBLEDAY

NEW YORK · LONDON · TORONTO · SYDNEY · AUCKLAND

Articles appearing herein have previously appeared in *The Washington Post* and *GQ*. "The Hoover: Called Up to Cooperstown" appeared in *The Baseball Hall of Fame 50th Anniversary Book*.

Published by Doubleday, a division of
Bantam Doubleday Dell Publishing Group, Inc.
666 Fifth Avenue, New York, New York 10103

Doubleday and the portrayal of an anchor with a dolphin
are trademarks of Doubleday, a division of Bantam Doubleday Dell Publishing Group, Inc.

Library of Congress Cataloging-in-Publication Data
Boswell, Thomas, 1948–
The heart of the order/Thomas Boswell.—1st ed.
p. cm.
Articles originally published in *The Washington Post*
and various magazines.
1. Baseball—United States. 2. Newspapers—Sections,
columns, etc.—Sports. I. Title.
GV863.A1B66 1989
796.357′0973—dc19 88-31172

To Wendy
Who has taught me
about everything—
except baseball

Contents

—————————————————————

—————————————————————

CONTENTS

Introduction

Talent writes with coffee. Genius writes with wine. That's how Ralph Waldo Emerson, one of the transcendental grape types, put it. I've never seen a wine bottle in a baseball press box, but I've thrown some ugly fits when the coffee ran out on deadline, so I know where I stand. Still, the daily sportswriter, the lifer on the beat, has consolations. After twenty years, even coffee grounds pile up.

This book, like *How Life Imitates the World Series* and *Why Time Begins on Opening Day*, is largely a collection of stories that have appeared in the *Washington Post* and various magazines. Naturally, I picked my favorites. However, a few sections (i.e., those without datelines) are new in the limited sense that I've rewritten or restructured previously published material in any way that pleased me. Whether the material is new or old, what I have tried particularly to do is unite or juxtapose stories in the hope of developing a topic or portrait a step further than journalism's daily slice-of-life necessities encourage.

Newspaper work can be a sort of writer's diary, a raw notebook to himself: This Is How It Seems Today. Only with time, and the variety of perspectives that it's bound to create, are we allowed to step back and see people and institutions as they transform before us. That's the fun of being in the trenches. It makes up for a hundred nights a year on the road and too much mediocre work. You imagine you can outwait anybody or anything. Sooner or later, the picture will come into focus. Then you have a shot at figuring out how it got that way.

That's one difference between a reality writer and a fiction writer. The beat journalist's ultimate goal isn't a dramatic or poetic effect, much as any writer lusts after such moments of luck. Rather, you seek a final portrait—or a small gallery of related and refracted portraits— which can be held beside the living face of your subject in the light of day without the work losing its integrity. "That's right" is what we're after, more than "That's beautiful."

In a sense, a daily sportswriter is like one of those monkeys chained to a keyboard trying to write Shakespeare by accident. It's not a bad methodology for those prone to coffee and facts, rather than wine and imagination. You hang around until the details, the telling episodes, the quotes and your own various best efforts at synthesis begin to make their own compelling case. "Collecting string," reporters call it.

Sooner or later, that string seems to bind itself into a coherent cord— an idea that doesn't embarrass you by snapping when you tug it. I still remember the day a veteran manager, whom I'd interviewed many times over several years, stopped talking and really looked at me. "You're still here," he said, surprised.

Like any professional reporter, I was going to keep scrounging string until I got him as right as I could. I choose to think he respected that.

That manager's boss, however, was a powerful owner whose basic nature I felt more ambivalent about each year. I gathered string on him, too. After about seven years, it started shaping itself into a noose. "Here comes the choirboy," said the owner, sarcastically, when he saw me one spring. "Who'd ever suspect a choirboy?" That remains my favorite baseball compliment.

During the seasons this book covers, 1983 to 1988, I collected a million words' worth of string—a thousand thousand-word stories, roughly speaking. Out of all that, one thread of an idea grew so strong that it now seems like a battleship chain to me. People change. And a lot more radically than we imagine. Either you change yourself or things change you. That's the choice.

The lasting power of baseball for me—beyond the tactical and technical fascinations of the game itself, even beyond the excitement of pennant races and World Series—is watching how the game illuminates and probes the faces of its changing people.

An English prof once wrote on a paper of mine, by way of critiquing my naïve notion that people were pretty much fully formed by voting age, "The biggest shock in life is watching how much your peers change. In twenty years, you won't believe it." Like anyone past forty, I believe now. There is no one Dwight Gooden or Sparky Anderson or Joe DiMaggio or Ozzie Smith. That's why we must keep going back to get another look, so we can sense the next twist of plot.

The Gooden of late 1985 was the definition of Too Good to Be True; a lifetime of circumstances had worked together to help him reach the apex of a 1.63 earned run average. The Gooden of early 1987 was such a different man as to be almost frightening. Here was a twenty-two-year-old trying to come back from drug rehabilitation, professional disappointment and every sort of growing pain and culture shock. Do we really alter this much—and in eighteen months? Is our clay so vulnerable to external events and undeveloped currents in our own natures?

DiMaggio at forty would have run from any reporter. DiMaggio, approaching seventy, waited in a hotel room to talk to me, giving his first in-depth interview since his divorce from Marilyn Monroe. After two hours, I was the one out of questions. Basically, DiMaggio just wanted to tell folks he'd grown to like 'em and even felt half at ease with them. As his fame slowly shrank to manageable proportions, the reclusive Yankee, with his habitual look of a hunted and affronted creature, gradually broadened until, finally, he could love being Joe D at twilight.

The Sparky Anderson of October 1984 looked like a worried, driven man who might burn out. Old friends were scared for him. Heart attack looked written on him. Somehow, by March of 1985, he was a significantly different man. And the change seems to have stuck. Sparky has remained the same new-and-improved, upbeat-yet-calm, philosophical-yet-competitive person right through the successes and disappointments of his Tigers' amazing 1987 pennant-race comeback victory and shocking playoff defeat.

It's one thing to see Earl Weaver on his home golf course in retirement with his goofball, nut-case gambling buddies. It's quite another—and a shock—to visit him a year later, after his old team has begged, bribed and badgered him into an attempt at a comeback—a return which, in his heart, he suspects is unwise. Finally, we see him going down with the ship as a twenty-five-year Oriole dynasty sinks toward last place. "Stick around long enough and you'll see it all," he says. "That's why you shouldn't stick around too long."

We pretend baseball is primarily a game of teams, when it's more about people. Ted Williams played in only one World Series; Walter Johnson, Hank Aaron and Rogers Hornsby in two each. Who cares or remembers? The team may be the individual's context, but its success is not his definition.

Each season, I find I have less faith in the hard certainty of baseball statistics and more in some attempt at commonsense psychology—murky as that area always is, for individuals or groups. The stats always come too late. They may measure everything, but they explain very little and predict even less. Because people insist on changing.

One summer day in 1987, I looked above Ron Darling's locker in the clubhouse of the New York Mets, who were in the midst of a miserable season as defending world champions. There lay a book titled *The Day They Scrambled My Brains at the Funny Factory*. That title ought to remind us, as it does Yale-student Darling, that statistics should not be confused with the men who create them. Baseball isn't a tabletop game and players aren't numbers. Sometimes they are guys whose brains get scrambled at the funny factory. Who knows why? Some players oversleep and miss games. Some cut rap records at noon but develop a headache by game time and miss a tough southpaw. Some cuss the manager or throw a firecracker at reporters. Some backstab teammates and threaten to settle differences with a punch. Some have wives who sue for divorce, claiming battery, or girlfriends who walk through airport metal detectors while packing pistols.

Every season, baseball tries to teach us that the game has a human, unpredictable heart. And is richer for it. Yet, every year, we insist the game should be less messy than the world around it. We pretend that potential is a hairsbreadth from performance, and that what's been done in the past should be readily duplicable on demand in the future.

The more we judge teams on paper, the more the sport insists that results be forged on the field by actual people. The game is a system in such flux that expectations are smashed to flinders. It drives some people batty. How on earth do preposterously ordinary teams like the '85 Royals, '87 Twins and '88 Dodgers end up as world champions?

"Stats are important. But the mind still rules the individual, and chemistry rules the whole team's mood," says Davey Johnson of the Mets, the only manager with a degree in mathematics. Or as Darling put it that testy summer of '87, "With computers, we think we know everything. What a guy hits with men on base on Tuesdays before Lent. But the stats couldn't tell me why I went from April 22 until July 7 without a win."

Human frailty, fluke injury, lost confidence and the unseen maze of the psyche cause the stats by which baseball lives and breathes to come into being, not the other way round. Those '87 Mets, coming off a 108-win season, were an ideal illustration. In the spring, the rotation of Bobby Ojeda (18–5), Gooden (17–6), Sid Fernandez (16–6), Darling (15–6) and Rick Aguilera (10–7) posed for a beefcake poster on motorcycles, in leather jackets over bare chests. Title: Kings of the Hill. Gooden spent April in drug rehab. Trying to pick up the slack, Ojeda pitched with a sore elbow and blew out his hinge for the season. With his team in need, Darling went seventy-five mysterious days without a win, although he was in perfect health. Three other starters ended on the DL.

That's how synchronism—and imbalance—can turn baseball's nice numbers on their heads. One man's drug problem can aggravate another man's sore elbow, which can strain a third chap's self-esteem, which can make the right fielder grouchy, which can get the second baseman a knuckle sandwich if he isn't careful. "This sport is confidence," says Johnson. "When a team has it, you exceed expected performance and win games you have no business winning. Last year [in 1986], I could've done almost anything and it would've worked."

If baseball in the eighties, with its bewildering succession of one-season winners and dethroned champions, has taught us one distinction, it's the difference between success and excellence. Many in sports think they are the same. They're not. There's no substitute for excellence—not even success.

Success is tricky, perishable and often outside our control; the pursuit of success makes a poor cornerstone, especially for a whole personality. Excellence is dependable, lasting and largely an issue within our own control; pursuit of excellence, in and for itself, is the best of foundations. If the distinction between success and excellence were easy to grasp, we wouldn't have found so many players, managers and teams in disarray in the eighties—particularly in baseball, but in all sports actually.

Whenever bad news hits the sports page, look for a "success story" gone wrong. Whether Billy Martin breaks another bone in another drunken A.M. brawl or Edward Bennett Williams blows apart his Oriole team's sense of financial fair play by paying Fred Lynn $1.2 million a year to malinger, look for people who wanted, more than anything else, to be known as "winners." Look, in other words, for people who saw a game as a way to fame. Look for people who judge themselves by what others think of them. From the day Dave Parker started wearing a Star of David around his neck, saying, "My name is David and I'm a star," it wasn't a terrribly long fall for him to plummet from potential Hall of Famer to stool-pigeon witness, singing on former friends in the Pittsburgh Cocaine Trial.

Whenever we see a player whose performance seems to guide us like a lodestar from decade to decade—whether it be Pete Rose, Carl Yastrzemski, Reggie Jackson or Tom Seaver—we always find a guiding passion for quality and a profound respect for the game. Over the long haul of a whole career, baseball selects for diligent craftsmen. In the end, the plodding Don Suttons, Phil Niekros and Tommy Johns pass the fly-by-nights. Don Mattingly and Wade Boggs—barely prospects when they arrived in the majors—keep getting better until they are batting champions. And Cal Ripken never misses an inning, even when his team is thirty games out of first place.

One midnight deep in July in 1985, I wandered into the Chicago White Sox clubhouse and, nearly two hours after the game, found Carlton Fisk—then age thirty-seven—alone in full weight-lifting regalia, pumping huge amounts of iron in deep squat thrusts. His body, drenched in sweat, did not in the least resemble the Fisk physique that I'd seen for a dozen years. The kid called Pudge had, somehow, gained at least twenty pounds of muscle and transformed himself toward the end of his career into a genuine hulk. Financially, Fisk was set for life. His White Sox were far from first place. What drove Fisk?

"Sometimes on the road I don't leave the yard until 1:30 A.M.," he said, recounting how he took his huge weight set with him to every city in the league. What nagged at Fisk was the sense that he'd left a project unfinished; he couldn't bear to leave it that way. Two years earlier, Fisk and Charley Lau had completely revamped Fisk's swing and made him a very dangerous man. "In Boston, I was a chopper, a real top-hand pull hitter. Everything hooked foul. Suddenly I was getting the bat head out in front better and getting more extension." The result: 26 homers, 86 RBI and third place in the AL MVP voting in '83. Then, just as he'd made his theoretical breakthrough, his old catcher's body let him down. More than 135 men have played 2,000 major league games. Only Bob Boone has ever caught 2,000 games. Fisk calls it "the Dorian Gray position." Not fair, screamed Fisk.

So he decided to race against time. Already five years beyond the age when the likes of Johnny Bench, Yogi Berra and Bill Dickey were on the slide, Fisk worked all winter getting a new body. Make it or break it. If he hurt himself, he could jeopardize his big contract. But he risked it. The goal: pure excellence. Finally, before the end, he was determined to do the thing properly.

In 1985 Fisk hit thirty-seven home runs at the age of thirty-seven; he almost became the first catcher ever to lead the American League in homers. Only those who've studied the inexorable decline of all great backstops know how unprecedented Fisk's season truly was.

Let's emphasize here that nobody, not even Fisk, is all one way or the other. Desire for success and love of excellence coexist in all of us. The question is: Where does the balance lie? In a pinch, what guides us?

To illustrate, listen to the best managers of recent times when they analyze a game. The voice could be that of Whitey Herzog, Dick Williams, Gene Mauch, Anderson, Weaver or Johnson, but the tenor of their comments is the same. They seldom look at the final score. Instead, they discuss how the game should have been played. Usually they shrug off defeats and will discuss what theoretical threads, what possibilities for improvements lay within that game. The win or loss, except in September and October, does not obsess them. Sometimes, not even then.

The second-rate manager, by contrast, is often fixated on the result. His teams, especially under pressure, seem burdened by his absorption with success when they should be focusing on the sort of quality play that would produce victory.

In sports, poise often is nothing more than the ability to row backward toward a goal, focusing on each stroke so intently that we ignore the finish line until we are past it. The instant a team stops living in the moment and starts looking over its shoulder, any disaster can happen. That's when managers preach a "return to fundamentals" and insist, "We have to get back to the things that got us here."

Success can burn up the person who achieves it. Excellence usually feeds whoever has it. For impatient, compulsive men, success may come quickly. But it doesn't tend to last very long. The pressure constantly to remain successful, especially in others' eyes, is exhausting, even killing. That is the real sadness in the New York Yankees of the Steinbrenner era.

An additional burden for the victim of the success mentality is that he's such a competitor that he is threatened by the success of others and resents real excellence. The person fascinated by quality is invigorated when he finds it in others; he can cope with being surpassed, since he respects the nature of the work itself. Don Sutton said of Sandy Koufax, "A lot of people get on top and try to keep others down. Koufax tried to help everybody else get up there with him."

No player in recent times has understood the difference between success and excellence better than Mike Flanagan. Iron Mike the Orioles called him because he would pitch a complete game when the bullpen needed rest, even if he struggled or lost. His personal ERA meant little to him. For years at a time, he would pitch through injuries, once making 157 straight starts. When his Achilles' heel snapped, when his knee blew up on a routine play, when his rotator cuff was frayed, when his elbow rebelled, he simply worked his way back to functionality as quickly as possible—once winning in the playoffs and Series while wearing a ludicrously large knee brace.

One night in 1983 Flanagan left the mound on a stretcher during the first game of a doubleheader. Early prognoses said that, despite his starting the season 6–0, his latest injury would keep him out the whole season. Flanagan went to stay at teammate Rich Dauer's house; they listened to the nightcap on the radio as the Orioles started a slop-tossing rookie right-hander who'd already been shipped back to AAA five times in his career.

The kid pitched a shutout. At his postgame press conference, the rookie was suddenly summoned away by a phone call from someone with an odd-sounding name—a phony monicker, as it proved, which the Orioles used as a secret password when they wanted to exclude outsiders. The phone call of congratulation to Mike Boddicker was from Flanagan. The Orioles won the World Series that season, with Boddicker the pitching hero of both the playoffs and Series and Flanagan back in the rotation, knee brace and all.

Sports reaffirms that, amid the pale pleasure of watching many good losers and bad winners, it is still possible to find good winners, like

Koufax and Flanagan. Think of a group portrait from all our major sports: Vince Lombardi, Dean Smith, Red Auerbach, Chris Evert, Walter Payton, Don Shula, Larry Bird, Joe Paterno, Tom Landry, Jack Nicklaus. They take their places perfectly next to the Herzogs and Weavers, the Andersons and Mauchs, the Seavers and Carltons, the Brocks and Aarons, the Roses and Schmidts of baseball.

As a group, they tend to be inordinately patient because they believe that, in the long run, they won't lose. If they are a bit uncomfortable and testy in the spotlight, it may be because they wish to hide how little our opinions of them matter in their eyes. At times they even seem to hum with a kind of suppressed but powerful inner arrogance that can taste like piety and make them a little hard to swallow.

Of whom do they remind us?

Perhaps the best and most rigorous teacher we ever had.

The math professor who taught us that it wasn't the answer to a specific problem that was important but, rather, learning to appreciate the interlocking coherence of the whole scientific view of the world. The English teacher who showed us the agonies of patience that went into crafting a poem so precise in its choice of words that we could read it a hundred times over fifty years and always find it powerfully true. The teachers, in other words, who taught us that love of learning—for itself—not love of grades, was the beating, enduring heart of education.

So too in games, the guiding principle that most often keeps people oriented through all their passages and changes is a governing passion for excellence. In baseball, that's what you discover at the heart of the order.

Heroes

The Clipper: Safe Haven at Last

WASHINGTON, July 1983 — In a parking lot beside RFK Stadium this week, two dozen middle-aged men, most of them dressed like Connecticut Avenue lawyers, chased one senior citizen as he left the Cracker Jack Old-timers' Classic. Pens and autograph pads in hand, the adults pursued the silver-haired sixty-eight-year-old man, just as they probably lapped at his heels during his days of legend from 1936 until 1951 when he was the Yankee Clipper and, some claim, the greatest player in baseball history.

"Joe, Joe," cried one fellow, "we played a round of golf together five years ago in Jersey." The hero stopped to sign. Finally, he was at ease with age and this endless foolishness called fame. At last, it was almost a pleasure to be Joe DiMaggio.

* * *

3

As DiMaggio opened his hotel door, he tucked in his shirt and buckled his belt. Once he might have been too formal or too leery to open his door when he was still in disarray. Now he takes things as they come and wonders why it took him so long to learn the trick. Now he'll let his hair down, to a degree, and chat for ninety minutes about almost anything.

DiMaggio knows many baseball fans were either children or unborn when he retired. They never saw him play. Since he's spent much of his life avoiding interviews, he's also left a spotty record of his thoughts about the game he loved. Many current fans have never heard him, either.

"It's only in the last few years that I outgrew that [reticence]," said DiMaggio. "It has been a tremendous change for me. I finally conquered that part . . . I find myself a lot more comfortable with people now. It gradually disappeared with the years.

"It sounds strange, but going through those TV commercials [over the last ten years] for Mr. Coffee and the Bowery bank in New York has helped a lot. I gradually broke down the barriers."

Perhaps sadly, it took DiMaggio sixty years to learn that even the simplest communication—outside, perhaps, the close-knit settings of family or long friendship—is a form of acting, a hard and conscious and practiced task of projecting some bearable public version of yourself.

"For a long time [until he was almost sixty], I would cringe, avoid crowds. It was not for reasons of being aloof . . . I just didn't feel natural. People said, 'You're so relaxed on the ball field.' I'd say, 'But I knew what I was doing . . .'

"Before a camera, or a group of people, I didn't have a performance to give. [So] I was very, very shy. I wanted to be away from people. I thought I didn't have that much to offer, that much to say, so I used to go into my shell."

What did he find that he had to offer?

"My gentleness," he said softly. ". . . I'm one of the easiest-[going] guys, and I'm patient with people. Usually I don't mind standing and signing . . . I think I should be flattered . . . the fans have been very good to me. Why not show up? I feel I owe something, as long as they want me.

"[Sometimes] I still balk. I hate banquets with a passion. There are certain people I don't ever feel at ease with . . . I don't do talk shows, though I don't mind sport shows . . . When a lot of people see you and start yelling, 'Hey, Joe,' that's embarrassing. But I'm oblivious to a lot of that now. I try to live a normal life."

Actually, DiMaggio is so infatuated with discovering that the public world need not be a recluse's nightmare that his schedule is now one long, leisurely but persistent round of appearances, cameo bows at old-timers' games and golf outings.

"I still have to work for a living," he exaggerated. "At least, I'm not really retired in the sense of doing whatever I feel like. Sometimes I wonder if I don't spend my life on airplanes. I took fourteen trips to New York last year."

If DiMaggio flies and appears and signs and generally circulates within the baseball world, then that's because he chooses to. Unmarried since he was divorced from his second wife, Marilyn Monroe, in 1955, DiMaggio leads an itinerant bachelor life, keeping a home in San Francisco, but materializing almost anywhere. The phone rings. "I'm heading to Vancouver tomorrow," DiMaggio tells an old friend. "They've built a new stadium. I'll take a tour around, see what it has to offer." Because of his large family—he's one of nine children and has a son, forty-two, by his first marriage, and two granddaughters—DiMaggio has relatives or friends almost anywhere you could stick a pin in the map.

DiMaggio is in no danger of being mistaken for the Electric Horseman. Perhaps it's a question of style, more than anything else. Where another man might seem to be flirting with the limelight so it won't forget him, DiMaggio is so confident of his place that his public appearances have the air of a royal favor. Perhaps a sense of self is as much a gift as a thing earned.

For instance, DiMaggio never reaches, and deigns to accept only a fraction of what is handed to him. When Grecian Formula offered him a quarter of a million dollars to pitch their stuff, DiMaggio declined. "It was a helluva lot of money and I had that beautiful pepper hair then," he said without a trace of anything in his voice. "It isn't that I don't like money, it's just . . ."

He shrugs. He can't explain. DiMaggio doesn't tint his hair and won't imply that he does. Just this week, Polident put out a feeler to see if he'd hawk their denture powder. "Tell 'em I've still got my own teeth," said DiMaggio to the middleman with a laugh. "Give that one to Martha Raye."

If the bustle of the world rolls off DiMaggio's back more easily than it did in his tormented decades as one of the country's dominant celebrities, it is, in part, a mere question of volume. The morning he separated from Monroe, photographers were perched in trees, watching the windows of their Beverly Hills house. He couldn't even leave his wife without answering reporters' questions on the way to the car.

Now his fame is almost old-shoe, a comfortable national institution like the way his name recurs as an American touchstone, whether in *The Old Man and the Sea,* "Mrs. Robinson," or the latest remake of *Farewell, My Lovely.*

A year ago, as DiMaggio was leaving Cooperstown after a visit to the Hall of Fame, he and a friend were deep in conversation and got lost. "That's the trouble with good b.s.," said DiMaggio. "You miss your turn."

Finally they hailed a fellow on a tractor to ask directions. The farmer, apparently unaware of DiMaggio's identity, leaned on the passenger door and, speaking across DiMaggio to the driver, began saying, "You go down about three miles . . ." Then, casually, in mid-sentence, he patted DiMaggio familiarly on the arm and said, "I see you, Joe," then finished his instructions. DiMaggio loves to tell this story. If only America had 200 million more such people of simple dignity, his life would be perfect. Even so, it's getting easier.

DiMaggio's present is easy to take and the past is now at a safe enough distance that redigesting it is all pleasure. He's reached the reminiscing age. Today's athletes say of the honors and records, "It doesn't mean much to me now. But I'll probably enjoy it when I'm old."

DiMaggio is enjoying it.

"You look in those old pictures at the people who attended ball games years ago. They came in straw hat, jacket and tie. Talk about a change. I know those were just the ways of the days. But now, when I see those pictures, I marvel at that. We weren't even aware of it."

DiMaggio knows it's baseball doctrine that pining for the old days gets you the raspberry. But he can't help it. He thinks his game was better.

"We only had sixteen teams then. It has to be watered down now. When they keep re-signing fellows like [Gaylord] Perry and [Jim] Kaat, what does that tell you?

"When I played ball, I played because I loved it," DiMaggio says later. "It gripes me when some of these [current] players find fault with the front office because the owner wants them to give 100 percent effort and gets mad when they don't . . .

"I played for the manager and my teammates, not for the owners. Of course, we didn't get no static from upstairs then," he says, in almost the only grammatical remnant of a childhood spent near Fisherman's Wharf in San Francisco.

For DiMaggio the game, at least as he remembers it, was an all-consuming craft—an art into which any man of honor would pour himself completely, defining himself by the pure hard line of his performance. "I wasn't one of those batting cage men. I went to the outfield every day and worked. I made a ritual of charging ground balls so I could adjust my way of straightening up to throw . . . Dom had ability, but he didn't have room to roam," he says of his brother Dom of the Boston Red Sox. "I did . . . I expressed myself . . .

"People say I was graceful. I was not aware of it. I did everything my normal way . . . I practiced hard. I was a complete player because I worked at it. I remember how good a fungo hitter Earl Combs was. He could put the ball just inches beyond your glove."

DiMaggio wonders if this generation has spent as many hours on baseball's vital details. He remembers working with a rookie named Reggie Jackson. "Reggie didn't mind working," says DiMaggio, "but his eyes must have bothered him even then. We'd come out two hours early. He'd pound that glove and the [fly] ball would land five feet away."

Finally Jackson could catch what he could reach, but his throws became a small symbol of the age to DiMaggio. "Getting rid of the ball quickly is how you throw somebody out. Reggie takes all that windup and the fans go 'Ooooh, aaah' because he had a strong arm. But he never threw anybody out. I guess it was more important to him to show off his arm." More to his taste is Steve Garvey, a player who has his full respect. "He's like Malicious [the racehorse]. He just keeps plodding along."

When it's time for DiMaggio to judge himself, he has a shocking preference. The fifty-six-game hitting streak is not his choice of monument. "Fifty-six is a helluva good record. Everybody's made a big thing of it. But the thing that's most important to me is that we won ten pennants and nine world titles in my thirteen years."

Only one unattained record still pricks DiMaggio to, if not pique, then an annoyed perplexity. New York brought him fame, wealth and an adoring media that gave him such an overlay of the mythical that it will probably remain forever impossible to judge where DiMaggio really belongs among the game's all-time top-ten players. But New York also brought him his cross—Yankee Stadium, a park whose Death Valley seemed constructed specially to thwart DiMaggio. Call it the House (Babe) Ruth Built and DiMaggio wanted to tear down.

"I don't like to say this about myself, but I would have hit 76 home runs [instead of 46] in 1937 if I'd played in a normal park," he says. "Mel Allen counted all the balls I hit to the warning track. I'll admit it got discouraging. I'd hit the ball 430 where it used to be 457 feet and the guy wouldn't even have to make a sensational catch . . ."

Within the last year, statistician Pete Palmer tabulated every home and away game of DiMaggio's career. Palmer found that in 880 games in Yankee Stadium, DiMaggio had 148 homers, 720 RBI and a .315 average. In 856 games on the road, he had 213 homers, 817 RBI and a .333 average. So it's likely that Death Valley cost DiMaggio perhaps 75 homers, 150 RBI and 20 points in average. In '37 DiMaggio had 27 homers on the road and 19 at home; Yankee Stadium probably cost him 10 homers and an outside chance at breaking Ruth's record.

If DiMaggio's words seem those of a prideful man, it is the last impression he would want to give, and a largely false one, too. DiMaggio has an enormous sense of himself and his deeds, but he seldom seems full of himself. He'll tell tales on himself.

"[Manager Joe] McCarthy wouldn't let me bunt. But once I tried anyway. I fouled the ball off so [wildly] that it tipped my nose. I almost decapitated myself. I said, 'That's it for bunting.' "

Before his last season, DiMaggio talked himself into coming back. "That was my first mistake," he says, leaving the exotic impression that it was his first basic mistake in baseball judgment. "I hit .263. I remember that average better than the good ones."

The next spring, in '52, he hung 'em up, though the Yankees told him he could play in any seventy-five games of his choosing, at no cut in salary. "It didn't take long for me to get over retiring," he says. "Within the year, I'd say, I went to one game and watched the St. Louis Browns play in '52. I stood way out in left field on a hill. Nobody saw me . . . My injuries were there. They were just too much . . .

"I knew my body. I understood myself."

The Wizard:
The Land of Oz

March 1988—If you dragged Ozzie Smith out of a plane wreck, he'd probably be filing his nails. If you dug him out of an avalanche, he might be humming. Nothing seems to ruffle his serenity. Not many shortstops wear a stickpin and French cuffs to the park. Like that cartwheel into a full backflip that has become his signature before World Series games, he is a combination of flamboyance and utter precision, apparent risk and real control. When it comes to sangfroid, he's an international jewel thief masquerading as a ballplayer; he could steal second and third in black tie. What the world sees of Osborne Earl Smith—born in Mobile, raised in Watts, scorned in San Diego, beloved in St. Louis and headed to Cooperstown—is exactly what he wants it to see. This is a man who's made himself, polished himself, down to the cuticles. If he has to go to Montreal to find the proper cut in a shirt, then let's go.

9

To the Wizard of Oz, image and reality are not terribly far apart. He wants to please, and not just from "Play ball" to last out but all the time, the way you're supposed to if you're the Real Thing. It's a project and worth the effort. If you ask him to be in Manhattan to shoot a magazine cover at noon, then a little thing like getting up at 5 A.M. in St. Louis and flying through a blizzard isn't going to stop him. "No, no. I'll be there. You don't have to reschedule." He'll get off the plane after five hours of delay without a wrinkle or a frown. Take him to a very-late-afternoon lunch—by now everybody's starving—and what does he do when a couple of stuffy joints turn his little party down? Does he take offense? Make a scene? Play the $2-million-a-year super-star? No, he stands in a cold drizzle, signs autographs for New York strangers (Mets fans, for crying out loud) and says, "Think they got a Wendy's on Park Avenue?"

Smith is the kind of guy who, when somebody rents a limo to drive him around town, gives the chauffeur a twenty-dollar tip out of his own pocket. Then he looks around to see what else he can do for the guy. Something a little personal. Something to remember him by. Hmmm, what about these steak knives which the maître d' at Smith and Wollensky gave Ozzie, and which he was too gracious to refuse? "I can't take these knives through the metal detector," says Smith, extending the Smith and Wollensky box to the driver. "But they're nice. You could give them to your wife."

"Thanks."

"Tell her I'm the Smith."

Ozzie Smith always gives his gifts with a story attached. He can't help offering an extra effort. The St. Louis Cardinals make sure somebody's assigned to drag Ozzie away from crowds, or he'll miss supper. He'll always spot somebody who'd really like those steak knives. When talent, style and decency collide, that's what happens. You get a poor skinny kid who, somehow, grows up to know his own value entirely. He finds it appropriate to dress with elegance and live unashamedly in a mansion, yet he doesn't forget the value of other people.

You get a common touch in an uncommon man.

That is one Ozzie Smith.

What would you think of a major league ballplayer who took the following positions in the space of a three-hour conversation?

• Major league umpires are incompetent and racially prejudiced. "The umpiring was better in college . . . Their judgment is bad, their eyesight is bad, their level of consistency is terrible . . . Since my contract, my strike zone has all of a sudden become a lot larger. I have to think a lot of umpires are trying to call me out just so they can show me that they're the boss."

• The national baseball press is almost as bad as the umpires and won't give his team a fair shake.

• His team is systematically undervalued and denied credit because its nucleus of everyday players is black. "I think we're hit with the stereotype of 'Cardinal runs' because we have a group of black guys in our lineup . . . It took me a long time to figure it out, but that's what people are getting at, that's why it's so different with us . . . We're not supposed to be able to do anything but run . . . Our club's had to apologize [for winning] for years. It irritates me . . . The double Vince Coleman slapped over third base with two strikes on him to win Game Three in the [1987] Series—if George Brett had done that, it'd be called 'an art.' It's different when we do it."

• He should've won the Most Valuable Player Award last year.

• His team lost the '85 World Series because of an ump's bad call. Then his team lost another Series, in '87, to an inferior team because, he suspects, the winners cheated, turning on air blowers when the Cardinals were at bat—"though I can't prove it."

• The former star slugger on his own team let the club down by not taking a painkilling shot so he could play in the World Series. "A lot of our players soured on Jack Clark when he didn't try to come back . . . [He] should have taken a shot . . . Everybody would have at least known that he had tried."

• His own manager, Whitey Herzog, also let the club down in mid-Series. "I felt that the team needed a vote of confidence—for the manager to say, 'You guys are as good or better than they are.' But Whitey kept saying, 'I don't know why we're here,' like he expected us to lose. I kept waiting for him to say something positive, but he never did. Maybe he figured we knew how he felt, and he was just trying to lull the other team to sleep. But some guys didn't understand that. We needed a boost."

• Bat corkers like Howard Johnson of the Mets should have asterisks beside their records so everybody knows they cheated.

• The New York Mets are disrespectful jerks, but the San Francisco Giants are worse. They're scared loudmouths. And by the way, Jeffrey Leonard should know that if he wants trouble, Mr. Leonard's the guy likely to get hurt.

• The San Diego Padres, the club he once played for, are still out to

11

get him. They wouldn't pay him what he was worth then because "I really don't think they wanted to pay a little black boy from Watts who did not hit home runs that much money." He's sure that, years later, one of their pitchers was ordered, by somebody, to hit him.

If you heard that this player was concerned that the CIA had planted eavesdropping devices in his glove, or that the KGB was putting arsenic in his sunflower seeds, you might not be surprised.

For more details, see his new autobiography, *Wizard*. It's all there, expanded tenfold. Yes, this is Ozzie, too.

On the back of his uniform should be the word "Shazam." Instead of "1," his number should be "8," but turned sideways, because the possibilities he brings to his position are almost infinite.

In a sport whose fans live to argue—and even relish the aggravation of cross-referencing its generations—the elders of the tribe show an almost unique deference to Smith. Few, if any, deny that he is the greatest defensive shortstop in history. "You feel he could field a ground ball while juggling three oranges and get the guy out without dropping a one," wrote famed sportswriter Jim Murray. Yes, magic and the circus are the right metaphoric ballparks for Smith. In childhood, magic fascinates us; so much seems impossible until it is explained. That's why, as adults, when someone does what's never been done, we return momentarily to the wonder of childhood. And that's why Smith often seems to border on the fictional. Other players talk about him like a cartoon hero or a movie character—it's always "Ozzie this" or "Did you see what the Wiz did last night?" Never a last name. Like Reggie, he's the only one.

Yet to understand Smith as a natural phenomenon is to deliberately misunderstand him—and wrong him—as much as if we thought the magician's tricks were done without endless practice. Smith is, by temperament, a student of the game who devises new ways to do the old. For instance, he was the first to realize that, on Astroturf, you could dig a ground ball out of the hole backhanded while skidding on your knees in a controlled slide, then pop to your feet and throw in one sudden movement. The effect is that of an arcade-game toy, grown to human size, springing out of the ground through a trapdoor. Smith also was one of the first to use the deliberate turf-hop throw to first, recognizing a millisecond edge when he saw one.

However, he is also, by acrobatic talent, an innovator who stretches the boundaries of infield play. Only a man who can take the field doing backflips could attempt the pivots at second base that Smith completes routinely. Dr. J brought terms like "hang time" and "degree of difficulty" to his dunks. Now Ozzie has introduced them to the double play. Smith's all-time-favorite showstopper displayed both his reflexes and his gift for improvision. He dove behind second base for a smash by Jeff Burroughs, but while Smith was in midair, parallel to the ground, the ball hit a rock and bounced sideways. Smith reached back and behind himself to the grab the ball—bare-handed. Then he did a somersault and came up throwing. Burroughs was out by days.

The last players who blended old-fashioned work and unique new gifts to create such a novel level of wonder were Willie Mays and Brooks Robinson. Defense has always been the province of stylists, back to Rabbit Maranville's basket catches. "People think that momentum in baseball is part of offense. Well, momentum works both ways," says Smith with pride. "We are the team that has proved that you can steal momentum consistently with great defense."

Because defensive statistics have always been deeply flawed and difficult to interpret, many in the game have simply given up considering them at all. Thus we overlook huge gaps in value between historic glove masters like Smith and merely mediocre men. In 1982, for instance, both Smith and Tim Foli of the Angels played in about the same number of games as shortstops, both for division champions. Smith had 103 more assists, a full 20 percent more. Yet that wasn't even one of Smith's best years. He threw out "only" 535 men. In 1980 he had set the record—621 assists. The runner-up that year had 529.

Get the big picture? Every year, Smith may make a hundred plays that good shortstops can't achieve. He probably steals 50 hits a year that nobody else can get and perhaps as many as 150—an incredible number—more than some poor shortstops. Toronto's Tony Fernandez is considered the American League's top wizard, and he averages about 450 assists. "The Next Ozzie"—Ozzie Guillen of the White Sox—hasn't gotten to 500 assists yet, much less 600.

Because defense is the cognoscenti corner of baseball, the poorly lighted room in the gallery, Smith has become all the more defiantly proud of his work: "I try to give people their money's worth. There have been nights when the team lost when fans came up to me and said, 'Your play is so exciting. It was worth it just to watch you." After he retires, Smith claims, he hopes people will be completely unable to find words to explain his play to the next generation. "I want them to have to put a tape in the machine." Only then will they see what and how.

Despite such pride and prowess, Smith was almost a cult figure in baseball until three years ago. His early batting marks (.211, .230, .222) consigned him to the nether reaches of the Miranda Line—the sarcastic baseball term for barely batting .200, named after good-field-no-hit 1950s shortstop Willie Miranda. Fair or not, the day Smith won an '85 playoff game with a home run (his first ever left-handed) may have been the moment he achieved credibility. America responds to a glove man who learns to hit the same way it does to a blond bombshell who publishes a volume of poetry. The shock is so great we don't demand too much of the rhymes. Well, we're not going to get rid of Ozzie now.

Not after he has raised his average for five straight years—.243, .257, .276, .280 to (trumpet salute) .303.

Not after he's lifted weights (and gained 25 pounds; he's now up to 167), so that last year he amazed everybody with 40 doubles and 75 RBIs.

Not after he was the leading vote-getter among the nation's fans in the 1987 All-Star balloting and runner-up in the 1987 National League MVP voting.

At the age of thirty-three, after ten sometimes overlooked years, Smith has become the all-purpose symbol of the feisty, paranoid, thrilling, innovative, controversial Cards. Yes, the Runnin' Redbirds, that star-crossed semi-team of the 1980s. In Missouri they'll remind you that nobody else has been to the World Series three times this decade. Other folks, not so generous, will point out that nobody else has blown two world championships either. If history confirms that the '85 Kansas City Royals and the '87 Minnesota Twins were the two worst teams ever to win the Classic, then it will not be overlooked that the Cardinals lost to both. "We're the team that got to the trough twice and couldn't drink," says Smith.

This is Ozzie's hour. In many ways he has been ready for it, overdue for it, for years. In other ways the spotlight catches him, and the Cards, at a mixed and troubling juncture.

An irony, not missed by Smith, is that he's been discovered by millions at a time when he is, in one sense, most vulnerable. In 1985 he suffered a torn rotator cuff in his throwing shoulder—an injury that can end even a nonpitcher's career. At one point, Smith vowed he would sit out two entire seasons if that was what it would take for the arm to heal without surgery.

Instead, he rehabilitated himself so quickly he never missed a game. Most fans, and even foes, didn't know he was ever hurt. However, his arm is now a slingshot, not a rifle. He positions himself to avoid long

14

throws and has developed the quickest release since Joe Namath faced a blitz. Still, Smith knows he'll never be the total defensive player he was from 1978 to 1985. "He's not the old Ozzie," says Herzog. "But he's still the best. And the old Ozzie didn't hit .300. So, overall, he's probably better'n ever."

But the old Ozzie never had to wonder how long his cuff, and his career, would hold out.

When you listen to Smith, you seldom hear a shrill grievance nurser. Only in extremis does that tone emerge. For instance, when he's trapped at his locker by dozens of reporters after the Cards have lost the sixth or seventh game of a World Series. Only then do you feel his enormous resentment. These people have never appreciated or understood me, his eyes say, but now they will not hesitate to judge. Then Smith speaks more and more quietly, almost a whisper, forcing his listeners to crush against one another to hear his edged words. He knows they will grant him his breathing space out of respect, and he seems to relish their discomfort. But far more often, Smith sounds like a serious yet cheerful man—a baseball Julius Erving, so polished, thoughtful and reasonable that he might well be a symbol for his whole sport.

Few men in sports, for example, can talk so easily or eloquently about the sources of their ambition. "When you're a kid, you become more daring than your friends, and something good comes of it," says Smith. "It's more 'I want to be special' than 'I know I'm special.' Where does that end up? The truth is, I don't know. How good can you be? I don't know. The only way you find out is to do it. You don't even know what you're reaching for. You just keep reaching. If there's one person in the world you don't want to cheat, it's yourself.

"It starts with yourself, then it carries over. You can't please others unless you're pleasing yourself . . . I feel sorry for players who let money be their driving force. If you do, you will never get the most out of your talent . . . I have one brother who could be an artist, if he put his mind to it. But he lacks the mental toughness. He gets bored very easily. See that?" Smith says, pointing at a huge restaurant flower arrangement. "I've seen him go out and pick dried flowers out of a vacant lot and make something that beautiful. He could be anything he wanted to be. But, for whatever reasons, he's just happy being himself. He works at a convenience store, like a 7-Eleven . . .

"You're not ever going to be able to put your finger on the difference. It really irritates me when people talk about how unusual it is that I've accomplished what I have in light of my 'humble beginnings.' That has nothing to do with it. Either you grab ahold or you don't. Either you say, 'I'm happy with this,' or you say, 'I'm going to get away from those conditions and do something more with my life.' I never thought about staying in that life. So you turn it [poverty] into a break."

The day Smith turned thirty, he'd never hit a lick. Never batted above .258 or had more than 50 RBIs. He'd had 30 extra-base hits in a year only once. Walks? Who'd walk him?

The idea that he could almost lead the league in doubles or be among the league leaders in hits and walks or—and this is a stunner—finish in the top four in the NL in '87 in runs produced (runs plus RBI minus homers) was unthinkable. Except to Smith. Remember: "You don't even know what you're reaching for. You just keep reaching." That's why, after the 1986 season, Smith went to New Orleans's Mackie Shilstone, the same muscle guru who worked with boxer Michael Spinks and basketball toothpick Manute Bol. "I gained twelve pounds the first week. And it was solid," says Smith, grinning. "Now, that's exciting." He was back on the program this winter, along with teammate Vince Coleman. He still can't hold the weight through 162 games, but Smith has reached the point where, approaching him in a locker room from behind, you could almost mistake him for Sugar Ray Leonard.

"What's next—.315?" says Smith mischievously.

This indefatigable attitude—the belief that a career-long Punch-and-Judy could remake himself into a clutch hitter who would produce more runs than home run champion Andre Dawson—has been the foundation for Smith's authority as the Cardinals' unchallenged team leader. He seems not so much to epitomize his team as to actually have molded it in his image over the past six seasons. Willie McGee, Terry Pendleton, Jose Oquendo, Vince Coleman and all those interchange-able Cards role players have arrived or blossomed since Smith came to St. Louis in 1982, in what was supposedly a very bad trade for a troubled Garry Templeton. Back then Templeton looked like ten times more of a Hall of Fame candidate than did Smith.

Now we look at the Cards and see Smith everywhere. He is the greatest defensive player on what may be the best defensive team ever. They steal. He stole forty-three bases in 1987. They peck, chop, bloop and beg walks from both sides of the plate. Now he does it as well as any. They have the game's best secret offense of bunts and sacrifices, hit-and-runs and extra bases that never show in the box scores. In five of six years (1982–87), the Cards have led the major leagues in ad-

16

vancing runners while making outs. The Cards are ardent about fundamentals, with Smith the taskmaker.

Lastly, Smith is stylish, cocky and quick to take offense at a slight. So are the Cards. Even Herzog, who seldom played the persecuted flatlander when he was losing to the Yanks every year in Kansas City, has gradually picked up the Ozzie tone of the defiant underdog. Smith admits that the Cards "have a bad rep with the umpires and some of the press." Mostly, they've earned it. When, at the '85 playoffs, pitcher John Tudor snapped, "Whaddaya need to get press credentials? A driver's license?" he was in fine Cardinals form.

Little shoulder. Big chip. That's definitely Smith, too.

The thought of leaving talent undeveloped and a place in baseball history unclaimed is intolerable to Smith. His brother at the 7-Eleven haunts him. So, perhaps deliberately, he nurses his grievances. He knows he needs them. *What might befall David if he became Goliath?*

To Smith's credit, there's hardly a weak gripe in the bunch. He really was an overlooked 135-pound high school shrimp who had to go to Cal-Poly to play. He really did have to learn to hit in the majors, and the Padres were lousy teachers. He really did play for a cheap organization that didn't know how uniquely valuable he was. The wife of the Pads' owner, during one salary fight, really did publicly offer him a job at $4.50 an hour to be her assistant gardener. Her usual pay was $3.50, she said, but she'd go up to $4.50 because Ozzie was a college man.

Smith is black in a sport so backward that Al Campanis was, in truth, one of the relative moderates on race relations. St. Louis does play second or third fiddle to National League teams in New York and Los Angeles. Smith does play one of baseball's more undervalued positions. The Cards' style of offense—the whole team, in fact—has been denigrated and explained away throughout the eighties. We're just reaching the point where the Cards are being seen as radically innovative, with up to six switch-hitters in the lineup and a defense of swift, gifted, fundamentally sound and intelligent players at every position; this defense, so far above previous standards of excellence, turns a staff of mediocre Cards arms into league-best pitching year after year.

As for the personal shots, Smith has some semblance of a point in every case. How *did* Andre Dawson win MVP? Dawson's team finished last. How *does* Jack Clark look himself in the mirror? For $1.3 million a year, don't you take a cortisone shot and at least try to be a designated hitter in the World Series? And how *did* the Twins play so much better at home?

The reason Ozzie harps and refuses to forget is because he isn't ready to stop being the Wizard of Ahhhs yet. Just watch. In a few years, the grudges will fade. The scary tone of paranoia will come under control. As the end nears and he admits it, Smith will not grasp so desperately at those last bits of neurotic fuel that help so many human engines run their best. Middle age is a fine time for perspective, but when wisdom and wealth come together—and too soon—they can be positively toxic to talent.

Years from now, the anger boiled away, all we will have left is a man who dresses like a prince, signs autographs endlessly and gives steak knives to his limo driver. Smith will also have a plaque in the Hall of fame and an hour's worth of highlight clips that will still be watched with wonder in fifty years.

Did he really do that? kids will ask.

Oh yes. Just pop in the tape.

Shazam!

The Hoover:
Called Up
to Cooperstown

As the Baltimore Oriole team bus rolled through Harlem long after midnight, Brooks Robinson tucked one foot under himself, propped his chin on his raised knee, leaned his forehead against the bus window, and looked into the steamy summer darkness. "Been coming this way for twenty years," said Robinson, who was then in his final season. A little of the syntax and twang of the son of a Little Rock, Arkansas, fireman still clung to his soft, rolling voice. "It never changes," he murmured, nodding toward a crap game going on in the crevice between two tenements. "That's an awful life to get born into and never get out of. Shows us how lucky we are. How grateful we should be."

The sentiment Robinson expressed that night was commonplace enough—simple empathy for the poor. What was striking was his lack of self-pity in considering himself lucky by comparison. That was hardly the most fortunate section of a blessed life. Just two years before,

Robinson had been on the edge of financial ruin. Not only was he broke but he was in debt as well, because of naïve business decisions. Others had made the money mistakes, dragging Robinson down with them. At every turn, Robinson's flaw had been an excess of generosity. How could he send a sporting goods bill to a Little League team that was long overdue in paying for its gloves? He'd keep anybody on the cuff forever. Said Robinson's old friend Ron Hansen, "He just couldn't say no." As creditors dunned him and massive publicity exposed his plight, Robinson answered every question, took all of the blame (including plenty that wasn't his) and refused to declare bankruptcy. He was determined to pay back every cent. With great embarrassment, he also returned tens of thousands of dollars that fans spontaneously sent him in the mail to soften his fall.

Just as twenty years of hard-earned baseball dollars trickled through his hands like a ground ball between the legs, Robinson's athletic skills also left him—suddenly and harshly. First his power, which led him to 268 home runs, disappeared. He couldn't even get his home run total into double figures. Next his average dropped through the floor. He batted .201 in 1975 and .211 in 1976. Though his marvelous soft hands and reflexes never really tarnished—even at the end he was a study at third base—his range diminished radically. He couldn't hold a job with his glove alone.

Finally, by his last season (1977), he was dead weight, a charity case of sorts. Robby had to approach the Orioles on a hat-in-hand, any-way-you-want-me basis as a player-coach just so he could stay solvent and try to start over. The free-agent era was only months old; the boom days ahead—million-dollar contracts for utility men and $2 million plus per year for a future Hall of Famer type—no one could have guessed. Back then a Brooks Robinson made only about twice the current rookie minimum of $62,500. One bad judgment—a failed sporting goods store—could take it all. That night in Harlem, the guy in the alley winning the crap game might have been in better shape than Brooks Robinson, a man who had never loved anything except baseball and had no solid future plans.

When the Orioles bus rolled to a stop in front of the Statler Hilton, it was the last time Robinson would return from Yankee Stadium as a player. Everyone piled off, Robinson carrying a case in his hand. "Here," he said to a reporter. "You left your typewriter under your seat."

Robinson left the game the way he played it—uncomplaining, smiling, teasing and being teased, pitching batting practice and picking up a typewriter for a reporter or a dirty towel for a batboy. Of all the game's greats, perhaps Robinson was least cursed by his own fame. He had great talent and never abused it. He received adulation and reciprocated with common decency. While other players dressed like kings and acted like royalty, Robinson arrived at the park dressed like a cab driver. Other stars had fans. Robinson made friends.

In the long run, that saved him. Though many were sad for Robinson back in 1977, few seemed as worried as might have been expected. "Brooks and [wife] Connie haven't changed their living style since the days we were making $6,000 a year in the minors," said Hansen. "His friends aren't millionaires and politicians, just average guys like me. People still love him just like they always have. He doesn't scare anybody. He's never snubbed anybody. For twenty years he has always had empathy for other people's feelings and now they are going to have empathy for his. Nothing really bad will ever happen to Brooks. Those who know him wouldn't allow it."

Other stars might be carried through hard times by their towns or former teams. That wasn't what Hansen meant. With Robinson, it went deeper. If Brooks's life could, in the broadest sense, go bad, then wouldn't our most basic verities, like casting bread on the waters, seem endangered?

The day Robinson retired, he was still at sea financially and personally. Yet the celebration for him in Memorial Stadium could not have been more joyful or devoid of any shadow. The biggest crowd ever to attend an Oriole regular-season game (51,798) stood and cheered in bright sun for a quarter of an hour as Robinson circled the field, standing like a ticket tape parade hero in the back of a Cadillac convertible, 1955 vintage, his rookie year. "Brooks, not retired, just called up to Cooperstown," said one bedsheet sign.

"Spent an hour combing my bald spot, so I could leave my toupee home," said Robinson, standing in the Orioles dugout as the microphone behind second base awaited him. "Now I think I'll just keep my hat on . . .

"Never in my wildest dreams did I think I would be standing here twenty-three years later saying goodbye to so many people," said Robinson when he took the stage. "For a guy who never wanted to do anything but put on a major league uniform, that goodbye comes tough. I would never want to change one day of my years here. It's been fantastic."

So Robinson quit, with barely a dollar to call his own and debts up to his neck, without even the sophistication or cunning to become a manager. And all the Orioles knew it. Robinson had given as much to baseball as a player could and was literally leaving it with nothing.

As a kind of compensation, it seemed everyone decided to leave him with their affection. "Around here people don't name candy bars after Brooks Robinson," said the day's master of ceremonies, Gordon Beard; "they name their children after him."

Even Weaver, the toughest of cusses, broke down in public for the only time in recorded baseball history. He told the crowd about Robinson's generosity toward a nobody manager who was a career bush leaguer. He talked about how he wondered, the first time he gave the take sign to Robinson, if he would obey. "And I've wondered every time since." He thanked Robinson for saving his job "several times over the years." Finally Weaver blurted out, "Thank you, Brooks. Thank you one million times."

To say that nobody knew how to react would be an understatement. "I thought of so many things while Brooks was riding around the stadium," explained Weaver later. "What I had planned to say didn't seem like nothin' to me. It wasn't true and honest feeling. So I just did it impromptu. I'd like to be like Brooks. The guys who never said no to nobody, the ones that everybody loves because they deserve to be loved . . . those are my heroes."

Somehow Robinson always elicited "true and honest feeling" from the people around him, even those never previously known to possess such things. Perhaps that was his gift. In a sense, his play was the least of him. That merely brought him to our attention so we could get to know the rest of him.

From 1964, when he was the American League's most valuable player, until 1970, when he was MVP of the World Series, Robinson was a living legend. Yet when, someday in a different century, an old man tries to explain to a small boy the power of Robinson's lasting fame, he may have a hard time translating the hero's statistics into a portrait of the man that seems consonant with his oversized myth.

Few players get to hear the words "the greatest at his position in the history of the game" while they are still in their primes. Robinson heard it routinely. Hyperbole and praise followed him around like spotted pups. Cincinnati manager Sparky Anderson said during the 1970 Series, "I'm beginning to see Brooks in my sleep. If I dropped this paper plate, he'd pick it up on one hop and throw me out at first."

For his first twenty-one professional seasons, Robinson got to show his skill. If his feet were slow, his reflexes were the fastest. If his arm was average, his accuracy and quick release were the best. Somehow he always seemed languid, especially as he threw overhand toward first; yet the fastest runners were out by larger margins when Robinson made his syrupy perfectos than when the most kinetic jack-in-the-box third basemen made similar plays as frantically as though they'd just sat on a cattle prod.

If Brooks's bat was merely good most of the time, it was at its best in the clutch. He drove in 75 runs 10 times, hit .280 7 times and had 20 homers 6 times. His 268 homers and .267 career average are a fair measure of his bat: useful, occasionally powerful, but not cause to lose your place in the hot dog line.

Above all, his glove was purple, like a standing invitation to a theme contest. On teams that had slick fielders like Luis Aparicio, Mark Belanger, Paul Blair, Bobby Grich, and Dave Johnson, you couldn't take your eye off Robinson. He overshadowed them all and sometimes forced you to watch the entire game through him. Others made difficult or acrobatic plays, even—a favorite baseball oxymoron—"impossible plays." Robinson made unthinkable plays. Shortstops steal singles. It seemed Robinson robbed a thousand doubles. Brooks Robby, indeed. Memory swears that he made a "Brooks play" at least once every other game. That is, when there weren't two in one game. Not semitough plays, mind you. An accidental swinging bunt, an almost sure scratch hit? As soon as you realized Brooks was at third, you barely bothered to watch. He went months at a time without having to stuff a dribbler in his hip pocket. No, we are talking here about discussion plays. Plays that demand comparison.

Thank heaven for replays. In Memorial Stadium, to this day, his Brooksobatics are still on display every night on TV sets above the concession stands as part of a half-hour recapitulation of Oriole history; and each night it is invariably Robinson's plays that bring audible gasps of surprise. They remain incomprehensible. You don't catch hard line drives in foul territory. You don't throw out runners with your feet in the coach's box. But it's on film. A perfectionist's archive. When the Hall of Fame asked for his glove after the 1970 Series, Brooks said, "Wait a year. It'll take me that long to get a new one broken in just right."

Despite all this, none of Robinson's plays seem to stand as sharp in retrospect as the person himself. After all, since Robinson's retirement, Mike Schmidt has built a record demanding that he, not Brooks, play for the celestial varsity. Mention Robinson in baseball circles and stories about his play almost never surface. Instead, there is always some anecdote about his nature.

"It's rough to try to replace an immortal, but Brooks did everything to make it smoother for me," recalls Doug DeCinces, who, on Brooks Day, tore third base out of the ground and presented it to Robinson.

"Every player I've ever managed blamed me at the end, not himself," Weaver once said. "They all ripped me and said they weren't washed up. All except Brooks. He never said one word and he had more clout in Baltimore than all of them. He never did anything except with class. He made the end easier for everybody."

Perhaps that's what amazes pro athletes more than anything: Robinson's ability to leave the stage as though it cost him nothing. In fact, it probably did cost him much less than many lesser athletes. Players with half Robinson's credentials had to swallow their bombast overnight. Brooksie—"Mr. Bad Body"—had always enjoyed pitching batting practice with his hat off to get a tan on his bald spot.

Gradually, in the early years of his retirement, Robinson's bleak money days became a thing of the past. To his own surprise, Robinson became a far more successful local baseball telecaster than he ever dreamed. A few guest shots turned into a regular job that kept him in the ballpark fifty times a year. His homespun tales were never the sort to attract the eye of network TV, but Robinson didn't care; and Baltimore found him as comfortable as one of his perfectly broken-in gloves. His analysis was perceptive and candid, sometimes even critical; but, as always with Robinson, his total absence of mean-spiritedness or any hint of ulterior motive protected him. "Brooks is entitled to his opinion," a chastised player would say. As likely as not, Robinson had been giving him batting tips before the game.

It is rare to find an announcer without ambition, without a need to fill air time and with no axes to grind. That's Robinson, who wouldn't take the managing job if offered and has no knack for grudges. He tells it as straight as he can, as long as he doesn't really have to hurt anybody's feelings. No job would be worth that to Robinson.

"You know, Chuck," Brooks will say to partner Chuck Thompson after a loud foul ball, "as an announcer I swore I'd never say, 'And there's the lucky fan who caught that one.' Ball comin' in there about two hun'ert mile an hour."

Later he'll say in an on-air aside, "Charlie [i.e., Thompson], been a couple of innings since we had any nachos in this booth. Think I'll go get us some."

Robinson also moved into an executive position with a petroleum company and joined a business management firm that specializes in helping pro athletes avoid exactly the sort of problems that had ravaged Robinson. Don't do as I did, do as I say.

If any baseball fairy tale ever had a perfect happy ending, it came on the last day of July 1983, when Robinson was inducted into the Hall of Fame. All weekend the highways were littered with cars, vans and buses loaded with orange-and-black-clad devotees making the pilgrimage to Cooperstown. In a normal summer, the Hall induction draws a crowd of perhaps five thousand, with Mickey Mantle long holding the record of nearly ten thousand. For Robinson, that Mantle's crowd was surpassed by several thousand.

"You really know how to make it tough on a guy," the choked-up Robinson ad-libbed as the crowd refused to end its ovation as he was introduced. "I realize I must be the luckiest man in the world. I've been given more than any human being could ever ask for."

In his closing remarks, Robinson seemed to be trying to say, in an oblique way, why his life had been so exemplary, so patient. "From the beginning, I was committed to the goodness of this game. I think my love for baseball has been the biggest thing in my life. This is the day for giving thanks. This is a life from which I want to give back."

Afterward Robinson stood in the streets of Cooperstown in a bright pink jacket, surrounded by people with block-lettered no. 5s on their chests. "The last five years have been as happy as the other twenty-three," said Robinson. "Everybody dreads retiring, but I'm having as much fun now as I was when I was playing. I can't believe it, to tell the truth."

That afternoon, Brooks Robinson seemed ideally of a piece with Fenimore Cooper Country. Mark Twain loathed Cooper's saga of noble savages and true-blue woodsmen from the bottom of his wise, mocking and bitter heart; Twain was a harbinger of a century that would find the word "virtue" almost impossible to pronounce without a knowing cough.

Brooks Robinson is a man who would be unpalatable, perhaps unbelievable, in fiction. Only reality, which refuses to play by any rules, has a place for him. In a fantasy creation, virtue of the sort attributed to Cooper characters is deeply suspect, since it's an unprovable author's contrivance. "One of nature's noblemen," Cooper liked to say of his favorite heroes. These days, that phrase has become a trendy sneer for cynics. We know, of course, that nature has no noblemen and could not create one if she chose, not even to play third base.

Hubris

99 Reasons
Why Baseball
Is Better Than Football

January 1987—Some people say football's the best game in America. Others say baseball.

Some people are really dumb.

Some people say all this is just a matter of taste. Others know better.

Some people can't wait for next Sunday's Supper Bowl. Others wonder why.

Pro football is a great game. Compared with hockey. After all, you've gotta do something when the wind chill is zero and your curveball won't break. But let's not be silly. Compare the games? It's a one-sided laughter. Here are the first 99 reasons why baseball is better than football. (More after lunch.)

1. Bands.

2. Halftime with bands.

3. Cheerleaders at halftime with bands.

4. Up With People singing "The Impossible Dream" during a Blue Angles flyover at halftime with bands.

5. Baseball has fans in Wrigley Field singing "Take Me Out to the Ball Game" at the seventh-inning stretch.

6. Baseball has Blue Moon, Catfish, Spaceman and the Sugar Bear. Football has Lester the Molester, Too Mean and the Assassin.

7. All XX Super Bowls haven't produced as much drama as the last World Series.

8. All XX Super Bowls haven't produced as many classic games as either pennant playoff did in 1986.

9. Baseball has a bullpen coach blowing bubble gum with his cap turned around backward while leaning on a fungo bat; football has a defensive coordinator in a satin jacket with a headset and a clipboard.

10. The Redskins have thirteen assistant coaches, five equipment managers, three trainers, two assistant GMs, but, for fourteen games, nobody who could kick an extra point.

11. Football players and coaches don't know how to bait a ref, much less jump up and down and scream in his face. Baseball players know how to argue with umps; baseball managers even kick dirt on them. Earl Weaver steals third base and won't give it back; Tom Landry folds his arms.

12. Vince Lombardi was never ashamed that he said, "Winning isn't everything. It's the only thing."

13. Football coaches talk about character, gut checks, intensity and reckless abandon. Tommy Lasorda said, "Managing is like holding a dove in your hand. Squeeze too hard and you kill it; not hard enough and it flies away."

14. Big league baseball players chew tobacco. Pro football linemen chew on each other.

15. Before a baseball game, there are two hours of batting practice. Before a football game, there's a two-hour traffic jam.

16. A crowd of 30,000 in a stadium built for 55,501 has a lot more fun than a crowd of 55,501 in the same stadium.

17. No one has ever actually reached the end of the rest room line at an NFL game.

18. Nine innings means eighteen chances at the hot dog line. Two halves means B.Y.O. or go hungry.

19. Pro football players have breasts. Many NFLers are so freakishly overdeveloped, owing to steroids, that they look like circus geeks. Baseball players seem like normal fit folks. Fans should be thankful they don't have to look at NFL teams in bathing suits.

20. Eighty degrees, a cold beer and a short-sleeve shirt are better than thirty degrees, a hip flask and six layers of clothes under a lap blanket. Take your pick: suntan or frostbite.

21. Having 162 games a year is 10.125 times as good as having 16.

22. If you miss your favorite NFL team's game, you have to wait a week. In baseball, you wait a day.

23. Everything George Carlin said in his famous monologue is right on. In football you blitz, bomb, spear, shiver, march and score. In baseball, you wait for a walk, take your stretch, toe the rubber, tap your spikes, play ball and run home.

24. Marianne Moore loved Christy Mathewson. No woman of quality has ever preferred football to baseball.

25. More good baseball books appear in a single year than have been written about footfall in the past fifty years. The best football writers, like Dan Jenkins, have the good sense to write about something else most of the time.

26. The best football announcer ever was Howard Cosell.

27. The worst baseball announcer ever was Howard Cosell.

28. All gridirons are identical; football coaches never have to meet to go over the ground rules. But the best baseball parks are unique.

29. Every outdoor park ever built primarily for baseball has been pretty. Every stadium built with pro football in mind has been ugly (except Arrowhead).

30. The coin flip at the beginning of football games is idiotic. Home teams should always kick off and pick a goal to defend. In baseball, the visitor bats first (courtesy), while the host bats last (for drama). The football visitor should get the first chance to score, while the home team should have the dramatic advantage of receiving the second-half kick-off.

31. Baseball is harder. In the last twenty-five years, only one player, Vince Coleman, has been cut from the NFL and then become a success in the majors. From Tom Brown in 1963 (Senators to Packers) to Jay Schroeder (Jays farm system to Redskins), baseball flops have become NFL standouts.

32. Face masks. Right away we've got a clue something might be wrong. A guy can go 80 mph on a Harley without a helmet, much less a face mask.

33. Faces are better than helmets. Think of all the players in the NFL (excluding your local team) whom you'd recognize on the street. Now eliminate the quarterbacks. Not many left, are there? Now think of all the baseball players whose faces you know, just from the last Series.

34. The NFL has—how can we say this?—a few borderline god-fathers. Baseball has almost no mobsters or suspicious types among its owners. Pete Rozelle isn't as picky as Bowie Kuhn, who for fifteen years considered "integrity of the game" to be one of his key functions and who gave the cold shoulder to the shady-money guys.

35. Football has Tank and Mean Joe. Baseball has the Human Rain Delay and Charlie Hustle.

36. In football, it's team first, individual second—if at all. A Rich Milot and a Curtis Jordan can play ten years—but when would we ever have time to study them alone for just one game? Could we mimic their gestures, their tics, their habits? A baseball player is an individual first, part of a team second. You can study him at length and at leisure in the batter's box or on the mound. On defense, when the batted ball seeks him, so do our eyes.

37. Baseball statistics open a world to us. Football statistics are virtually useless or, worse, misleading. For instance, the NFL quarterback-ranking system is a joke. Nobody understands it or can justify it. The old average-gain-per-attempt rankings were just as good.

38. What kind of dim-bulb sport would rank pass receivers by number of catches instead of by number of yards? Only in football would a runner with 1,100 yards on 300 carries be rated ahead of a back with 1,000 yards on 200 carries. Does baseball give its silver bat to the player with the most hits or with the highest average?

39. If you use NFL statistics as a betting tool, you go broke. Only wins and losses, points and points against and turnovers are worth a damn.

40. Baseball has one designated hitter. In football, everybody is a designated something. No one plays the whole game anymore. Football worships the specialists. Baseball worships the generalists.

41. The tense closing seconds of crucial baseball games are decided by distinctive relief pitchers like Bruce Sutter, Rollie Fingers or Goose Gossage. Vital NFL games are decided by helmeted gentlemen who come on for ten seconds, kick sideways, spend the rest of the game keeping their precious foot warm on the sidelines and aren't aware of the subtleties of the game. Half of them, in Alex Karras's words, run off the field chirping, "I kick a touchdown."

42. Football gave us the Hammer. Baseball gave us the Fudge Hammer.

43. How can you respect a game that uses only the point after touchdown and completely ignores the option of a two-point conversion, which would make the end of football games much more exciting?

44. Wild cards. If baseball can stick with four divisional champs out of twenty-six teams, why does the NFL need to invite ten of its twenty-eight to the prom? Could it be that football isn't terribly interesting unless your team can still "win it all"?

45. The entire NFL playoff system is a fraud. Go on, explain with a straight face why the Chiefs (10–6) were in the playoffs in 1986 but the Seahawks (10–6) were not. There is no real reason. Seattle was simply left out for convenience. When baseball tried the comparably bogus split-season fiasco with half-season champions in 1981, fans almost rioted.

46. Parity scheduling. How can the NFL defend the fairness of deliberately giving easier schedules to weaker teams and harder schedules to better teams? Just to generate artificially improved competition? When a weak team with a patsy schedule goes 10–6, while a strong defending division champ misses the playoffs at 9–7, nobody says boo. Baseball would have open revolt at such a nauseatingly cynical system.

47. Baseball has no penalty for pass interference. (This in itself is almost enough to declare baseball the better game.) In football, offsides is five yards, holding is ten yards, a personal foul is fifteen yards. But interference: maybe fifty yards.

48. Nobody on earth really knows what pass interference is. Part judgment, part acting, mostly accident.

49. Baseball has no penalties at all. A home run is a home run. You cheer. In football, on a score, you look for flags. If there's one, who's it on? When can we cheer? Football acts can all be repealed. Baseball acts stand forever.

50. Instant replays. Just when we thought there couldn't be anything worse than penalties, we get instant replays of penalties. Talk about a bad joke. Now any play, even one with no flags, can be called back. Even a flag itself can, after five minutes of boring delay, be nullified. NFL time has entered the Twilight Zone. Nothing is real; everything is hypothetical.

51. Football has Hacksaw. Baseball has Steady Eddie and the Candy Man.

52. The NFL's style of play has been stagnant for decades, predictable. Turn on any NFL game and that's just what it could be—any NFL game. Teams seem interchangeable. Even the wishbone is too radical. Baseball teams' styles are often determined by their personnel and even their parks.

53. Football fans tailgate before the big game. No baseball fan would have a picnic in a parking lot.

54. At a football game, you almost never leave saying, "I never saw a play like that before." At a baseball game, there's almost always some new wrinkle.

55. Beneath the NFL's infinite sameness lies infinite variety. But we aren't privy to it. So what if football is totally explicable and fascinating to Dan Marino as he tries to decide whether to audible to a quick trap? From the stands, we don't know one thousandth of what's required to grasp a pro football game. If an NFL coach has to say, "I won't know until I see the films," then how out-in-the-cold does that leave the fan?

56. While football is the most closed of games, baseball is the most open. A fan with a score card, a modest knowledge of the teams and a knack for paying attention has all he needs to watch a game with sophistication.

57. NFL refs are weekend warriors, pulled from other jobs to moonlight; as a group, they're barely competent. That's really why the NFL turned to instant replays. Now old fogies upstairs can't even get the make-over calls right. Baseball umps work ten years in the minors and know what they are doing. Replays show how good they are. If Don Denkinger screws up in a split second of Series tension, it's instant lore.

58. Too many of the best NFL teams represent unpalatable values. The Bears are head-thumping braggarts. The Raiders have long been scofflaw pirates. The Cowboys glorify the heartless corporate approach to football.

59. Football has the Refrigerator. Baseball has Puff the Magic Dragon, the Wizard of Oz, Tom Terrific, Doggie, Kitty Kat and Oil Can.

60. Football is impossible to watch. Admit it: the human head is at least two eyes shy for watching the forward pass. Do you watch the five eligible receivers? Or the quarterback and the pass rush? If you keep your eye on the ball, you never know who got open or how. If you watch the receivers . . . well, nobody watches the receivers. On TV you don't even know how many receivers have gone out for a pass.

61. The NFL keeps changing the most basic rules. Most blocking now would have been illegal use of the hands in Jim Parker's time. How do we compare eras when the sport never stays the same? Pretty soon, intentional grounding will be legalized to protect quarterbacks.

62. In the NFL, you can't tell the players without an Intensive Care Unit report. Players get broken apart so fast we have no time to build up allegiances to stars. Three quarters of the NFL's starting quarterbacks are in their first four years in the league. Is it because the new breed is better? Or because the old breed is already lame? A top baseball player lasts fifteen to twenty years. We know him like an old friend.

63. The baseball Hall of Fame is in Cooperstown, New York, beside James Fenimore Cooper's Lake Glimmerglass; the football Hall of Fame is in Canton, Ohio, beside the freeway.

64. Baseball means Spring's Here. Football means Winter's Coming.

65. Best book for a lifetime on a desert island: The Baseball Encyclopedia.

66. Baseball's record on race relations is poor. But football's is much worse. Is it possible that the NFL still has *never* had a black head coach? And why is a black quarterback still as rare as a bilingual woodpecker?

67. Baseball has a drug problem comparable to society's. Pro football has a range of substance-abuse problems comparable only to itself. And, perhaps, the Hell's Angels'.

68. Baseball enriches language and imagination at almost every point of contact. As John Lardner put it, "Babe Herman did not triple into a triple play, but he did double into a double play, which is the next best thing."

69. Who's on first?

70. Without baseball, there'd have been no Fenway Park. Without football, there'd have been no artificial turf.

71. A typical baseball game has 9 runs, more than 250 pitches and about 80 completed plays—hits, walks, outs—in 2½ hours. A typical football game has about 5 touchdowns, a couple of field goals and fewer than 150 plays spread over 3 hours. Of those plays, perhaps 20 or 25 result in a gain or loss of more than 10 yards. Baseball has more scoring plays, more serious scoring threats and more meaningful action plays.

72. Baseball has no clock. Yes, you were waiting for that. The comeback, from three or more scores behind, is far more common in baseball than football.

73. The majority of players on a football field in any game are lost and unaccountable in the middle of pileups. Confusion hides a multitude of sins. Every baseball player's performance and contribution are measured and recorded in every game.

74. Some San Francisco linemen now wear dark Plexiglas visors inside their face masks—even at night. "And in the third round, out of Empire U., the 49ers would like to pick Darth Vader."

75. Someday, just once, could we have a punt without a penalty?

76. End-zone spikes. Sack dances. Or, in Dexter Manley's case, "holding flag" dances.

77. Unbelievably stupid rules. For example, if the two-minute warning passes, any play that begins even a split second thereafter is nullified. Even, as happened in this season's Washington–San Francisco game, when it's the decisive play of the entire game. And even when, as also happened in that game, not one of the twenty-two players on the field is aware that the two-minute mark has passed. The Skins stopped the 49ers on fourth down to save that game. They exulted; the 49ers started off the field. Then the refs said, "Play the down over." Absolutely unbelievable.

78. In baseball, fans catch foul balls. In football, they raise a net so you can't even catch an extra point.

79. Nothing in baseball is as boring as the four hours of ABC's "Monday Night Football."

80. Blowhard coach Buddy Ryan, who once gave himself a grade of A+ for his handling of the Eagles. "I didn't make any mistakes," he explained. His 5–10–1 team was 7–9 the year before he came.

81. Football players, somewhere back in their phylogenic development, learned how to talk like football coaches. ("Our goals this week were to contain Dickerson and control the line of scrimmage.") Baseball players say things like, "This pitcher's so bad that when he comes in, the grounds crew drags the warning track."

82. Football coaches walk across the field after the game and pretend to congratulate the opposing coach. Baseball managers head right for the beer.

83. The best ever in each sport—Babe Ruth and Jim Brown—each represents egocentric excess. But Ruth never threw a woman out a window.

84. Quarterbacks have to ask the crowd to quiet down. Pitchers never do.

85. Baseball nicknames go on forever—because we feel we know so many players intimately. Football monikers run out fast. We just don't know that many of them as people.

86. Baseball measures a gift for dailiness.

87. Football has two weeks of hype before the Super Bowl. Baseball takes about two days off before the World Series.

88. Football, because of its self-importance, minimizes a sense of humor. Baseball cultivates one. Knowing you'll lose at least sixty games every season makes self-deprecation a survival tool. As Casey Stengel said to his barber, "Don't cut my throat. I may want to do that myself later."

89. Football is played best full of adrenaline and anger. Moderation seldom finds a place. Almost every act of baseball is a blending of effort and control; too much of either is fatal.

90. Football's real problem is not that it glorifies violence, though it does, but that it offers no successful alternative to violence. In baseball, there is a choice of methods: the change-up or the knuckleball, the bunt or the hit-and-run.

91. Baseball is vastly better in person than on TV. Only when you're in the ballpark can the eye grasp and interconnect the game's great distances. Will the wind blow that long fly just over the fence? Will the relay throw nail the runner trying to score from first on a double in the alley? Who's warming up in the bullpen? Where is the defense shading this hitter? Did the base stealer get a good jump? The eye flicks back and forth and captures everything that is necessary. As for replays, most parks have them. Football is better on TV. At least you don't need binoculars. And you've got your replays.

92. Turning the car radio dial on a summer night.

93. George Steinbrenner learned his baseball methods as a football coach.

94. You'll never see a woman in a fur coat at a baseball game.

95. You'll never see a man in a fur coat at a baseball game.

96. A six-month pennant race. Football has nothing like it.

97. In football, nobody says, "Let's play two!"

98. When a baseball player gets knocked out, he goes to the showers. When a football player gets knocked out, he goes to get X-rayed.

99. Most of all, baseball is better than football because spring training is less than a month away.

The 40 Fiats
of Chairman Boz

April 1988 — In the spring, the fanatic mind runs not to daydreams of playing baseball but rather to ideas that would fix it. Restore the sport to itself. Slay the unjust. Raise high the incorruptible. You know, the usual stuff. All serious fans long to be the commissioner of baseball, if only to straighten things out once and for all. But sooner or later they realize that might not be enough. What the game really needs is a good five-cent benevolent dictator.

Me, for instance. Would a forty-year-old man who keeps a giant four-foot-in-diameter papier-mâché baseball beside his front driveway do anything to hurt the game? Of course not. And to prove it, here is a list of my first 40 fiats, once I'm appointed Supreme Being of Baseball:

1. The home plate ump shall have a button. If a batter takes more than thirty seconds to adjust his uniform, tighten his batting glove, wiggle his toe, call for time and otherwise delay the game, the ump shall push the button. The button will open a trapdoor to a pit, full of reptiles, under the batter's box. This shall be known as the Rickey Henderson Hole, in honor of the potential Hall of Famer whose career was tragically cut short. Carlton Fisk and Cliff Johnson: consider yourselves warned. The trapdoor will also work for home run trots, but with bigger reptiles. Jeffrey Leonard gets a free trial.

2. Pete Rose shall manage the Cincinnati Reds on the same basis that a Supreme Court judge holds tenure. For life. Reggie Jackson shall be given sole custody of the Oakland A's. Why make a guy with a 180 IQ wait to own a team? This would be too good to miss. Jim Palmer shall get to manage. He deserves it, heh, heh, heh. Jim Rice shall smile and tip his cap to the crowd before he is permitted to bat. Steve Carlton shall be allowed to make more comebacks only if he promises not to say one word. Joaquin Andujar shall have a new uniform number: ? ?. No one shall have to room with George Bell on the road.

3. There shall be special New York Rules. George Steinbrenner shall never fire Billy Martin. Ever. And Billy will know it. This is what you call finding a punishment to fit the crime. Both ways. Addendum: Uniform no. 1 for the Yankees will be unretired. Immediately. Codicil: No one from, or in any way affiliated with, New York City shall be allowed to use the phrase "subway series" until one actually occurs. (Penalty: Take the subway from Shea to Yankeee Stadium.) Rider to the Rules: Darryl Strawberry will be traded for Dave Winfield. Darrylberry the Dim deserves both Billy and George. Winnie, who's become a winner, would think he'd gone to heaven to play for Frank Cashen and Davey Johnson, two of baseball's brightest men. Finally, all Yankee Stadium personnel—especially cops—shall be replaced immediately by people with a certificate documenting their planet of birth.

4. The team with the better regular-season record shall get the home field advantage in the playoffs and World Series. Too late? Oh, no, because . . . next . . . we will replay the 1987 postseason under the new rules.

In the future, any World Series in which the Boston Red Sox win three games shall be declared complete. In accordance with this ruling, official records for 1946, 1967, 1975 and 1986 shall be corrected. Johnny Pesky, Bill Lee, Bill Buckner and John McNamara, you owe the game's new despot a real nice dinner.

5. A. Bartlett Giamatti, president of the National League, and Dr. Bobby Brown, president of the American League, shall be the Democratic and Republican presidential nominees in 1988. In case of a tie, Commissioner Peter Ueberroth gets the job. Why do we get a top heart

surgeon, a former Yale president and a *Time* magazine Man of the Year running baseball, but we get Pat Robertson and Gary Hart as candidates to run the country?

6. The mound shall be raised back to 15 inches, where it was for decades. Let's see if anybody can throw a fastball anymore.

7. There shall be punishments for bird-brained teams. The Blue Jays must wear dog choke collars until further notice. The Cards shall wear whine detectors, devices similar to smoke detectors, which shriek when Whitey Herzog or any of his Birds break into their patented paranoid alibi rap. The Orioles must write on the blackboard 1,000 times: "We are awful. Very slowly, we will try to get just a little bit better, not all at once." Edward Bennett Williams must initial all 1,000.

8. Only nicknames shall be allowed on the back of uniforms hereafter. Instead of Jim Dwyer: Pigpen. Floyd Rayford: Sugar Bear. Give us Chicken Man and Oil Can. Who knows "Davis"? But Chili, Storm and Eric the Red are easy. This would have been especially helpful in the old days. We could have known the difference between "Puddin' Head" and "Available" Jones or "The People's Cherce" and "Mysterious" Walker. Pittsburgh low-budget GM Sid Thrift's name shall be legally changed to Sid Cheap.

9. The designated hitter shall be put in both leagues and left there. Watching pitchers hit fifty times a week for the sake of two moments of strategy *isn't enough fun*. Sorry, this is my dictatorship. (All anti-DH rebels caught plotting to overthrow the chairman will be forced to have dinner with Dick Williams.)

10. The umpire shall confiscate *every* bat used to hit a home run. It will be sawed apart and inspected after the game. Any player found corking will be suspended for 10 days without pay. At $8 a bat for about 4,000 major league home runs, this will cost $32,000 a year— about half the minimum salary for one rookie player and a tiny price to learn the truth about the quality of the modern hitter. Any player who's absolutely certain he'll never hit a home run, and thus never risk suspension, shall be left alone and allowed to put wolfbane and cat's eyes in his bat if he wants. Every pitched ball used to record a strikeout will be confiscated and inspected. Ump, just toss that little baby to the ball bailiff while the next hitter comes to the plate. Nobody'll even notice. Same penalties for scuffing, spitting, etc. That's another 20,000 balls a year—maybe $78,000 a season. Or about $3,000 a team—half the price of another usher.

11. The fans shall decide who among the over-the-hill gang stays. Any player over forty years old must first receive permission from the fans, by ballot, to continue playing. This will be called the new Go Away rule. If Willie Mays and Pete Rose simply will not retire, we can retire 'em ourselves. Aren't our memories of them public property? The oldster with the most votes would win the coveted "Say Hey, Go Away" Award.

12. No player shall earn more than 100 times the salary of the average American worker. Sorry, guys, too many of you are already over that now. Whenever a player goes free agent and voluntarily changes teams, he must, henceforth, wear at least one piece of his previous team's uniform. Last year, Reggie Jackson, for instance, could have worn an Orioles cap, a Yankee jersey, Angel pants and those nice Day-glo yellow A's socks. Finally, any free agent earning $1.5 million a year shall laugh at all practical jokes played on him by new teammates. Penalty: Wear a Kirk Gibson mask all season.

13. Owners shall not be tolerated lightly. Any owner who ever again says he's losing money shall be forced to sell his team immediately—for his original purchase price (translated into '88 dollars with inflation factored in). Gee, everybody sure got quiet. Could that mean that, looked at from all sides, owning a ball club is basically a bonanza?

Augie Busch shall never again be allowed to ride his Clydesdale-drawn beer chariot around a World Series field unless he holds the reins himself.

There will be fewer owners, not more. Back to twenty-four teams. There aren't enough major-quality pitchers to stock twenty-six teams. The Seattle Mariners should be disbanded first. Make them all free agents. Nobody would notice. Not even owner George Argyros. As winner of the Worst Available Dome/Worst Available Owner combo contest, the Astros and John McMullen will also be sacrificed.

14. The All-Star Game shall be abolished. Pick the teams; just don't play the game. Anything that produces two good games, no great ones and twenty-three bombs in the last twenty-five years should be discontinued. Nice idea. Lousy reality. No old-timers' games shall be played unless all proceeds go to indigent old-timers. All other codger con games will be banned.

15. Let there be interleague play. We've talked about it for twenty-five years—now we will have it! It's perfect with twenty-four teams, but it can be done when baseball expands to twenty-eight teams, too. (Okay, so expansion is inevitable—but not until after the reign of Chairman Boz.) Take the Orioles—and twenty-eight major league teams—as an example. The Birds will play their six American League East foes 13 times each season—the same as now—for a total of 78 games. The O's

41

also will play each American League West team 6 times a year—just one 3-game series in each town. (Scarcity increases demand.) That's another 42 games. Finally, in odd-numbered seasons (e.g., '89), Baltimore plays 6 games versus each National League East team. In even-numbered seasons (e.g., '90), the Orioles play 6 times against each National League West club. That's 42 interleague games a year. And 162 games in a season, same as now. The current lack of interleague games is insane. No other sport would dream of it. The owners are just keeping it as a rainy-decade moneymaking gimmick if they ever need it.

16. The visiting team's general manager shall be put in charge of all electronic scoreboards, exploding displays and public-address system noises—including trumpet charges and train locomotives. Let's see how long the Minnesota Twins keep their toys the first time Frankie (Nervous Breakdown) Viola gets hit with a 111-decibel Tarzan scream in the middle of his windup.

17. No instant replays shall be allowed inside the ballpark and no NFL-style instant replay to change the umpire's decision—ever. Leave human error (the Denkinger Factor) intact. It is important that children understand that the game is not so serious that we can't, occasionally, allow the wrong team to win.

18. Let there be lights for Wrigley Field, for crying out loud—and not just for eight games a year. What's all the fuss? Be honest. Who doesn't like night games better than day games? Man, it gets hot in July. If you can get a weekday afternoon free, go swimming, play golf or have a stroke in your garden. Don't sweat your brains out in the bleachers. For those who must suffer, God created Sunday afternoon games. That's enough. Sensible teams long ago went to Saturday night games because people prefer them. Baseball is night baseball and has been for decades. Let those who refuse to learn from the Chicago Cubs be condemned to repeat them.

The only people who really want day ball in Wrigley Field are sportswriters (great deadlines—the Chicago scribes get home for dinner and the visiting laureates have more time on Rush Street).

All weekday World Series games shall be at night. All weekend World Series games shall be in the day. It's cold in October. Play a couple in sunshine, but don't get carried away.

19. On an intentional walk, the ump shall simply wave the batter to first base. We don't have to watch four stupid pitchouts. Yes, it will be a terrible sacrifice for purists—once every 119 years we will not get to see Rollie Fingers strike out Johnny Bench in the World Series on a fake intentional walk.

20. There shall be no balks whatsoever. Let pitchers do anything to any base. Steals are nice, but we have too much of a good thing. Modern runners have outgrown the ninety-foot base path. Games take forever. Too many dull pick-offs. Without balks, mediocre thieves would disappear. Good riddance. However, the great ones would remain, but at a lower level. The best would probably still steal 50 to 75 bases. But not 75 to 130, which is just too many.

If a top base stealer gets a good jump these days, he can steal second cleanly even if the pitcher picks him off—he simply steals on the first baseman, not the catcher. What, you ask, if the pitcher steps toward home, then throws behind his back or across his body to first base? You kidding? Thief'd be safe at second by ten feet. Just imagine it. Note: Steals of third base would be unchanged, because there's already no balk to second base. We'd be unifying the rules.

21. There shall be a demerit system for managers. Any manager who is fired three times shall be forced to go to Manager School for a year before he can be rehired by the old-boy network. After a fourth firing, two years of school, and so on. Under this system, John McNamara would be able to speak French and, by now, Don Zimmer could name all the continents.

Frank Robinson, Joe Morgan and Don Baylor have the right of first refusal on all open managerial positions in baseball until such time as all three are hired.

No manager, especially Tom Lasorda, shall be allowed to wear a baseball uniform in the dugout unless he's still a player. What's with this, anyway, guys? Would Don Shula wear shoulder pads on the sideline or Pat Riley put on yellow-and-purple shorts?

22. Rosters shall go back to twenty-five men. Come on, collusion isn't enough? However, the team itself, by secret vote, gets to elect its own twenty-fifth man after the manager has chosen his twenty-four.

23. Henceforth, the players themselves shall be allowed to choose their own between-innings music. Disc Jockey of the Day. Battle of the Bands. This would get serious fast. Steve Garvey could play whatever he heard in the elevator that morning. Charlie Kerfeld could give us the Screaming Blue Messiahs with "I Wanna Be a Flintstone." Classic suggestions? Vida Blue: "I Wore My .44 So Long, I Made My Shoulder Sore" (Howlin' Wolf). Lou Gehrig: "Takin' Another Man's Place" (Aretha Franklin).

24. Some old traditions shall be restored. No doughnuts or iron bats in the on-deck circle. Swing three bats. It didn't hurt Babe Ruth, and tradition counts for a lot in this game.

All mascots shall be banned except the Phillie Phanatic. Even he gets one week of probation to remove the off-color stuff from his act. The Chicken shall be shot on sight.

Other old traditions shall be destroyed. The seventh-inning stretch shall be history. Even football fans are smart enough to figure out when they want to stand up.

The National Anthem shall not be sung. "O Canada," okay. "America the Beautiful," maybe. But, be warned, the czar is leaning toward a simple "Play ball."

On second thought, any singer who picks the National Anthem shall perform above the Henderson Hole. Umpire's judgment. Crowd may boo or cheer to influence his decision.

25. Bob Costas and Tony Kubek shall get a new partner—Tim McCarver. This trio will broadcast all national TV games for the rest of the century. Anyone who says they are too esoteric, funny, enthusiastic or sarcastic gets his season ticket revoked. Howard Cosell and Joe Garagiola get to do the backup game of the Game of the Week. Thus, if the power of mass prayer has any validity, the main game will never again be rained out.

26. There shall be some changes in how the Hall of Famers are picked. The thousand-plus members of the Baseball Writers of America who are allowed to vote for the Hall of Fame shall have to prove (a) that they are still alive or (b) that they have attended an actual baseball game within the past decade. They shall also be asked to spell M-A-Z-E-R-O-S-K-I.

Neither Nolan Ryan nor Bert Blyleven shall ever be allowed into the Hall of Fame—they don't deserve it. Exception—Ryan and Blyleven can go to Cooperstown if both Jim Kaat and Tommy John, who have had better careers, are put in before them. Entering the '88 season, Ryan was 261–242 with a 3.13 ERA. Blyleven was 244–209 with a 3.14 ERA. Kaat retired at 283–237 with a 3.45 ERA, while John is now 277–216 with a 3.26 ERA. John has as many 20-win years as Ryan and Blyleven combined. Pitching is about winning. Style points don't exist.

27. Any player who refuses to speak to the press during the regular season shall be forbidden to grant any interviews or sign any book contracts in the postseason. This just in by unanimous ballot of the Baseball Writers of America: Dave Kingman, who has contacted every team looking for a job, shall cover the Tigers for the *Detroit Free Press* for one season. It won't be too hard for a bright guy like Dave. About two hundred times a year, counting spring training and the postseason, he'll do an 800-word early-edition "plugger" story, followed by a 1,000-word "running" story while the game is in progress. Then he finishes up his workday by writing a new 1,000-word final-edition story on deadline at midnight, plus maybe a 600-word sidebar for the 1 A.M. edition. During the season, Dave will toss in maybe fifty long features, too, not to mention his Sunday notes column every week. Spending 125 days on the road away from family shouldn't bother him. And he won't forget to cover all the news—like if some millionaire slugger starts following a 90-pound woman reporter around screaming obscenities at her. Maybe he'll even make some news—if Willie Hernandez pours a bucket of water on his head.

28. No more domed stadiums may be built. Whenever artificial turf surfaces must be replaced, they must be replaced by grass. But then, you already knew that. When a team from a grass home park has to play on Astroturf on the road, it shall get to use an extra "short fielder" on defense, just like in coed softball.

29. All symmetrical modern parks shall have grapefruit-sized holes in their outfield walls, like Swiss cheese, so that the occasional 'tweener to the fence sometimes gets stuck inside momentarily. Maybe we can't have wall ivy or a Green Monster in every city, but the game's nonsense factor needs to be improved. The Twins shall be required to fix the Metrodome roof so a normal human can catch a fly ball without 3-D glasses and a hard hat. However, once the ceiling's repainted, critics of the stadium shall shut up. It's exactly the sort of weird idiosyncratic park—with its Plexiglas fence in the left, its big "Baggie" in right and its bizarre caroms in the corners—that we'd protect with a vengeance if it had been built in 1918.

30. Revenue sharing shall be instituted for all teams. This was baseball's best economic option a decade ago, and it still is. Revenue from every ticket should be split 50–50 between the home and visiting teams. (The current home-versus-visitor split is close to 90–10.) This does not mean all teams will have equal revenue. For example, if the Dodgers draw 3 million home fans at $8 a ticket, that's $24 million. They keep half—$12 million. The Dodgers, a famous team, would probably draw 2.25 million on the road. Total road gross (at $8 a head) is, therefore, $18 million. They get half—$9 million. Total Dodger revenues: $21 million. By contrast, the Braves only draw 1 million home fans at $8 a head. Gross—$8 million. They keep $4 million. A dull team like the Braves might draw 1.75 million on the road. Gross—$14 million. They get $7 million. Annual Brave revenues—$11 million.

So an excellent team with superior marketing can have twice the annual ticket take of a poor team in a weak market. That's fair. This isn't baseball socialism. However, my system would be far better than the current setup, which lets clubs like the Yanks operate with five times the income base of the have-nots.

31. The bleachers shall be brought back. Henceforth, one-tenth the seating capacity of all ballparks shall be designated as bleachers. These bleachers shall be sold on game day, not before. The price will be $1 for anyone under 18 or over 65. Everyone else will pay the regular price. Franchises will be allowed to designate 25 games a year as no-bleacher dates, giving them their previous sellouts. Bleachers will make the majority of games available to potential new young fans and loyal older ones. This is called m-a-r-k-e-t-i-n-g.

32. No fielder shall be allowed to use a glove that is larger than a base.

Graig Nettles, a genius with a human-size glove, shall be paid to take infield practice before games until he's sixty years old. Some pleasures are too good to lose.

33. The umpires shall not recognize fan interference on a foul ball. Civil laws (e.g., assault and battery statutes) are sufficient.

34. The major league players and management shall contribute on a 50–50 basis to a pension plan for minor league players who have four or more years of pro experience. The cost: $1 million per franchise per year. That veteran minor-leaguers have no pension and no benefits when they retire is baseball's greatest shame.

35. Salary arbitration shall no longer be in the hands of labor ne-gotiators, many of whom know nothing about baseball. Let the umpires be the arbitrators—they're already called the Ol' Arbiters. What else do they have to do all winter? Who knows the game better? Besides, think how dramatically the players' behavior would improve if umpires set salaries. Along with their new power, umps shall have new con-straints. First of all, no major league umpire shall be allowed to consist of more than 49 percent body fat. Under no conditions are John McSherry and Eric Gregg permitted to work on the same side of the infield. Hey, you in the blue muumuu, mix in a salad.

Each year, the worst umpire in the majors, as determined by player ballot, shall be sent back to the minors. Each year, the best umpire in AAA, as determined by ballot, shall be sent up to the major leagues.

Furthermore, postseason umpires shall be chosen on merit. Oh, you thought they already were? Finally, one set of umpires for both leagues. At once. This is ridiculous.

36. There shall be a Lee Lacy Law: just as hits and errors are flashed on the board, the offical scorekeeper will also be in charge of announcing all outfield throws that miss the cutoff man.

37. No beer shall be served before the first pitch or after the top of the seventh in any park. Any drunken fan who thinks he's tough and goes on the field during a brawl shall be given a catcher's mitt and be forced, under penalty of the Henderson Hole, to warm up Nolan Ryan before his next start.

38. The central combatants who start any baseball brawl shall be forced to have a real fight—three rounds, headgear, 16-ounce gloves, 15-by-15 ring—before the next game between the two teams. It would be something to watch while the grounds crew chalks the batters' boxes. (No extra admission charge.)

Any team that hits a batter with a pitch shall have to send its pitcher up to hit the next time its DH is scheduled to bat.

39. Any Cleveland Indian season-ticket holder shall get a free ticket to one World Series game. Thirty-three years without a single postseason game is enough.

40. Nobody shall report to spring training until March. There's no agony like getting the baseball juices started in mid-February, then having no significant games for seven weeks. In addition, Opening Day will be a national holiday. For children. Like us.

The Heart
of the Order

DH: Carl Yastrzemski

Captain Beefheart

BOSTON, September 16, 1983 — Monday night in Fenway Park, Carl Yastrzemski hit five home runs and made a marvelous catch in the ninth inning to save a no-hitter.

Yastrzemski's first home run of the night was a 420-foot line drive over the Baltimore Orioles bullpen off Jim Palmer, a gentleman who will someday join Yaz in the Hall of Fame.

As the forty-four-year-old jogged the bases, the fans cheered and the sky cried. The instant the ball left Yaz's bat, the rain began, as though even the New England weather wanted some tangible way to pay its respects to the leaving legend.

Yastrzemski's other home runs that night, and his great running catch in defense of Billy Rohr, were all bubbles rising from the past, figments flashed on the vast center-field screen as the Red Sox appeased their crowd during a long rain delay with an old movie about the 1967 Impossible Dream Season.

There was the twenty-eight-year-old Yaz in his Triple Crown glory slugging one pitch after another into that same distant bullpen in a long-ago September, cramming the pennant down the throats of Jose Tartabull and Dalton Jones whether they wanted it or not.

As the twelve-foot-tall mythic Yaz on the screen made his tumbling catches, played caroms off the Monster, threw out runners at all available bases and catapulted those home runs with his chiropractor's dream of a swing, the clouds were not the only source of tears in Fenway Park.

It's tough enough to lose a dignified man who's become a worthy institution when you make it easy on yourself and turn your eyes away, allowing him to slide into retirement only half-noticed. But it's genuinely hard to watch the gimpy, creaky old man fighting to go out with style while the image of his own youth flickers on the screen in double size, taunting him and us with our mortality, reminding us of what we are about to lose.

That night, the rains washed out what would have been Yastrzemski's 453rd home run (17th on the all-time list), his 3,413th hit (7th) and his 1,843rd RBI (9th).

The next evening, in the makeup, Yastrzemski pinch-hit in the ninth inning with the winning run on second base. A mere single was needed. His grounder was stabbed at the last second before it could escape into center field and the old man was thrown out at first base by a step. As an obligatory but taken-for-granted postscript, the Red Sox lost in the twelfth. That's the hard world of fact in which even legends must live.

These days, Yaz is trying to bring it to the wire with panache. Perhaps as early as Saturday, he will break the current all-time record for games played (3,298 by Hank Aaron). It's fitting that Yastrzemski—the man of Polish farming stock—should hold the record for endurance. It suits him better than any other mark. Except for '67, he was never a great player, just a very good one who squeezed every drop of production from his talent.

His Red Sox are back where he found them twenty-three seasons ago: players fighting, after their fashion, to stay out of last place, while management fights, in its fashion, to keep them there.

When the season began, Yastrzemski's goal was "not to be a detriment" to a team he thought might win a pennant. Now that team should worry about being a detriment to Yastrzemski. He is batting .281—just 5 points below his career average—and he's also got 10 homers, 24 doubles and 55 RBI in just 342 at bats. In other words, when he plays, Yastrzemski's production at forty-four is almost identical to his career figures. "This is the way I wanted to go out. But there's still a ways to go."

Yastrzemski must help now with all the last-minute preparations, like a man arranging his own funeral. A front-office man asks him how many seats the family will need for the season-closing "Farewell Yaz" game. "Better make it sixty, with all the in-laws," says Yastrzemski. "My dad says we'll have twenty-one Yastrzemskis in the same place at the same time."

Asked if he dreams about a final at-bat home run, like Ted Williams, he says, "I tried to get a home run for my three thousandth hit and it took me twelve at bats just to get a single. I've learned that lesson."

Yastrzemski knows that his baseball legacy is safe. He's one of those figures who transcended his stats. Yaz batted under .280 twice as often as he hit .300 (13 to 6) and he drove in fewer than 75 runs twice as often as he drove in 100 (11 to 5). He hit more than 23 homers only 4 times in 23 years.

Yet, like Pete Rose, Yastrzemski has managed to leave a personal image of himself that surpasses his professional abilities. Yastrzemski can even put his place in the game into words.

"I'd like to be remembered as a winner," he said this week, sitting by his locker. "Someone who made things happen that helped the team win. But I hope I did it with class. Stan Musial was an idol of mine as a boy. I tried to model myself after him, to a degree.

"Given some ability, and I'm not what you'd call a big specimen, I've gotten the most I possibly could out of it.

"I always see ballplayers come back and say 'if.' Retirement won't be hard for me, because that will never be there for me. 'If I'd worked harder, if I hadn't retired too soon . . .'

"When we have those reunions of the '67 team, most of those guys who've been retired for years *are younger than me*. Almost all of 'em. Their biggest thing is always 'if.' You can see that they haven't accepted it [retirement]. They always pull for me and tell me, 'Keep going.'

"That applies to everything. You want to live so you don't have to say, 'If I'd just given myself a fair chance to succeed . . .' "

If anything galls Yastrzemski it's the team's collapse this year.

"We've had sixteen straight winning seasons here and I'm very proud of that," says Yastrzemski, whose clubs have been 257 games over .500 since '67. "This year feels miserable. I can't imagine how bad it must have felt my first six seasons."

Only Yastrzemski knows how deeply he is gnawed by the Sox failure to win a World Series. He is all ballplayer and sees his world in terms of hanging curveballs, not literary metaphors. "I don't think about all that stuff . . . I'm a quiet farm boy. I guess it just wasn't meant to be. In '67 [in the Series], Bob Gibson in the seventh game was too much. The guy was just great. I accept that.

"But in '75 everything went against us." Yastrzemski gives a recitation of umpires' calls and unlucky hits. Then he pauses and the *real* old wound rises to the surface. "I'll never forget that slop curve to [Tony] Perez." It's nice to know Yastrzemski will never forgive Bill Lee, either.

Catcher:
Gary Carter

Hero's Heart

NEW YORK, October 1985 — Everybody looks Gary Carter in the eye these days. They want to know what manner of man lurks inside. When you catch with one knee wrapped like a mummy, when you can't run right or squat right, when you've lost twenty pounds and ought to be exhausted, how in the name of common sense do you hit 13 home runs and get 34 RBI in September in a hairbreadth pennant race?

How do you have the greatest clutch month of your life, with 8 outright game-winning hits, when you ought to be in traction? How do you amass 32 homers and 99 RBI when you've had one lousy injury after another since Opening Day?

Look deeper. Some people have *eyes* of different colors; it's rare, but there's a name for it. Carter has *one* eye of different colors. As far as he's been able to find out, that's so rare there isn't even a term for it.

"I'm just unique." He grins, squinting that right eye whose iris is halved on a perfect diagonal, one half pure brown, the other pure green.

Just above that eye, the New York Mets All-Star catcher, cleanup slugger and all-purpose hero has another mark of distinction: an old, deep scar like a saber slash that runs three inches across his forehead to the top of his nose.

"Who says you can't run through a brick wall face first?" he asks with a snicker so kidlike that it's easy to forget that this is a man who plays the position of pain and eats it up.

"The Expos tried to make me an outfielder in 1976. I went for a fly ball full-speed and split my whole face wide open on the bricks. I thought I was dead. You could see my skull."

Must have been a vital game. "No. Just spring training in Winter Haven." He shrugs. Bizarre as it seems, athletes really *can't* explain why they try to run through brick walls in spring training games. "That's how I play."

Heroes never know why. That's what makes them ambiguous, powerful, even mysterious. Just unique, like that eye.

On Opening Day this season, in his first game with the Mets after being traded for Hubie Brooks and sundry others, Carter was hit on the elbow with a fastball. Naturally, at least for him, he won the game with a tenth-inning home run. Then he won the next day's game, too. Say hello to New York City, Gary, where they love guys like you who say, "Challenge me. Please."

Carter will play about 150 games this season—only slightly above his iron-man average—and not one has been pain-free. When it wasn't a cracked rib, it was a bad ankle. Then his right knee deteriorated so badly, from leading the league six times in games caught, that doctors told him to put the miserable wheel up on their arthroscopic rack and do a full 1,500-game check—*snip, tie, wash. DL.*

Carter refused.

For ten years in Montreal, he waited to win the pennant that was always predicted, the title that would be built around his toughness and brains, his enthusiasm and leadership, his home runs and cannon throws, his dugout banter and schmaltzy interviews. Never happened. One man with guts out of twenty-five wasn't quite enough.

The Expos always whined that it was really Carter's fault that they didn't win. They stabbed at his broad back constantly, talking about how he was unpopular because he made his teammates look bad by comparison. Always smiling and signing autographs. Always in shape and sacrificing for the team. Always raising money for leukemia, crippled children, cancer research or the boys' clubs. Always drinking milk while they were out . . . well, we now know what at least some of them were doing.

"He's always promoting himself and showing us up," the Expos said. How true.

This is no new Carter who's batted .344 the last six weeks. Every time someone says, "Lights, camera, pressure," Carter accidentally starts hitting line drives through walls. In his only two postseason series he hit .421 and .438. He was most valuable player twice in the All-Star Game. Last year he tied for the NL lead in RBI with 106. But this has been his best year. "Not big hits," says teammate Tom Paciorek. "*Unbelievably* big hits."

"I have to ask myself how many more times I'm going to have this chance to win it all," says Carter, thirty-one and in his eleventh full season—old age for a catcher. "I've had enough cortisone shots in the knee for a whole team, but I can't think about that. I'm glad I didn't have the surgery. Maybe someday, in my wheelchair, I'll look back on this and say it was worth going through a little pain and agony to reach out and take something that was finally within your grasp."

That's how Carter talks. Smart, like the four-year National Honor Society student he was. Florid, like the jock romantic he is, full of purple sentiments. Self-congratulatory in the sense that his words could be translated as "Ain't I one courageous dude?"

But the "pain and agony" are documentable truths, not locker-room pap. This man is burning up his baseball body at double or triple speed. And that wheelchair isn't all joke. He already has caught 1,400 games and had surgery on his *other* knee. The NL record for games caught is 1,861, so we know the species limit.

"It makes me sick to hear Carter get ripped," says Mets manager Davey Johnson. "I see the foul balls off his fingers and the tape all over him. When you *catch* like he catches—hard-nosed and every day—then you can talk all you want. You've earned it.

"He gave ten years of his life's blood in Montreal," says Johnson. "Now they're makin' up stories about him being a bad influence. They're burning him every chance they get. Bush."

Some people have a hard time liking big handsome hulks from Southern California who star in three sports at *Sunnyhills* High and turn down a scholarship to be the quarterback at UCLA. They gag at somebody who blocks the plate, ignores injuries, nicknames himself "The Kid" and gives hundred-word answers to three-word questions.

In a world that's often too bad to believe, they fear people who seem too good to be true. For them, virtue will always seem more threatening than vice, because it's less accessible. They'll mistrust the heart of Carter, the humor of Rose, the dignity of Garvey. In this, heroes are no help at all because they can never really explain.

First Base:
Rod Carew

Taken to Heart

May 16, 1983 — Because of his pride, intelligence, sensitivity and, perhaps, because of his vanity and stubbornness, too, Rod Carew takes everything to heart and keeps it there. At times, he seems to be the only man in baseball capable of hitting .400 and being melancholy at the same time.

"I'm hurt by what's said about me . . . Maybe I'm too sensitive, but that's the way I've always been," said Carew, the California Angel who bears seven batting titles and one cross—the fixed thought that he's unappreciated.

"I think in my career I've played the game as intelligently as anyone. I do what I'm capable of doing. I know my limits and I don't try to go beyond them," said Carew who, at thirty-seven, is hitting .411 and, simultaneously, threatening to retire because he is disgusted with "unfair" criticism.

"Sometimes it seems like all I hear is how I don't drive in enough runs, don't hit home runs . . . don't hit well under pressure. Or else somebody's knocking me as 'aloof and moody.' I just get sick of it. Maybe it doesn't bother some other guys, but it hurts me . . . I'm human . . .

"What about the rallies I get started and the ones I keep going? It's always my RBI or runs [scored]," said Carew, who in sixteen seasons has driven in more than 70 runs only three times and scored more than 100 runs only once. "My [career] on-base percentage (.395) is one of the highest. But I can't drive myself in . . . I just want credit for what I've accomplished."

Of all the outstanding players in baseball, few are as much of a pleasure to watch, or as hard to evaluate, as Carew. It is easier to appreciate the artistry of what Carew does best, hit singles, than it is to decide where those one-base hits place him in the history of his game.

As a batsman, a student of a rigorous and changing craft, Carew stands alone in his generation as Ty Cobb and Ted Williams did in theirs. No hitter in the game is more watched and discussed at the technical level than Carew. His style is intensely individual, matched to his personality and unconventional to the point of being unique.

"Carew never swings at bad balls, he never lets his ego interfere with playing the game his way, he never overswings," said Charley Lau, batting coach of the Chicago White Sox. "Mechanically, he's fluid, with no tension. He barely uses his muscles.

"The worst thing you can do is think you have a book on him. You can't go with a pattern to Carew, because he'll recognize it very quickly and then he's got you. You have to disguise your ideas, save 'em for an important situation."

Last season, for instance, Baltimore became convinced Carew could be confounded by a diet of slow and slower curveballs; he hit .219 against the Orioles. This year, Baltimore has tried more of the same. The result: Carew is 15 for 25 (.600) and another "pattern" has been unraveled.

On a team full of star hitters, each Angel sees a different, distinctive quality in Carew. To Bobby Grich, it is Carew's stillness at the plate, his "quiet" gestures, that are most striking, as well as the way "he hits with his hands, not his body. And he almost never pops a ball up." To catcher Bob Boone, it's a mystery how a man can be a master of six stances and switch from one to another within the same at bat; what hand-eye coordination, a pure inexplicable gift, that must require.

Pitcher Tommy John likes to needle Carew about his knack of hitting fastballs on the fists with the label part of his bat, yet still dumping the ball over the infield for a soft bloop hit. "Rodney's secret is that he cheats," said John, for Carew's benefit. "He corks his bat. Other players cork the barrel. I think Carew corks the handle."

Perhaps it's Fred Lynn, the other batting champion on the team, who perceives Carew's innovations most clearly. "First, he bunts better than anyone else, even with two strikes. That distorts the whole infield and creates wider angles for him to hit the ball through. It's like he's always hitting with the infield pulled in. His bunting creates holes.

"Also, he's the only hitter I've ever seen who has an inside-out swing that puts topspin on the ball. Usually you only get topspin when you pull the ball. As he swings, Carew's hands are way out in front of the bat, and the barrel is actually lying below the plane of the swing. Then he snaps his left hand from completely under the bat to completely over it."

Thus Carew has invented a swing that incorporates almost every advantage that a contact hitter could want. He can wait until the last instant to commit his wristy, inside-out swing. He's snake-quick because he uses little body movement and relies on reflexes, not muscle. His bunting and his unique knack for hitting smashes past a drawn-in left side complement each other.

What Carew's swing does not allow him to do is hit with power. Of his 2,757 career hits (31st in history), 78 percent have been singles; Carew has only 85 homers and he knocks a ball out of the park about once a month.

It is Carew's perverse misfortune that he has accomplished so much that he has moved his name into a class where it may not belong. When a player has the highest career batting average (.331) since Ted Williams retired, and when he wins seven silver bats to move into the same batting champion category as Ty Cobb (twelve), Honus Wagner (eight), Rogers Hornsby (seven) and Stan Musial (seven), then the standards by which he is measured tend to change.

Instead of being judged only in relation to the innate limits of his talent and physique, a player is inevitably measured against the achievements of those whose statistical company he keeps.

For instance, Cobb, Wagner, Hornsby and Musial hit not only for average but, by the standards of their eras, for power and run production. All of them won titles for total bases, slugging percentage and RBI as well as batting average. Carew hasn't won any of these, and almost certainly won't. As he said, "When I try to jerk a ball out of the park, I only hurt myself. I tried to do it on Monday night and I pulled a muscle in my back" (forcing him to leave that game and miss the next).

Carew is a finesse player, and a fragile one; he has missed an average of twenty-six games a year with injuries, usually minor, nagging ones. He asks for a night off more often than most stars because he knows he must be in perfect working order to ply his delicate craft. Also, he'll rest against tough left-handed pitchers.

All this contributes to the perception that Carew plays only when he feels like it, and when it suits the interests of his batting average. Adding to Carew's image problems are other elements of style, and a couple of nagging numbers. Carew is meticulously neat, hates to get his uniform dirty and considers it the height of poor judgment for a great hitter to injure himself while playing defense. Thus he almost never dives for a ground ball and moves aside to play many hard ground smashes sidesaddle.

In short, it's all too easy to see Carew as a sort of baseball lyric poet with extremely clean fingernails. The fact that he has one RBI in 50 at bats in 4 league championship series and one RBI in 13 All-Star games also gives fodder to those who want their hitting heroes to be macho.

Despite the sport's inherent bias toward muscle, it should be noted that, over his career, Carew has averaged nearly a full run produced per game (.973). Only a dozen active players, names such as Schmidt, Jackson, Rice and Murray, have done better.

It is Carew's misfortune that, as he approaches his 3,000th hit, he continues to be placed under a scrutiny that, while it may be fair, hardly seems as generous as befits a man so elegant.

Second Base: Bill Ripken

Heart's Delight

BALTIMORE, July 12, 1987 — Cal Ripken, Jr., has been in the major leagues six years. He still drinks milk. Bill Ripken has been in the bigs one day. He drinks beer. As he walked out of the Baltimore Orioles clubhouse Saturday night, he heard Alan Wiggins say, "Way to pick it, Bill." "Thanks, Wiggie," shot back Ripken, like he's been there years. "Don't drink all the Schlitz," said Wiggins.

Calvin and Bill (only outsiders call them Cal and Billy) are brothers, the first siblings ever to play in the majors with their father as manager. Even so, it would be a mistake to mistake them. You'd want Cal to date your sister. But she'd probably want to investigate Bill first. It's not that Bill's so handsome, not with all those scabs, even on his forehead, from his reckless abandon. But there's something unique about a cocky, gravel-voiced twenty-two-year-old who mixes gall and charm. Ask Bill about his first play, a room service grounder, and he says, "Nice to get

63

Sunday hops on Saturday night." That puts him ahead of both father and brother in colorful career quotes.

"Everybody loves Bill," says his sister Ellen. He's the Ripken with the pizzazz, the one they tell the stories about. When cops were rousting Ellen and a girlfriend outside a clubhouse in Richmond, taking them for groupies, Bill heard the voices, walked outside in just a towel, said, "Got it under control, sis?" then turned around and walked back inside. Problem solved.

"Mom cried when she found out that she was pregnant with Bill. It was a surprise," said Ellen as she sat in the box seats behind home plate in Memorial Stadium during the seventh-inning stretch watching her little brother's major league debut. "But Dad told her, 'Don't worry. He'll be the joy.' I'm not tellin' any tales out of school, am I, Fred?" says Ellen, turning to brother Fred. "A few years ago Mom and Dad were in a restaurant and Bill was being his usual outgoing self and Dad wrote on a napkin and passed it to Mom, 'Told you he'd be the joy.' You remember that, don't you, Fred?"

"Was that the same night," asks the demythologizing Fred, "that Bill threw the birthday cake in that guy's face?"

Mother Vi, Ellen and Fred barely watch the historic game, focusing far more on Fred's cute daughter—the first grandchild in a family that believes profoundly in family. "The one and only grandchild," says Vi, as though others better get on the stick. Yet the split second a grounder heads toward Bill, Vi yells, sharply yet routinely, "Come on, hon." Before the play's even over she's turned away, knowing the outcome.

The rest of baseball thinks the three-Ripken phenomenon defies all odds. Yet the family seems incredibly blasé. Their sense of the baseball order is so ingrained they find it hard to think any other way. If a player's good enough to make the majors, he should make it and will. If he isn't, he shouldn't and won't. If Bill deserves it, he'll get it. If he doesn't, he shouldn't. What's the issue? If Bill hit .190, it almost seems the family would prefer him in AAA. Isn't that the way it should be?

"I'll go get examined one day and find out what's wrong with me," says Cal Sr. "Maybe in twenty years when I'm in a rocking chair, all these things will have some meaning in a different way. Right now I got twenty-four people to take care of."

"Cal [Sr.] and Bill are going to have a lot of media, fans, even players, questioning all this. So they have to be formal, even more professional, than they are," says Vi. "You wouldn't believe how many people say, 'It has to be pull, not ability.' Average fans relate to their own experience, like the Little League dad who coaches his sons, so they can't conceive that in the professional world discriminations of talent really are made impartially."

If anyone thinks the Ripkens are tittering with delight these days, then they haven't analyzed the pressure in the situation. "I can imagine it," says Roy Smalley, Jr., whose father was a big league shortstop and whose uncle, Gene Mauch, managed him. "My biggest accomplishment in baseball was beating all the shit. I took in Minnesota my first two years there. When you're demonstrably disliked en masse because people think you're getting to play on your name, it's ego-deflating and embarrassing. You want to make it quit, silence everybody, right now, today. And it can't be done that fast.

"I still run into fans who think I married Calvin Griffith's daughter . . . This game'll thrill you to death and make you sick to your stomach. On bad days, you find out how much people like to yell at ballplayers. The family connection is just more ammo.

"The flip side is that playing for Gene was fun and I can imagine how much fun it would have been to play for my dad," adds Smalley. "Talk to Bill Ripken in a couple of years. I bet he'll say he wouldn't trade this."

"Many players would end up hating the game if they were in the situation Bill is in," says Orioles coach Elrod Hendricks. "It's a double whammy. His father is the manager. And he plays next to his brother, who'll probably be in the Hall of Fame. Bill can't possibly live up to the comparisons with his brother.

"I've heard it enough already. Even before spring training. 'Why doesn't he hit with power like his brother?'" says Hendricks. "But Bill is so strong-minded—much more like his daddy than Cal Jr.—that I think he'll close his eyes and ears to it and get through it all."

Hendricks's real fear is that Bill will suffer a syndrome he's seen often in the eighties. "All our young guys who've gotten big buildups —Mike Young, John Shelby, Storm Davis, Dennis Martinez, Ken Dixon—were asked to do things in the majors they'd never even done in the minors. All you heard was twenty wins or forty homers. When they didn't live up to [false] expectations, people said, 'He's a bum.' They ended up doing less than they were capable of."

If anything, the Orioles are giving Bill no buildup whatsoever. The line is that Pete Stanicek is the future at second base and Craig Worthington at third. Ripken projects as a scuffler.

Yet the whole family has a way of consistently exceeding predictions.

As recently as two years ago, when Earl Weaver returned to manage and Bill was having his second injury-ruined season in the minors, who truly expected that July 11, 1987, would get into the record books?

Who'd have believed the father would become a respected manager, widely perceived as much more competent than the team he inherited? As for skinny Bill, that's even more of a shock. At six feet one, he's filled out to 180 pounds and arrives in Bal'mer with the reputation of being a superb fielder and a heady, fairly durable leader. Somehow, his average has improved as he's gone up the ladder. At Charlotte .268, then .286 at Rochester this year with eight straight hits recently. Is this the kid who needed two years to get out of rookie ball?

The Ripkens' future is uncertain, to say the least. The father could end up fired because of his players. Even if Bill gives his best, his Orioles career might be brief. As for Cal Jr., if his dad were fired, would he re-sign with the Orioles? Conceivably, all three Ripkens could be gone next Opening Day. Or all could be fixtures. These delicious yet tense days for the Ripkens should be taken for what they are worth and savored. After all, it's not every father who, even for one sweet summer, gets to gaze on either side of second base and see his pride and joy.

Shortstop:
Don Mattingly

Heart and Soul

It's tough to win a batting title your first full season, follow that with a Most Valuable Player Award and still remain somewhat unknown. To do so while playing for the New York Yankees ought to be impossible. But then, Don Mattingly's a tough guy. Tough to know, tough to predict, tough to evaluate. Toughest to get out.

Most twenty-four-year-olds would recall the winter night when they received the MVP plaque as one of glory. Mattingly says, "I don't remember much about it, except our son Taylor lost his pacifier and we were up all night with him. That'll bring you back to earth."

Just when you think you have the Don of the Bronx pegged as a phlegmatic stoic, he comes to a banquet after the Super Bowl wearing punk sunglasses and a headband with "Steinbrenner" on it. "Did it because Pete Rozelle was there," he says. That argument with George

III over his new $1.37 million contract—close to a million-buck raise in a year—couldn't have anything to do with it?

If you guess along with Mattingly, you'll be the one who gets burned. That's the pitchers' book on the compact five-foot-eleven, 185-pound first baseman—little good it does them. Mattingly takes things as he finds them, then reacts. Except, occasionally, when he gets a step ahead of you, sets you up, and leaves you wondering, "Who's behind that mask anyway?"

Ask what pitcher and what pitch are hardest for him and he pulls a perfect Mattingly. "John Candelaria. Haven't got a clue to him yet. And high fastballs on the inner half. Write that down." True, Candy Man owns him. But the pitch Mattingly hits best is the fastball in his wheelhouse. If he tells this white lie often enough, some dumb pitcher somewhere is going to believe it.

Nobody has figured out Mattingly yet, that's true. Two years ago, he was just a prospect who'd hit .283 as a rookie but with no power (4 homers in 279 at bats). Then the Yankees hoped he might be a perennial .300 hitter. Now that estimate's radically revised.

"Who do you compare him to?" says former Yankees star Roy White. "Compare him to anybody you want. Stan Musial, Ted Williams, Joe DiMaggio."

For historical reference, the Musial analogy works. Left-handed hitter. Eccentric closed and coiled stance. Sprays the ball. Tons of doubles. Not too many walks. Hard to strike out.

"He doesn't look like Musial, but he hits like him," says Orioles manager Earl Weaver. "Musial was the best at adjusting once the ball left the pitcher's hand. He'd hit the pitcher's pitch. Williams was the best at making them throw him his pitch. He didn't believe in adjusting. If it wasn't what he wanted, he knew enough to walk to first base. That's why he hit .406.

"Once every coupla games, a Musial or Mattingly is going to adjust and put that tough pitch in play instead of walking and you're going to get some extra outs. But he's also going to drive you crazy by popping a perfect fastball on the fists down the left-field line for a double."

The difference between Stan the Man and Mattingly is that, at similar ages, Mattingly is undeniably ahead. Sure, Musial averaged 209 hits, 79 extra-base hits and a .352 average in his first two big years. But Mattingly has been in that stratospheric range, too, for the last two years: 209 hits, 77 extra-base hits and a .333 average.

Plus.

Plus, Mattingly hit 23, then 35 homers and drove in 110, then 145 runs. When Musial was twenty-three, twenty-four years old, he was a comparative stripling, hitting about a dozen homers and driving in 80 or 90 runs.

"The power's been evolutionary. A surprise, I never expected to hit thirty-five," says Mattingly. "I learned the weight shift from Lou Piniella. He taught me to use my body more, look for pitches, set up pitchers and pull the ball."

The last Yankee to drive in more runs than Mattingly was DiMaggio in '48. Nobody in the American League has led the majors in doubles back to back since Tris Speaker. Special players do special things. Immediately.

Another Mattingly distinction is a Gold Glove. "Day game after a night game. Mattingly's still out there taking his hundred ground balls," says coach Jeff Torborg. When Mattingly botched one last July, it ended a streak of 1,371 plays without error. Try that playing catch.

Sometimes he sneaks out to shortstop during the New York Yankees' batting practice to take grounders and fire clean, accurate, right-handed pegs to first base. Usually nobody notices him because he's built like a shortstop, moves nimbly like a shortstop and wears an inconspicuous infielder's number—23.

Because Don Mattingly throws left-handed, very few people realize he is out at shortstop—learning, polishing, plotting, dreaming.

"He's always wanted to play shortstop right-handed. It's his fantasy," says Roy White. "It's amazing to watch him. You know, he looks like a pretty good shortstop."

Encircling Mattingly in comparisons only highlights his glow. He's Wade Boggs with power. Eddie Murray with hustle. George Brett but younger and in a home run park with Rickey Henderson on base and Dave Winfield on deck.

None of these parallels charm Mattingly much. "I appreciate it . . . but it doesn't help me on the field. So let it go. I'd compare myself more to Bill Buckner. He's consistent, hard-nosed, good in the clutch. I love the way he plays. If it's biting it takes, then it's biting; if it's scratching, then scratch . . . I'll take a ground ball off the chest, get my uniform dirty."

Why Buckner? When Mattingly was a teenager in Evansville, Indiana, Buckner was hitting .300 for the Cubs, the Midwest's darlings. Why the passion for consistency—the neither-rain-nor-sleet approach to performance? Well, (okay, laugh) his dad was a postman.

Mattingly's the easiest sort of player to praise—the quiet gamer with eye black like a punt returner and low, unstylish stirrups below his pants. "Half the time you forget he's even here," says White.

"What I do on the field, that's me," says Mattingly. "If I take care of my game, everything falls in place. The game is the thing you can control. Especially in New York, where so much stuff can clutter you up."

Like Ron Guidry, who clings to the bayou, Mattingly is defiantly anti-style. Just by existing, Mattingly is a standing critique of Henderson. A Yankees prankster has tacked a sign above Henderson's locker here: "O Lord, help my words to be gracious and tender today, for tomorrow I may have to eat them." No one ever snipes at Mattingly.

As they say, no brag, just fact. "I feel like I earned the MVP. I've worked hard," says Mattingly, "I kind of expected it. If I didn't win it last year, I didn't know when I ever would. I don't know if I'll ever do that again."

Don't bet against him. He adjusts. Mattingly abandoned a written "book" on pitchers. "Too monotonous . . . Actually, they're all tough, or none of them are. I get everybody or everybody gets me." What he really discovered was that a chronicle on catchers helped more. When lefties troubled him, he found a way to trouble them back: though he hits 60 points less against them, he slugs more homers in far fewer at bats.

If Mattingly has a flaw, it's probably ineradicable because it runs to the core. Will he, like Buckner, be too tough to stay in one piece? Last spring, arthroscopic knee surgery. This spring, a bone bruise to the thumb that has him benched. So far, not much. But will it add up?

Come back in 2001 for that. Then we'll really see how well he stacks up with Musial. For now, let Scott McGregor speak for a multitude of pained pitchers who have gotten to know Don Mattingly far too well, far too quickly. "How does he strike me?" says the Oriole. "All over the place. He just waxes you and goes home."

Third Base:
Wade Boggs

Heartburn

BOSTON, July 26, 1987 — As he pitches batting practice to the Boston Red Sox, Bill Fischer feels like Igor, the aide to Dr. Frankenstein, who watched a monster as it was created a bit and a piece at a time. For three years, Fischer has watched Wade Boggs re-create himself. Now the Wadester or the Boggman is almost ready to erupt. When Fischer arrived, Boggs was still a purist, a fanatic about hitting nothing but line drives. "He'd even get furious if he hit a liner in batting practice that had the wrong spin," says Fischer. "He hated those topspinners that dove." As for fly balls: totally anathema.

A man who eats chicken before every game, sits in the same spot in the dugout before every at bat and crosses the foul line at precisely the same minute each evening is clearly a perfectionist, a person who wants to control every situation and eliminate surprise. In his early days, Boggs may have been the most boring man in baseball—proof that almost any quaiity, taken to its apotheosis, can become fascinating and approximate a virtue. Studying him at bat was like watching a computer purr. He'd swing at a first pitch, or a bad pitch, once a week and pop up to the infield once a month.

Even with two strikes, he was, statistically, twice as likely to get a hit as to strike out because of his compact, almost defensive swing. He'd rather demoralize than demolish. For every hit, he'd make just as many loud outs. For him, a bad swing was a slump and a soft out a cause for revenge.

Yet, with the years, Boggs has learned to dream of living dangerously. A bit at a time, he's turning slugger—an idea so contrary to his nature that some doubt he'll ever execute it. "There's no question that Boggs hits the ball farther and harder than Jim Rice or Dwight Evans or Don Baylor," says the old pitching coach Fischer. "He has titanic power that he hasn't shown yet. But he will. He regularly hits the ball onto the roof in Chicago and into the waterfalls in Kansas City. He'll hit ten home runs in one round of batting practice. He'd win any home run contest he ever entered."

How many homers could Boggs hit?

"As many as he wants."

"He outdistances any of us," says Baylor, who has 330 career homers. "It's not close. He has great arm extension and he finishes very high —just like a golfer who hits it three hundred yards. Look above his locker. Two pictures. One of extension, one of a high finish. Until you see it every day, you don't realize how strong he is. It seems like he can hit it as far as he wants to. Yet he never loses his form. His head isn't flying out like a pull hitter's.

"Boggs can be the one slugger who can also hit .350 to .370."

Since no such Ultimate Weapon has existed in baseball since Ted Williams, it would be extremely wise to require Boggs to do these things before giving him credit for them. Nonetheless, signs and omens are at hand. In his first five seasons, Boggs hit only 32 homers in 2,778 at bats—about one a month. Of course, he did manage to bat .352—the fourth-highest mark in history behind Ty Cobb, Rogers Hornsby and Shoeless Joe Jackson. Last winter, facing arbitration, the Red Sox told Boggs they couldn't pay a $2-million-a-year type contract to a singles hitter. Boggs told them to "bat me third" instead of leadoff and watch the home runs fly.

The Red Sox believed him. They also suspected he might never hit those home runs unless he was properly paid for them in advance. This is an enormously proud man who spent six wasted years in the minor leagues—during which he never missed a batting title by more than four points in any full year. Yet he never got a shot at playing in Fenway Park. Seems unbelievable now; but it's fresh as yesterday to Boggs. "Nobody can take a batting title away from me. You don't vote for that. There are no [front office] politics," Boggs says, tight-lipped under his red mustache. "You have to work hard for everything you get in this life, but you don't always get what you deserve . . . If I'm obsessed with being the best, then it's because I don't want anybody to take anything away from me."

So the Red Sox carved out a contract Boggs could love. And as soon as the opportunity presented itself, Manager John McNamara moved Boggs into the third hole—residence of Williams, Babe Ruth and their kin. No more leadoff man. Since then Boggs has batted .390 with 40-home-run power. It's almost as though he'd been so hurt and squelched at Bristol and Pawtucket that he refused to provide services until they were paid in full. Or maybe it just took him until he was twenty-nine to put all the bolts in his neck and screws in his forehead.

At the moment, Boggs is hitting .366 with 17 homers, 27 doubles, 5 triples and 135 hits. That projects to the old Boggs, but with a new gland. "Yes, I can keep hitting home runs, if I keep deciding to hit fly balls," he says. "But fly balls are also outs. Line drives are hits." In other words, Boggs will hit home runs just as long as it doesn't detract from his image: the Man Who Really Might Hit .400. The Wadester may be coming, but not without a price in personality adjustment. Boggs wants it all. No wasted motion or emotion. No slumps, flaws or vulnerability.

When he went 0 for 11 recently, including 0 for 6 in one game, some turned to the Book of Revelation. Sure enough, there it was. One of the portents for the end of the world. The next day, Boggs shaved his full beard, months in the growing, and immediately whacked up a double, a triple and a disabled pitcher in his next game. "One inch to the right, and it would've missed his pitching hand," said Boggs, ever sympathetic, "and I'd have had a hit."

To others, Boggs's evolution is a drama. To him, it's just evolution. "This is a man who does not shun a day's work," says McNamara. "He's made himself into a great third baseman," says longtime Coach Johnny Pesky. "Those plays he made in the World Series last fall were typical of what he's been doing for two years—turning plays that would make Clete Boyer or Brooks Robinson proud . . . He's worth every cent they pay him. He was born with a great talent and he's developed all of it."

"He's such a competitor and has such great work habits that he just

73

keeps getting better at everything," says Baylor. "Every young player should watch Boggs and [Don] Mattingly."

At times, the game seems utterly simple to Boggs. Two books sit on his coffee table at home: *My Turn at Bat*, by Williams, and *The Art of Hitting .300*, by the late Charley Lau. The first governs Boggs's head, preaching patience, selectiveness, study of pitchers' habits and the need to wait until the last instant. The second is his guide to modern batting mechanics. Lau's best disciple, Walt Hriniak, is Boston's batting coach, so Boggs stays close to the source. Finally, Boggs's father was a renowned fast-pitch softball player in Florida, so the little boy had to master the quick inside-out swing needed to hit a 100 mph pitch from just forty-five feet away.

Add to this Boggs's 20/10 eyesight—the same one-in-a-million score that brought Williams so much pride—and you have a man suited to unique feats. No wonder Boggs can shrug and say, "Everybody asks me 'why' about everything. I have no idea. I see it. I swing. I hit it.

"People want one secret. They want to say, 'It's like this.' Well, it's not 'Pass go and automatically collect $200.' Hitting is never the same two days in a row. It's intangibles, so many intangibles. Is the wind blowing in? Where are they pitching you? With me, it's here, there and everywhere. Never a pattern. Where is the defense? Some play me to pull, some pitch me away. If there were one way [to hit], then everybody would be great . . .

"Sometimes you have a fight at home and go oh for four. Next day it's patched up and you go four for four . . . Don't say luck doesn't matter. No matter how much you prepare, you can't eliminate luck. A perfect swing can be a line drive right at somebody and an imperfect swing can be a bloop hit . . . I had twelve diving catches made against me in one week early this year. Daryl Boston dove four rows into the seats to take a home run away from me. They never even out—not even close. You lose far more hits than you get."

And what if he could leave aside those thoughts of silver bats and, perhaps, a .400 season? Boggs may be working on that project as we speak. "I bat too many times a year to hit .400," he says. "I'd like to hit once a week—like the NFL where you play 16 games. The day I play 120 games in a season is when I'll have a chance to hit .400." Thus Boggs has moved the quest for .400 into a late-career holding pattern. "Rest when you're tired, take care of your injuries," he says, fantasizing about the joys of baseball old age. "Especially, miss that tough left-hander who can bring you down for three or four days afterward."

Entering this season, only three pitchers have had any success with him: Don Sutton (6 for 31), Matt Young (1 for 19) and Dan Quisenberry (2 for 19). In other words, one right-hander, one left-hander and one submariner. "I guess maybe they're the select few of each group," says Boggs, laughing.

Much amuses Boggs, who is not given to the outright laugh. Those who try to search out all the obscure records that he breaks particularly tickle him. He calls them "fossil hunters." When did a major leaguer last have 240 hits before Boggs did it in 1985? Answer: 1930. Who last had 200 hits and 100 walks in the same year before Boggs did it in 1986? Answer: Stan Musial, 1953. When the proper fossil is unearthed, his name is usually Tris Speaker or somebody else who gets his fan mail forwarded to Cooperstown. So far, wherever Boggs has gone, someone has trod before. "I have not broken any new ground," he says. Nonetheless, you get the feeling that he expects to explore the uncharted before he's finished. "I want to be the best," Boggs says, leaving his time frame vague. "That is the bottom line. That's what drives me."

With that, he heads back to the batting cage to add a stitch here or there. Fischer, who once set a major league record of going 84 innings without walking a man, lays pitch after pitch right where Boggs wants. The line drives crash off Fenway's walls and fences. When one pitch is low, breaking Boggs's concentration, Fischer apologizes. Behind the cage, McNamara and Hriniak observe every pitch closely—a support system if they should be needed. The wind blows in, hard enough to make the flag snap. "Last one," says Fischer.

Boggs uncoils and the ball bores its way through the wind—over the right-center-field fence, over the bullpen and well into the bleachers, an easy 420 feet. Boggs doesn't notice, walks away taking it completely for granted.

But it makes you wonder.

Left Field:
Pedro Guerrero

Warrior's Heart

July 1985 — Even in a complex age we still sometimes meet a man as simple and hard as the poverty that made him. Crush a thousand men and 999 may die, but the one who lives will be special. One of nature's crueler laws. Pedro Guerrero's last name means "warrior" and that's close enough.

When you are born poor in San Pedro de Macorís in the Dominican Republic, you fight upward or you sink down. You succeed or you cut cane for a lifetime.

"I always know I am going to make it in the major leagues someday," says Guerrero, who signed a pro contract at sixteen and this year, at twenty-nine, may be the most valuable player in the National League. Why? Guerrero's handsome, smooth face grows implacably quiet. "Because I could not go back. There was nothing."

Twenty years ago, Manny Mota of the Los Angeles Dodgers played winter ball in his native Dominican Republic. To the children who swarmed around him he threw coins. Now the children of San Pedro de Macorís have grown up. A dozen of them are in the majors—more big leaguers than have been produced by any city of its size on earth, Joaquin Andujar, George Bell, Tony Fernandez, Julio Franco and Juan Samuel among them.

How many children, like Guerrero, looked at Mota, Rico Carty, Juan Marichal and the three Alou brothers and said, "That's the way out," we cannot know. We only meet those very few, like Guerrero, who are so exceptional that learning the game with a guava-tree limb for a bat is no hindrance.

Today Mota is the Dodgers' hitting coach, leaning on the cage. Guerrero is their hitter, launching practice pitches into the Veterans Stadium upper deck with a swing both savage and compact. Many, looking at Guerrero's .326 batting average, his 28 home runs, his 70 RBI and his $7 million five-year contract, call this a success story. Guerrero knows better. He goes back to San Pedro de Macorís every winter. The poor come to him, a steady stream it sometimes seems. To beg.

"I can't find a way to say no," he says. "They know I am rich. And I know how poor they are. They come to my house, stop me on the street. I'm a real soft touch. I don't think that's bad.

"They all tell a story. About their mother or child who is sick. I know some are lying, just to get the money. Just like anywhere else—good people, bad people. Some are the ones who boo me at the ballpark.

"It bothers me," says Guerrero, "that I cannot tell who is telling the truth, who really needs the money and how much."

So what does he do?

"I guess." He shrugs. "Some ask for fifty dollars and I give them twenty-five. Some ask for twenty-five and I give them a hundred.

"But to everyone at least I give something," says Guerrero, who funds eleven youth teams. "I will do anything for that little town."

"Pedro never forgets his friends," says Mota. Or his parents, for whom he has bought a home, or his brother, who lives in his L.A. condo, or even rookie teammate Mariano Duncan—yes, also from San Pedro—who lived with Guerrero and his wife, Denise, for three months.

Let's be honest. Guerrero is no saint. Just a proud, driven and simple man, remember. He is as vain as he is handsome, posing in front of mirrors without knowing it for minutes at a time, seemingly transfixed by his own beauty. He expects special treatment from the Dodgers and gets it. After the strike, Guerrero missed the first game back and the

Dodgers weren't even going to fine him until the NL made it a mandatory policy for any AWOL players.

True, Guerrero loves food too much; he ballooned to 218 pounds once last year, and someday the massive chest and buttocks that are now his power source could become his enemy. True, he spends his money as generously on himself as he gives it to others; he loves jewelry and lives in affluence near Dodgers owner Peter O'Malley. No Dodger would emphasize such nagging demerits against a loyal team man who plays hurt, hard and smart.

Perhaps one story says enough about Guerrero as a player. Save it for *The Natural II*. Last month, Guerrero's bad back, which sometimes goes out of place and spasms, had a spell so severe that Manager Tommy Lasorda told Guerrero to leave the game. "Let me give it one swing," said Guerrero. One swing. More like a half-swing, as Guerrero reinjured his back. The result: one 430-foot game-winning homer over the center-field fence. Guerrero needed forty seconds to *walk* the bases, then was out of the lineup more than a week.

Such heroics, everything in fact that Guerrero has done this year, have been a joyous vindication after nearly a season and a half of frustration. In '84 Guerrero was weighted down by excess poundage, by the expectations attendant on a $1.25-million-a-year deal and, finally, by the pressure of being shifted from the comfort of the outfield to the embarrassment of third base.

Many a star, coming off back-to-back 30-homer, 100-RBI years, would have nixed the position switch. But Guerrero gritted his teeth through 22 errors and six months of Chavez Ravine boos. "I try not to listen to the boos," he said. "Every day I read the letters from Dodger fans—twenty-five to fifty of them—all telling me, 'We are with you. Those who boo are not the true Dodger fans.'"

On June 1 this year, Guerrero was headed toward another season of humble 16-homer, 72-RBI power stats. Finally the Dodgers admitted they'd been dumb. Lasorda gave Guerrero a reprieve to play left field, saying, "We know you're willing to play third, but we'd rather have your bat than your glove."

His dignity, his performing grace, in a sense, restored, Guerrero homered in his first game and hit 15 home runs in June, winning NL player of the month. Then he batted .460 in July.

"You know that nursery rhyme, 'Thirty days hath September, April, June and November,'" says Lasorda. "Well, I changed it. I knew June was Pedro's favorite month, so I told him that in the U.S., June had sixty days. I'd see him in July and say, 'Well, Pedro, it's June 52 and I see you're still hot.' "

To Guerrero, it does not mean a great deal that he leads the league in slugging and on-base percentage. His play comes from deeper sources. As he says of one Dominican team owner who once gave him a few much-needed dollars during his bush-league days, "He showed me he cared about me before I was famous. He buy my heart."

The things Pedro Guerrero wants most, money no longer buys. That, perhaps, is why he gives away his millions so freely. "Winning honors is nice," he says, "but I remember my rookie season ['81] when we won the World Series. That was the best.

"I play for the ring," says Pedro Guerrero, "and the sweet champagne."

Center Field:
Eric Davis

Heart Stopper

CINCINNATI, May 7, 1987—Every spring brings its baseball phenoms. But Eric Davis is a phenom raised to a higher power. The familiar problem of how a gifted man turns potential into reality has redoubled urgency these days whenever the Cincinnati Reds come to town. "Eric Davis has more raw talent than any player I have ever seen in my life, including Willie Mays," says Reds manager Pete Rose. "I wouldn't be surprised at anything he does. Well, except hit .400. Too hard . . . The things he can do, it's scary. And I get to write his name down every day."

"There's one like Eric Davis every fifty years," says veteran Dave Parker, who, some thought, was that "one" fifteen years ago. "It's a thrill to watch him. They should make me pay. I just hope he stays healthy and hungry so he can reach his full potential—which is unlimited."

While many leap to praise, some cover their eyes, recalling Cesar Cedeño and Bobby Bonds a generation ago. "We're jumping the gun on Eric Davis," says New York Mets manager Davey Johnson. "It's not fair to him. That kind of potential can be a kiss of death. When people lead you to believe you're that good, before you really are that good, it's an albatross around your neck. We give superstar accolades before the production comes—then the guy has to live with it. He can't even enjoy the game. It scares me. In a way, I'm glad he's on some other team. It is pressure. Hell, he's still learning who Eric Davis is . . . He reminds me of Bobby Bonds. Remember Bonds?"

In the midst of all this stands a tall, slim, bow-legged wraith from Los Angeles who runs as fast and hits a ball as far as almost anybody who has ever played the game. In his last 508 at bats—slightly less than a full season—he has 39 home runs, 93 stolen bases, 125 runs scored and 98 RBI.

Yes, Mark Fidrych, Fernando Valenzuela, Dwight Gooden and Roger Clemens, meet Eric Davis. What you were to pitching, he is to playing. We've had more than our share of media novas on the mound in recent baseball history—barely known hurlers who looked as though they might make the marks of Walter Johnson and Sandy Koufax seem dusty and small. For a while they made us hold our breath, conflicted, waiting for some reassurance of mortality, just as we wished for a legend in our time.

However, it's been many a year since an everyday player stood this large, escaping definition for a few weeks or months as we wondered where his exploration of unknown territory might take us all while it lasted. Fred Lynn, simultaneously a rookie and MVP in 1975, had no aura of the limitless. Maybe Reggie Jackson, when he hit 47 homers at age twenty-three and stayed ahead of the Ruth-Maris pace until August, was the last such creature back in 1969.

It's one thing for baseball fans to pick up the paper every fifth day and find out that a Fidrych has pitched another shutout before 50,000 or that Valenzuela has a long scoreless inning streak. It's an entirely different, and more intoxicating, experience to check the box scores every day and say, "My Lord, he did it again. Who is this guy?"

That's how it is right now with Davis. When he hit three home runs on Sunday in Philadelphia, giving him 5 for the weekend (2 grand slams) and 12 homers in the Reds' first 25 games, his teammates almost ignored him. "When I came back to the dugout, they told me, 'We're not impressed,'" said Davis. ' "We've seen you hit three in a game before. Show us four.'"

Yes, Eric, show us more.

Agog with word of his Philly show, the universal baseball media descended on Shea Stadium to watch Davis cope with Broadway, the Big Apple, the megamedia hoedown. Yeah, show us. And he did.

He leaped above the center-field fence to rob his old hometown buddy Darryl Strawberry of a home run. He stole three bases in the span of four pitches—one on a pitchout and another on a perfect ankle-high peg to third by Gary Carter. His routine three-hop grounder directly at second baseman Wally Backman was the shock of the night, however; the Met took two quick steps in, fielded the room-service bounce and fired fast and hard to first base. Davis beat it cleanly for what could only be scored as a hit.

On a night when he barely touched the ball with his bat, he dominated a 2–0 game between what may be the National League's two best teams.

Last year, in 415 at bats, he had 27 homers and 80 steals. That's 40 home runs and 120 steals for a full year. You don't have to be much of a fan to know that combo has never been done. This year, in 93 at bats, he's hitting .409 with those 12 homers, 27 RBI, 28 runs and 13 steals. For a full year, that projects to . . . well, it doesn't project to anything. It's nonsense. More than 70 home runs, 170 RBI, 180 runs, 80 steals. Wayne Gretzky stats for baseball. But these are the days for talking nonsense about Davis. Is this a man who'll bend our statistical definitions of the game? Could this twenty-four-year-old who was only a rumor last summer and an insider's tip as recently as a month ago combine speed and power, the two aphrodisiacs of the sport, at a level that has never been approached?

Say it slowly: 50 homers and 100 steals. That's the fantasy. Babe Ruth and Ty Cobb together, with Mays's glove.

Davis doesn't just hit home runs. He hits five-hundred-foot home runs. To the opposite field. "The one he hit in Montreal I still don't believe," says Rose, the primary authenticator and purveyor of Davis mythology at the moment. "Over the runway in the upper deck in right center."

Davis doesn't just steal bases. He takes them instantly, without even waiting for a pitch, almost as though he were collecting mail. Pitchouts and perfect throws to third by Gary Carter, they mean nothing to him. Career percentage: 90. That includes pick-offs.

In the outfield, he makes us beg for quantification—just how fast does he run and how high does he leap? He doesn't know and won't say. He was nip and tuck in some impromptu off-season dashes with the likes of Rickey Henderson, Tim Raines and Bo Jackson. As for altitude, basketball was his first love; there he jackknifed his six-foot-three, 185-pound frame high enough for backward two-handed tomahawk dunks.

It's in the seeing that Davis really tantalizes us. Look at such garden-variety eighties phenoms as Kirk Gibson and Bo Jackson and, though you see the obvious potential for an MVP-type season, you also see the holes and the limits. With Davis, there is still that glimmering promise of an almost frightening synthesis.

He stands at the plate as languidly, almost asleep as the pitch is delivered, as Hank Aaron. He holds his hands in close and slashes his wrists like Ernie Banks. His build, with that twenty-nine-inch waist and those huge forearms ("They're corked," says Rose) are pure George Foster from his year of 52 homers and 149 RBI. The long legs and the gait that never seems to touch ground evoke Willie Davis. His bat extension through the hitting zone—like a golfer trying for maximum arc for a long drive—is so pronounced that it may in time qualify as a signature; but Frank Robinson managed it nicely, too.

Quite a fancy pedigree of mannerisms. "Oh, it's glaring. Written all over him. Hard to miss him," says the Mets' Johnson, even as he tries not to overstate. "Lean and lanky, a young George Foster with speed. Might hit one six hundred feet. But he can jump-start you, too. He's electrifying."

Already Rose says things like, "Oh, he's going to put up big numbers. He can be as good as he wants to be. With a player like that, you just put the ball in his court. However much money he wants to make, however many home runs he wants to hit, that's what he can do."

So Eric Davis, who struck out so much that it took him almost seven full seasons as a professional to hold on to a major league job, now has baseball's Midas touch. Luckily for Davis, he seems enormously wary of the cult growing around him. Phenoms are common. Careers are rare. He says he wants a career.

"I want to become the best player and person I can be," he says softly. "I see a lot of myself in Darryl [Strawberry]. But he's more vociferous than I am. I'm more laid back. I don't predict what I'll do."

Davis has had the good fortune of failure in the minor leagues—at Eugene, Cedar Rapids, Waterbury, Indianapolis, Wichita and Denver. Where Bo Jackson, for example, must make his mistakes in the American League, Davis made his almost in solitude.

"When you can deal with rejection, it makes you a better person," he says, thinking of the two years he was shipped back to the minors and last spring when he lost a regular job that he'd won. "You have to learn to roll with the highs and lows. Like last month, when I struck out nine times in a row. I looked at it as oh for nine, not nine strikeouts. I hope that's maturity. If I'd done that a couple of years ago, I don't know if I'd have bounced back as well . . . In baseball, you evaluate when the season is over."

Those, such as Davey Johnson, who like Davis's easy manner, almost wish the world had not found him so fast. "Look how long it took people to catch on to Aaron and Mike Schmidt," says Johnson. "Maybe it helped them." But anonymity is impossible for Davis now. Every day Rose says something like, "Every time Eric sees a slow curve, it becomes a souvenir. I don't know what these scouts are looking at. Nolan Ryan threw two fastballs past him, then he hit a slow curve into the third deck."

If it's true that modesty is the only sure bait when angling for praise, then Davis has mastered the trick. He has a natural nervousness when watched and just a hint of shyness when talking about himself. He has a ten-month-old daughter, and diapers can help humility. All around him in the Reds locker room are mammoth egos delighted to put him in his place. Parker calls him "my son" and has given him the heart-to-heart talk on the mistakes of his own career—plagued by poor work habits and high living. Johnny Bench and Joe Morgan come around to say the right word.

Most people invent themselves as they go along; Davis is in the midst of the process. "I have a lot to learn," he says. But he's also curious, wondering, like everybody else in baseball, just what this somewhat slow-to-blossom but oh-so-splendid center fielder can accomplish.

"I'd like to sit back and see what I do," he says. "I don't know exactly what it'll be."

Right Field: Fred Lynn

Heartbreaker

BALTIMORE, July 1986 — What could be better for the mental muscles than wrestling with a problem that has perplexed you for a dozen years and that leads you to different answers—to a different balance of opinion—every time you approach it?

For example, Fred Lynn.

Near the Baltimore Orioles' training site in Miami is a restaurant done in a baseball motif. Three walls are covered—floor to ceiling—by huge action photos. The owner could've chosen anybody who ever lived. He picked Babe Ruth, Roberto Clemente and Lynn. That's how lots of people—those who have voted him to nine American League All-Star teams—feel about Lynn, one of the game's vivid, graceful stylists.

Often it seems there are two Lynns. One was rookie of the year and MVP in 1975—an unmatched feat—then won a batting title in '79 with a .333 average, 39 homers and 122 RBI. That fellow has, for the last

85

month, been carrying much of the load in keeping the Orioles alive in a pennant race. In 24 July games he has 22 RBI and 8 home runs. When Lynn hasn't won games at bat, he has saved them in center— running into fences and sliding all over the Memorial Stadium grass to snare toe-high liners.

Now for the bad news: the other Lynn. On Sunday he gambled for an extra base, jammed his shoulder sliding and left the game. "We don't know how he is yet," said Manager Earl Weaver. "I hate to even ask . . . You're gonna blow out if you play ball like Lynn does. Some guys like Eddie Murray are not overhustlers. They save a step here and there. They seldom get hurt and only get embarrassed a couple of times a season. Lynn's not that type, and you can't change him."

"Freddie has always played for the moment," said the Orioles' Mike Flanagan. "A lot of people enjoy watching that." But it's a mixed blessing. He has missed 325 games in 12 years, sat out most of 50 others and averaged 468 at bats a season. Because of injuries, most of them minor but nagging, he has spent 20 percent of his career benched. Because of all those pulls and sprains, Lynn has hit more than 23 homers just once, driven in more than 86 runs twice and really had only two genuinely eminent years.

Yet when he plays, he's silk. Per 600 at bats, he averages 100 runs, 36 doubles, 26 homers and 100 RBI, hitting .293. But he has never had 600 at bats. In fact, he has made it to 500 only once in the eighties. Naturally, when Lynn sits, everybody talks. And the questions are always the same.

Why does he insist on running into walls and taking extra bases, even when his managers and teammates always make it clear that they wish he wouldn't? Why does he prefer not to play when he's only at 80 or 90 percent efficiency, insisting that another man at 100 percent can do just as well? Doesn't he know that a great player's presence means more than mere stats? Why, for years, has he taken days off against tough left-handers, with pennants on the line? Why isn't Lynn, who knows how easily he gets hurt and how slowly he heals, more careful?

If you want to start an argument, bring up Lynn. Four weeks ago, after Lynn had missed seventeen games with a sprained ankle and flu, I wrote: "Lynn only plays when he feels perfect. Firemen go into burning buildings for $25,000 a year, but Lynn won't go into center field for $8,333.33 a day if his ankle hurts. Asked recently to pinch-hit with the bases loaded, Lynn said he didn't feel up to it. A potentially serious injury is one thing. But sore ankles and sore throats are the things pros play through; that distinguishes them from amateurs who play for fun, not for a living."

Weaver called my column "the most irresponsible" ever written about his team. Coach Frank Robinson told me, "Thanks, he [Lynn] needed that." And, in fact, the next week Lynn was the American League's player of the week.

Obviously, it's hard to find a calm middle ground on Lynn. Perhaps Carlton Fisk, his teammate for six years in Boston, does it as well as any.

"How bad did you nail Freddy, anyway?" Fisk needled me.

"Maybe a six on a scale of ten."

"That's about right," said Fisk.

Okay, so maybe I got the "six" upside down.

"Remember," continued Fisk, "Freddy was a huge success with enormous expectations right away. He had to be perfect to live up to what he was supposed to do in Boston. So maybe he never wanted to go out there when he couldn't be that great all-around player.

"Also, most of his game is in his legs. If he can't run, he can't play the game the way he wants to. And most of his injuries are to his legs, or his back, which hurts when he runs.

"I remember what Gene Mauch said when Lynn had his best year in California," recalled Fisk. "People said Lynn looked like he was enjoying the game again. Mauch said, " 'I think it's a case of Freddy reveling in his own good health.' "

Lynn has always played for the moment and for himself. He would no more pass up a chance to leap above the wall to steal a home run than a child could resist such a thought in his dreams. In pursuit of those moments of pure athletic fulfillment, Lynn, who went to Southern Cal on a football scholarship, is utterly fearless.

Sometimes Lynn does not return from his adventures in one piece. Then he feels the high demands of his public and the pressure of his critics. He loathes the thought of a hobbled, unworthy, embarrassing performance, even if it might help the team, even if he is being paid millions to provide it.

Early in his career, Fisk faced the same dilemma. He loved to block the plate like a hero. The result: his body was becoming a wreck. A decade ago he gave up blocking the plate, even if it meant the game. Someday Fisk may set the record for most games as a catcher. Pride was the price of durability. "But some people can't turn it off and on," said Fisk.

Fred Lynn has always wanted to have it both ways—seize the moment and also perform only at his best. It's the sort of choice we'd expect more from an artist than from a pro athlete. He has done it his way and, as usual when you make that stubborn decision, paid a big price.

Right-handed Pitcher:
Doyle Alexander

Heartless

DETROIT, September 1987 — The silver snakeskin cowboy boots, the old blue jeans and the soft, weathered leather jacket sit in his locker like a gunslinger's holster hooked nonchalantly to the peg above a hallway door. Comfortably used, but threatening. Independent, fascinating, insolent.

Extend your hand to shake Doyle Alexander's pitching hand and you can wait for a while. Slowly he turns his head, pretending not to see you. When he turns back, he still ignores your hand and looks you hard in the eye instead. Then, the instant you pull your hand back, he puts his forward and you have to shake on his terms. He's just changed speeds on another hitter and won again. If you're insulted or defensive, then he's happy. Because he's in control.

"Ask a couple of questions?"

"You can ask."

Answer? We'll see about that later.

People ask Alexander questions these days. He's the hottest pitcher in baseball. In 9 starts as a Detroit Tiger, he's 8–0 (1.40 ERA). Toss in 5 scoreless outings and a 28-inning scoreless streak. Yes, people want to know Alexander better. That's to say, they want to know him at all. He's a mystery man. Tall, lanky, put together wrong with big hips and narrow shoulders. A mustache, narrow eyes and low brow add to the incongruous look. He's a mystery pitcher, too. "Goofy windup, all those pitches from all those angles," said four-time batting champion Bill Madlock. He gives the old guys a headache and the kids a nervous breakdown. "He entices hitters with their own pitch," said catcher Mike Heath. Nobody's got Alexander figured. "That's the way I like it," he said.

Instead of no. 19 above his cubicle, there might as well be a lyric from an old TV show, "Have Gun, Will Travel," identifying the knight without honor in a savage land. Since 1971 Alexander has been a Dodger, Oriole, Yankee, Ranger, Brave, Giant, Yankee (again), Blue Jay, Brave (again) and now a Tiger. That's ten teams. He's pitched decently, sometimes very well, for all of them. Yet he has been traded seven times. Twice teams released him. Twice he went free agent. Not everyone likes him. But the feeling is mutual.

Years ago, Baltimore general manager Hank Peters called him "one of the most disagreeable individuals I've ever known." But then Peters is management. Alexander never has had an agent. In fact, he loves to trade left hooks with the boss over millions of bucks. Result: he's a very rich 173–145 pitcher. If you want a hired gun, especially in September, you can't do better. Do not ask Alexander to sign autographs or charm the press or attend functions. He will not do it. Or apologize. He lives in Texas, not in the town where he works. He's paid to pitch.

On the mound, Alexander feels no "pressure" because he could not care less whether the Tigers or the Blue Jays—or for that matter, the Giants—win the World Series. He's played for them all. He's a student of baseball, not a fan of it. Like a sniper inspecting a scope, he watches for lethal details—a changed batting stance—not for excitement.

Nobody tells the thirty-seven-year-old what to do. Or what to throw. He calls his own game. Every pitch. The catcher puts down a sign. Then Alexander brushes his glove against his chest to add or on his thigh to subtract. On most pitches he's shaking off his own catcher, telling the crowd that, basically, his battery mate hasn't got the foggiest idea. What does Sparky Anderson think of the system? He rolls his eyes. You need Alexander the Great badly enough, you let him do it his way. You can always hire the catcher a good therapist.

Doyle and his managers give each other a wide berth. Billy Martin got rid of him twice, called him "gutless." Martin loathed the detachment, the absence of loyalty. Most of all, he hated the way Alexander saw him without adolescent romance—no respect for the no. 1 on his back, no need to call him "Skipper" or seek approval. Martin assumed the pitcher mocked him behind his back. And he was probably right. In their last chapter, Martin did a slow burn as Alexander returned to beat the Yankees in big games. The final score is important to Alexander.

That's why these days are doubly sweet to his dour nature. He has points to prove. Last year he wanted to leave the Blue Jays so badly he made up a handwritten list of "Reasons for Leaving Toronto" and gave it to a columnist. Surprise. He got traded to Atlanta.

Last winter he decided to go free agent and leave Atlanta, too. He even turned down a two-year $2.3 million contract. Then every team in baseball turned him down. "Monopolistic owners," he said. This May he returned to Atlanta for a paltry $400,000, with $200,000 in incentive clauses. Perhaps by coincidence, he pitched like $400,000, not $2.3 million. His record: 5–10. You get what you pay for? As soon as Atlanta traded him for John Smoltz, eureka, nothing but zeros.

With Alexander, the money may be important, but so's the principle of the thing. Once he punched a dugout wall and disabled himself; he sent the club a check for his month's pay.

These are the days when baseball is a joy, a child's game once more for the grown men who play it. They get carried away by crowds and glory. In many cases they care so much they fail. Maybe that's why Alexander has long been almost unbeatable in pennant races. He avoids the spotlight, even when it seeks him. He barely knows what city he pitches for. After all the trades and, he says, "all the lies" that surround that long list of leavings, baseball is now 99 percent business to him.

Sunday, in a game his team desperately needs to win, the crowd will roar and the batter will try to swallow the lump in his throat. As Alexander gives his own sign—some weird slider, slop curve or even knuckleball—then goes into that goofy windup which looks like a ladder collapsing, it will be High Noon in the baseball season. Alexander will be a man with a big, if bitter, edge. For better or for worse, he will care less than anyone.

Left-handed Pitcher: Tommy John

Heart Transplant

NEW YORK, July 1987 — The rule in baseball is that stars should retire on top, or somewhere near it, with their dignity intact and their image still resplendent. Those who linger interminably, bouncing from team to team, injury to injury and folly to folly, deserve the ridicule they get.

Tommy John is the exception that proves the rule. He never worried about acquiring dignity, considering modesty far more important; and he was so mediocre for so long and excellent for so short a time, he never really managed to acquire a hero's image. Embarrassment has been his companion for a quarter-century, so he laughs along with the rest when he disables himself covering first base or slips and breaks his hand playing catch.

As his recompense, it seems John is to be allowed to go on forever. At age forty-four and in his twenty-fifth major league season, if you count the one he missed with a supposed career-ending injury, he'll probably never get to 300 wins or Cooperstown. Who cares? Certainly not John. He seems blithely determined to keep sinkerballing (and some say scuffballing) the New York Yankees toward pennant competition, carrying baseball's most glorious franchise on the sport's least impressive shoulders.

Tommy John, who pitched for Modesto, Madison and Fort Lauderdale in cameo rehabilitation stints the past two seasons, was the Yankees' Opening Day starter in Yankee Stadium in 1987. Tommy John—a man who has worn six big league uniforms, who has been released outright once, who has been a free agent three times, who even retired once to coach college ball—is, at the moment, rock-solid in the New York rotation. Why not? While almost every other pitcher in baseball gives up gophers, John kills 'em. Can't hit what you can't excavate. A long blast off John only bounces twice before it gets through the infield.

What's the big surprise? John was 5–3 with a 2.93 ERA in 71 innings last year. Only injuries stopped him then. When healthy, he was as good as ever. Get accustomed to having him back. John's already talking about next season.

Usually, when we see a baseball player who simply won't retire, who insists on making comebacks even though he's been rejected, we wish he would just, please, take himself off the stage. Seriously, Reggie, Tom, Lefty, Don and Phil, aren't a plaque in the Hall of Fame and a multimillion-dollar bank account enough for you guys? Aren't 300 wins or 500 home runs sufficient in the adulation department? After you've gotten the last conceivable milestone record, why don't you leave gracefully?

John, however, completely escapes this category. His ego has always been so small he could hide it in his glove. A funny, eccentric chatterbox, he was always loved by everybody, but nobody ever bothered to salute. Though he is twenty-fifth in the history of baseball in games won (271), nobody's holding any breath for 300. John was disabled three times last year, and the Yankees hold their breath on every rocket through the box at the man.

As for Cooperstown, it's probably just a romantic fancy. Would the facts stand for it? John had one fifteen-victory season in his first dozen. Nine years after setting foot in the majors, he was 84–91; we're talking long, long-term mediocrity. His lengthy and barely distinguishable career was considered over, ended by injury, before he ever figured out his true pitching style and finally became a star—well, a semistar—for four lovely twilight years when he went 80–35.

Then, just as he discovered what it was like to pitch in the playoffs (five times) and the World Series (three), the magic left him and age tore him down. Since the end of 1980 he's pitched for the Yankees, Angels, A's and now the Yankees again. His 57–62 mark tells the truth. He's hung on by his fingernails for years. Once he even asked to pitch for a friend's semipro team. That's why baseball insiders are so happy (and dazzled) to see him now.

"I swear he's throwing as well now as he was in '80 [when he won twenty-two]," says catcher Rick Cerone. "It's hard to believe. In fact, he's got two new pitches: a cut fastball on the fists to righties and a change-up. So you might have to say he's got better stuff now. One thing we know for sure: as long as he can throw a ball, it will sink."

"He never threw hard, but now he's throwing just as not-hard as he ever did," says bullpen coach Jeff Torborg. "People ask what difference it makes whether he throws a sinker seventy-six miles an hour or eighty-two. Well, a harder sinker is a heavier sinker. And he's got it back."

How did John get reborn last season at age forty-three, a birthday Steve Carlton and Joe Niekro haven't even reached yet? He stopped acting like an old man, for one thing, and started lifting weights two years ago. Not three times a week, like some players, but every day—even in the morning before he pitches at night. "I discovered all those 'lat' muscles in the back below the shoulder. I wasn't even using them," says John.

Just as vital, John unearthed a mechanical flaw and restored his money pitch, the sinker—or, as frisking umpires might say, his defaced spheroid. Maybe Tommy doesn't cheat. Perhaps Gaylord didn't, either. It's possible it wasn't even John who suggested that Rick Rhoden leave notes in his glove for the umps who have been examining him of late—messages like, "Right church. Wrong pew," and "Warmer." Whether or not sandpaper is next to godliness for an old hurler, it's certain that any pitch, legal or nay, requires good delivery.

"I was totally messed up," John says. "I knew it, but that didn't solve it. Gene Mauch told me, 'In your best years, it looked like you were handing the ball to the catcher. You're not now,'" says John. "He couldn't find words I could translate into mechanics."

Finally an old coach, Tom Morgan, told John, "Come over to my house and we'll play catch. Let me show you something I think I see." When you make friends as John does, advice arrives like the morning mail. What Morgan saw was a frightened old pitcher trying to be so fine—allowing himself two inches of error, not a foot—he was cutting himself off, not extending, not pulling down through the ball at the last instant. The old knack returned almost instantly.

Since then, gravy. Now John worries only about developing more new pitches and convincing others he really should jog and sweat more than young pitchers—running alone in a conditioning program they won't touch. He'd also like to pitch live batting practice to subs so he could discuss the fine points of "getting inside" on the fists with them. Heck, they might learn something. But they don't want their timing destroyed by John's craft. So he shrugs and fine-tunes in games.

John broke in against the Washington Senators in 1963 with a kid Cleveland shortstop named Dick Howser behind him. Since then John has been traded three times, once as a young throw-in. John even claims to be baseball's first right-handed southpaw. In 1974 with the Dodgers, he had a tendon from his right forearm transplanted into his left elbow. Nobody had ever tried that; the surgeon told him flatly he would never pitch again. Instead, John, who had never won more than 16 games, came back and won 20 in three of the next five seasons. His golf game even got better; a weakened right side, don't you know.

That operation, so long ago, reminds him of Scott McGregor of the Orioles, a very John-like pitcher who is on the brink of release by a team that considers him washed up at thirty-three. John never even came back from his historic surgery until he was thirty-three. All his best deeds came afterward—and all those still to come.

None of this, absolutely none of it, surprises John. In baseball, he's old and wise, not old and obsessed. "The only thing that ever burns inside me," John says, "is Szechwan food." As he sees it, the moral of his career is that, if it can happen in baseball, it'll happen to Tommy John. So why stop now?

One-handed Pitcher: Jim Abbott

Heart of Gold

HAGERSTOWN, Maryland, July 1988—Face it. A kid born with one hand is never going to pitch in the big leagues. It was a nice fantasy. Everybody loved Jim Abbott when he won the '87 Sullivan Trophy as America's top amateur athlete. But now he's pitching to grown men.

Obviously, international competition bothers Abbott a lot. Take him out of the small pond of college baseball—where he was 26–8 at Michigan (3.03 career earned run average) and, last month, became a no. 1 draft choice of the California Angels—and the truth starts to come out. When he's facing Cuba, Japan and Taiwan—average age about twenty-eight—we've seen a much different Abbott for two summers.

Last year, he had an ERA of 0.00 in three appearances in the Pan American Games. He also became the first U.S. pitcher to beat Cuba in Havana in twenty-five years.

This summer, the U.S. national team—collegiates headed to the

Olympics—are barnstorming. And, as usual, Abbott is getting his ears pinned back. His ERA is 0.00 again. He's given up four hits already —in three games.

Just when you think Abbott has surpassed all rational expectations, he moves up a level—and gets better.

Olympic coach Mark Marquess, whose Stanford team has won back-to-back NCAA titles, said, "As a person, they told me Abbott was the All-American boy—almost too good to be true. But he's surprised me. He's better than that, if a person can be . . . As a pitcher, he didn't have a great junior year [this season]. I expected him to be a polished left-hander. What I didn't know is that, right now, he's the hardest thrower on my staff . . . The Japanese [hitters] aren't going to be divin' in on him. He brings it too hard."

Once upon a time, being America's best Olympic pitcher meant little. Now, after the '84 Olympic team sent Will Clark, Mark McGwire, Cory Snyder, Barry Larkin, B. J. Surhoff, Mike Dunne and others to the majors in a hurry, the Olympic team is a Grade A pedigree. This year, Abbott and second baseman Ty Griffin of Georgia Tech have been the showstoppers so far for a nice 13–3 squad.

To understand Abbott, it helps to watch him on a 102-degree day in a small Maryland town in the foothills of the Shenandoah Mountains when he's not even scheduled to pitch. The grandstand is standing room only—that's 6,500 in Hagerstown—and the PA system plays "Some Kinda Wonderful." Abbott heads to the bullpen to do some work. Others think he's almost the finished product. He thinks he's only halfway there.

"You develop to your [level of] competition. You learn to do what they force you to learn," said Abbott. "When I went to Michigan, I just had a fastball. Then a curve. I added a cut fastball, which is my slider. Now I'm working on a straight change-up and slow curve. And I know I have to learn to pitch inside. That's the big thing."

In college, with aluminum bats, low and away is the key location. In pro ball, with wooden bats and a generation of Jose Cansecos who feed off any pitch that lets them extend their huge arms, the inside corner, especially for a left-handed pitcher, is the heart and soul of success.

"It's totally different," says Abbott. "You gotta hit some people. In Japan [on a five-game tour], I hit a guy flat in the face. I'd never done that before. But I have to get over it. It's part of the game."

In the bullpen, the dust hangs heavy in the air, the catchers don't want to crouch and even the billboards seem to shimmer with a wavering desert-heat quality. Abbott works through his entire repertoire, throwing almost machine-gun fast. Fastballs and sliders—in, down and in, and then far enough inside that you can see imaginary hitters skipping rope, sucking in their guts, diving under the low bridge. Jim Abbott has had to overcome a lot; if hitters have to overcome some heat in their kitchens, the six-foot-three, 200-pound kid with the choirboy face might not mind as much as you'd think.

Abbott's glove stays on his stump of a right hand, just six inches from where his left hand ends his balanced follow-through. If a batter were at the plate, he would pluck it off and put it on his left hand in one motion after every pitch; Abbott has done it so quickly and smoothly for so long that some fans barely notice his handicap. "He's an average fielder. I expected below-average," says Marquess. "They bunt on him. He throws them out. Next case."

It's the line drives through the box that scouts worry about. "That question grinds at you," Abbott said. "I'll try to do the best I can. I can talk till I'm blue. That doesn't prove anything. But I think I can [protect myself]."

Is it possible that the worst danger is actually almost behind him—the lethal aluminum bats that create liners faster than any in the major leagues? "That's possible," he said, grinning.

Finally, pouring sweat, Abbott switches to straight change-ups. They're raw. Some bounce. But they're all low; and his motion is almost the same. Already it could be a waste pitch.

These days, Abbott is a twenty-year-old in a sweatbox laboratory. The U.S. national team plays a schedule that would exhaust any minor league team. Six-hour bus rides, twelve-hour flight to and from Japan, seldom two nights in one town and never three. The minors can't be this hard, not with 4:15 A.M. wake-up calls and big-time media in every town. After a 6 A.M. flight, they got to Durham, North Carolina, at 9 A.M. only to find their hotel rooms would not be vacated for several hours. "Is this how the U.S. Olympic basketball team travels?" asked Abbott.

Even when they got to the Durham Bulls park—yes, where the movie was made—they found out that, as Abbott said, "The Bull is really in foul territory." Another Hollywood trick.

Abbott and his teammates are meeting real baseball this summer, not college ball with training tables and more days off than games. The question isn't Can You Play, it's Can You Play Every Day? Play exhausted. Play depressed. Manage your body, your mind, your time. Some are chewed up. Some eat it up.

So far, and it's early, Abbott seems to like the learning process. He's fascinated to face an entire Japanese team—the defending Olympic champions who beat the United States in the finals in Dodger Stadium in '84—full of high-fastball guess hitters. He and Andy Benes, the no. 1 pick in the whole draft, marvel at a team so disciplined that players will "start swinging while you're in your windup so they can get out in front of your best fastball," even though they may look ridiculous—fooled by ten feet—on a change-up.

This summer will seem interminable, and sometimes demoralizing. Those seven straight games in August with Cuba, then the World Championships in Italy (with Cuba on hand again), will be man-sized work. "Cuba is better than some major league teams. No question," said Marquess.

By deep September, when the United States plays the first of five games that could win it an Olympic exhibition-sport title, this team—and Abbott—will be either worn to a frazzle or partway to grown-up.

Many questions will be asked about this Olympic team. But no one will face as many as Abbott, who has fascinated baseball fans with his unique personality and his unique liability. For now, why not look at it this way: some athletes seem followed by a special destiny that seeks them even as they pursue it. For example, Abbott has the inside track on the first-game Olympic starting assignment. Circle the date. September 19. Abbott has until then to finish becoming a man at his game.

September 19 is also Abbott's twenty-first birthday.

P.S.: The U.S. Olympic baseball team won first prize at Seoul, Korea. Abbott won the championship game. In fact, he saved the game—and the Olympics—with a great defensive play. One-handed.

Coach:
Stump Merrill

Heart's Desire

March 1986 — When Stump Merrill's wife, Carole, heard that he'd been named first base coach of the New York Yankees, she said, "What does a first base coach do beside pat the guys on the rear end?"

"Nothing," he answered. "How about some practice?"

It's taken Carl Harrison Merrill twenty years of hard work to win the honor of doing nothing much down round first base at Yankee Stadium this season. When they play the anthem on Opening Day, nobody will stand taller in his pinstripes than the five-foot-eight former catcher.

When you play your college ball for Maine, when you hit two home runs in your six-year minor league career, when you manage seven more seasons in the bushes, when you officiate high school basketball and coach football at Bowdoin in the winter to earn extra bucks, it's a long way to the House That Ruth Built.

Even to the coach's box. They say the only thing on a baseball field that gets noticed less than the first-base coach is first base; it's the ideal job for an international fugitive. But when the opener comes, Merrill's big league debut won't go unmarked. The Yankees' first game is scheduled at Fenway Park and many friends from Merrill's tiny hometown of Topsham, Maine, will note the moment with an approving New England nod for a task completed.

"Yes, I'm very excited," Merrill said. "I think I've accomplished something, a reward for the long hours and all the years I've put in.

"Now, if I can just survive a few more weeks," he said, laughing, as though New York fired first-base coaches as fast as managers.

At forty-one, Merrill has lots of rewards for his years in baseball. No pension or job security. A master's degree from Maine that he's never used. Thousands of days away from his wife and two kids. A degenerative arthritic knee ("two zippers, two 'scopes") that makes him a prime candidate for an artificial knee.

And a smile lit from within.

"My wife says, 'Are you ever going to put all that education to work?' " Merrill said. "Everyplace I've been, people say, 'What are you doing here?' But I don't think I'd do anything different. I've never wanted to do anything else except come to a ballpark. I've never had trouble getting up in the morning and going to work. There's an awful lot to be said for that. I tell her I'd be a miserable SOB in a real job."

All Merrill truly regrets is that he couldn't share his daughters' youth. He's never dragged his family on the road with him during schooltime. "We don't want our kids to go to fifteen schools. The value of a quality education for them exceeds the things I'm doing."

That modesty doesn't mean Merrill undersells his own ambitions or skills. "My father died when I was fairly young. I remember two things he told me: think positive and think big."

When Merrill interviewed for a high school coaching job fourteen years ago after one last blown knee ended a dogged career in the minors (one season with more than 15 RBI), he was asked his ultimate goal.

"Major league manager," he wrote.

Pretty brash for a guy who played four years of pro ball before he hit a home run. "Every day I'd come to the park and the guys would say, 'This is Stump's day for the homer.' When I finally hit it, in Reading in '69, I was running so hard I was halfway to third before I realized it was out of the park. My roomie ran out of the dugout and, just like we planned, I slid into home plate and he called me safe.

"Managing in the majors was utterly unrealistic then. Even now it's probably a million-to-one shot.

"But," says Merrill, "I'm on the dance floor."

Maybe only Merrill knows how close he came to missing his dance. From Batavia to Portsmouth to Bakersfield to Eugene to West Haven to Nashville to Columbus, he pitched BP and gave pep talks, hit fungoes and mothered homesick youngsters, warmed up wild pitchers and watched a thousand bush league cow-milking contests.

What kept him going was that though progress was slow, it was progress. Then in 1982, sixteen years after turning pro, the real blow came. After finishing second, first, first and first as a manager, Merrill somehow got on the wrong side of the Yankees' brass. He was sent *backward*, from AA to A. He was knocked flat.

"There were long nights soul-searching," he said. Back at the bottom of the minor league barrel in Fort Lauderdale, people *really* told Merrill, "You don't belong here."

Instead of quitting, going back to the relative safety of college coaching, Merrill "kept my mouth shut and waited for a break . . . I'm a big believer in fate and hard work. I think I learned from it, became a little better man."

Perhaps the truth is that Merrill simply loved the game too much to leave it. Last year, the Yankees' AAA managing job came open and a surprised Merrill found himself at Columbus in charge of their top prospects. His team finished first (the fifth time in seven years) and his managing record reached 584–382.

Now New York's camp is full of players who've had Merrill at some stop. Most cite the same quality: honesty. "Stump is a straight talker and a judge of people," coach Jerry McNertney said.

Suddenly the stumpy one's opinion is sought in the same breath as that of coaches lower on the totem pole than he—fellows such as Whitey Ford and Merrill's good buddy Catfish Hunter.

"People seem to think I know more than I did a year ago," he said.

What does the future hold?

"Can't wait to start the season," he bubbled. "Can't wait to find out what we're holdin'."

No, Stump—long-range future.

Merrill shrugged and grinned. One arm leaned on his fungo bat. His foot was on the top step of the dugout to take weight off that bad knee so he could pitch a little BP soon.

"Maybe," he said, "they'll bury me in a pine box with high stirrups."

Manager:
Davey Johnson

Heart of a New Machine

NEW YORK, May 1985 — In baseball, if your voice shatters the crystal, they call you Whispering Phil, and if your mug makes mothers cover their babies' eyes, they tag you Handsome Jack. So it ought to give fair warning that Davey Johnson's nickname was Dumb Dumb.

The inside joke in his All-Star days with Baltimore was that Johnson actually was the smartest Oriole. Nobody else had the brass to second-guess Earl Weaver. In fact, Johnson actually got himself traded because he just couldn't resist challenging Weaver to tests of brainpower.

Johnson still wears cowboy boots and plays the "Aw, shucks" role with his drooping eyelids and weak chin. But he's starting to blow his cover. The forty-two-year-old New York Mets manager is the Columbo of skippers. He may even be the new wave.

Since Johnson arrived last spring, the mysterious Mets, in first place in the National League East despite a team batting average of .225, have stood every law of baseball probability on its head. Perhaps only Johnson, who has a mathematics degree from Texas's Trinity University and keeps a computer, not a fungo, next to him in the dugout, really knows what the word "probability" means in baseball.

For twenty years, professors have been muttering from ivied campuses about the revolution that would hit baseball if the game ever got a manager who grasped the sport from both an athlete's and an academic's point of view. Johnson may be the first hybrid.

He started in four World Series, made four All-Star teams and tied Rogers Hornsby for the all-time season home run record for a second baseman (forty-two). He's all ballplayer—tough, tangy, scarred and very stubborn. He's been beaned and released, put in the doghouse and sent back to the bushes. He knows clubhouse politics and dugout emotions. But he also puts on the take sign "because of Professor Ernshaw Cook's theory of favorable chance deviation" and sees the end of a slump "because we're on the upslope of the sine curve."

Consider the following numbers. In 1984–85 under Johnson, the Mets have been outscored by 18 runs. But they've won 29 games more than they've lost: 113–84. In one- and two-run games, the Mets are 70–37. In all others, 43–47. The Johnson Mets are 23–2 in extra innings. To a stat freak, all of this is almost hallucinatory.

At first it was thought to be beginner's luck. Then it was a streak. Now, after two hundred games under Johnson, it's possible—just possible—that what we have here is a man ahead of his time.

You can mumble about great relief pitching, good defense, a deep bench and team spirit—all of which the Mets have—but something else is going on here, too. For a century, teams' records in close games have mirrored their record in lopsided games—regardless of type of personnel. Bullpen, schmullpen. And clubs that got outscored have rarely gotten above .525 for very long.

Johnson, who is a licensed pilot and who made his first million dollars in real estate, not baseball, isn't giving many clues to his methods. His office bookshelf gives hints of his personality: *The Hidden Game of Baseball* (exotic stats), *Computer Baseball*, *Radar Gun Readings*, *The Talbot Odyssey*, *The Salamandra Glass*. But show that you have even an inkling of what he's talking about and he stops talking about it.

For example, Johnson mentions Cook's cult tome on higher mathematics, probability and baseball. When someone says he has a copy and could Johnson explain it more, it ends the subject.

"The fallacy of the book is that it assumes players are machines," he says. "For example, Cook says if the count is 2–0 on a hitter with an

103

average under .250, you should put on the take till he has *two* strikes. What he doesn't take into consideration is that you could destroy a player's confidence that way.

"You can only do that stuff in game-on-the-line situations."

And, specifically, what game-on-the-line situations?

Sorry, Davey just remembered an urgent meeting.

Even Johnson's coaches aren't quite sure what he's up to, although they like the results. "Late in a close game, he looks for every little edge," said coach Mel Stottlemyre. "He believes a great deal in match-ups in game situations. He has a list of which hitters he won't allow to win the game against certain of our pitchers. And vice versa for our hitters against their pitchers.

"I see other teams not concerned with those things. You can call it 'outthinking' the other manager if you want to. I think we get the better of the late-game matchups," said Stottlemyre. "Davey doesn't make a lot of [overmanaging] moves in the first six innings, but when the game is close and it's late, he takes over completely and does exactly what's best for the team, regardless of [players'] feelings. The players accept it because he'll take them aside and explain it."

"It's gotten past the point where you can explain our record [in close games] just by pointing at our bullpen, or our good pinch-hitting or the way we all persevere," said pitcher Ron Darling, a Yale student. "I think [Johnson] has taken some strategic stuff to a higher level. In the games we win, it always seems like it's one big hit that does it, or one big inning."

Like Weaver, Johnson loves to study pitcher-versus-hitter matchups over a career. "But I thought Earl abused the [matchup] 'cards,' " said Johnson. "I believe more in who has the hot hand." As an example, last year Johnson told Keith Hernandez, "You're hitting .138 off Nolan Ryan for your career. Let me give you a rest here." Hernandez said, "I'm comfortable hitting off Ryan. The stats don't show atom [hit right at 'em] balls. And I've hurt him late in games."

Johnson relented, and "I won the game with a homer," said Hernandez.

Can it be proven that Johnson's bookish theories and his old-salt knack have combined to make him the sport's breakthrough prototypical manager? No, of course not.

For fifteen seasons, Weaver's teams won about five games a year more than the stat formulas said they should have. And they did better in the tight going than should have been possible. Fifteen years isn't coincidence.

Maybe these mysterious Mets have some curious blend of factors that no one will name. Or maybe they've just been lucky and the clock will toll midnight on their hairsbreadth escape act soon.

Whatever the case, Dumb Dumb Davey Johnson is going to be a closely watched man until the verdict is final.

"The dugout guys and the scientific fellas with all the numbers have always been real far apart," said Stottlemyre. "I don't know if Davey is the first one to bring their ideas together.

"But he might be getting closer."

Owner: Edward
Bennett Williams

Fighter's Heart

WASHINGTON, August 1988—Of all his Orioles, Edward Bennett Williams liked Jim Palmer the best and never hid it. Palmer's style, wit and brains, not to mention his eight 20-win seasons, were the sort of qualities Williams admired. EBW was sure that the Best were really all one large club under the skin. That Palmer loved to needle and argue, test authority and challenge his bosses also went down smoothly with Williams, who never met a Supreme Court justice or U.S. president who daunted him. The spice of a little insubordination whets the intelligence.

Jim Palmer stood in the most remote back corner of St. Matthew's Cathedral yesterday, paying his last respects to the owner he found so powerful and fascinating. "It was impossible for him to have any contact with you and not leave an imprint," said Palmer.

Sports figures like Palmer and John Riggins, even commissioners like

Peter Ueberroth and Pete Rozelle, were barely worth mention among the dignitaries—the senators and bishops, educators and attorneys, journalists and businessmen—who filled St. Matthew's yesterday, the crowd spilling back down the front steps toward the blocks of black limousines.

Games were just a sliver of Williams's diverse life—one in which he seemed to create a symbiosis of all the major mainstream power sources in his society and age. How many others felt so at home at a 6 A.M. mass and a 10 P.M. prizefight, with a murder trial and a little political fund-raising mixed into the meat of the day?

For Williams, everything illuminated and nurtured everything else in his life. The certainties of his Catholicism steeled him for the stresses of his law practice. The passion for competition that drew him to sports served him just as well in business, where he fought to the limit for every edge. The charm he laid on a jury worked in Democratic back rooms, too.

None of Williams's worlds, however, seemed to draw him more strongly in the last decade of his life than sports. He understood athletes, especially great ones, and they understood him, too. They were akin in their need for a simple result—a win or loss—and a level of commitment to a goal that many people would find frightening.

"Time isn't the same for everybody," said one eulogist at Williams's memorial. "Ed's clock ran faster." Certainly, Williams squeezed in more, started earlier, trained harder, pushed himself beyond reasonable limits—just as every singular athlete must.

"You always felt how much he wanted to win," said Palmer. "This year was awful for him [with the Orioles losing]. He told me after the 1984 season, 'That was the worst year of my life.' And after 1985, he said, '*That* was the worst year of my life.' It wore him down."

Williams understood how to run the good race, fight the good fight. In defeat, knowing he'd done his best, he could be gracious and even humorous. "He told me he lived by the expression 'No indecision and no regrets,'" said Palmer. "He didn't second-guess himself. He just took his best shot."

Williams could drive too hard for some tastes and had little use for relaxation; the reward for good work was more work. The goal, the end, obsessed and fed him. Any athlete understands the glory and the burden of working for decades to perfect a gift.

Like his athletes, Williams took the world much as he found it—accepted the game as played—and simply tried to play it better than anybody else. The point of the game, the shape of the field, the nature of the rules only interested him secondarily—after the results were in and he'd won again.

Like many athletes, he had little patience with those who couldn't match his sacrifices or intensity. If you were in the game, you had to play it his way. When a person constantly wishes to raise the stakes, the higher the better—a murder trial, a presidential election, a Super Bowl trophy, a World Series ring—nothing is more irritating than reminders of one's own humanity. Just as many athletes ignore their injuries, pretend that they simply do not exist, Williams was able, somehow, to function for eleven years with little or no visible concession to his cancer. If this was not a kind of athletic feat, what is?

Finally, like any athlete, Williams never wanted to retire or even slow down. Would Pete Rose ever voluntarily stop going to bat or Sonny Jurgensen want to throw his last pass? Williams kept booking hours and brainstorming over how to improve his star-crossed Orioles. For him, life, like a game, was a never-ending process of competing, succeeding, then setting the next goal. One great season only opened the possibility for a better one—a new personal best.

That is not the only way to live. But it is one of the most productive and dramatic. For a man blessed, apparently from youth, with the almost limitless power of rock-solid faith—in himself, his church, his country, his vocation, his family, his teams—it created a life of monumentally big achievements.

None need mourn a life so large and full, but many of us, for a long time, will seek to understand it.

President:
Lee MacPhail

Old Sweetheart

March 1986—Lee MacPhail holds three big league records that may never be broken. He has visited at least two art museums in every major league city. He has been to the symphony in all of them, too. And while on airplanes between those towns, he has read at least one biography of every American president, two on most.

Who knew Seattle had two galleries, Dallas a symphony or Polk a biographer? And you thought Joe DiMaggio's fifty-six-game hitting streak was safe.

Once, on an all-star tour of Japan when he was American League president, MacPhail got wind of a Rubens exhibit. "Bet we won't see any ballplayers here," MacPhail joked to a friend. The next thing MacPhail knew, six-foot-five, 240-pound Jim Bibby of the Pittsburgh Pirates was tapping him on the shoulder to exchange notes on the use of chiaroscuro.

MacPhail likes to tell the Bibby story because he prefers that the laugh be on him. It's part of a modesty that runs so deep and is so genuine that MacPhail has become a kind of reverse Teflon man. Public *praise* won't stick to him. In fact, if he's famous for anything, it's the pine tar bat decision that left him so reviled in Yankee Stadium that he now feels "uncomfortable" about returning to the park where he was once general manager. Talk about backward.

For forty-five years gentle, unpretentious, upright little Lee MacPhail has changed and improved everything in baseball that he has touched; his fingerprints are everywhere these days. Find some boring, tiresome and enormously important area of the old game that's in decent working order, or headed that way, and it probably bears MacPhail's stamp.

Look at issues as diverse as drug testing, salary arbitration, long-term contracts, free agent signings and last-second labor settlements, and MacPhail has played the role of the creative conciliatory conservative.

Last week at a testimonial dinner in Dallas, Commissioner Peter Ueberroth called MacPhail "the best man in the game." Nobody disagreed. "You've had a lot of the good things in life, so we're not giving you anything," teased Ueberroth. Then MacPhail learned that a $100,000 academic scholarship in his name would be established at his alma mater, Swarthmore.

"We had to find things to give him that he couldn't refuse to take," said Ueberroth. "When he retired as AL president, they tried to give him a very expensive watch. He said, 'I already have a watch my father gave me.' "

MacPhail's father, Larry, is in the Hall of Fame, and it's a safe bet the son will be, too, someday. There the similarities end. The controversial old man, who brought night baseball to the major leagues and was president of the Reds, Dodgers and Yankees, was sarcastic, rough, abusive and brilliant. The camouflaged son, who ran the Yankees and Orioles and has taught the ropes to three grateful commissioners, is refined, wise and so calm that butter wouldn't melt in his mouth.

Now that he's retired, credit has started to catch up with him. Not that he would care, or even accept it if it were forced upon him. This is a man who was so embarrassed at getting credit for settling the strike of 1981 that when everybody said he "won" the '85 strike for the owners, he called the settlement a personal failure and apologized.

Let's pin down this MacPhail guy.

Whose idea was it, anyway, to start negotiating drug-testing clauses into individual player contracts? At the moment, that's the only drug policy baseball has, and it's one that may accidentally work. If players wish to sign away their civil liberties for a few more dollars, that's their business. About 350 have. This way, however, the union was saved embarrassment. Who'd want to bargain away constitutional rights?

MacPhail can't remember the source of this idea. Of course, it came out of the Player Relations Committee, which he ran in 1984–85. Probably coincidence.

How come baseball's owners finally stopped bidding like crazy for mediocre free agents this winter? Why did they stop offering long-term contracts of more than three years? Why did they decide it was time to let players know they weren't afraid of arbitration?

Could it be because, in his farewell speech, MacPhail begged the owners to follow his advice in these three areas? Maybe the reams of statistical evidence his Player Relations Committee gave to document these points had some slight effect.

"I emphasized that long-term deals had proved to be a disaster," he said. "In '85 we paid almost $30 million salary to men *who didn't play a game*. Also, long-term contracts were cited in arbitration. We were building up a record against ourselves."

Speaking of arbitration, it will change significantly next year, thanks to MacPhail. That's when the new criteria for eligibility—the core of the labor battle last summer—kick in.

Of the 160 players who could have filed this year, 55 wouldn't be eligible under the new rules. Some of last month's biggest winners—young Orel ($1 million) Hershiser and Bret ($925,000) Saberhagen and others who went all the way to the arbitrator—would not have had that huge leverage in their dealings.

How much will the new MacPhail guidelines save the owners? Probably at least $5 million a year immediately, not counting long-range ripple effects. "Or $10 million?" said MacPhail's successor at the PRC, Barry Rona, mischievously. "Because of Lee, the days of knee-jerk capitulation are over. The owners are no longer afraid of the process."

MacPhail "can choose any role he wants in baseball anytime he wants as long as I have anything to say about it," said Ueberroth. "Everything he touches goes well. The man has integrity. I came into this game trying to find out who the competent people were. He's the top."

MacPhail, sixty-eight, tried to retire once before, after a decade as AL president during which that league went from second-rate to top dog once more. MacPhail was implored to return as PRC chief for the '85 labor battle. He scoffed, saying the post was too controversial for an old softy like him, more the sort of job for his dad. He'd go to the symphony and the art gallery while the battle raged.

"I wouldn't take that job unless all twenty-six teams asked me; and I've never seen all twenty-six agree on anything in my whole life in baseball," he joked.

Two days later, twenty-six telegrams were put on Lee MacPhail's desk. They all began: "Dear Lee, please . . ."

Commissioner:
A. Bartlett Giamatti

Poet at Heart

NEW YORK, August 1988—When he speaks, A. Bartlett Giamatti has the resonant, commanding voice of a man accustomed to the lectern and podium. As a professor of literature at Yale, as president of Yale and as National League president, his idiosyncratic and often pyrotechnic gift with the language has been a source of power. Giamatti could charm a subpoena server or bamboozle a Supreme Court justice. He can say nothing and make it sound good, or say something and knock your socks off.

Once in a great while, however, Giamatti's voice leaps an octave and, for a second, becomes a high-pitched, childlike celebration of delight. When this happens, the subject is usually his lifelong infatuation with baseball.

That passion—not his academic books like his new *A Free and Ordered Space*, or any single accomplishment in his two years as NL president

113

—is the reason that, a week from now, Giamatti will probably be elected the next commissioner of baseball. The sport's owners hired him in '86 because he had brains and energy. Now they want him to be the boss because they sense how deeply he has fallen in love with their game. Giamatti's long affair with baseball has turned into a marriage.

"When I took this job, I'd seen a lot of baseball in my life, cared about it and thought I knew about it. Well, I was in the second grade in some respects," said Giamatti this week, sitting behind his large antique wooden desk overlooking Park Avenue.

"I was happy to accept this incautiously made offer by the National League because I wanted to learn new things about something I cared about. And I care about this," said Giamatti, his voice shooting upward on the last five words. "How people go about their pleasure is as important to me as how they go about their work . . .

"The largest thing I've learned is the enormous grip that this game has on people, the extent to which it really is very important. It goes way down deep. It really does bind together. It's a cliché and sounds sentimental, but I have now seen it from the inside . . . I think I underestimated the depth of this historical enterprise."

Suddenly the voice goes up, as though Giamatti were surprised with his own unabashed, unqualified words. "And," he said, "baseball is very good. It is not life-threatening. It is not a pollutant. It is an unalloyed good. Of course, there are passions [involved]. But passion is good if it is directed toward a noble end.

"There's nothing bad that accrues from baseball. [Realizing] that has been the most rewarding part of all this."

Sports commissioners are supposed to rhapsodize. However, a fellow who, within two minutes, drops references to Marcel Proust, Robert Frost, *Rashomon* (the Japanese film) and the Heisenberg principle (physics' uncertainty principle) might be expected to protect his intellectual flanks a trifle better.

That Giamatti will be Peter Ueberroth's hand-picked successor as commissioner is almost certain. But would Giamatti make a good commissioner? Several years ago, he laughed uproariously when it was suggested that he might be, at one and the same time, the most overqualified and underqualified man on the list of possible replacements for Bowie Kuhn.

Certainly, Giamatti and Ueberroth are almost antithetical. From negotiating TV contracts to marketing to dealing with drug testing to supervising crowd control, Ueberroth came to his job with enormous experience. In everything, he was a problem solver, unencumbered by

114

theoretical baggage. Tough, combative when necessary, imperious when opposing bossy owners, Ueberroth operated on the inductive theory that what works is probably what's right.

Giamatti is the deductive type. A flashy, deep thinker with a passion for logic and justice, he wants to figure out, by mind muscle, what is morally and theoretically correct, then pursue it. For years, when they were both at Yale, Giamatti relished playing the liberal devil's advocate to conservative Judge Robert Bork in friendly dinner debates.

Some would say such abstract thinking can make for poor policy. And they might cite Giamatti's contributions to the new balk rule and his thirty-day suspension of Pete Rose as examples.

Giamatti may or may not be qualified to handle the business of baseball—labor-management wars, ownership infighting, public relations damage control, etc. However, he is probably already better qualified to oversee the integrity of the game on the field than any commissioner in decades. Teachers are learners, first, and Giamatti studies baseball like a future general manager. He already leaves Kuhn and Ueberroth in the dust as a monologist on technical trends of the game. His idea of heaven is to grill scouts or umpires for "all their bottled-up wisdom."

In the last twenty years, baseball has been lucky in its commissioners. When the game faced lawsuits, Supreme Court cases and congressional scrutiny of its antitrust exemption, it had a lawyer on top: Kuhn.

When baseball faced an economic crisis that demanded lower salaries, higher attendance and increased TV revenues, baseball had a leader who was a master marketeer, a TV old hand and (perhaps) a co-conspirator in a perfectly orchestrated example of monopolistic collusion.

Does baseball need a thinker now?

The guess here, perhaps the hope, is that the game will be fortunate again. What will face Giamatti in the nineties?

In large part, it will be the theoretical questions baseball has shoved aside because of its turbulent eighties.

Is there enough talent available to make expansion a wise course? When and where should it take place? Should there be realignment and new divisions? What about wild cards—the worst idea ever to haunt baseball salons? When, if ever, will the DH rule be unified? What financial structure can be built to stabilize salaries at a tolerable level? How can teams share revenues to a greater degree? As new parks are built, how can baseball respect its traditions by moving back toward grass, back toward irregular fence configurations and away from domed parks?

Giamatti calls the 1890s "the great age of baseball invention," when the "basic grid of the game was set." The 1990s may be an era of reinvention for baseball. Will the sport of the future be played on grass or turf; inside or outside; with pure pennant races or wild cards; with ten men on a side or nine; with flawed umpires or robotic instant replay; with safe stadium conditions or rowdy crowds like those that infest soccer; with twenty-six teams in two leagues or thirty-two in four?

A sport cannot ask itself questions more basic. If baseball ever needed clear thinking, concise arguing and depth of passion, too, it is now.

Fan:
Jeff Wickstrom

Song from the Heart

BALTIMORE, September 9, 1987 — Most men lead lives of quiet desperation. Jeff Wickstrom sings the national anthem at the top of his lungs from coast to coast at his own expense. Last night he completed one of baseball's oddest odysseys. This summer he's sung the anthem at all twenty-six major league parks. He's done it thirteen times at home plate in a tuxedo before cheering crowds. A dozen times he's sung along in the stands because teams wouldn't give him a microphone, even for his standard fee—nothing.

And last night, three thousand miles from home, when his grand finale was rained out, he stood in the Memorial Stadium parking lot in Baltimore and paid homage to Francis Scott Key and "the home of the brave," one last time. "An inauspicious ending," he said, laughing, "to what, realistically, is probably the highlight of my life."

Wickstrom, forty-one, a carpenter, lives with his wife, Ann, in Seattle

117

and sings in the local opera chorus for fun and the odd dollar. In his time, he says, he has been a graduate student in history at George Washington University, studied voice for five years, done odd jobs as a knockabout and been an alcoholic. He's not a kook or publicity hound. At least not yet, although you cross your fingers when a man gets a sniff of fame.

This summer, Wickstrom guesses he's spent $15,000, not to mention lost wages, so that he could, just once in his life, do what he'd always dreamed of: stand in front of thousands of people and make them shiver, maybe even cry, when they hear him sing. "I'm in debt," he says. "I'm almost at the max on both charge cards. Sold my stocks. I've got a '74 MG that I've kept in good shape that I'll probably sell when I get back home. I didn't make one cent. And I have not gotten any singing offers. My dream is to be a professional operatic tenor. But, realistically, I don't think I will be. Robert Merrill's not in danger. Still, I wouldn't trade this summer."

At Shea Stadium, a small group of college boys changed "Jeff-rey, Jeff-rey," when he returned to his seat after his swift, robust classical rendition of the anthem. "People appreciate not hearing all that pop garbage. I liked Jose Feliciano until I heard him do the anthem at the World Series. So often the anthem is just butchered," Wickstrom said.

At Candlestick Park, Giants star Will Clark introduced himself and shook Wickstrom's hand in congratulation. No other player said a word all summer. But one was enough for Wickstrom, a fanatic Giants fan for twenty-five years. That day the crowd stood and cheered as he walked up the aisle to his seat. "My wife was in tears," said Wickstrom. "She'd never experienced anything like that. Well, neither had I . . . She's considered a saint—by me. We met in the chorus of *Aida*, right onstage . . . Luckily for me, she understands the singer's crazy desire to perform."

Who doesn't want to step out of the chorus? But how many find a way?

Wickstrom did it out of annoyance, after hearing an especially awful anthem at a minor league hockey game two years ago. "I called the team and said, 'I sing in the Seattle Opera chorus. I know damn well I can do better than that.' I thought they'd want an audition. Instead, they said, 'Can you do it tonight?' I got up my courage. The fans went wild, like, 'Where did this guy come from?' And the general manager said, 'When can you come back?'

"Life's short," he said. "I was forty. This was a way I could have my moment. You have to push. You can't just wait." He pestered anybody and everybody until he'd sung for the Mariners, Seahawks and SuperSonics. (Only the SuperSonics didn't ask him back.)

One night he sang for the Mariners at 7:30 P.M., drove across town for the second act of *Tosca*, ran next door to do the anthem for a minor league hockey game, then finished *Tosca*—all the time dressed as an 1800s Roman policeman in tricornered hat and brass sword. "I was lucky," he said. "In the chorus, sometimes you're dressed as a peasant."

Local TV crews, on the lookout for the offbeat, discovered him. "I found out what can happen when the media notice you," he said, with mixed meaning. This summer's quixotic tour has generated plenty of news stories and TV bites. Celebrity fades quickly; for him, it's just about over.

Wickstrom would love to be "America's designated anthem singer. I'd take that." But there is no such job. So the gray rain in Baltimore yesterday was a fitting prelude to what has been called the melancholy of all things completed.

"My wife says she's a little concerned that, now that our 'tour' is over, the high point of my life will have been completed," said Wickstrom. "I know what she means. But I think that the reality of my life will descend on me with such suddenness when I get back to Seattle that it will force me to make decisions real fast. I've got to pick up my hammer and pay some bills."

Wickstrom is in debt. But he's proud of himself, for reasons he can't exactly express. On Mother's Day at Comiskey Park in Chicago, an elderly lady stopped him after his anthem. Her family had asked what she wanted for the holiday; she said something fascinated her about going to hear this singing carpenter.

"She told me I was wonderful and asked for my autograph," said Wickstrom. "I was so excited I was trembling."

Wickstrom remembers her name: Connie Adducci. And he remembers that, in the middle of the game, she brought him a homemade hot dog. "You look like you're hungry," she said.

"No question," said Wickstrom, seeming well fed at last, "Connie Adducci was the highlight."

Five Octobers

1984:
The Year the Cubbies
Lost the Pennant

When Tim Flannery's ground ball trickled into right field, knifing under Leon Durham's glove and through his Cub heart, baseball's decade of romantic good luck was finally snapped.

From the moment Carlton Fisk's home run hit the foul pole in the sixth game of the 1975 World Series until Durham helped doom his 1984 Cubs one victory shy of a pennant, everything that a baseball fantasist might have dreamed up actually became a tremulous reality. For ten magic years, baseball had a shimmering quality of wish fulfillment. The "national pastime" once more became a living theater, a renewed source of myth and a sharp restorative for jaded modern appetites.

In 1974 you had to explain why you were a baseball fan. By 1984 you had to explain why you weren't one.

For a decade, baseball produced one borderline-impossible pennant race or media-dream World Series or larger-than-life protagonist on top of another. In 1978 the Red Sox and Yankees had the best pennant race in their league's long history, yet in 1980 and again in 1982 other teams—first the Yankees and Orioles, then the Orioles and Brewers—battled almost as well. Three times in five years the two most famous franchises in the sport—the Yankees and Dodgers—met in World Series that were a transcontinental variation on the old Bronx-to-Brooklyn Subway Series of the fifties. When Cincinnati's Big Red Machine wasn't provoking comparison with the celestial 1927 Yankees, then baseball was enthroning the Long-suffering Phillies ('80) or the Po' Li'l Orioles ('83). Such morality-play championships were fitting finales to seasons filled with ethical undercurrents. Characters like Reggie Jackson, Billy Martin and George Steinbrenner assumed a symbolic role in society like placard-bearing actors in *The Pilgrim's Progress* (Vanity, Vice, Vulgarity).

By '84 baseball's run of luck had reached the ridiculous. The U.S. President once announced Cub games for five years. The Vice President, captain of his '48 Yale team, played in two College World Series finals and could perhaps have been a major leaguer. The president of the Olympic Organizing Committee, encouraged by some to run for the Senate, considered it a proper career step to become baseball commissioner. Syndicated columnists of all political stripes, from George F. Will and James J. Kilpatrick to David Broder and Scotty Reston, were glad to carry their teams' colors in public.

Each spring in the early eighties the bookstores bulged with more tomes on the sport: novels, essays, retrospectives, biographies, confessions, coffee-table glossies, team tell-alls, collections of quotes, diaries, poems, statistics. When Earl Weaver retired, a biography *and* autobiography appeared almost instantly. An umpire (Ron Luciano) had to write a *sequel* to his life story. An eccentric Kansas schoolteacher (Bill James), who views the game through the prism of box scores, became a bestselling guru. Otherwise normal citizens became "sabermetricians" or formed "Rotisserie Leagues" or joined exotic camp fan clubs like the Mayo Smith or Emil Verban societies. The common thread was that everybody treated the game with respect (at the least) or reverence (at the worst). Even Howard Cosell, a front-running, trend-spotting, bandwagon-jumping expert, dropped "Monday Night Football" but stayed with baseball telecasts.

Each season the sport broke attendance records—crowds were up over 50 percent from the end of '74 through '83. A new network TV contract was signed—for a *billion* dollars. The bumptious game even decided, at least in theory, to expand eventually by six more teams.

As the NFL went through a mid-life crisis of rules changes, oversaturation and paralyzing parity, baseball held an old-fashioned revival meeting. "Come back, America," might have been the catchphrase of a cautious game that thought "reform" meant rolling back change: revoke the DH, go back to grass, refurbish old parks. While other leagues like the NFL, NBA and NHL struggled to discover their identities—doubling and tripling their bizarre playoff formats—baseball went forward by going into reverse. Of course, that's the norm for religious rebirths.

It was a double-edged coincidence that baseball's vigor dovetailed with the dominant political taste of the eighties—Ronald Reagan's rejection of "malaise." Baseball is an apolitical, open-ended source of metaphor; the story of Babe Ruth's life doesn't belong to any party or ideology. In sports, as in few other corners of our world, we agree to settle for disconnected, inconclusive insights rather than insisting on correct and final canons. Nonetheless, the dominant cast of mind in any era likes to bend rich symbol systems to its own uses, so in the eighties baseball has, inevitably, been enlisted as an argument for a return to traditional values.

Perhaps a more basic reason that baseball struck a chord is its tendency toward insularity. All games offer an alternative reality. You live in the game while the game lasts. However, among our games, only baseball offers a cocoonlike continuum where the fan can dwell almost indefinitely if he wishes. As novelist Robert Coover put it, the game can be turned into as complete a refuge as you require, almost a year-round fantasy zone. From games on radio and TV to trips to the park, from newspapers, magazines and books to make-believe leagues and endless statistics, from winter trades to hot-stove free-agent arguments, baseball can envelop a person to an almost alarming degree. Anything can become an obsession, but baseball in particular appeals to the fanatical personality. And it's an especially congenial companion in today's introspective, isolationist mood.

Thus for many good reasons (and a few not so appealing), baseball had reached the point not many months ago where it was the designated hot property in sports.

Then just in time, just as the most preposterous and trendy of miracles—a World Series in Wrigley Field—might have brought the sport into the scalding glow of media overkill, Leon Durham and the

Cubs saved the day. Just when being a baseball fan might have devolved into orthodoxy—as being an NFL fan was an obligation of citizenship only a few years ago—the game dropped everybody flat. Just when a Tiger–Cub World Series seemed like the perfect antidote to a "disappointing season," the Cubs went and committed Harry Caray. Instead of salvaging the season by reaching the Series for the first time since 1945, the Cubs provided the perfect final downer for a drab year.

Somewhere the Oldest Fan is muttering, "Now we'll find out who's been along for the ride and who's on for the duration."

The whole '84 season was, in a sense, a test of devotion and discernment for the ardent fan. As a rule, baseball offers a daily density of pleasure that draws us to the box scores in the morning and keeps us up hovering by the radio round midnight. The game promises, and usually delivers, a flow of detail and drama that builds throughout the summer, creating true tension. Talk about foreplay. Make you crazy, man.

Last season was, by this day-to-day standard, a dud. The pennant races went to sleep early, and nobody left a wake-up call. The only close struggle in the AL West was among teams so ordinary (the Royals and Twins) or so disgraceful (the White Sox and Angels) that it was almost unseemly to follow the proceedings.

Seldom has a season been so dull in progress—yet so memorable in reprise. The game didn't offer any of its Big Three enticements: a truly historic pennant race, World Series or record performance by an individual. But it provided almost everything else.

Above all, 1984 was the season of hidden shocks. There is no way to quantify surprise, so it can't be proved that last year was more numbing to our sense of reality than any other. But it certainly seemed that way. Can anyone think of a season in the past thirty years that remotely approached it for events that on Opening Day would have been dismissed as laughable, preposterous, beyond fantasy?

Since division play arrived in 1969, baseball has never produced a group of winners half so unexpected as the Cubs, Padres, Tigers and Royals—clubs that finished fifth, fourth, second (6 games behind) and second (20 games behind) in '83. Can one person step forward anywhere and prove that he wrote these four names on a piece of paper —much less bet on all of them? A bookie would have given you 50,000 to 1 on that parlay. Just as staggering were the collapses of the defending champs—the Orioles and White Sox (both fifth place) and the Phillies and Dodgers (fourth).

By coincidence, the White Sox went from 36 games over .500 to 14

126

games under—a plummet of 50 games—while the crosstown Cubs went from 20 games under .500 to 31 games over—a rise of 51 games. To see any team rise or fall that much in a season is an anomaly, but for two in the same town to go in opposite directions is unprecedented. Of course, if you're a Chicagoan, you could just say your city won 170 games in '83 and 170 in '84, so what's all the fuss?

The final standings show that baseball has moved into a new age, joining the NFL in a period of dubious parity. While football has deliberately jumped into the questionable embrace of enforced mediocrity, baseball has done so by accident. What the college draft, profit sharing and a restrictive free-agent policy have done to the NFL, baseball has done to itself through the natural workings of an almost completely free marketplace.

At the moment, baseball doesn't have any team of dynastic proportions. With a little luck, almost any club can wake up one day and find itself in the World Series. Seldom, if ever, have such thoroughly ordinary teams as the '83 Phillies and '84 Padres made their way into the Series. The "names" on both teams were oldsters past their prime who survived one last pennant race out of pride. For the past two years the postseason has been dominated by teams with players "of a certain age"—Pete Rose, Tony Perez and Joe Morgan in '83, then Steve Garvey, Graig Nettles, Goose Gossage, Ron Cey, Gary Matthews and Larry Bowa last season. They have almost nothing in common except the flinty and determined look in their aging eyes. They're young and yet, suddenly, they are not. They look at you hard. They're the superstar rejects.

Long ago Branch Rickey said, "Better get rid of 'em a year too soon rather than a year too late," and that's been the front-office rationale for tightwad ingratitude ever since. Recently, those rich castoffs have been having the last word. "The same *teams* don't always make it to the playoffs," said Cey last fall, "but it looks like the same *people* do. Maybe this is more a sport of special individuals and less of rich organizations than some think."

These days, even the best teams are uniquely vulnerable. "We look great now," said Sparky Anderson after his Detroit Tigers had won the fifth and last game of the World Series, "but Baltimore looked great last year and Milwaukee looked great the year before that. The American League East is a scary division to manage in."

Baseball lives in a time of lowered expectations now that we've learned how difficult it is to build and maintain a better-than-good team. As soon as a team gets very good, the payroll becomes prohibitive;

the best a club can hope for is simply to hold itself intact. The free-agent money dries up, and the team falls easy prey to injury and stagnation.

It's obvious in retrospect that baseball was a game of divisional dynasties from 1969 to about 1980. Now all that's changed. In the past six years only two NL teams—the Mets and the Giants—have not been to the playoffs. And in the AL, eight teams have won divisions in the past four years. The Tigers, who eschewed the free-agent sweepstakes after their Series triumph, look like another team that can't afford to make the jump from good to great. Nobody can. Only one team—Steinbrenner's Yankees—tried to go the whole nine yards and buy up talent at every position. The result: internal chaos; an insane, self-perpetuating salary structure; a roster bottleneck that prevented young players from developing.

The corollary to this can't-spend-too-much theory is that almost all second-division teams realize they must join the multimillion-dollar bidding to some degree. Look how quickly the Padres, Cubs and White Sox bought the last key pieces to their off-season puzzles. The rewards are too great not to play big-money roulette, and the punishments for being really awful—like the Indians and Giants—are too great as well.

On the other hand, were the old days really so wonderful? How much fun was it to watch the Yankees and Royals meet in the playoffs four times in five years? Or see the Reds against the Pirates or Orioles against the A's three times?

The new trends have their bizarre charms. Like the Kansas City Royals. Sure, the Cubs were cute. But the Royals were beyond belief. In a sense, their victory in the American League West was the most ludicrously titillating event of the whole season. The Royals were the worst team in baseball history ever to win anything. Nitpickers will say that one team—the '73 Mets—won a division with 82 wins, 2 less than K.C.'s total. But would any true fan really claim that the Mets, while mediocre, were as genuinely bad as the Royals? Not with Tom Seaver, Jerry Koosman, Jon Matlack and Tug McGraw on the mound.

The Royals became the only team in history ever to finish first despite being outscored for the season (by 13 runs). This is the team that phoned Bucky Dent in retirement at his Florida baseball school and said, "Bucky, we've had a couple of injuries. Well, actually, about five injuries. How'd you like to come play shortstop for us? Tonight?"

Down the stretch, when they pulled away from the California Malingerers, the Royals' starting lineup contained these seven names night after night: Pat Sheridan, Greg Pryor, Lynn Jones, Darryl Motley, Jorge

Orta, Onix Concepcion and Don (On) Slaught. Manager Dick Howser called them his "spare parts" in spring training, but by September they were the whole engine. The starting rotation of Gubicza, Leibrandt and Saberhagen looked like a berserk Scrabble rack.

What the gritty Royals did was unprecedented. They were a losing team (in '83), a decimated team (three players sent to jail), a written-off team, *before* the roof caved in. Yet, with children on the mound and nobodies everywhere, with six shortstops in one season and enough injuries to stop two good teams, they won their division.

That these Royals could beat the healthy and wealthy Angels head to head when it counted in September amounted to a baseball parable. Who could be on the side of the Angels—the Me Generation nine?

If one team makes the blood boil, it's the Angels. They ought to give their fans a rebate. The next time an Angel cheers for a teammate, they ought to stop the game and give someone the ball. For three years this rich club has played as if it thought hustle and morale were diseases requiring inoculation.

This is a team that had a 500-home-run hitter (Reggie Jackson), a man with seven batting titles (Rod Carew), a nine-time All-Star (Fred Lynn), a six-time All-Star (Bobby Grich), a four-time All-Star (Bob Boone), an '83 All-Star (Doug DeCinces), another past All-Star (Brian Downing), a centerfielder with 48 steals (Gary Pettis). They also had a starter with 255 wins (Tommy John), a fellow who hit .336 (Juan Beniquez), three solid starting pitchers (Witt, Zahn and Romanick) and three decent relievers (18–9 and a 2.51 ERA in 117 appearances). Toss in a passable manager (John McNamara), a top front-office mind (Gene Mauch) and all the money in the world.

What have you got? A .500 record.

The Angels arrive at the park on time, smooth and tuck in their uniforms, give a presentable effort and make sure they get the best table at the best restaurant in town after the game. It's a heavenly life for them. But it's hell to watch.

After I wrote such slander about the Angels in the last week of the season, their general manager, Buzzie Bavasi, called me and said, "I'm mad at you. Why didn't you write that a month ago when it might still have stirred them up and done some good?" Owner Gene Autry was on the phone next, saying, "They aren't all like that. But in general, you're right."

The Angels-Royals juxtaposition proved once more that no matter how much talent you have, baseball is still a battle of one-run games. It's in the nature of the sport. The teams that play better as teams—

with hustle, intelligence, cohesion, unselfishness—do better in tight play. In one-runners, the Royals were 26–21, the Angels 22–30. There's your season.

While teams with some of that spirited dynamic, like the Twins, could stay in contention, a team totally without it—the White Sox—disappeared. In a season full of almost utterly unaccountable individual performance, none was more stunning than the collapse of White Sox pitching. The same trio of LaMarr Hoyt, Floyd Bannister and Rich Dotson which was 43–5 after the '83 All-Star break was 41–44 for all of 1984.

Which proves?

That he who builds his house on the notion that hurlers can be consistent from one year to the next will soon be sleeping in the street. The White Sox probably should have been a caution to all the teams that went auction-crazy over free agents Bruce Sutter and Rick Sutcliffe after the '84 season. No veteran pitcher is worth the long-term dollars those two were offered.

If anything, individuals were even more unpredictable last season than teams. Did anyone anywhere predict that Tony Gwynn of San Diego and Don Mattingly of the Yankees would be batting champions? The tubby Gwynn, with his high-pitched voice, friendly good manners and thirty-one-ounce Little League–size bat was the most delightful surprise. "You'd never pick him out of a crowd, would you?" says Padre coach Harry Dunlop. "He's got a body like Yogi Berra, Thurman Munson and Bill Madlock . . . You just can't tell about this game."

Can one fan anywhere claim that he predicted Ryne Sandberg of the Cubs and Willie Hernandez of the Tigers would be the MVPs? Did anybody even pick one of them?

Reliever Hernandez, acquired in a barely noticed trade from Philadelphia, won both the MVP and Cy Young awards, a silly injustice that would be comparable to Dustin Hoffman winning the Oscars for both Best Actor and Best Actress for *Tootsie*. Relievers should be eligible for either MVP or Cy Young (probably the latter) but not both.

While Hernandez had his season in the sun after several workmanlike years, Sandberg looks like a full-blooming Natural. Nobody knows where these freaks of nature come from or why they're touched by greatness. Look them in the face and it's clear that they don't know either. They look like everybody else in their world, but they're better. Sandberg, the so-silent Swede from Spokane, son of a mortician, can't give you a clue. He just has the gift, or it has him. Cardinal manager Whitey Herzog calls him "the best baseball player I have ever seen."

George Brett tells Sandberg, "I watch you every afternoon on cable TV. You're my idol."

If the natural players have an indefinable grace and efficiency of movement, then the natural pitchers have a special leverage that seems to transform their bodies at some crucial instant from muscle and bone to elastic and steel. They become daredevil slingshots, hurling the ball as though heedless of their arms. Case in point: Dwight Gooden, teenager bucking for legend.

We all spotted him before the season, right? We knew that sure, after a year and a half in A ball, he could come to the majors with the Mets at age nineteen and become the first pitcher in history to average 11 strikeouts per 9 innings (276 K's in 218 IP).

What really underlines the amazing quality of '84 is that Gooden was not indisputably the best first-year pitcher in the game. The other great rookie—a lefty who is still basically invisible up in Seattle—is named Mark Langston, and he also won 17 games and also won the strikeout title in his league (204 in 225). Watch this space for further developments. For about 15 more years and 4,000 strikeouts?

Sutcliffe, of course, is another one we all spotted. Lots of pitchers start the season 4–5 for the Cleveland Indians, get waived out of the AL without a blink and then go 16–1 for the Cubs. It all happened so fast that we sometimes have to pinch ourselves as a reminder that nothing comparable has ever happened to any pitcher.

Beneath the exterior of the '84 standings, many such remarkable stories were woven. Alvin Davis drove in 116 runs for Seattle, while another rookie, Philadelphia's Juan Samuel, almost became the first man ever to have at least 70 stolen bases, 70 extra-base hits and 70 RBIs. (He missed by one RBI.) Sometimes it seems that even inveterate fans forget how capricious their sport can be; if we dreamed more wildly in the off-season, we might double our pleasure and come closer to forecasting the future, too. After 1983, for instance, Atlanta gave away forty-four-year-old Phil Niekro while the New York Mets tried to trade away Dave Kingman and couldn't. Niekro went 16–8 as a Yankee and made the All-Star team, while Ding Dong Kingman proved there is no justice by driving in 118 runs for the A's.

Despite the 1984 success of those two veterans, we're seeing one of our generational changings of the guard. Names that have been on our tongues for fifteen to twenty years are disappearing in a rush: Rose, Morgan, Perez, Jackson, Yastrzemski, Singleton, Palmer, Jenkins, Niekro, Seaver, Carlton. They're either gone or going.

Their replacements in our national portrait gallery seem extremely promising. In just the past two seasons the American League has seen the emergence as full-time players of Mattingly, Alvin Davis, Julio Franco, George Bell, Rich Gedman, Greg Walker, Tim Teufel, Mike Boddicker (20–11), Bud Black (17–12), Frank Viola (18–12), Langston (17–10) and Storm Davis (14–9). Waves of talented new AL pitchers, like Roger Clemens, Mark Gubicza, Bret Saberhagen and Rick Romanick, are flooding the mound. Proven stars like Cal Ripken, Kent Hrbek, Wade Boggs, and Tom Brunansky have played only three full years.

The National League has its fresh faces—Gwynn, Sandberg, Samuel, Chili Davis, Johnny Ray, Gooden, Tony Peña, Jesse Orosco, Ron Darling and Alejandro Peña (ERA champ)—but, on the whole, it's the AL that has depth in new talent.

This one trend is so large and undeniable, it has been almost universally missed. Quietly and quickly the American League not only has caught the National in quality of play, but has now clearly moved into the lead. Maybe even a sizable lead.

"The American League now has most of the best players," says former NLer Sparky Anderson, who's managed for fifteen years, nine in the National, six in the AL. "As Joe Morgan says, 'The change has changed.'"

"Look at the final All-Star team this year," continues Anderson. "Two NLers [Sandberg and Mike Schmidt] out of nine. Same the year before. The AL just has the players with the big numbers, and those are the stars."

Most dazzling is the AL's complete superiority in power hitters.

The AL has four times as many legitimate home-run hitters as the NL. Go on, attribute that to the DH. It just gets worse. Much worse. The top five sluggers in the NL had a total of 150 homers. The top five men on one AL team—the Boston Red Sox—had 154. That's right. The Red Sox had more quality power hitters than the entire National League. Don't try to cop that old Fenway Park plea, either. Homers come just as cheap in Wrigley Field or Atlanta Fulton County Stadium, and a half-dozen other NL parks are perfectly reasonable long-ball parks, too.

"The National League never wanted interleague play," needles Anderson. "Now they better jump for it if they get the chance, 'cause pretty soon it's going to be the American League that thinks it's too good to play 'em."

Perhaps the strangest aspect of the entire 1984 season—and the core reason why the whole year seemed so flat at the time—is that there was not, in a sense, a single truly important game during the whole regular season. "Play ball" was hollered 2,105 times, and not one of those contests was awaited with any real national passion.

In the absence of any ongoing drama, the doings of the Cubs became the game's official summer saga. Perhaps a perennial losing team touches a far deeper chord in people than any mere winner could. You learn wisdom in defeat, not victory. George Allen, with typical football myopia, said that losing is like dying. Cub fans know he had it wrong: losing isn't like dying; it's like living. So what? It ain't so bad.

Maybe Chicago's feelings about the Cubs were summed up by a sign in a restaurant near Wrigley Field. "Any employee wishing to miss work because of death or serious illness," it read, "please notify the office by 11 A.M. on the day of the game."

By the time the postseason began, the Cubs were practically the nation's mascots. Perhaps those ten years of fantasy baseball had the whole country primed for an orgy of paeans to day baseball, old brick outfield walls and "Take Me Out to the Ball Game" during the seventh-inning stretch.

Then, just in time, the Cubs came to the rescue. The ancient order remained intact. The Cubs proved they were still the Cubs. The ivied park with its cheerful message—you don't have to go to the World Series every year, or even every lifetime, to be cherished—was safe.

How the Cubs trashed those three final games of the National League season—the only three really meaty games of the whole baseball year—must have been preordained, because it was done so neatly, like a ritual suicide. The Cubs won Game One, 13–0, for a perfect dose of overconfidence. They also won Game Two, 4–2, thanks to enough pixilated good fortune to make anyone believe that the ghosts of long-dead Cubs were doing their work. At least one lifelong fan in Wrigley Field knew better. As his team left for San Diego, Tony Epifano looked down at the jubilant scene and spoke the words of a lifelong Cub fan: "This is terrible. They're going to lose three in a row, and I won't be able to bear watching it."

Of course, the Cubs napped through Game Three, losing 7–1. By the time they woke up in Game Four, they were in a war. And Steve Garvey wasn't on their side.

Yes, the Padres carried Garvey off the field that night. It was either that or just bow down and kiss his feet as he trotted home. Four straight run scoring clutch hits. Five RBIs. Sudden-death game-winning homer in the ninth. Can you break a Cub's heart? Or does that just come with the uniform?

Maybe baseball's dime-novel decade really ended then. Fisk hitting the foul pole started it, and Garvey's almost equally dramatic home run ended it. The proper popular ending, of course, would have been for Sutcliffe to win the final game and for the Cubs to win the Series.

But ground balls don't have hearts.

Except for folks in San Diego, who really wants to remember Game Five? Who wants to remember the seventh inning? Durham getting down on one knee so that there would be exactly enough room between his big knee and his big leg for that little ball to pass through? That was the end of what had been a 3–0 Cub lead in the game. Suddenly the Padres were even, then ahead.

So it was over. Not just the game, but the season. And perhaps not just the season but a period of frolic baseball health.

Now it's back to reality.

One of baseball's eerie qualities is that whatever the sport needs, it seems to get. Just when the game was going through radical dislocations off the field (testing the loyalties of its fans with player strikes and drug busts and million-dollar contracts to stiffs), the game *on* the field surpassed itself. In a sense, baseball forced us to forgive it for its growing pains as it entered its modern age.

When the game sorely needed a decade of magic, it arrived. Just when the sport might have alienated an older generation of fans, it fascinated a new one that enjoyed watching the kaleidoscopic tumult. The baby boomers, the weaned-on-TV generation, the computer kids with the microsecond attention spans—they all found baseball more appealing in its new jazzed-up, controversial garb.

Now, as Bowie Kuhn leaves and Peter Ueberroth arrives, baseball appears ready for a few years of sane shakedown. Owners know that their revenues must be better shared and that cable TV superstations must be regulated. Players realize, even though their union won't say it, that salaries must soon top out or the game's health will be badly damaged.

What baseball needs now, it seems, is a moratorium on its recent convulsions. No more strikes, please. No more batting champions going to prison. No more palace revolts against a good commissioner. No more lawsuits and franchise raiding. No more tenfold salary growth in a dozen years.

Anarchy is exciting, but a strain. And it goes against baseball's grain. Needed now is a period of restraint and compromise and order. Hello, dullness, my old friend.

Fortunately, what baseball needs it almost always gets. God knows why.

1985: The Hallowed and the Hollow Men of Summer

Put a few million bucks in a man's pocket and you will see his true colors soon enough. He'll tell the world to go to hell, if that's what's in him. Or he will treat his fortune as a blessing to husband, if that's the kind of man he really is.

Handling great prosperity can reveal character as much as handling poverty. In the Caribbean they say, "The higher the monkey climb, the more he expose." That's been baseball's underlying theme for a decade: Trial by Wealth.

The charms of the game itself have only been heightened by the addition of one extra wild-card player: Mr. Money. Since 1976, when free agency began, baseball has been a fascinating moral laboratory. It's as though we had been allowed to watch an experiment in human nature conducted under almost scientific conditions.

What would happen if we took 650 major-leaguers (with salaries averaging $50,000 a year) plus 26 owners (with franchises worth $10 million on the average) and made them vastly richer each year? No matter what these human guinea pigs did, wise or foolish, we'd mushroom their net worth each season anyway—until the players made $360,000 a man and the clubs were worth $50 million apiece. We'd reach a point where a player (Baltimore's Eddie Murray) would actually earn more in one game ($16,049.32) than the average worker earns in a year. As a further perverse twist, the public would indulge the flaws and foibles of all concerned as though they were aristocracy, since millionaires are America's only royalty.

How does a person or institution react to such sudden, vast and largely unmerited good fortune? What games does the psyche play on a man whose good luck outraces his imagination? Is it heaven or hell when we wake up in a world where all fifteen pool balls go into the pockets on the break shot?

The first decade of free agency is history now, and most of the results of our "Twilight Zone" experiment are in hand. When we look back, we realize that the most important baseball stories of 1985 all involved watershed events in baseball's relationship to Big Money. On the surface, the Players' Strike, the Cocaine Trial, the Pete Rose Record and the Royals' World Championship seem unconnected. But let's look again.

Ten years ago, we had three basic questions about what the death of the reserve clause would do to baseball. How would it affect the game as a viable economic industry? How would it affect the players, for both good or ill? How would it affect teams as competitive entities?

• What was the One-Day Strike but a tragicomic culmination of the petty, greedy, interminable tug-of-war between labor and management over divvying up a billion-dollar TV contract? August 7, 1985, will probably be remembered as the day when the last pieces of debris from baseball's financial explosion finally came back to earth. Just when the worst disaster in the game's history seemed possible—a second season-raping strike within four years—everything fell in place for a solution that should leave the game in frolic health by the time (1990) the next labor contract comes due.

• What was the Cocaine Trial but courtroom theater, where we learned again that great riches can bring great pain and even greater humiliation? Stool pigeons, reformed addicts and peddlers who could have spent years in jail (but for immunity), all took the witness stand. No installment of that old TV series "The Millionaire" ever turned out more tragically. When we look back at the greatest and most promising players of recent years, it's a shock to see how many had their lives or careers scarred by too much cocaine or liquor. Only a fraction of the casualties have reached the public record, but what a list it is: Dave Parker, Keith Hernandez, J. R. Richard, Lonnie Smith, Steve Howe, Garry Templeton, Ron LeFlore, Darrell Porter, Willie Wilson, Willie Mays Aikens, Vida Blue, Tim Raines.

• What were the splendid career achievement records of Pete Rose, Tom Seaver, Phil Niekro, Rod Carew, Nolan Ryan and Reggie Jackson if not testimonies to men who knew that real accomplishment was a harder and rarer thing than merely grabbing cash and celebrity? If the Free Agent Era has a human message, it's the encouraging news that most men seem more addicted to developing talent than to wasting it. The lure of doing a difficult thing well may be more basic, at least among top-level ballplayers, than the temptation to buy a cheap thrill in a gram bottle.

• What Rose represented at the individual level, the Royals symbolized as a team. When Kansas City fought off match point six times in the playoffs and World Series, what better illustration of how often the same old reassuring values resurface when baseball selects its champions? Look at Series winners like the '83 Orioles, '84 Tigers and '85 Royals. How can we miss the moral? It's easier for a camel to pass through the eye of a needle than for a rich and self-satisfied team to win the Series.

In a sense, each of these focal points of 1985 also marked an end to old business and pointed the way to new questions.

Before baseball's next labor showdown, in 1990, what can the game's owners do to stabilize their economic house? We've had enough breathless panic and bad blood for one revolution. What can players do—as a union and individually—to minimize the traumas that sudden wealth can inflict? Finally, with ten years' worth of hindsight, what team-building lessons can franchises take from this period of auction-mentality bidding and demolition-derby competitive balance?

Whatever else Peter Ueberroth may do in his five-year term as baseball commissioner, however much you distrust his grandstanding about mandatory drug testing, however suspicious you are of his ulterior political motives, the new man has already earned his salary. The old game has never seen a bluff like the bully-pulpit con that he ran to help beat the strike. Within baseball, it's hard to find anybody who will give Ueberroth credit for preventing that labor disaster. The new boss made enemies in almost every quarter—bless his heart. Outside baseball, it's hard to find anybody who doesn't give him praise. For once, the truth is *not* in between. Give Ueberroth plenty of kudos. Above all, *please* don't give the credit to anybody else. No one else deserves it.

If Bowie Kuhn had been commish, the sport might *still* be on strike. When a strike neared, Kuhn always pulled his head inside his shell. Ueberroth stuck out his neck. Kuhn worked behind the scenes. Ueberroth stole the scenes. Kuhn sided with the owners when they fabricated tales about red ink. Ueberroth ordered his employers to "open their books" and prove their claims. Kuhn said, "No comment," and watched it all on TV. Ueberroth was on every network, with a multi-headed peace plan. Kuhn wouldn't use the power he had. Ueberroth pretended to powers that nobody thought he had, intimating that he could unilaterally appoint himself as the owners' negotiator and accept the union's terms.

Kuhn played Clark Kent. Ueberroth looked for a phone booth.

Kuhn, who angered no one except the fans, was beheaded anyway —the 1981 strike tarnishing his whole reign as commissioner. Ueberroth, who angered everyone except the fans, ran the risk of marching to history's guillotine, accused of being a meddler. Instead, because he had the gumption to talk straight and blow holes in the phony arguments used by both sides, Ueberroth helped embarrass and buffalo both sides into a quick solution.

In the long view, Ueberroth's dramatic May decision to force the owners to open their books paved the way for a settlement in August. Even factoring in all the owners' bookkeeping tricks, the players could see that their hands were finally reaching the bottoms of the owners' deep pockets.

In the short run, Ueberroth pressured both sides to settle. In retrospect the Ueberroth Plan was very close to the final settlement. In fact, its basic points show us the outlines of how a ten-year argument was finally settled. The commissioner, a free-market man, told the owners to drop their various sneaky proposals for a team salary cap like the one in pro basketball. They did. He also asked them to get their sticky fingers off free agency, a system that increased fan interest and promoted balanced competition from the day it was born. They did. Finally Ueberroth asked the owners to stop asking the players to solve their (the owners') financial problems. This was an important philosophical point. The owners had to admit, once and for all, that the sport's red ink was all their fault, that the union had never done anything wrong and that it was the owners' responsibility to restructure their own financial empire.

All that done, Ueberroth started swatting that smart, wiseass, intransigent players' union in its greedy snout. Ueberroth told the players they couldn't realistically have both free agency and the current system of arbitration, in which teams and players both submit salary figures, with the arbitrator choosing one. It amounted to an economic whiplash that owners couldn't be expected to have the self-restraint to escape.

For years the union had refused to accept the reality that baseball was an oligopoly. In most businesses, you try to drive your competition out of existence. In baseball, every team has to be fairly strong so that the whole league can survive. Until Ueberroth exposed the error of its ways, the union had always pretended that baseball was a standard total-competition marketplace.

It isn't, insisted the new commissioner. Baseball has a right to create a system in which weak teams can compete. If that impinges on old-fashioned free-enterprise theory, then so be it.

Just as the owners backed off their salary cap and free-agency rollbacks, so the union did what it said it never would. It changed the arbitration ground rules, making the process available to fewer players beginning in 1987. As for that billion-dollar TV contract, both sides just haggled that rascal right down the middle.

When we look at the whole arm-wrestling match between players and owners since the day in 1974 when Catfish Hunter was declared the first free agent, there is really only one possible overview. To paraphrase what Huck Finn said about kings: All baseball owners is mostly rapscallions.

It would be difficult to find a single instance in this whole era when the game's owners told the unvarnished truth. Their brazen lies about the depth of their wealth were, in retrospect, scandalous—a kind of grand theft.

Even now the owners' claims of hard times are, at bottom, a deceit. To illustrate, take the example of Edward Bennett Williams, who bought the Orioles for $12.2 million in 1979. He could have sold the team for $50 million in 1985. Such franchise appreciation is fairly typical. Could it really be shown that *anybody* in baseball lost money when the value of franchises is rising far faster than money is being "lost" on the books? Ninety percent of all baseball owners either make money or get filthy rich. What about the other 10 percent? It's their tough luck. When did capitalism start guaranteeing profits?

At the moment, owners require even less sympathy than usual. Perhaps somewhere an impartial observer can be found who believes it was pure coincidence that not one significant free agent signed with a new team last winter [1985–86] and that not one signed with his old team for more than three years. Presumably the owners conspired like crazy to pull off this coup—although what might be called an unspoken "conspiracy of common sense" is remotely conceivable. Whichever the case, the result is the same. The owners managed to curb the salary explosion just before it started to pinch them in the profits. 'Nuff to make you cynical.

Will the owners continue to Hold That Line on free-agent bidding? Probably not. Sooner or later a George Steinbrenner or a Ted Turner will finish licking his wounds from past free-agent embarrassments and decide once more that he can buy a pennant. In the long run, collusion isn't the owners' best solution. They need another method—a legal and permanent one. NFL-style revenue sharing: that is the central economic problem which the owners must solve in the eighties.

The real engine that has propelled baseball's salary rocket—and that may do it again—is the imbalance in wealth among teams. The day the Yankees, Dodgers, Cubs and Braves are only twice as rich as the Mariners, Indians, Giants and Pirates—rather than four or five times so— is when baseball's salary graph will start to level off. At present, rich clubs spend with impunity indefinitely. If the rich weren't *so* rich, they'd be restrained by the marketplace. A dollar badly spent in the past would prevent a future free-agent adventure.

These days, the duty of the devoted fan is simple. When you hear the words "revenue sharing" and "baseball" in the same sentence, please salute.

The ugliest side of baseball in recent years has been the way in which many ordinary fellows, with no particular claim to a blessed life, have accepted their inordinate—almost ridiculous—good fortune as if it were their due. Health, cash, glamour, adulation, youth: sure, we'll take it. But sign an autograph, give to charity, hustle in a lost cause, risk injury for the team, give an interview, show some modesty, admit a mistake or be humble in failure—forget it.

The manners and morals of ballplayers have, in all likelihood, remained largely unchanged in the last few years. Geneticists insist that the species alters slowly. Yet when a young millionaire forgets to run out a ground ball, or charges five dollars for an autograph (as some do), or asks to renegotiate an already embarrassingly inflated contract, or demands to be traded from a bad team, or nurses a minor injury for weeks or in any other way proves himself to be less than a paragon, it sure stinks to high heaven, doesn't it?

Maybe a fat paycheck and a famous name shouldn't bring a special set of onerous responsibilities along with them. But they do.

Since the day federal arbitrator Peter Seitz liberated the baseball serfs, ballplayers have performed for higher stakes and been judged by higher standards. Anyway, that's what the judge told Willie Wilson before he threw him in jail in 1983 for attempting to purchase cocaine. "Role model," the judge said. In this harsh and heightened light, those who succeed can seem artificially heroic, and those who fail can appear unrealistically contaminated.

Sometimes it's impossible not to personify baseball. The game almost seems to have a speaking voice. During the same September when the game was having its ugliest scandal since 1919, Pete Rose reached the final days of his twenty-three-year assault on Ty Cobb's career hit record. The two events seemed to exist to comment on and complicate each other. In fact, the night Rose broke the record, the man who batted next, Dave Parker, had testified in the Cocaine Trial earlier that day. Such a juxtaposition has a silent eloquence almost too edged for words. Yet the easy Rose-Parker symbolism may be more ambiguous than it seems.

It's indisputable that Rose's 4,192nd hit—like Tom Seaver's 300th win, Rod Carew's 3,000th hit, Reggie Jackson's 525th home run, Nolan Ryan's 4,000th strikeout and Phil Niekro's 300th win—was a statistical monument to a strong and basically estimable personality. Each of those men illustrated a virtue that a whole character might be structured around: Rose, enthusiasm; Seaver, practical intelligence; Carew, art for art's sake; Jackson, pride; Ryan, conditioning; Niekro, patient humility.

On the other hand, the men who found themselves snared in the Curtis Strong trial were not, on the whole, a sleazy bunch. Keith Hernandez, Dave Parker and Enos Cabell have, at various times, heard themselves called "team leaders." Ironically, Parker considers Rose his hero and exemplar. Hernandez says his cocaine hang-up was the nightmare mistake of his life. Cabell was the only witness to hint at a darker and more ambiguous side of the truth: he took cocaine because (as many players believe) it helped him play better.

We laugh when a player throws a spitball or puts too much pine tar on his bat. But if the same player runs the risk of addiction by using an illegal drug to heighten performance, we label him a jock leper.

In a world of gray, Rose is our man of sharp, clear colors.

The pertinent lesson within Rose's story is that none of his motivations for playing was affected one iota by whether he made $10,000 a year, or a million, to play the game. His goal was excellence itself, personal identity through concrete accomplishment. When the next generation of ballplayers—those who'll grow up with the notion of huge wealth accompanying success—look for a lodestar, they couldn't do better than this old Red.

Rose thinks he plays for victory and a paycheck. But he doesn't. He has accidentally, through some gift of nature, stumbled onto a far higher notion of his calling. Some have played the game as well as Rose has, but no one has loved it as much. For more than twenty-five years, no detail, no subtlety, no outward paradox, no hardship that the game presented has offended or bored him. He has accepted the sport as a given and made it his lifework to understand the thing and be in harmony with it.

Because he has loved the game for its own sake, on its own terms, the game loves him back and cannot cease rewarding him. Rose was born to play baseball, we say. What we didn't realize, but now suspect, was that he may have been born to manage it, too. For all those years—the sweltering doubleheaders in St. Louis, the raw, mist-swept nights in Candlestick Park—Rose never could keep his eyes off the field. While others wool-gathered, he gathered the game—one fact, one connection, one insight at a time. Baseball's ultimate doer also was its best watcher. Now managing seems so natural to him that he can't even explain it. And seldom tries.

Each year a few more players seem to grasp some of the lessons that Rose came by instinctively. Fewer players switch cities to go free agent; more put down roots and identify with one team. Fewer go for the last dollar on a contract; more opt for the quality and type of life they prefer. Some are even learning generosity. Eddie Murray of the Orioles has quietly funded a summer camp for children.

At the moment, baseball is intensely concerned with the mechanics of drug testing. To a degree, though, cocaine may already be a dead issue in baseball. Surely no player will ever be dumb enough to kid himself that cocaine is nonaddictive. No player can doubt any longer that he might be a target in a prosecution. And finally, no player—after the witch-hunt atmosphere in Pittsburgh, where even Willie Mays's name was besmirched—can doubt that even if he doesn't end up in jail his reputation could be badly damaged, perhaps by something that does not even medically qualify as a drug problem.

In the long historical view, the players of the last decade may eventually be looked on with a bit of pity. They were given something they weren't remotely prepared to handle: the level of freedom that a million bucks brings. If they'd had more in their heads, they might have put less up their noses. Perhaps the surprise is that so few ended up in rehabilitation centers and courtrooms.

"Let's not lose our bearings," the game sometimes seems to say. "In the midst of all the money, all the fame, all the pure whirling foolishness, let's remember what is important."

And what is important? At least in baseball, it is the daily doggedness, the occasional brilliance and the sincere craftsmanship of the truly committed individual. It's Rose, against all common sense, sending himself to bat in Chicago after he has tied Cobb's record; the whole baseball world wants him to break the record at home in Cincinnati. He just doesn't think that feels right. He thinks it'd be better to win the game. It's Phil Niekro, on the last day of the season, not only winning his 300th game but becoming the oldest man ever to pitch a shutout. At forty-six, he also fulfills a career-long dream: to win a game without throwing a knuckleball. (Okay, he threw one or two in the ninth inning.)

When we speak of teams, what's important is somewhat more complex and considerably more vague. It's the harmony of purpose and the deep internal familiarity that raise a group of men to a level of excellence transcending any individual consideration. At its best, baseball offers us the exceptional man as the centerpiece of a group that truly seems to achieve a collective personality.

In other words, we get George Brett risking his neck to dive hell-bent into the concrete mouth of the Kansas City Royals' dugout to try to catch a pop-up that the rest of the planet considers meaningless. And we also have coach Lee May right there, poised to catch Brett when he does something nobody dreamed he'd ever do. Thanks, we needed that.

Let's hear it for a loaf of Brett, a slice of Biancalana and a pound of Balboni. Everything the past decade raised on high, the Royals brought low. The Royals have their Rolls-Royces, too, no doubt. But let's pretend they don't. Let's take them at the mythic level, which, once you get to the World Series, is where a team sees itself.

Were these Royals the worst team ever to win the World Series? Well, let's hope so. These guys deserve to be remembered. If they aren't the worst, let's say they were anyway. This is a club that merits more than "Well, sure, they were pretty mediocre, but somebody sometime probably had even less measurable talent and more luck."

No, no, no. That won't do. Instead, let's see the Royals as the pleasing culmination of an eighties trend: the fulfillment of the romantic team project. In a period that places so much dollar emphasis on the individual, it's interesting that one undermanned or historically frustrated team after another keeps winning the Series.

The Phils, Dodgers, Orioles, Tigers and Royals of '80, '81, '83, '84 and '85 have been almost identical in team psychology. All had failed (more than once) when they were younger and thought to be much better. After they were discarded—no longer thought a prize commodity —they won. Only Detroit was a favorite through the postseason.

"We came to play," said Royals designated hitter Hal McRae, "not to feel sorry for ourselves."

Baseball may have reached the point where, because of money, the greatest enemy a player can have is expectation. Hardly any team repeats now. Is it possible that being filthy rich, as well as an overdog, is a new burden teams have felt only recently?

Conversely, the player who (in reality) has everything desperately needs to play behind the illusion that he has been denied something —"our championship." Take my villa on the Côte d'Azur, but gimme that Series ring!

While other teams have embraced free agents, or at least sought "the right free agent" to fill a weak link, the Royals' general manager, John Schuerholz, hasn't bought that theory at all. "I think the interaction of your players among themselves is more important now than it ever was. You can't say what makes good chemistry within a group of people. But you better pay attention to getting it, and then to keeping it."

The last three World Series winners have not gotten a significant contribution from *any* big-name free agent. (The '84 Tigers bought Darrell Evans, but he had a negligible season that championship year.)

Baseball may have needed a decade to come full circle. The game's old ways really may have been the best way: for owners, players and team builders too. Grow your own talent. Pay the guys who deserve it. Don't roam for a few dollars more. Pay attention to your craft, not the things that money can buy. Build a team with an internal identity, not a bought box-office image.

And, yes, remember that the grass is almost never greener on the other side.

It's taken baseball quite a while to realize what aristocrats have always known: money is the least important thing on earth . . . once you have enough.

1986:
Ultimate Red Sox

ACT I

HAVERHILL, Mass., July 1986—Whether he's watching them on cable TV, or listening on the car radio, or rising at 6 A.M. to buy the morning paper to get a late score, the Sheik is, to say the least, worried about his Red Sox. "The league must be pretty weak this year if they can be so far ahead," mutters Irving (Sheik) Karelis, the jeweler in this calm/nervous town. A couple of times a day he says it. Always exactly the same words: "The league must be pretty weak this year."

The words sound disparaging, but they're not—just a Red Sox fan's bizarre form of extreme optimism. Faith in the Red Sox themselves is, of course, never permissible. The Red Sox used up their lifetime supply of second chances a generation ago.

Now they're an old New England habit—an addiction like cigarettes that you never completely break, no matter how often you try or how long you go without them. The gnawing's always there, ready to catch you in a weak moment.

The Sheik grew up on the Red Sox in the 1920s and '30s, then pitched in the minors for them in the '40s after some people called him the best curveball pitcher the University of New Hampshire ever had. For forty years, since he retired with fond memories of striking out Ted Williams and Joe Cronin, of beating Don Newcombe head to head in eleven innings in the minors in Montreal, Karelis has followed them with duty, sorrow, knowledge.

Not once in his whole life, and he's old enough for Medicare, have the Boston Red Sox won a World Series. This could be the year, although Karelis will not hear of it, growing grumpy if you talk about Series tickets or plans for a trip to Shea Stadium in New York during October.

So what if the Red Sox have a seven-game lead over the Yankees in the AL East as baseball pauses for the All-Star Game. "They haven't even won the division yet . . . Only July," mutters the Sheik. "Lots of weaknesses . . . Long way to go."

"Sheik, this is their year. Everything's falling in place. Can't you just enjoy it?" But he won't listen. "The shortstop is terrible . . . They got no backup catcher . . . Seaver's awfully old . . . Stanley's erratic . . . How can you count on somebody named Oil Can? . . . The key will be how well Hurst comes back."

Each day, new difficulties introduce themselves to Sheik on the streets of Haverhill as he talks to his buddies at the Haverhill Country Club or Karelis Jewelers. They're all duplicates of him—frightened fatalists. Doctors, lawyers, writers and businessmen—guys with degrees from Harvard and MIT who can tell you every pitch of the previous night's game and who go by silly nicknames such as Tank and Moose—all recite their litany as Angie brings them their cheeseburgers between nines. "Buckner's ankle's bad . . . Armas looks old . . . Baylor might wear out."

Unlike fans of a normal team, you don't root for the Red Sox. You simply suffer with them, accept their fate, curse them and love them again—like flawed chlidren. So Karelis and millions of others like him are caught in a sweet-and-sour dilemma. Should he, and they, hope, one more time? The conflict, the psychological denial, is so great that Sheik always refers to the Red Sox' lead as "seven games" when it's nine or "six" if it's eight. Without hope, there is no true suffering, only melancholy.

The Red Sox Problem runs so deep, is so in the region's grain, that it even affects those who care nothing about baseball. It's part of a common history that is deeper than sport.

Once upon a time, the World Series seemed to have been created expressly to glorify the Red Sox. Furthermore, Fenway Park, in particular, appeared destined to host more Series celebration than all America's other ball yards put together. The first Series was won by the Red Sox in 1903. And, starting in Fenway's inaugural season of 1912, the Red Sox began a hegemony that, by 1918, had added four world titles in a span of just seven seasons. In 1918 Babe Ruth won half of the Red Sox' four Series victories. The next year he emerged as the greatest slugger in history as a Boston outfielder. So, in 1920, the Red Sox sold—not traded, but sold—Ruth to New York. Since then the Yankees have won thirty-two pennants, the Red Sox three. Since then New York has twenty-two world titles. Boston has none. You could say Red Sox fans do not like Yankees. Religious differences. Of course, it's all a Puritan fable about selling your soul to the devil—guilt, expiation and endless remorse. Today's Red Sox probable: Original Sin.

From Maine to Connecticut, millions of otherwise sensible people continue to play their ritual roles in the Red Sox chorus. That's why, when Karelis's wife, Ellie, mentions a plan that starts at 8 P.M., Sheik just says, "The Can's going tonight," and she knows the evening's agenda is set in stone.

This isn't domestic tyranny. It's just—and all New England knows this—that 1986 has turned out to be "one of those years." In the last sixty-eight seasons, the Sox have only been in a hot pennant race about nine times. So, when it happens, everybody knows the symbolism of the thing, makes way before it and prepares for the autumn shriving.

Of all the Red Sox stumbling blocks in the next four months, none will be greater than the difficulty that young Boston ballplayers will have in comprehending the strange ebb and flow of public moods that will surround them. It will be all too easy for them to see pessimism and defeatism on every side when, in fact, the passions and loyalties of their fans are deeper than any mere rooting.

If the Red Sox began to doubt their followers, even think of them as a millstone, perhaps they should think of Sheik watching them on the cable. Roger Clemens is pitching. That's who Karelis and generations of schoolchildren hereabouts have dreamed of being—the twenty five-game winner who will make null and void the decades of disappointment.

"The league must be pretty weak this year," Karelis says.

"Do you think Clemens's arm will hold up?" someone asks. "He's never lasted two hundred innings in a season in his life."

"He's got to get more on top of his breaking ball if he's going to keep it low," says Karelis technically.

The Sheik does not answer the question, pretends it never was asked. In the crowded Red Sox dugout, which now contains the population of the six New England states, there are some things that are just too serious to discuss.

ACT II

BOSTON, October 21, 1986 — Oh no, not again.

As matters now stand, the only responsible adult position on the World Series is to root, root, root for the Red Sox like a ten-year-old kid.

For the 90 percent of fans who are nonaligned observers—being card-carrying members of neither the Red Stocking nor the Metropolitan party—now is the time to cast independence aside. Register Red Sox. Call relatives, pester acquaintances, hand out leaflets on street corners.

Got friends in Hong Kong? Send a telegram: "Pray for Bosox."

Why take sides now? Doesn't the true fan stay a step removed from partisanship, preferring instead to enjoy the whole sport and cheer for whoever is most worthy? Doesn't the entire game offer more if we don't lapse into a narrow adoration? Well, sure, usually.

Aren't the Mets a fine team, nice guys, a classy franchise with a great future? They certainly are.

Under any normal circumstance, the Queens contingent could be endorsed. But these are not normal days.

Enough is enough.

The Mets won a Series in '69. That is a long time ago. Still, any Mets fans over thirty have memories. And any Mets fans under thirty can just calm down and wait.

Seventeen years is not sixty-eight years. Old people in this town, ardent Red Sox plain folk, are in danger of going to their reward without a single season that ended on a note other than defeat. That is excessive.

What would be far more excessive—beyond any definition of cruel and unusual baseball punishment—would be for the Red Sox to lose this year.

Because this season has, in every sense, been perfect for a Red Sox title. The team finished fifth in '85, so the redoubled pleasures of underdoghood are firmly in place. Splintered by injuries, the club was dismissed as a pretender in July. Yet it endured. By now everybody knows the legend of the Disneyland Weekend. The youngest living fans will retell it to tatters when they're old. From complete collapse to the best comeback in postseason history. Nobody has ever returned from 1–3 in games and three runs down in the ninth. Nor from the potential last strike of the season.

If, with all this in place, the Red Sox also were to blow a two-game lead in the World Series, it would simply be too ugly to embrace as sport. Make merry and mock as much as we wish, many simple people would take such a thing entirely too much to heart. Like me.

Look around the diamond at the Red Sox. See if you really want them to bear the stigma of squandering this Series.

Catcher Rich Gedman is a stoic, durable, self-made player. This summer his father and stepsister died. At the pennant celebration he showed little emotion. If he let go, he didn't know what might come out. And he didn't want to find out. Not yet.

First baseman Bill Buckner looks as if he's held together by wire. You've seen him: the guy's going to fall apart like a cheap Christmas toy the day after the Series. Second baseman Marty Barrett is your basic feisty, brainy, underrated infielder who'll probably end up a manager for twenty-five years. Shortstop Spike Owen is a humble, cheerful young Seattle Mariners reject who's gotten the scapegoat rap here for his nervous (five error) fielding in the playoffs; he's answered with a 12-for-27 bat. Third baseman Wade Boggs's mother was killed this summer in a car accident.

Jim Rice, in danger of joining Rod Carew and Ernie Banks as a Hall of Famer who never played in a Series, has outgrown his grouchiness and become a team man. Next to him we find Dave Henderson, a Kingdome escapee, who hit a home run that will stand beside those of Bobby Thomson and Bill Mazeroski. In right field there's Dwight Evans, the classy fifteen-year veteran who, Boston knows, has two special children at home.

Pitcher Bruce Hurst, a Mormon, was called gutless for years because he acted too civilized to suit his bosses. Calvin Schiraldi had the no-heart tag as a Met and was the least effective pitcher on the Pawtucket staff in midseason. Oil Can Boyd was suspended and rumored to have a drug problem this summer. The problem: his hyperactive metabolism, combustible personality and scrawny physique made him look like the public's stereotype of a ballplayer with a drug problem. "Test me. Every day if you want," Boyd said, to clear his name. And came up clean every time.

Matters have gone beyond the point where more shrieks of "Another Boston Choke" are amusing or acceptable.

"They can't lose, can they? Just tell me they can't lose," begged a woman who has followed the Red Sox for thirty years.

I began a dissertation.

"Can they lose?" she threatened, in the tone Sir Laurence Olivier used in *Marathon Man* to ask, "Is it safe?"

"They can't lose," I answered, to save my life.

But could the Red Sox lose? Could they become the second team ever to win the first two games in their foes' yard, then fritter away the crown?

Did the third pitch to the Mets tonight fly out the park? Did the first four New Yorkers to face Oil Can in Fenway score? Wasn't the final score an ominous 7–1?

Put it this way, Game Four is all but lost. Hello, Al Nipper. Game Five is probably history, too. Dwight Gooden, with revenge in his eye. The Series goes back to Shea, Mets ahead, 3–2. Even if Roger Clemens wins Game Six, then who's on the hill in No. Seven but The Can't, the human ham radio who picks up every distracting signal in an alien park.

That's vintage Red Sox Think.

You're up, 2–1. You can close it out at home. Your three aces will all pitch fresh, while the other guys will all pitch tired on short rest. And you are certain that you are dead.

This simply must not be allowed to happen. How could any commissioner ever again call baseball a family game?

Enough's enough. Register Red Sox. Cable Hong Kong. Is it too late to start a chain prayer?

ACT III

NEW YORK, October 24, 1986—Limpin' lizards, here comes Bill Buckner. What on earth are we to make of the Boston Red Sox player who has become the symbol of the Agony of Victory?

He crawls on his belly like a reptile. He couldn't run any worse if his feet were on backward. That isn't Billy Buckshot praying; he's walking. The man is a child's Christmas toy. No matter how you put his body together, he still plays baseball.

What's the count on Buckner? Two arms, two legs, no ankles. Laugh, laugh, I thought I'd cry. Who else falls down, then does the backstroke under a pop-up?

When it comes to visual memories of the 83rd World Series, Buckner may hold the patent. Buckner crawling after a ground ball on his knees. Buckner diving for a popped-up bunt and giving it a Bobo Brazil head butt. Buckner carrying his sickly bat out to the foul line during pregame introductions as a public statement that, damn it, he will break out of his slump.

Buckner belly-flopping across home plate, helmet over face like an eleven year-old, then lying there waiting for an autopsy. "I didn't slide," he said. "I died."

Buckner says he's not really that slow going from home to first, "it's third to home that takes twenty minutes."

In Boston they say he wears so much tape that "he looks like the Invisible Man out for a walk."

He ices so many parts of his body after every game—both feet, one knee, one shoulder and his hamstrings—that he has been asked if he's a devotee of cryogenics, the science of freezing a body until a cure for what ails it comes along.

"The way he runs is the theme contest of this World Series, isn't it?" wrote Leigh Montville in the *Boston Globe*.

At first glance and second, too, Buckner is both amusing and inspiring. He's very kind of blood-'n'-guts. He's the willingness to endure any amount of pain and any potential for embarrassment or failure just so he can say he played the game.

But Buckner, and his situation, also are more complex than that.

Is he playing hurt?

Or is he hurting the team?

Is he unselfish or very selfish?

Is he a hero or a hot dog?

Is he the worst player on the field in this Series—an utter liability on offense, defense and the base paths who should be on the bench in New York tonight in Game Six so Don Baylor, who at least has joints that move, can play first base?

Or is he an inspiration, the symbol of everything the Red Sox are about and the last man you'd want to remove for the sake of some dry strategy?

Is the brown-haired man with one high-topped black shoe incredibly courageous or amazingly foolish?

The answer, please.

All of the above. Though probably quite a bit more of the good stuff.

It is unlikely that any man so hurt—at least so conspicuously hurt— ever has played a major role in a Series. Or been so determined not to get off the stage, no matter what the cost to himself. Or maybe his team.

This postseason has been agony for Buckner in more than one sense. It's not the pain. He's used to that. He's taken an anti-inflammatory drug for the last ten years of his sixteen-season major league career, although he knows doctors don't like that.

He has had nine cortisone shots this season. The X rays of one ankle show bone virtually against bone. After the season he'll have spurs and chips removed. He has studied up on plastic ankles. No, it's not funny.

Buckner knows all the stories about players who called it quits rather than risk permanent injury. Buckner openly courts an invalid old age and perhaps middle age, too. "I think it's worth it," he says.

But is it worth it if he bats .174 in the Series and .196 for the post-season? Is it worth it if he has no walks, 4 RBI and only one measly extra-base hit (a double) in 51 at bats in October?

Is it worth it if he botches a pop-up and a bunt that should be a double play? Is it worth it if he reaches nothing at first base?

Above all, is it worth it if he is 2 for 11 in the playoffs and 1 for 10 in the World Series with men in scoring position?

In short, to be honest, is it worth it if he's worthless?

What makes all this so wrenching, so unfair, is that the sophisticated statistical studies of baseball in the eighties have, basically, unearthed only two men who, throughout their careers, have consistently proved that the word "clutch" can have an empirical basis: Eddie Murray and, to an even greater degree, Buckner.

No other player in baseball raises his level of performance so consistently when the pressure is greatest, the game situation most dire and the team in the greatest need.

Quoth the 1986 *Elias Baseball Analyst*: "Has batted for higher average with runners on base than with the bases empty in eight of last nine seasons." With runners in scoring position in recent years, Buckner has batted .430, .341, .220, .325 and .320. His slugging average rockets up even more in such spots.

That's why it's so painful to watch Buckner's defensive swings and the weak pops and grounders they are producing now.

Ever since he hurt his Achilles' tendon in Game Seven of the AL playoffs, he really has been a shadow of a ballplayer.

Buckner just says he's stubborn. His grit, however, puts Red Sox manager John McNamara in a tough spot. When a man gives this much for the team, how do you take him out, even if you should?

When McNamara fills out his lineup Saturday before the Red Sox face left hander Bob Ojeda in Game Six, he'll choose between his head and heart.

With no DH spot, should it be the rusty but healthy Baylor at first?

Or should he gamble on Buckner one more time, in the vital no. 3 hole where he can kill rallies, and at first base.

As of now, McNamara says, "If he's hobbling like he has been, he'll be playing." If so, hold your breath. He may play funny, but he doesn't deserve a sad end.

ACT IV

NEW YORK, October 28, 1986—The dark cloud suddenly disappeared here just before noon Tuesday, right on time for the sun to shine on the New York Mets' World Championship parade. The chill drizzle crawled northeast up the coast, headed for Boston, just in time. For sun to bathe New England on this day would be like wearing a white tux to a wake.

"Concentration is the ability to think about absolutely nothing when it is absolutely necessary," says the Mets' Ray Knight, the most valuable player of the World Series. That would seem to be just the prescription for fans of the Boston Red Sox—which is to say, most of the country's baseball-viewing population for the previous ten days or so.

Although New Yorkers may not wish to hear this, their victory celebration gives little sustenance to most of those whose passions became involved with the 83rd World Series. Let's just say it. For 162 games the Mets were superb. But in the playoffs and Series they proved again that it's as important to be lucky as to be good. When the Mets give high fives, they should fold their fingers over in a prayer of thanks.

If Bob Stanley and Rich Gedman hadn't been equal co-conspirators on a wild ball or passed pitch—it wasn't any one thing—the Mets would have lost this Series in six games and faced a lifetime of choke questions. If Bill Buckner had not botched as easy a play as any that was ever muffed on a great stage, Game Six would now be in the eleventh inning with Rick Aguilera (Series ERA 12.00) facing Stanley (Series ERA 0.00). Buckner's plight should remind us all never to neglect the Modified Cub Factor. The only ex-Cub in the American League Championship Series: Donnie Moore. The only ex-Cub in the Series: Buckner.

Unfortunately, it is a strain to give the Mets full credit—and they deserve plenty. There's good reason. The Mets are always cocky, occasionally bush. Before the bottom of the sixth inning of Game Seven, the Mets trailing, 3–0, the scoreboard screen replayed Buckner's Game Six extra-innings error. If that's not unsportsmanlike, what is? The

Mets immediately scored three runs to tie the game. Two innings later, during Darryl Strawberry's home run trot, a camera panned the Red Sox dugout—live. Not nice.

While the Mets' victory was a kind of baseball perennial—we kept coming back . . . this team has character . . . and, oh yeah, it helped that we were better than them, too—the Red Sox defeat will live, vivid and symbolic, growing in the retelling for years.

The Red Sox became the second team to win the first two Series games in the other club's park and still be defeated. They became the first to have a two-run lead with two outs in the last inning and nobody on base and lose. Of course, they were also the first gang to get within one strike of a world title and fail.

How many times did the Red Sox seem to be over the hump, finally and forever?

• When they thumped Dwight Gooden in Game Two. Then rousted him again in Game Five.

• When they led, 2–0, at the midpoint of Game Six with a rested Roger Clemens working on a no-hitter. Who knew he had a blister forming, something that only happens—is this Red Sox, or what?— when he is throwing too well.

• When the Red Sox retook the lead, 3–2, by the seventh-inning stretch of that sixth game. Go on, bring in rested Calvin Schiraldi and his 1.41 ERA.

• When Dave Henderson, for sweet justice sake, went deep to open the tenth and the killer bees, Boggs and Barrett, raked a double and single for a 5–3 lead round midnight on Saturday.

• When Mookie Wilson fouled off pitch after two-strike pitch that could have been the last strike of '86 until, finally, his classic nine-pitch at bat became a feature-length movie, starring Stanley, Gedman, Buckner, Manager John McNamara and the man who wasn't there, Dave Stapleton.

• When Dwight Evans and Rich Gedman homered back to back early in Game Seven, the latter blow bouncing out of Darryl Strawberry's glove over the fence. Major curse-busting omens there, it seemed. How could we forget, however, that the '75 Red Sox also took a 3–0 lead into the sixth inning of the seventh game?

• When Mets manager Davey Johnson, desperate, yanked his red-hot long reliever, Sid Fernandez, to send up Lee Mazzilli (a .173 hitter right-handed) to face Bruce Hurst, who had retired sixteen of the first seventeen Mets.

154

Then single, single, walk, single, liner to right and the game was tied. It was Keith Hernandez's two-run single in that sixth that sent Shea Stadium into a full meltdown. All that was left was the emotional disintegration of the Red Sox bullpen, whose occupants are a mite too young or too old for such moments.

Finally, when Boston started the eighth inning single, single, two-run double to cut New York's lead to 6–5, millions were on the same page. Oh, we get it. All the pain was for this. Wait sixty-eight years? Sure. For this we'll forgive everything and call it a square deal.

A quaint fiction exists that Red Sox fans would all catch pneumonia if they didn't have their premonitions to keep them warm. Phooey. New Englanders are not fixated on defeat and are relishing this year of Patriots, Celtics and Red Sox supremacy with no discernible damage to their worldview. If anything, Red Sox fans invest their hearts too much. It has been said that if the Red Sox cared as much as their fans, they would not have failed to win a world title since Woodrow Wilson's term.

That is incorrect. Because they do know their fans—love them and hate them and understand them—the Red Sox care more than other teams, or care in a slightly different and more burdensome way. That, as much as the bullpen's arms or McNamara's strategy, is the reason that the final game, the final out, the final strike of the World Series have always been too much for the Boston Red Sox.

And probably always will be.

The lesson is the same for every generation of Boston fans. Because the Red Sox try so hard and come so close and always fail at the very last, because they truly suffer for their sins and would never forget them even if they were given that privilege, only one response to the team is allowed.

You must ignore the cold fall mist on your hair. You must concentrate very hard. You must think of nothing. You must forget. Then, come spring, you must forgive them again. And although it does not seem possible, love them—as you would blood kin—just a little more.

ACT V

"For weeks, I would wake up in the middle of the night and that's all I would see . . . . I don't think I will ever watch those last two ball games again. Once was enough."

—JOHN MCNAMARA, a Red Sox goat

155

"It hurts a lot more to lose than it feels good to win."

—BRUCE HURST, a Red Sox hero

BOSTON, February 15, 1987—Filene's is a big store. But when you put a couple of Boston Red Sox players on a pedestal in the lobby, it gets small in a hurry. You could wait an hour and not get Marty Barrett's autograph.

Marty Barrett? When a pint-sized second baseman bats .433 in the World Series for the Red Sox, he has to be careful. He could wake up and find out he's governor of Massachusetts.

There's no place in America better than New England to be a hero. And maybe no place on earth worse to be a goat.

For men like Barrett, Wade Boggs, Roger Clemens, Dave Henderson, Don Baylor, Dwight Evans and Bruce Hurst, this has been a winter of glory and solicitude. In the phrase "near miss" they stand for the "near." That they came so close, did such deeds, then still had their prize ripped from them makes them twice as sympathetic to the public mind. Though guiltless, they've been denied. The fan knows his own level of pain and disgust and imagines that theirs must be ten times as great.

"Everywhere you go, ever since the parade the day after the Series, people say, 'Great. Wish you could've gone all the way, but you had a wonderful year,' " said Barrett, who set a record with 24 postseason hits. "I'll be in Burger King and a guy'll say, 'Hey, aren't you . . .' He may not know my name, but he'll say, 'We feel for you. You had some tough luck. We're with you.' "

If Hurst goes into the 7-Eleven in his hometown of St. George, Utah, for a five-minute errand, he ends up spending an hour. It's not so much the autographs as it is the reliving. Tell us again how you almost beat the Mets three times all by yourself. Not your fault, Bruce. You just ran out of gas in that last game.

If Boggs is out on his boat fishing near Tampa, he'll hear a motor and know what it means. You can spot his rusty hair a long way off. In the middle of a lake it's "Sign this" for the American League batting champion who became Mr. Leather in the World Series.

Even whimsy has crept in. "Think what Hendu Henderson's life would be like if we'd won the sixth game," said reliever Joe Sambito. "He doesn't become a Red Sox until August. Then he saves the season with a home run when we're down to our last strike in the playoffs and hits the homer that wins the Series. When we lost, it was like a voice from above saying that they're not ready just yet for a statue of Dave Henderson in the Boston Common."

You must stand close to the Red Sox a little longer if you want to hear the other currents flowing underground, beneath the wisecracks and square shoulders. What is more complex than coping with great success or great failure? Coping with both at once.

Most of the Red Sox gathered recently at a downtown banquet. Black tie. Sellout crowd of twelve hundred at ticket prices worthy of a World Series. Pride, disgrace, testiness, impatience, worry for the future—all were mixed.

There was Clemens, the happiest of men, you'd imagine. Yet he was fanning a feud with Hank Aaron, who'd said that, as a pitcher, Clemens didn't deserve the MVP award as much as everyday player Don Mattingly of the Yankees. "If that opinion came from a classy person like Reggie Jackson, I'd take note. My idol was Reggie," said Clemens. "But some people will do anything for some cheap publicity." A year ago, Clemens was an unproven youngster coming off shoulder surgery. Now he's calling a man with 755 home runs a cheap publicity hound.

Boggs used the banquet to make sure everybody knew he had demands to make. "I don't want to bat leadoff anymore," he announced. "I've always been knocked for not driving in runs. I just haven't had a chance. It's time for Wade Boggs to move on, and that means hitting third."

One of the people who's surprised already is Manager John McNamara, who, until Boggs's proclamation, thought that Bill Buckner, who had 102 RBI last year, was his no. 3 hitter. But then McNamara has had one surprise after another all winter. In late January he learned that center fielder Henderson had gotten a knee checkup (after waiting two months) and would need arthroscopic surgery.

That was nothing compared to the Rich Gedman Surprise. On January 7 at 11:20 P.M., McNamara turned on his hotel TV in New York to make sure that his All-Star catcher—and the most irreplaceable regular on the team—had come to contract terms before the midnight deadline for free agents. "They mentioned all the ones, like [Yankees pitcher Ron] Guidry, who were not signed. They didn't mention Gedman. I assumed, going to bed, everything was okay."

Then he found out Gedman was probably lost and, at the least, could not negotiate with Boston again until May 1.

To this day, Gedman's defection is a mystery. "Nobody understands it," said Don Baylor. "They were very close at 6 P.M. Then neither side picked up the phone for six hours. Then it was midnight. Too late."

New England opinion in polls was four to one on management's side. What's so bad about a two-year contract for $1.65 million? With each week, the shock at Gedman's loss sinks deeper. Will the son of owner Haywood Sullivan inherit the job? That's twenty-eight-year-old Marc Sullivan—career average .200, credentials nil.

"I'd want Rich Gedman back," said McNamara. "The only club that ever won a pennant in April was the '84 Tigers. He can come back in May, far as I care."

One reason for Gedman's strange departure is never mentioned. Maybe he just can't stand it. Maybe he has to escape. Born in Worcester, Massachusetts. Lives in Framingham. Gedman is the Red Sox player most in touch with Red Sox history, Red Sox suffering, Red Sox jinxes. And although the public considers him blameless, he knows that, within the game's dugouts, he's the man most blamed for the Red Sox' Series defeat.

We take you back to Game Six in Shea Stadium, Boston ahead, 5–3, in the bottom of the tenth with two men out, nobody on base and Calvin Schiraldi on the mound. Three singles make it 5–4, Mets at the corners. Mookie Wilson fouls off a pair of two-strike pitches.

Then a run-scoring wild pitch by Bob Stanley ties the score and a routine grounder by Wilson, right at Buckner, goes untouched between his feet for a game-losing error. That final Mets rally, aided and abetted by the Red Sox, will be remembered a hundred times more than the heartbreak of Game Seven. Those are the fifteen minutes that will make New Englanders wake up in a sweat for generations.

"I can accept it all . . . the [Mets'] hits, all right, fine," said McNamara. "And errors remain part of the game. But to tie the [sixth game] on a wild pitch—that's what remains vivid. If they'd just earned that run." Then he added, "Or a passed ball, whichever it was."

Baseball insiders say passed ball. They say that Stanley will spend decades living down Gedman's mistake and an official scoring misjudgment. A million replays show the pitch didn't miss being a strike on the low-inside corner by more than six inches.

"Everyone tried to have me blame Gedman," Stanley has said this winter. "I would never do that. They might as well blame me. They did all season." All career, Stanley might have added. Only his wife has blurted out stronger feelings: "Geddy blew it."

If Gedman leaves Boston, the passed ball that he was never charged with will be forgotten in his new town. In the Back Bay, never.

Discontent would not touch what this winter has meant to many Red

Sox. This is a team that both feels for one another and fears for one another. Oh, they worry about Stanley, who threw The Pitch, and even about Gedman some. But Stanley's a wealthy veteran used to the unfair abuse of Boston jock life and Gedman may skip town. You don't fret over Jim Rice (.161 playoff batting average, zero Series RBI) because his ego could survive an 0-for-1987—and he has that glare. It's Schiraldi, who lost both the sixth and seventh games, old Buckner, who made The Error, and McNamara, who will be second-guessed until Doomsday, who concern them most.

"It's tough to talk about what happened [to them]. Heck you don't even want to think about it," said Barrett. "You know when you're in that kind of showcase if you do good, you'll be great forever. Do bad and that'll be remembered forever. Somebody told me about a guy who made a bad play and, when he died fifty years later, that's all anybody mentioned."

Fred Snodgrass? Snodgrass's Muff in 1912? "That's right," said Barrett. "There's a good chance Bill Buckner will be like that. And after all he's accomplished . . . a batting champion."

What if it had been you?

"If it had come to me, I'd have caught it," said Barrett, grimly. End of discussion.

Buckner is going to be remembered for one thing. And it shouldn't be that. "It's bothered me," says Baylor, almost insulted that his game would have shown such poor judgment in picking its victim. "Pressure, like that last out, is what you train for. When Henderson came over from Seattle, I told him, 'Welcome to the big leagues.' Until you get in a pennant race, the playoffs, you're not playing baseball . . . The real players rise. It comes out . . . They say the Fall Classic is a spotlight. It can be. Or that light can get very dim."

Buckner's saving grace is that he was already America's Wounded Warrior—the Red Sox' Badge of Courage. "Buck's going to come out okay," said Sambito, remembering the ovations for him on parade day. "Fans sympathized with him all Series long. People in their chairs felt the pain with him. That'll help . . .

"It's Schiraldi who got so down on himself that it worried me. After he lost in the playoffs, I told him, 'Calvin, you're the best we have. Put it out of your mind. Come back in the morning. You can be the hero tomorrow.' And he was."

So what happened after Schiraldi's defeat in Game Six? He came back the next day ready to redeem himself. And it rained. He had a day to sit in a New York hotel room and think. When Schiraldi took the mound in the seventh inning of the seventh game, score tied, he was a wreck. Ray Knight, the first batter, hit a home run.

Perhaps a measure of the offseason agony of Buckner, Stanley and Schiraldi is that, as the winter has lengthened, they have all gone underground, refusing interview requests and avoiding Red Sox public functions. The man who grasps their feelings best may be Baylor, the Judge, whose kangaroo court helped turn the Red Sox into a cohesive and truly committed team in 1986. "I've checked the pulse around Boston ten or fifteen times. Well, maybe two hundred times," he said. "Ninety-five percent say, 'Great year.'

"I can't agree."

The blessing and curse of artists, and many ballplayers, too, is that the best of them are so inner-directed, so accustomed to living by their own arrogant self-judgments, that they are incapable of forgiveness by popular vote. Baylor and McNamara have talked several times, once a whole afternoon, trying to work out their feelings.

"Hell, I hate to lose at gin rummy," said the manager. "I'll never get over it. To come that close . . . It's going to keep coming up forever. It's just something we'll have to face. Unless it really gets shoved down my throat, I think I can be more patient in March than I was in October."

Still, it's not the world that tasks McNamara or invades his dreams.

"People tell me it made them become baseball fans," he said. "It'd be nice—no, that's not me—I wish I could be as satisfied as they are. It's difficult to stomach." And he's off in a reverie, back in his mind to the tenth inning of October 23, midnight approaching. "You'd think one of 'em would hit a ball at somebody. Not one of their hits was very hard. Then those three pitches for the last strike . . . The decisions I made, I haven't had trouble sleeping with 'em. That's not what bothers me. It's . . . that it happened. How could that happen?

"Somebody told my wife it was 250,000 to 1 that could happen."

With the months, McNamara has built his tactical defenses for all the moves for which he was second-guessed then, now and probably always. "If I felt I were wrong, I would have a tough time. But I'd do the same things. It didn't work. But that's not the point. Baseball people tell me, 'What you did was right.' But what good does that do?"

It does McNamara enormous good. He doesn't want a lifetime of self doubts.

Of all McNamara's debatable or dubious decisions, and there were a dozen—why didn't Gedman sacrifice, why did Clemens come out with the blister, why use Al Nipper in relief in a one-run game—two are already Big-Time Lore. First, should Dave Stapleton have replaced Buckner in the field in Game Six? No one will ever neglect to mention that Johnny Mac put him in for the final outs of all seven previous Boston postseason wins. That's self-incrimination. "If Buckner hadn't gotten to the [Mookie Wilson ground] ball, that's a different matter. But he did. Buckner has the better hands," said McNamara, almost admitting that, although his decision may have been flawed, events did not expose it—Buckner's limited range.

Next, should he have pinch-hit Baylor for Buckner in any of three different bases-loaded situations, including the tenth inning of Game Six? Buckner stranded all nine men. "I've never asked about that," said Baylor. "And I hope he doesn't bring it up."

"Turn it around," said McNamara. "Would I have pinch-hit Buckner for Baylor if the pitcher had been a righty? No. Because I had faith in both of 'em . . . How about the time in Detroit when I pinch-hit Gedman [a lefty] against Willie Hernandez [a lefty]? Grand slam."

When all the logic-chopping and rehashing is done, McNamara knows he'll no more be finished rolling his stone up the mountain than will Buckner when he explains for the millionth time how a grounder got between his legs. It's not what happened to McNamara, Buckner, Stanley and Schiraldi that matters—neither the ridiculous weight of importance put on such matters, nor the unfairness of being judged for a whole public lifetime by some ground ball or wild pitch. It's what they do with it that is, and will be, of interest.

Each Red Sox must find his own ways to deal with what may have been, all factors considered, the most brutal team disappointment in baseball history. "It took me until ten days to get over it," Baylor said recently. One day he and Dwight Evans realized that neither had watched the replay of the Red Sox win over California in Game Five of the ALCS when they did to the Angels what the Mets did to them: get down to their last strike of the season, then win by miracle.

"Watching it brought back the memory of sitting on that bench as we were being overrun by police," said Baylor. "We were all crammed together in one third of a dugout, on top of each other. All of a sudden, we were a real team, everybody screaming, 'Make the last at bat a good one.' " Baylor picked a curve off his toes to light the fire. "I'm not supposed to touch that pitch ever. But I hit it out of the park," he recalled, still incredulous.

Like every Red Sox, Baylor will have to make his peace someday with those old Series tapes of what may, in time, be the sport's most famous defeat. Will he ever review those last two tortures?

"Eventually," he said. "But they might go into the archives for a while."

No glass in sports has ever been more perfectly divided than the one from which the Red Sox now drink each day. Whether they view it as half-empty or half-full is their problem or their solution.

1987: The Mysterious Case of the Cards, Jays and Twins

PART I

ST. LOUIS, July 3, 1987—When the history of baseball in the 1980s is written, one club will stand out as a complete anomaly—a team that was not only different from others, but also a mystery to itself.

Year after year, the St. Louis Cardinals make us scratch our heads. Whatever we foresee from them, we get the opposite. And never more so than in 1987. No wonder Whitey Herzog claims that his first rule of managing is "Try not to be too damn smart."

Coming off a 79–82 season, the Cardinals were expected to do zilch. They were dead last in baseball in scoring in 1986. By a lot. A few days into the 1987 season, catcher Tony Peña was hit by a pitch and knocked out for a month with a broken left thumb. Then the Cardinals lost pitching ace John Tudor to a freakish broken leg. Next Tom Herr missed three weeks. Tudor's replacement, rookie Joe Magrane, got rolling (5–1), then got a sore elbow. Some nights, Herzog had only twenty healthy players. Seriously, what is Byron Lee Tunnell doing in a big league rotation?

So what have the Cardinals done? Why, they have the National League's best record (47–29) and have pushed those cursed New York Mets six games behind in the standings. They've also drawn fans to Busch Stadium at a pace (36,446 per date) that could eclipse every attendance record in the sport except those of the Dodgers.

The more you look at St. Louis, in this or any year, the less sense the club makes. In an era of homers, the Cardinals hit almost none. In a period in which teams desperately seek starting pitching, the Cardinals barely appear to care, settling for defense and a deep bullpen instead.

Cardinals starters like Tunnell, Tim Conroy and Greg Mathews simply follow in the tradition of Steve Mura, Dave LaPoint and John Stuper, who may have been 60 percent of the worst rotation ever to win a World Series title. Herzog took the Kansas City Royals to the playoffs three straight years with starters like Al Fitzmorris, Doug Bird, Jim Colborn, Andy Hassler and Rich Gale. What we have here is a man who's repeatedly proved he can finesse the most important figure in the sport—the starting pitcher.

The Cardinals' style of play seems like a typographical error —1890s, not 1980s. It's stolen-base, sacrifice-bunt and hit-and-run baseball. Yet somehow they transform one-run theory into big-inning practice. Herzog does everything to give away outs, yet gets runs.

At the moment, in the Year of the Home Run, the Cardinals lead the majors in scoring—yes, they've gone from twenty-sixth to first. Yet they are next to last in baseball in homers. Could a team that won't hit a hundred homers win a world title in a season in which many teams will hit two hundred?

Almost every year in this decade, the Cardinals have stood logic on its head. This is a team that had the best full-season record in the NL East in '81, yet never made the playoffs—you can look it up. When these guys are expected to fail, they win the World Series ('82) or come within one out of doing it ('85). But when they're expected to win, they lose. Both of their eighties pennants have been followed by 79-win seasons.

Don't ask Herzog, the man who deals the Cards, what's going on. He's as bamboozled as the rest. In 1985 his bullpen wasn't supposed to survive the loss of Bruce Sutter, so the Cardinals didn't blow a ninth-inning lead all year until the sixth game of the Series. In 1986, with Joaquin Andujar traded, Cardinals starters were suspect, so they came through dandy (3.37 team ERA), but the hitting took a hike. Big deal. In 1987 it figured the Cardinals wouldn't hit enough to carry their respectable pitching. A lot we know. For the moment, the Cardinals' lineup looks like one of the best of its type in history.

The team batting average is .286 and starters Coleman, Herr, McGee, Oquendo, Pendleton and Smith are switch-hitters. Tell somebody that in fifty years and they'll never believe it. Plenty of teams have none. Two is a ton. Six, all legitimate hitters, is inconceivable. When Clark started taking swings left-handed in batting practice this week, Herzog exploded, "Oh no, not you, too."

When posterity is told that every Cardinals player, except Clark, is a possible Gold Glove defender, that may be hard to swallow, too. But it's true. Bloops and grounders are futile against St. Louis. Either hit a rocket or take a right turn at first base.

The St. Louis defense underlines just how ungifted the team's starting pitchers are. With what may be the best total defense in history behind them, plus a spacious park, they have allowed more hits per inning than anybody except Montreal. The St. Louis ERA is 4.14, even with the Wizard of Oz and Co. on hand. At least the St. Louis hurlers are brainy. They know they can't strike out many (last in the NL), but at least they walk very few (third best) and also avoid their foes' power, allowing the fewest homers.

Nobody questions where the Cardinals get their brains or their style—it's from that generally styleless and definitely "not too smart" Herzog. This is a guy who, when offered a "lifetime contract" by ancient owner Gussie Busch, asked, "Whose life we talkin' about?" Herzog talks in aphorisms; it just comes natural for him to say, "Two things in baseball don't mean squat: last year and yesterday. Tomorrow means a lot." He lets you work out the toughies, like, "Wait for the prom, miss the dance."

Perhaps what the Cardinals do best in the Herzog era is forget. They forgot the injustice of the 1981 split season and shocked everybody in 1982. They forgot two dispiriting years and Sutter's defection to win a pennant in 1985. They forgot the humiliation of looking like unsportsmanlike chokers in blowing the 1985 Series. And now they've forgotten that the Mets beat them by 28½ games last year.

"The Mets don't do that much," Herzog will say. "They just hit the long ball and they've got starting pitching. They had a bullpen . . . last year." Get that knife in and turn it, Rat. "Oh, I think everybody

hates the Mets," he adds. "They always seem to say the right thing—
to rub people the wrong way."

Herzog teams can be counted on to be tight-knit, extremely cocky
and a tad paranoid on the subject of never getting enough credit. For
example, when the 1986 season went down the tubes, the Cardinals
hung together and played 10 games over .500 in the second half to
finish third. "That was important. We didn't quit," said Clark. Teams
that do give up when they're out of the race—witness the '84, '85 and
'86 Orioles—quickly lose their team character. The more you quit, the
better you get at it, until no collective fiber remains.

Herzog's teams are always quick to take up the gauntlet. When the
Mets' Howard Johnson popped off about Danny Cox hitting him with
a pitch, the right-hander all but promised to drill Johnson at their next
meeting. "If he wants to start, he knows where to find me," said Cox.
"In fact, I'll give him a hand." Of course, the 225-pound Cox is the
same fellow who used a Series off day to fly a thousand miles just so
he personally could beat the living tar out of a man he thought was
wronging his sister.

The Cardinals are as bristly as Herzog's haircut on issues of pride.
Ask Pendleton about a stellar defensive play against the Mets this week
and he says, "It'll never be on 'This Week in Baseball.' We make plays
other teams can't touch, but we're never on that show." Gee, could
"TWIB" come out of New York?

No Cardinal ever misses a free shot at New York or the Mets. "The
Cubs are our big rival," says Herzog, consigning the Mets to second-
class foeship.

To be a Herzog Cardinal is to be a blunt, buck-stops-here type.
Herzog confronted Mathews not long ago, chiding the southpaw for
letting an 11–8 rookie year go to his head. "You need to pull your belt
up tighter, son. You're laggin' behind," said Herzog, before sending
him to Louisville for a reality check. Mathews is back now, winning,
and says shamefacedly, "I was living the [got-it-made] life."

Herzog, however, is also the warmest of managers, especially to players who ride the bench, as he did for eight journeyman seasons in the
majors. "Whitey came up to me one day," says Tito Landrum, "and
said, 'I should have started you today. You hit the ball hard against
this pitcher three of four times the last time you saw him.' I was impressed because the game he was talking about was a year and a half
before. Even I hadn't remembered it."

The net result is a team of unusual cohesion, purpose and resiliency.

"So many people worry about what they don't have," says Ozzie Smith, the clubhouse leader, "rather than what they do have. When Tudor and Peña and Herr went down, we focused on the weapons we had left."

These days the scuttlebutt is that the Mets will, sooner or later, run St. Louis down on sheer talent. Herzog lets this impression rest in place. "We're struggling. Our pitching has to get better than it's been. They've got Mr. [Dwight] Gooden back and we won't have John [Tudor] until August. We have to hold on until then."

The Mets, perhaps a little blithely, buy into this scenario. They won two of three head-to-head games in Shea Stadium this week. In one win, the Diamond Vision board displayed a medley of Three Stooges comedy routines, put to a song called "The Curly Shuffle," just before the winning rally.

" 'The Curly Shuffle' might have played a big role tonight," said Mets manager Davey Johnson, deadpan. "We haven't played [that video] all year and we haven't done very well. I don't know why they took it out [of the Diamond Vision routine]. That's probably been our problem."

Somewhere hidden in Johnson's joke is an assumption about the Cardinals: that they aren't terribly threatening. Just get that "Curly Shuffle" straightened out, then run 'em down.

A vote of league players would probably agree that the Cardinals, even in first place, are not the NL East's real front-runner at the moment. It's widely presumed that the St. Louis pitching just can't hold up in the midsummer heat and that its hitting has already peaked.

Yes, that's what's expected of the Cardinals. However, the Mets, Expos, Cubs and other clubs should remember that if St. Louis fulfills other people's expectations of it, it'll sure enough be the first time.

ST. LOUIS, October 15, 1987—Maybe now, about five years late, the St. Louis Cardinals will start to get their due. Maybe three pennants in six years will do the trick, not to mention the 1981 season when they were robbed of a playoff berth in the split-season fiasco. This is one of American sport's special and distinctive teams. They're worth scads of conventional champs, because they're willing to go against the grain of their whole game.

Before Game Seven of the 1987 National League playoffs, Cardinal veteran Tommy Herr looked out at the field and took inventory. "Everybody says we don't have Jack Clark," he said. "But look what we still have left."

Ozzie Smith is likely to end up in the Hall of Fame. Willie McGee, a past MVP, drove in 105 runs. Herr and Terry Pendleton have been as good defensively as any second and third baseman in the league. Both switch-hit, hit-and-run, steal and drive home as many base runners as almost anybody in the league—Herr 81, Pendleton 84. (Andre Dawson drove in 88 runners.)

Vince Coleman may steal more bases than any man in history. He and McGee give the Cardinals the best outfield range in baseball. Nobody contests that St. Louis has the best infield leather—maybe ever. Tony Peña may have the best arm of any catcher. Reliever Todd Worrell has more saves plus wins in the last two years than anybody in the league; he's a Goose Gossage–quality closer. Behind him, Ken Dayley (2.66) and Ricky Horton are as good as any second-line relief.

John Tudor is 43–10 since early 1985—that's a better percentage than Dwight Gooden, Roger Clemens or anybody else. Big Danny Cox is a horse who's at his best under pressure. Joe Magrane, an overpowering six-foot-six southpaw, is as good a future twenty-game prospect as exists. Greg Mathews (young and left-handed) and Bob Forsch (old and right-handed) are as dependable as any fourth and fifth starters—your basic dozen-game winners. The Cardinals come from so many angles with so many different styles that they make foes feel like they're caught in a revolving door. Smoke, hooks, change-ups— this staff has everything from both sides.

Just because you don't know fleet little Curt Ford and big Jim Lindeman does not mean they aren't prime prospects. Jose Oquendo is the best utility man in baseball—playing every position except catcher. When the Wizard of Oz retires, he'll step in and the Cardinals will only miss half a beat at shortstop. These three all made key playoff contributions—to the Giants' amazement and the Cardinals' amusement, since they expected it.

How could the Cardinals outlast the Mets with only 20 RBI from Clark after the All-Star break? How could they double-whitewash Montreal, 1–0, 3–0, in a crushing final week doubleheader? How could they win the playoffs without Clark and with only one steal by Coleman and Smith (who had 152 this season)? How could they not only hold the Giants scoreless the last 22 innings, but let only one Giant reach third base?

They're lucky. They're gutty. Whitey Herzog is a genius. The Giants choked. The Cardinals always bring out the worst in their foes. Yes, we hear all these things. And Herzog goes along with it all, feathers in his catlike grin, saying, "I don't know what we're doing here," and "I don't even know who I'm starting in Game One of the World Series." The poor pathetic, plucky Cardinals, the only team in baseball that, with a rabbit ball, couldn't even hit 100 homers. And now, Clark, who hit 35 of their 94, is useless.

There's only one possibility that the Cardinals and Herzog never mention, never allow on the table. No, they never tell the truth. The St. Louis Cardinals won the National League pennant for the same reason they won in 1982 and 1985. Because they are a great team. The best team of the 1980s so far, by a clear margin. Not great in the ways that fans, foes and critics are accustomed to appreciating. But just as formidable as a club with 200 homers and a pair of 20-game winners.

Even Herzog calls his team "a bunch of dinkers and dunkers." How can you love a lineup full of men trying to hit ground balls? It's almost un-American. How can you love a pitching staff that hates strikeouts and low-hit games and prefers that you pound the ball all over the lot—so Ozzie can turn singles into double plays and triples can go home to die in McGee's glove?

The perfect Cardinals inning won this playoff. We take you back to the seventh inning of Game Three. Oquendo nudges a pool-cue liner over short. Ford breaks his bat chunking a flare over second. Dan Driessen and Vince Coleman hit five-hoppers through the pitcher's legs into center. Ozzie beats out a bunt. Herr lays down a dead-fish sacrifice. A pinch runner steals a base. A Lindeman can of corn becomes a sacrifice fly. Only the last lazy fly travels 200 feet in the air. Result: Four runs. A 6–4 lead. And a comeback win that leaves the Giants nearly crazy.

The point is that the Cardinals did exactly what they were trying to do. Those bunts, quails and sacrifices were as deliberate, as skillful and as lethal as a Will Clark grand-slam homer.

When the baseball got tight and strategic, the Giants couldn't score a run, catch a fly ball in the lights, make a decent throw to the plate, block a curve in the dirt, pitch around a no. 8 hitter with first base open or build a rally without a home run.

What about the Cardinals? McGee was turning two-run 'tweeners in the alleys into outs. Pendleton was forcing a lead runner at third by two inches on an almost perfect bunt. Smith was flying over runners, turning three incredible seventh-game double plays. And Tudor and Cox were teasing hitters into submission.

Come Saturday, America will wonder how the halt and lame Cardinals, without Clark and with McGee, Pendleton and Mathews still at half-speed, can dream of stealing a world title.

Those better-to-be-lucky-than-good Cardinals won't be giving away any secrets. Really great teams never do.

PART II

DETROIT, October 4, 1987 — The Toronto Blue Jays huddled together as though for warmth, fifteen or sixteen of them jammed, shoulder to shoulder, in one end of their dugout. Throughout the ninth inning they might have been a still life, without a lip, much less a limb, moving. No chatter, though they were just behind by one run with a season at stake. Everyplace you looked, faces worthy of an emergency room.

When it ended, this seventh loss in a row, by an agonizing 1–0 score on a wind-helped homer that cleared a fence by inches, the Blue Jays barely stirred. When their place in history had finally been secured (next to the Phillies of 1964), the Blue Jays did not smash their traitorous bats in the rack. Instead, they watched Frank Tanana, who'd pitched a shutout, who'd preyed on their anxieties with curves, as he leaped into his teammates' arms and rejoiced as only a hometown Detroit boy could on such an undreamable day.

Gradually the Blue Jays left the dugout and began the rest of their lives. All except one. George Bell stayed on the top step. A half-dozen teammates touched him, tried to squeeze an arm or shoulder of the man whose 47 home runs carried them for seventh months and whose 2-for-26 slump sank them in the last seven days. Finally, alone, Bell slowly put his face in his hands as the cameras clicked like a tiny firing squad. Before the game, he had stormed, "Get those cameras out of my face." Now, at least, he would steal what they sought: an image of his sorrow.

What had happened to Bell and the Blue Jays has been almost too cruel to credit. Even Larry Herndon's division-winning homer Sunday was the kind that is often caught here atop the nine-foot-high fence— that is, if Bell had not misjudged the ball and never summoned a proper leap.

"That was like robbin' a bank," the Tigers' Sparky Anderson said, "and no one even remembers to call the cops."

A clean getaway, indeed. But not without casualties. The same Blue

170

Jays who led the 1985 American League playoffs three to one, then lost the last three, have swallowed another pill of bitter history: a 3½-game lead blown in the last eight days. Only the Phillies, who lost 10 in a row to fritter away a 6½-game margin, did worse.

"I'm not going to sit around and care about what people say about the Toronto Blue Jays," said veteran Lloyd Moseby. "You don't care about losing [years] unless you're a loser; 1985 isn't even in my mind. I just want to go home."

But how much solace will await them there? How many fans can resist rising to the bait of a word like "choke"?

"People can think what they want," said the Blue Jays' Rance Mulliniks. "A winner is not someone who wins all the time. It's someone who always battles to get back up off the floor."

Perhaps no team has ever flopped with such dignity as these Blue Jays. "I don't know if baseball can get any better," said Toronto manager Jimy Williams of the seven Blue Jays–Tigers meetings in the last eleven days—all one-runners. "We actually played well. We just didn't hit." Not after catcher Ernie Whitt broke two ribs and joined Tony Fernandez (dislocated fracture of the elbow) on the bench. "I'm very proud of them," said Williams.

If there's one mystique in baseball that never fades, it's the assumption that courage not only exists, but, in moments of enormous crisis, is almost palpable. Old salts even look for ways to measure it. Anderson learned such a trick years ago. When he goes to the mound in a crisis, he casually "takes hold of the pitcher's shirt real lightly above the heart." In the cloth he can feel the pitcher's heartbeat.

"You can never put courage into a human being, but you can find out if it's there," he says. "Some guys, that heart is flying so fast it's like an anxiety attack. You know they'll never cope with those situations . . . I've misjudged players' talents, but I've never been wrong about what I call the Look. I've never been wrong about who I could take with me into the trenches."

Anderson studies his men's faces. Darting eyes worry him. But the ones who get calmer, who "seem to be drawing from within"—they may have the Look. And he seldom loses faith in them. In the 1975 Series, Anderson's slugger Tony Perez endured what Bell has recently suffered—an oh-fer that rivaled Gil Hodges's for the worst Series slump ever. Anderson got the demons in the open, because he was sure Perez could deal with them. "I told him, 'Doggie, keep it up. Hodges is in sight. Just think, only four more outs and you've set a whole new record.'" Perez hit a vital homer in the seventh game.

Certainly no one found the right relaxing note to play for Bell and Co. In games like this weekend's, it is far easier to have adrenaline than good sense or poise.

"Look, I think Bell should be MVP, but the pressure of having that whole team on his shoulders finally got to him," said Detroit's Bill Madlock. "He was pressing."

Someday baseball fans may remember only Tigers courage. They will see Kirk Gibson's ninth-inning game-tying homer last Sunday that began this long comeback just as the Tigers were about to trail by 4½ games. And they may remember only Toronto's fainthearted moments, like the game-ending grounder between Manny Lee's knees Saturday.

The Blue Jays' hearts may have fluttered too fast in the last week, but their shirts are far from empty. When the last days of this pennant race are remembered, let us hope it will not be some corny catchphrase like Pholdin's Phils that will remain but, rather, the memory of seven head-to-head games that may've been as exciting as any World Series. Some even suspect that the real 1987 Classic has just been completed.

PART III

MINNEAPOLIS, October 23, 1987 — Throughout the evolution of major American professional team sports, only baseball has escaped the curse of the distorting, infuriating, far-too-important home field advantage. That is, until the 1987 Minnesota Twins arrived.

In the NBA and NHL, contending teams play the entire regular season for only one basic reason: to get the home field advantage in the playoffs. For example, the Boston Celtics recently won 39 consecutive games at home. Redskins coach Joe Gibbs would sooner give up his headphones than give away the RFK Stadium crowd in the postseason.

No statistician or psychologist would deny the large and measurable advantage in these sports of having huge, long-toothed, often profane crowds on the shoulders of visiting teams. According to the '87 *Elias Baseball Analyst*: "Home teams won 54 percent of all major league baseball games over the past five years, compared to 58 percent in the NFL, 60 percent (of games played to a decision) in the NHL and 64 percent in the NBA." (Of all teams, the Minnesota Twins had the biggest home field edge over the period from 1982 through 1986, playing 15.8 percent better at home than on the road. This season, it's been an amazing 35 percent better.)

Now the field pox may be contaminating baseball. Since the turn of the century, baseball teams have searched for every possible home field edge—and failed to make it into anything terribly significant. Watered base paths, sloped foul lines, asymmetrical outfield fences, towering outfield walls and vocal home crowds have simply spiced the sport, not twisted it.

Home teams have won only 53 percent of all World Series games. In fact, 55 percent of all Series have been clinched on the road! This mirrors baseball's annual regular season home edge—55 percent or less. In other words, just about the margin you'd hope for: enough to enliven discussion but not enough to define the sport.

Baseball has been so immune to home field factors that, for generations, nobody has questioned the practice of giving the odd-game edge to the American League in odd-numbered years and vice versa.

Even the arrival of artificial turf did not change the natural order of baseball things beyond a speed/turf team like the Royals or Cardinals being helped a bit by a spacious pool table field or the Houston pitchers growing arrogant in the Astrodome. It felt acceptable. Still, what these three teams attempted was stretching the envelope. They were getting close to a feeling that "home" carried a special and dubious meaning.

Now something new has happened. It's called the Thunderdome. And it's as potentially bad for the sport as a whole as it is fun for the one twenty-sixth of the game that resides in Minneapolis.

First, the Twins have artificial turf, which has been shown to be an edge in itself. Turf teams adjust to grass better than grass teams adjust to turf. It's a statistical fact.

Second, the Twins have accidentally introduced a completely unfair and capricious element—the only ball-colored Teflon ceiling in existence. Perhaps this is a matter of taste, but the feeling here is that the winds, fog and cold of Candlestick Park constitute a *legitimate* home field edge. If you're tough enough to learn those elements, and endure them a whole season, then more power to you. However, a trick roof seems like just that: a trick. Every ballplayer learns about wind-blown pop-ups and cold hands. Only a Twin spends enough time in the Metrodome to learn how to catch invisible fly balls.

Finally, and perhaps more important, the Thunderdome is the first baseball park that has duplicated smaller indoor arena noise levels—as high as 118 decibels in this Series.

Cardinals manager Whitey Herzog says the Metrodome is five times louder than Busch Stadium. Cardinals fans sounded as if they were cheering from inside their cars in the parking lot; everything's relative. Those Homer Hankies in Minnesota also feel as if they are on top of you. Cardinals fans did their pom-pom number, too, but they felt remote and unthreatening. Close stands help.

As for the public address systems at these parks, both are infernally loud and obtrusive—inexcusable. The Cardinals played the Budweiser beer jingle seven times during one rally. The Twins are far worse. They not only play mega–rock 'n' roll, but offer ear-splitting locomotive effects and Tarzan screams in mid-inning. Something's gotta be done and fast. For starters, Peter Ueberroth should ban any artificial noise pollution during innings.

Several American League teams also charge that the Twins steal signs with a center-field camera. The Twins were once caught with a TV monitor in their dugout; it was removed. Does anyone really think Minnesota—56–25 at home and 29–52 on the road—is in the Series on any basis except its home field play?

Most important, baseball should recognize immediately that, in the future, the home field edge in the playoffs and Series should be given to the team with the better regular-season record, just as currently exists in every other pro team sport. It's ludicrously anachronistic to see the Twins, with the ninth-best regular-season record in baseball (85 wins), getting an extra home date against both the Detroit Tigers (no. 1 in wins) and the Cardinals (no. 3).

The most lasting memory of the '87 Series probably is already locked in place, no matter who wins. This will be the Home Field Advantage Classic. If the Twins come back to win, that legacy will be a dead certainty, since that outcome would make this the first Series in history—since 1903—in which every game was won by the home team.

We may not be able to blow off the Metrodome roof or order the Twins to paint their ceiling, but Ueberroth should clamp a muzzle on mad organists and start working toward a 1988 postseason in which the home field advantage, if we're going to be stuck with one, at least belongs to the proper team.

MINNEAPOLIS, October 25, 1987—Woebegone no more.

The Minnesota Twins called an impromptu team meeting this evening a few feet from first base to discuss exactly how it felt to be champions of the world. Kent Hrbek, born and raised in these doleful athletic regions where much goes right, but never totally, initiated the gathering by gloving the last out of their 4–2 victory over the St. Louis Cardinals in Game Seven of the World Series. That will get you a quorum real quick.

Manager Tom Kelly, a Minnesotan by temperament, if not birth, did not attend, preferring to watch others celebrate. That's how Minnesotans usually do it—except tonight. The first two Twins to celebrate were Hrbek and catcher Tim Laudner, the only locals on the roster. That tells you how much this evening meant to a self-deprecating state that sells sweatshirts with a picture of a snow shovel and the inscription "Minnesota Aerobics." How nice and well behaved are people here in the northern steppes? Of a crowd of 55,376, only one fan tried to run on the field, and he was gently tackled by police and apologized as he walked soberly back to the stands.

Long after this game, thirty thousand or more fans still stayed in the Thunderdome stands, waving their Homer Hankies, or perhaps wiping away a tear with them. Almost every Twins player came to the mound, to the microphone, to share. "Ever since I was a little boy, I've dreamed of driving down Hennepin Avenue in a victory parade," bellowed a hoarse Hrbek, his voice rising and crackling as he yelled, "And I get to do it!"

Recent events have been a shock and test of character for Minnesotans. They are constitutionally unsuited to unadulterated pleasure. It goes against the German and Scandinavian roots that permeate this region so deeply. It's said that Minnesotans greet all human experience with one of three expressions. "You betcha" covers everything that's good or not too bad. If the neighbor buys a thirty-foot python as a pet or the boss arrives at work in leather and chains, they say, "That's different." And if the python eats the house, or the boss burns the factory, the Minnesotan says, "Whatever."

Even the bedsheet signs here reflect these attitudes: "Pinch Me." "Is This Great or What?" "Wanted: Homer Hankie—Will Swap Four Vikings Season Tickets."

So these last nine days have tested and tried Minnesotans almost beyond the limits of north-country endurance. Last weekend, for instance, tickets to Games One and Two of the Series were being scalped for $800 a pair. "The Pope Needs a Ticket," said one sign. Cars downtown honked all day. Police enforced laws against passengers leaning out the windows of moving vehicles.

By this Saturday, however, after three losses in St. Louis, a frost had settled. Scalpers were dumping tickets for half of face value or even giving some away. To kids. (That's the Twin Cities.) Shops in downtown malls had posted signs saying, "Sorry, Twins merchandise is NOT returnable."

By the fifth inning of Game Six, with St. Louis ahead by three runs, the Thunderdome was a nice quiet place to read a good novel. Ever hear of Bud Grant? Only an hour (and a Hrbek grand slam) later, cops with toy dead cardinals taped on the bills of their blue hats were joining a conga line of fans by the beer stand.

By this evening the pendulum of civic schizophrenia had swung again. "Compassion, please," said one sign held by a ticket searcher.

This region has long had America's friendliest and most unashamedly fickle fans. They enjoy, but do not trust, victory. They endure, but do not truly suffer from, defeat. On the other hand, they're human. They'd really like to get to chant something stupid, such as "We're number one," at least once per lifetime.

That's why Kirby Puckett grabbed the mike when it was all over and told the crowd, "A lot of people doubted us. Well, we're number one in the whole world." He expected a Dome-splitting roar. He got almost nothing. Minnesotans—with their witty, civil signs like "Kelly has a well-tuned Viola"—cheer their players, not themselves.

This was a night of glorious agony. The Twins and their fans had every right to feel the ghosts of their bleak history reaching up to tie their shoelaces. Willie McGee and Jose Oquendo made fabulous catches to rob Twins of doubles. Vince Coleman threw out two runners at the plate. Puckett got himself eradicated at third. Why, the Cardinals even slapped Frank Viola around like a bass fiddle with four singles for two runs in an inning.

Who wouldn't be spooked? But omens can change directions. As Whitey Herzog goes, so go the Cardinals. In Game Six, he showed patience with John Tudor when he had a 5–2 lead and fresh bullpen. As Herzog said later, "Bam, bam, bam—it went so fast." So tonight Whitey shifted tactics. Get somebody up at the first hint of trouble. That didn't work either. Danny Cox replaced Joe Magrane, who'd been pitching better than any Cardinal in the Dome. He got two outs and one defeat.

By the time Todd Worrell arrived, the situation was already in flames. When he walked Roy Smalley to load the bases, the decibel meters here broke. Finally, when Worrell reached a full count on Greg Gagne, the worst Twins hitter of the Series, the state of Minnesota made a definitive decision.

It donated its hearts to the Twins. Forget the "sirs" and "thank yous" and being hospitable to tourists. Minnesotans informed the Cardinals that they wished them all to drop dead forthwith.

Maybe Gagne's grounder over third base was the kind that Terry Pendleton got his Gold Glove for fielding. But that's something for Missourians to chew as offseason solace. Just as they can mutter about Jack Clark and how the Twins became the only team ever to grab a Series without winning on the road.

Minnesota doesn't want to hear it. Too many good teams, too many good politicians, have come up short. If a team with 85 wins, a team that gets outscored for the year, a team with only two starting pitchers, happens to catch some breaks and play like hell and win it all—well, it's about time. You betcha. That's different. When Gagne's foot reached first base a yard before Tom Lawless's throw, that was enough, the final wonderful straw. All heaven broke loose. For once, the good guys, the nice state, the team that said "please" for so long were about to finish first. And Minnesota, bad manners or not, could scream "We're number one" all night.

And right through the long, cold winter, too.

1988:
Minds over Mastodons

NEW YORK, October 10, 1988—Leadership among ballplayers, as among politicians, is as important as it is indefinable. The gift expresses itself in many styles. But, once it exists, the team bends to the leader and the whole game, in turn, bends toward that team. Kirk Gibson, who is batting .182 in the National League playoffs, is such a leader, perhaps the best in baseball at this moment. What Reggie Jackson and Pete Rose, Willie Stargell and George Brett have shown us in recent Octobers, Gibson is showing now. He's what players call "Big Time." Others play the game. He means to change it.

October 10, 1988, was a big-time day for Gibson and his Los Angeles Dodgers. A few minutes before 1 A.M., he hit a home run over the center-field fence to win Game Four, 5–4, in 12 grueling and amazingly convoluted innings that required 4 hours 29 minutes. "About time I did something," growled Gibson, who'd been 1 for 16.

A few minutes after 1 P.M. on the same day, he hit another monstrous home run to provide 3 vital runs for L.A. in its 7–4 victory in Game Five. Now, thanks to Gibson's leadership, his example, his demands and his play, the Dodgers are one victory from taking a pennant away from a far more gifted New York Mets team that beat the Dodgers 10 times in 11 meetings this season.

In his final act Monday, Gibson beat out an infield hit in the ninth inning, then stole second base to set up the Dodgers' last insurance run. Before he got to second, he knew he'd aggravated the hamstring pull that has left him gimpy for a fortnight. As he hobbled off the field, waving for a pinch runner, the Shea Stadium crowd gave a momentary, spontaneous cheer of delight that Gibson could bedevil them no more.

Gibson saw it for what it was. "The notion of respect" came to his mind, he said. Of course, he now despises every Mets fan even more. Cheer my injury, will you. "Those are the sort of things that inspire me," he said wolfishly.

This is Gibson's leadership style: a stubble beard, a perpetual limp, a recklessness that borders on deliberate injury and a complete refusal to be embarrassed by the fact that his all-America football physique obviously is not intended for baseball. Nothing about the game looks natural to him. His speed is an explosion, often slightly misdirected, necessitating bizarre last-minute corrections. His spectacular catch in left field on Saturday was a one-man, three-ring circus—part clown, part trapeze artist, part juggler. His slides resemble safety blitzes. His stance and swing are always grim, mechanical, graceless and, when he finally connects, ferociously powerful.

Sparky Anderson did Gibson the injustice a decade ago of comparing him to Mickey Mantle—a natural ballplayer. It's taken a thousand games of sweat and hundreds of games on the disabled list, but Gibson has survived to be Gibson, a sort of laconic punk-cut road warrior. "Sometimes the Man Upstairs tortures me terribly, but then He puts me through wonderful times like these," said Gibson. "I guess it's like fishing. You wait thirty-six hours for one muskie, but it's great when you get him."

On his homers, which made losers of Roger McDowell and Sid Fernandez, Gibson did an almost unique thing in sports. In a moment of joy and vindication, he showed nothing. He jogged the bases—not too fast, not too slow—as though it were spring training. Then, when he reached the dugout, he exchanged hand slaps with a trace of a smile so faint that only his teammates, looking into his eyes, could see it.

Oh yes, the New York Mets watch Gibson. They see what he does for the Dodgers and what he is doing to them. "That team really seems to revolve around Gibson. He's not a guy to show anybody up. He's not out there to style. He's a gamer," said Wally Backman, aware that some of his Mets are stylers. "Now all their guys are gamers. On paper, their lineup doesn't [match up] with ours. But they're busting their butts, being aggressive, making things happen. That's the way we should play."

Since Gibson arrived this spring as a free agent, the Dodgers, so often accused of being too mellow, have aped his approach. When Mike Scioscia ripped Dwight Gooden for a two-run homer with nobody out in the ninth inning of Game Four to rob the Mets of a win and force extra innings, there was Gibson pounding Scioscia when he got to the dugout.

Even the Dodgers pitchers now act a little crazy, with no sensible big league respect for their bodies. When L.A. ran out of pitchers in Game Four, who started warming up but Orel Hershiser, the slim superstar with the accountant's face who had pitched seven innings the previous day. Orel, what are you doing, son?

Gibson makes everybody think it's 1908 again and the game is being played for blood and honor. Hershiser came in and got the last out, with the bases loaded, for a save.

Now the whole Dodgers team has the gung-ho fever. Was it really just six months ago in Vero Beach that a Dodgers prankster put eyeblack inside Gibson's hat rim? Gibson tore the clubhouse up, left camp, criticized his teammates and said that wasn't how he played baseball, like it was some Sunday picnic for laughs. They could be goof-offs. But include him out.

Thanks largely to Gibson, these are different Dodgers. They even amaze Manager Tommy Lasorda. "I looked up in the eighth inning today," said Lasorda, incredulous, "and Hershiser's down in the bullpen throwing *again*. What have I got to do, throw a lasso around him? Well, hell, he's already hot and we get in a jam, I'd have brought him in."

That's how John McGraw and Pepper Martin talked. And Kirk Gibson. Does the players association know about this?

Beneath everything, the secret of Gibson's effect on the Dodgers is a quality that he has developed only in recent years. Beneath his hard exterior, an emotional, almost sentimental interior has been appearing as his hairline recedes—especially where teammates are concerned.

"I think what happened to Jay Howell inspired some of us," said Gibson. "We don't feel he's a cheater. We don't want him to feel he let us down. We've been saying we want to take the Series back to L.A. and he's going to be the guy to nail down the last game.

"You create these crazy scenarios," added Gibson sheepishly.

To remind his teammates of how much grief Howell would take if they lost, Gibson wore the initials *JH* on his sleeve. After Gibson limped off the field in the last inning, Scioscia told him, "If you don't play tomorrow, I'm going to wear *KG*."

It's not hard to figure out why.

Just a case of follow-the-leader.

NEW YORK, October 11, 1988 — Maybe this will make up for the intentional walk to Jack Clark. The walk that never happened. The walk that Tom Lasorda never ordered in the National League playoffs in 1985.

Different circumstances reveal different slices of a manager's skill. Nobody's got it all. You just hope that, over the long haul, you get the chance to show the strong as well as the weak.

Tactics have never been Lasorda's trump suit. But he has never been the bumbler many cast him to be after Clark took Tom Niedenfuer to Pasadena to win the pennant for St. Louis. Now a playoff has rolled around that casts Lasorda in the best possible light.

No team has ever needed pep talks and pap, pats on the back and screams in the face, more than these underdog Los Angeles Dodgers.

When they had their hearts ripped out in NLCS Game One by Gary Carter's down-to-the-last-strike bloop, Lasorda had the answer before Game Two. Somehow he got wind of a ghosted column by David Cone in the *New York Daily News*—three thousand miles away—and long before game time, he had copies of the ill-advised masterwork pasted all over the Dodgers' clubhouse. Complete with appropriate highlighting.

Bench jockeying is almost a lost art, but Lasorda, who can outcurse any man in baseball and loves to prove it, revived the form that night. Cone lasted two innings. Lasorda should have been awarded the poor kid's ears.

The Dodgers got the bank-vault-from-the-top-story dropped on them again in Game Three when Harry Wendelstedt gave Jay Howell the heave for using pine tar. Once again, a Dodgers lead—4–3 in the eighth—went up in a forest fire of Mets hits.

181

Lasorda was the perfect motivator, the perfect intuitive psychologist again. Talk about the wrath of the righteous. He praised National League president A. Bartlett Giamatti to the skies while damning every aspect of his decision to uphold Wendelstedt and suspend Howell. Everybody uses pine tar, Lasorda insisted, although, of course, they don't. It doesn't give a pitcher an edge, he said, although, of course, Howell would never have bothered to use it if it didn't. "What is a resin bag for?" Lasorda asked with Socratic eloquence. "It's so the pitcher can get a better grip on the ball."

By Monday, Lasorda had topped himself again. He was in heaven. "A chemist called me," he said. "Do you know what pine tar is? It's liquid resin."

Most managers fear more than anything else the charge that they have lost a crucial game. Let the players lose it, many bosses think. Just don't let me leave myself naked before mine enemies. Sunday night, Lasorda left himself with nary a thread. And he pulled it off. He used two starters in relief, including his potential Game Six and Game Seven pitchers. He used seven pitchers in all and he sent an eighth back to the hotel to get his sleep for Game Five. With his ninth pitcher, Howell, suspended, Lasorda had nobody left.

N-O-B-O-D-Y.

"I told the guys on the bench that if Hershiser walked in the tying run and we had to keep playing [several more innings], that they could just wear black armbands during the next game," Lasorda recalled.

Why black armbands?

" 'Cause I'd have killed myself.

"How could I walk down the street the rest of my life with everybody pointing at me saying, 'Do you know what he did to his team? Do you know what he did to Orel Hershiser?' "

When you're hot, you guess right. As 1 A.M. approached in the twelfth inning of Game 4, Lasorda called for Jesse Orosco —not his favorite reliever—to face his old Mets mates Keith Hernandez and Darryl Strawberry, a lefty against lefties. Orosco walked Hernandez, then threw ball one to Strawberry. Lasorda, who usually goes to the mound only to remove pitchers, visited Orosco—neck veins bulging, jaw flapping, eye to eye. You'll never see a better chewout. Lip readers had a field day.

"I just gave him a little encouragement," Lasorda said the next day. "Just a few words to let him know we were all behind him."

Lasorda gave such a pep talk before Game Four that Hershiser, who'd thrown 118 pitches the night before, walked up to him and said, "I'm ready." "What for?" said Lasorda. "For the bullpen," said the man whose September feats will go straight to the Hall of Fame. As if that weren't enough, Hershiser sneaked out of the dugout in the eighth inning of Game Five and warmed himself up.

Lasorda is proud of himself. Just as he wept publicly after his Clark gaffe, he's busting his buttons now. Asked how Hershiser got his nickname, "Bulldog," Lasorda says, "I gave it to him. When he first came up, I gave him a talk so good I wish I had it on tape. At the end, I told him, when the P.A. announcer says, 'Now pitching for the Dodgers, *Orel* Hershiser,' do you think that scares Dale Murphy? From now on, you're Bulldog Hershiser."

Lo, Hershiser, who once pitched like a puppy, has become his name.

Former Orioles John Shelby and Rick Dempsey arrived in Los Angeles in demoralized states. Lasorda's positive thinking, his ego-boosting, doesn't work on everybody. But it was what they needed. Shelby, in particular, once took failure to heart for weeks; now he ends Games Four and Five by making exactly the same sort of shoestring catch he failed to make to end Game One. Is that partly Lasorda?

The round manager has now taken the Dodgers to the playoffs six times in twelve years—little credit he usually gets for it. Some might think that this team, because it was won with mirrors and because it has reflected so well on Lasorda, might be his favorite.

Ask him and you get pure Tommy—a story that is such a perfect mix of shmaltz and truth that you want to hug him with one hand and cover your wallet with the other: "When I was fourteen years old, somebody asked my father which of his five sons he loved the most. I knew he was gonna say me. But, instead, he held up his hand and said, 'Which finger do I love the best?' "

The previous day, Lasorda had told the same exact story. But that time, he said it was his mother.

LOS ANGELES, October 16, 1988 — It's never happened before in the World Series.

That's what you wanted to know, isn't it? Now don't you feel better? That's why you, and everybody else who watched Kirk Gibson's home run on Saturday night, felt so perplexed with amazement.

Nobody—now let's word this exactly right—had ever before hit a ninth-inning home run to turn defeat into victory in the World Series. Let alone with two out. Let alone with two strikes. Let alone with injuries to both legs so bad he could barely limp around the bases.

In eighty-five Series, you'd figure everything has transpired. Don Larsen's perfect game and the Black Sox' imperfect fix. Bill Wambsganss's unassisted triple play and the 10th-inning, final-game fly Fred Snodgrass dropped to blow the 1912 Series. The Athletics' 10-run inning to wipe out an 8–0 lead. Reggie Jackson's five home runs.

From Mickey Owen's passed ball to Bill Buckner's boot; Mazeroski's homer to Don Denkinger's blown call; the Babe's called shot to Fisk's foul pole polka; the Big Six's three shutouts to the pebble that finally gave the Big Train a Series win, baseball has consistently suspended disbelief in October.

But only one man knows how Gibson feels: Cookie Lavagetto. His two-run double with two out in the ninth inning of Game Four in '47 ended Yankee Bill Bevens's bid to pitch the first Series no-hitter and gave Brooklyn a 3–2 win.

Which Dodger was better? Kirk or Cookie? Both had two-out, two-run hits to turn a loss into a win. They're the only pair to do that in the last inning. Is a homer by a star better than a double by a journeyman? Is breaking up a no-hitter better than dragging yourself out of an ice bucket, shot up with Xylocaine and cortisone, to beat a pitcher with 45 saves?

Take your pick.

Lavagetto's hit tied his Series, but the Dodgers lost in seven games. Maybe that gives Gibson a potential edge.

Nobody's saying that Gibson's homer is on the short list of Greatest Series Moments. It was only Game One—though it certainly seemed to carry weight into Game Two. The Dodgers waltzed so blithely— 6–0 behind Orel Hershiser—that Gibson stayed frozen in carbonite for an extra day, hoping to play in Oakland.

Other famous game-winning, last-inning homers in the Series have all come with the score tied. Sorry, Casey Stengel (inside-the-park in '23), Tommy Henrich ('49), Dusty Rhodes ('54), Eddie Mathews ('57), Bill Mazeroski ('60), Mickey Mantle ('64) and Carlton Fisk ('75), that's not quite the same.

Those in Dodger Stadium on Saturday night, especially the Athletics, know the difference. Some mortal Dodger, in the grip of hero worship, wrote "Roy Hobbs" above Gibson's locker. However, even *the Natural*, dedicated to the proposition that mythic excess is art, would not have dared to pull a stunt like Gibson, who is baseball's halt and lame Unnatural. Only real life can end this way and get an Oscar.

Gibson's homer did not short-circuit a light tower and burn Chavez Ravine to ash. It just scorched Dennis Eckersley, Tony LaRussa and an Oakland team that would like to get its foot out of its mouth and Gibson's boot off its neck.

Even now, a day and a game later, what Gibson did bestrides this World Series, just as his two game-winning homers within thirteen hours against the Mets defined the National League playoffs.

"I don't think I'll ever see anything like that again for as long as I live," said Dodger Dave Anderson.

"Excited? I was going to run around the bases with him," said Mickey Hatcher, king of the L.A. Stuntmen. "I figured they'd have to get a wheelchair out there for him. My first reaction was to go out and kiss him. But the guy doesn't shave."

It's impossible not to acknowledge the Hollywood-script quality of the whole evening. Gibson was a mystery man all night, back in the clubhouse getting shots and ice. He hadn't even been able to bear taking practice swings in his living room in the morning, with the pain in his bum right knee far surpassing that of his healing left hamstring.

"I didn't even think the guy could walk," said Brian Holton. "I'd forgotten all about Kirk," added Hatcher. "I didn't even see him all night," said Steve Sax.

But Gibson was still hoping. When broadcaster Vin Scully said on TV that Gibson was gone for the night, Gibson growled, "Bullshit," and broke out of his ice wrap like the Thing coming to life.

Gibson, reduced to "visualizing" his swing for three days, started hitting off a tee and, as the ninth inning began, had the bat boy fetch Tommy Lasorda. "I told him, 'If you get [Mike] Davis to hit for [Alfredo] Griffin, I can hit for the pitcher.' He took off for the dugout. I guess it was what he wanted to hear."

With Davis, a home run threat and former Athletic, at bat, Lasorda deked Oakland nicely by sending the weak Anderson out on deck. Eckersley pitched too carefully and walked Davis, assuming the Dodgers had no power left. "You can't walk the tying run," said Eckersley; ". . . that's why I lost."

As Gibson did a jig of pain after each lunging swing, and even tried a half-speed jog to first on one foul dribbler, the A's continued to pour fastballs at the outside corner. "He didn't look too good on his swings," said Hassey, the catcher, yet he kept ticking off fouls.

185

But the Dodgers adapted by running. On the first steal attempt, Gibson finally had a decent swing, poking a foul to left. Oh, so that's their game, thought the A's. Can't allow a hit-and-run double to the opposite field.

So they changed plans. On the first slider, Davis stole second and the count ran full. Suddenly, LaRussa had to face a decision with historic overtones. In the 1985 playoffs, in this ballpark, Lasorda pitched to Jack Clark in just such a spot, top of the ninth, with first base open. Next pitch, home run. Season over. However, in 1947, the Yankees intentionally walked Pete Reiser, whom they feared, to get to Lavagetto. The Reiser run beat them.

With hindsight, the A's may remember Game Five of the '84 World Series, when Goose Gossage talked Dick Williams into letting him pitch to Gibson with Detroit ahead, 5–4, in the eighth. "Ten bucks says they pitch to me," yelled Gibson to Sparky Anderson. "Ten bucks says they don't," yelled back the Tigers' manager.

They did. Gibson went into the upper deck for three runs and the icing on a world title.

Now it is easy to say you should let Eckersley pitch to right-handed Steve Sax. But, at the moment, Hassey thought "we can freeze Gibson" with a backdoor slider—a pitch that looks like a low outside fastball for a semi-intentional walk, then snaps back to nick the corner and end the game, unhit.

"I tried to make a nasty pitch," said Eckersley. Instead, it proved to be "the only pitch he could hit out."

Already, the home run, probably not a 400-footer, is growing by the hour. Now Sax says Gibson "hit it with one hand." There's a palm tree, about 500 feet from home plate. If it ever dies, folks here will swear Gibson killed it. That won't be true. But if the burly A's somehow lose this Series, there won't be much doubt who killed them.

LOS ANGELES, October 17, 1988—It's hard to gaze at the sun, or Orel Hershiser, for too long. Everybody is looking at him. But how many can see him through the blaze of his brilliance?

Every Dodger, of course, breaks his vocabulary to do justice to Hershiser in this Year of the Bulldog. Both his athleticism and competitiveness are praised to the nth degree. In just a few weeks, he has grown superhuman.

"There really is a Big Dodger in the Sky and I think he's come down and taken over Hershiser's body," said Los Angeles manager Tommy Lasorda after Hershiser's eighth no-run job in ten starts.

"After the Series, the league above the major leagues will draft Orel no. 1," said Mike Marshall after Hershiser blanked Oakland on three hits and got three himself in World Series Game Two. "Then he'll be the top pitcher in the Ultra League."

Rick Dempsey calls him "overpowering and devastating," then recalls seeing Hershiser bet $5,000 on a single hand of baccarat in Atlantic City. "Win or lose, you can't tell what he's going to do, or how he feels about it. He's kind of bookworm-looking. But he's one of the toughest characters I've come across."

Suddenly, he's 007 Orel. A scratch golfer. A pool shark. Could have played pro hockey for the Flyers. Look how he's hit and run the bases and fielded. One Dodger says Hershiser seems "incapable of a bad game," while another says, "He's so capable of doing anything he pleases, it's almost sickening."

And Lasorda has renamed him again:

Orel Shutout Hershiser IV.

At the other extreme of necessary misperception, the A's are in a state of denial, refusing to believe their eyes. They say nice things, then add provisos. Manager Tony LaRussa compared Hershiser to "several guys in our league whose ball moves like that." Dave Parker said, "I haven't seen anything real exceptional in this Series so far." Come again? And Dave Henderson adds, "It isn't like he blows you away. It isn't like he has Roger Clemens stuff."

While Mark McGwire was muttering, "He doesn't intimidate you," only Jose Canseco had the good grace to say, "It's the first time in my career I've ever had a guy throw me only fastballs. And I still can't believe I didn't hit even one hard. If he can get away with that to me, he can do it to anybody. He definitely had me mumbling to myself."

While the Dodgers see Hershiser's 67 straight scoreless innings and first back-to-back postseason shutouts since Sandy Koufax in 1965, the A's see a merely mortal foe.

Unfortunately, both these views miss the most moving part of what Hershiser has accomplished. For this brief time when he can do no wrong, he has given us a glimpse of human perfectibility.

This tall, gangly man with the innocent face, the elf ears and pointed nose, the pinched lips and narrowed gaze, has taken a very good but not great ten-year pro career and raised it to the heavens of his game. By persistence and good fortune, he has reached a peak of performance that, even if it is temporary, has never been surpassed. Not by Christy Mathewson when he pitched 3 shutouts in one World Series. Not by Grover Cleveland Alexander when he pitched 16 shutouts in one season. Nobody has ever been better. Because you can't be better than a 0.29 ERA over 97⅔ innings.

Cut from his college team, Hershiser reached the majors as a marginal reliever and never cracked a starting rotation until he was crowding twenty-six. After one wonderful year (19–3 in 1985), he slipped right back to mediocrity, going 30–30 the next two seasons.

When Dwight Gooden or Roger Clemens goes 24–4, we know why. Each is sighted and tracked like a celestial object from the day he signs his first contract. When every game is a potential no-hitter, when 20 strikeouts is a sane possibility, the huge majority of mankind may feel awe, but not kinship. Hershiser, however, is one of us. Not by some trick of facial appearance, but by the whole reality of a career where San Antonio was almost too tough and the escape from Albuquerque was a battle.

That Hershiser has handled his long and wearying hour upon the stage with such gentle grace brings dignity to us all. His split second of prayer in victory seems guileless. His exhaustion running the bases is real. His grin when his parents get to throw out the two first balls is ripe for the photo album. He sees Kirk Gibson playing in agony and, like a kid, he races to bullpen to warm up—anything to help the team—the day after he's pitched. And then the day after that, too.

Could it cost him millions if he hurt his arm? Of course. Was it foolhardy courage? By baseball standards, sure. Pure pitching Russian roulette. And he's still spinning the chambers, pitching every game on short rest and threatening to start Game Seven on just two days. But his example had such force that, by playoffs' end, Gooden pitched in relief.

Hershiser has been that rarest combination: a modest yet charismatic performer. "I was extremely tired . . . I was winded from running the bases so much . . . I wouldn't say I threw superb," he said after resting between innings with towels soaked in ammonia around his neck to revive him on a hot night.

While he has laughed about his hitting and joked about giving Lasorda gray hair by sliding while going first to third, Hershiser still throws his shoulders back just enough to make the massive A's understand his intentions. He means to take them all on and beat them—a case of mind over mastodons.

Others lie and say they feel no pressure. Hershiser says, "These early leads my team's gotten me [the last two starts] just put the monkey on my back. It's my burden to carry. If I get more than three runs, I feel like I would let the team down if I lost."

One moment, Hershiser is joking about being so excited by Gibson's Game One homer that he forgot to take films of the game home so he could study the Athletics. But the next minute, he's playing big-time mind games with the A's, saying that "I really didn't want to expose everything [tonight]. You gotta have some repertoire left . . . Oakland won't know what to look for in Game Five."

Right now, Hershiser is a conundrum—a phenomenon that should not exist. "I have never seen anybody pitch like that and continue it. It is just unbelievable," said Lasorda. "How's he different [in recent weeks]? He's more confident. He has more control. He has greater pitch selection and greater command of those pitches. And he gets it where he wants to get it every damn time. I can't believe a pitcher can be this good."

Orel Hershiser is never going to be this good again. Nobody else has been, so why would he? And he probably knows it. That's why his dignity, modesty and unselfishness in handling this blessing have been a sort of gift to everyone, not just fans of the Dodgers. It's enough to make anyone root for a fifth game, just to see him one more time.

OAKLAND, October 19, 1988—To anyone who has ever tried to play the game of baseball without any visible talent, the Los Angeles Dodgers' lineup in World Series Game Four was a source of potential lifelong inspiration.

To anyone who has ever felt unjustly used, slandered, cursed by dumb bad luck and punished far beyond the dimensions of one's misdeeds, the name Jay Howell will bring an equal dose of pleasure.

Perhaps some team in some Classic at some time has fielded a weaker nine than the Dodgers did in this game. In fact, Kansas City won a world title in 1985 thanks to the noble efforts of gentlemen like Buddy Biancalana, Darryl Motley and Pat Sheridan.

Still, the Dodgers of October 19, 1988, really are special. Only the truly terrible could do something as truly wonderful as their 4–3 victory over the Oakland Athletics. Okay, change "terrible" to "undermanned." Still, doesn't it feel as if the Dodgers deserve some higher praise—even if it's a bit backhanded—than merely being called another "underdog"?

They were underdogs before Kirk Gibson, Mike Marshall, John Tudor and Mike Scioscia (who went out in Game Four) were hurt. Now they're about one sprained ankle from being the Philadelphia Phillies.

They're also one victory away from being world champions. On Tuesday evening here, the Dodgers took the Bash Brothers' best roundhouse left hook to the jaw—a sudden-death home run by Mark McGwire. Wednesday night, the Dodgers got up—hopping mad as usual at the universal slights to dignity that surround them—and jabbed the A's into a bloody mess for fifteen rounds, before knocking them stiff as an East Bay mackerel with an uppercut to the heart from their former teammate Howell.

Perhaps some player in some postseason at some time has suffered more, and deserved it less, than Howell. But that's real doubtful.

He's been called a "high school pitcher" in print by a wet-behind-the-ears Mets pitcher. He's been convicted of breaking the rules and suspended from the National League playoffs for the most minor and debatable of infractions. He's been called gutless about three different ways by the Athletics' Don Baylor in one of the most uncalled-for attacks ever to sour a World Series stage.

And when he's finally gotten a chance to pitch, he's been quadruply cursed. One save turned into a squander when his center fielder dropped a bloop. Then, after a ten-day layoff, McGwire dropped the big one on him in Howell's first game back in Oakland since his trade.

If Howell were a rotten son of a gopherball, that might be one thing. But he's about as good as they come. Honest. How many players say, "Yes, I used pine tar. Lots of guys do. But I was wrong." He's a standup type who faced every question about McGwire.

This night, he even turned the other cheek. Given an open podium to blast Baylor, Howell said that just because somebody said something "nasty" about you didn't mean you had to answer them. But then, Howell had already given an answer of considerable eloquence.

When he got McGwire to pop up with the bases loaded to end the seventh inning, that was his opening presentation. When he snapped a slider past the bat of Jose (0 for 14) Canseco for a third strike with a man on base in the ninth, that was his display of the evidence in his defense. And, when he drew a pop-up from the Cobra, Dave Parker, to end it, that was his summation to the jury: the American public.

Even A's manager Tony LaRussa, a lawyer, said, "That was one really tough save."

Actually, all the Dodgers, not just Howell, saved themselves on this night of many memories. The fuse was lit when they sat around, minutes before the game, watching a pregame show on which Bob Costas took the self-evident position that these Dodgers, in their current disarray, might be the worst lineup ever to take the field in a World Series.

"They were screaming so loud I couldn't even hear," said Lasorda. " 'We'll show 'em.' "

The Dodgers lineup for this game combined this season for 37 home runs and 301 RBI. That's fewer home runs than Canseco had by himself. And it is 16 fewer RBI than the Oakland trio of Canseco, McGwire and Dave Henderson.

Someday we can tell our descendants that the Dodgers beat the A's with Mickey Hatcher and Mike Davis batting third and fourth. Davis had two homers this season; Hatcher had one.

To a degree, teamwork, strategy and an acute self-knowledge can count for more in baseball than in almost any sport—as the Dodgers are on the brink of proving. "This team is very similar to the '79 Orioles. Nobody respected us and we knew it," said Rick Dempsey. "This team has the right amount of Indians and the right amount of chiefs. We all try to set up the chiefs. That's usually enough because we have such good pitching."

In this game, facing Dave Stewart, the only man in baseball who has current back-to-back 20-win seasons, the Dodgers' Indians had to try to set up other Indians. The chiefs were all sick.

For seven innings, they made Stewart's life a nightmare out of *Gulliver's Travels* with pesky little hitters—taking pitches, fouling off strikes, flicking line. drives and playing hit-and-run. They got four runs—on a passed ball, an error and two ground outs—but it could easily have been more, because most of their line drives were caught.

Could such a frail attack possibly be enough to beat an opponent of which Lasorda has said, "They're a very, very tough team that can really blister . . . They can mash you all over the place?"

For the Dodger irregulars—who call themselves the Stuntmen—it was an inning-by-inning act of prayer, first to keep winner Tim Belcher intact into the seventh inning, then to bring Howell home in one piece. "You can keep good hitting down," said Dempsey. "But you feel like you're standing on the edge of the cliff the whole game."

Before this game, Hershiser, who will try to end one of baseball's most amazingly improbable postseasons here Thursday night, said, "I hope we have a few more miracles left in our bag."

In this fourth game, Howell was asked to provide that miracle. And he did. Maybe because no one in baseball has ever deserved it more.

OAKLAND, October 20, 1988 — Orel Hershiser and Kirk Gibson will take the bows and Tommy Lasorda will make the speeches. And they should. You can't pitch more gamely than Hershiser or lead more bravely than Gibson or prime the psychological pump better than Lasorda.

But Mickey Hatcher is, and always should be, the symbol of the world champion Los Angeles Dodgers of 1988.

For Mike Davis and Tim Belcher, for Alejandro Peña and Tim Leary, for Rick Dempsey and Brian Holton—for all the Dodgers that nobody knew or respected until the last two weeks—Hatcher's the crooked-smiled, hyper-hustling emblem.

This World Series—the fourth in a row that has left fans stunned with incredulity and gasping for historical perspective—began with Hatcher racing around the bases with his arms above his head like a madman after hitting a home run that even he could not believe. And, of course, this Series ended the same way, with Hatcher lighting a Dodgers forest fire with a two-run homer off Storm Davis in the first inning, then beating out an infield hit with a head-first dive just before a killing two-run home run by former Athletic Mike Davis.

"Mickey exemplifies what our whole team is about," said Gibson, who was limited to his pinch-hit home run in Game One. "Nobody has given us credit all year, but we've accepted what we had to do to win. Mickey had to take my [no. 3] spot in the batting order [in the Series] and he's probably done it better than I could have done it."

Actually, Hatcher probably did. He batted .368 and slugged .737. He drove in five runs and scored five. When his homers didn't start a game, his hit-and-run singles were at the heart of key rallies. Hatcher also made a great diving catch in the outfield and, to the disbelief of the A's, turned two Oakland line drives off the distant outfield walls into singles.

In other words, while Oakland outfielders were acting cool, consistently jogging to balls and allowing extra bases, or throwing to the wrong bases, Hatcher was leaning and breaking on every pitch, just like an infielder trying to get a jump.

While the Oakland superstars were trying to hit home runs to polish, or preserve, their images and their pre-Series predictions, Hatcher was battling his brains out to hit a few line drives. The net result? Hatcher had 14 total bases. That's the same number Jose Canseco, Mark McGwire, Dave Parker and Carney Lansford had combined.

To know Hatcher's slightly askew approach to baseball and life is to know the best about the Dodgers. No, not the pious, long-winded, self congratulatory side of the Dodgers that has not gone away, not even in this lovely moment. What Hatcher captures is the exuberant, fundamentally savvy, comedic, yet fiercely determined side of the Dodgers that has always made their bus rides and training camps and dugout banter worthy of an R-rated Bill Murray movie.

Once upon a time, in spring training in Vero Beach, Florida, a decade ago, an unknown but audacious young Hatcher cut the seat out of Lasorda's pants. At the time, Lasorda was the manager. When you play baseball the way Hatcher does—sliding on your face, slapping singles to the opposite field and searching for a defensive position where you can hide—playing jokes on the manager might not seem too smart.

But Hatcher knows his place. And laughter is part of it. For most of his ten major league seasons, his position might as well have been described as "chemist," because aiding team chemistry has been one of his main jobs. "During a game, Mickey is dead serious. He can't stop pacing the dugout. Everybody pushes him out of the way and yells at him to sit down," said Gibson. "But that's just his hyper nature . . . He's a big part of our mix . . . and with this mix we're world champs."

Hatcher knew Lasorda would retaliate for the Pants Attack. The Dodgers closeness comes from Lasorda's somewhat bizarre blend of profanity, combative temper, affection, loyalty and bottomless enthusiasm. In other words, he wants you to cut up his pants. It means you love him. And he will prove that he loves you in return: by ordering that you be killed.

Lasorda ordered a young pitcher named Hershiser to "hit that Hatcher right in the head or you won't make the ball club."

"Yeah, Tommy'll deny it now," says Hatcher. "He's always saying, 'You're the biggest liar.' But at least Hershiser yelled, 'Watch out' and threw it over my head."

At the moment, Lasorda and Hershiser are both grateful Hatcher's head remains in one piece. In the great tradition of World Series stars like Dempsey, Bucky Dent and Ray Knight, Hatcher decided to play the best baseball of his life at the best possible time: when scores of millions are watching.

Thursday night, the mightily muscled one—well, actually, the slope-shouldered guy with the folksy smile—did it again. We thought Canseco's grand slam and the game-winning blows by Gibson and McGwire were hit a long way. Hatcher's blow, unleashed through Oakland's supposedly cement-like air, made them all seem short. We're talking 420 feet, minimum, and maybe 430.

More important than the two runs was the tone of defiance Hatcher had set. See, he was saying to the makeshift Dodgers lineup, I hit one home run all year. Now I have two in the World Series. Get the message.

Of course, the thirty-three-year-old utility man, turned superstar by necessity, ran the bases as though he were one leg of a mile relay team. Does he think his bat is really a baton? On the other hand, Hatcher may just be proud of his speed. Or what used to be his speed when he played wide receiver for Oklahoma in the 1976 Fiesta Bowl.

Back in Los Angeles, A's Manager Tony LaRussa insisted, "The Dodgers are much more than emotion. We're going to have to deal with a good team, not just a bunch of big hearts."

But then, the Dodgers still figured to get Gibson back. Who knew Mike Marshall, John Tudor and Mike Scioscia would go down? For three days here in Oakland, the Dodgers really have been just a bunch of big hearts, plus a superbly deep staff of pitchers.

"Everybody calls us underdogs," said Hatcher. "I suppose you'd have to say that we are. We're not a team of stars. Forget [hitting] .400. We just play hard. We know that it's always better to make an aggressive mistake. That's how we've played all year and we know it works. That's why, as a team, we don't feel we're underdogs."

The Dodgers have Heroes, like Hershiser, with a capital *H*. But they also have the Stuntmen—the role players among whom Hatcher is the king. If it were necessary to be riddled with bullets, then hurled through a plate-glass window to win a game, then, metaphorically, that's just what they want to do.

Long after Thursday evening's 5–2 victory was in the book, with the notation "Game-winning RBI—Hatcher," the boss of those Stuntmen was still trying to figure it all out. "I was missing something in baseball. I was missing something in my life. I didn't know what it was. Now I have it," he said. "Was this supposed to happen or what?"

Falling off mountains and getting stabbed by spies is easy work compared to what these Dodgers have done. The stunt they pulled on the A's in this World Series matches any in the history of baseball for degree of difficulty.

OAKLAND, October 21, 1988 — By the time a baseball season reaches October, the sport has, gradually over seven months, developed an entire set of mythological characters who, for that one season, have a talismanic quality.

To a large degree, the playoffs and World Series are an acting out of the oldest of battle scenes as a central hero or two, an Achilles or a Hector, come out from each camp for combat. Who will remain a charismatic figure? Who will become human?

That all heroes are flawed is an idea that, in battle or sport, seems to flee from our minds as though some primitive response required that one figure step forward and let his courage and poise inspire the entire group. So what if this year's legend can become next year's goat? At least in baseball, the Season is a symbolic unit which players not only respect, but to which they ascribe an unnamed power.

That's what's behind the clichés: "It's his year . . . The hot hand . . . Team of destiny."

At times, it can all start feeling very ancient, territorial and psychological. Of course Orel Hershiser bows his head for a moment in triumph and sings hymns in his trance between innings. Of course he kneels when he reaches base. He is in touch with his heritage: the man who, for a time, is favored by the gods.

The 1988 World Series began with four men—two on each team— who stood so far above all others that what befell them carried disproportionate weight.

The Athletics had Jose Canseco, the first player to have 40 home runs and 40 stolen bases in the same season. He epitomized the A's: intimidation through size with grace. One Dodgers scout, in a pre-Series meeting, actually said his goal was "to bring Canseco down off Mount Olympus and compare him to somebody in the National League."

Oakland also had Dennis Eckersley, a baseball phoenix reborn as a relief pitcher. Left on the ashcan by the Cubs, he'd not only saved or won 49 games, but also saved every game in the American League playoffs. Nothing in baseball is harder than getting the last out. It's been such a mental block for pitchers for a century that it is accepted dugout law that the invisible wall exists. The man who can smash it—time and again—somehow has appropriated the right to claim victory.

Though the Dodgers were the inferior team in talent, they had the ultimate suit of armor: Hershiser. Good pitching may or may not stop good hitting, but players believe that it does. So the best pitcher in a Series is the ace of trumps. Hershiser entered the playoffs with the longest streak of shutout innings in baseball history. Thus he was the ace of all aces. Then, against the Mets, he raised the mythic ante even higher by starting three games, saving another and sneaking into the bullpen to warm up in yet another game. When he should have been exhausted, he shut out the Mets in a winner-take-all game for the pennant.

Concerning Hershiser, the battered word "awesome" was in every mouth. And awe is reserved for heroes.

Los Angeles also had as symbolic a warrior as the game has seen in years: Kirk Gibson, a footballish fellow who seems to maim himself so his deeds will become doubly charged with leadership value. Playing in pain against the Mets, Captain Kirk, going where no man had gone before, hit two game winning home runs within 13 hours—one at 1 A.M., then one at 1 P.M.

The Athletics' great mistake in the World Series was their assumption that their own magic, their aura of collective power, was insuperably great. Canseco talked openly about dominating a quick five-game Series. Don Baylor, a mythic leader in other years but a slightly embittered man as his glory days wane, impugned the courage of the Dodgers' key relief pitcher. He might as well have said: "We have the shield of Eckersley to protect us. You only have this timid person named Jay Howell. I know him—a mere mortal."

In Game One, Eckersley faced Gibson.

A Gibson who could barely stand.

Down to his last strike, Gibson hit a home run that, in some still photos, seemed to have been struck with one hand. No player, not in the entire twentieth century, had hit a sudden-death homer to turn a World Series defeat into victory. Gibson became a redoubled myth. Until such time as Eckersley could undo the damage, he had been exposed as vulnerable. And Eckersley never got another chance.

As an added twist, Gibson's blast upstaged a homer by Canseco. And not just a homer, but a grand slam. Wouldn't such an act affect the pecking order in a band of a lions or tigers? Might it not bear upon some atavistic part of a man?

196

In Game Two, Hershiser demonstrated how—if your deity dues are all paid up—you can slay a dragon, cut a Gordian knot or clean the Augean stables. He not only pitched a shutout—his eighth unscored-upon outing in ten starts—but had as many hits that game as the whole A's team. That he fielded and ran bases stylishly moved him to an even higher level of grudging respect. Not just a pitcher, but an athlete.

Canseco went into a slump that would reach 0-for-18 by Series end and his fielding became a tad sulkish, too. Within days, Canseco was saying he was "only a third-year player" and "carrying a team" was too much to ask of him. His team wasn't playing like the real A's." As for himself: "I'm still learning." Mythic apprenticeship is hard work, especially your first brush with an evil spell. So far, Canseco's doing nicely.

The final weapon in the Dodgers' arsenal of ideas was their team notion that no defeat can demoralize them. Why? Because, in their collective humility before the gods of talent, they freely admit their weaknesses. As compensation for their lack of skill, they were granted superhuman resiliency.

Neither a lucky bloop by the Mets' Gary Carter, nor NL President Bart Giamatti's stern sentence when Howell was found to have pine tar in his glove during the National League Championship Series nor Mets pitcher David Cone's atonement for his Dodger-bashing in a newspaper column could deflect them.

When Mark McGwire homered to end Game Three—only the seventh sudden-death homer in Series history—the Dodgers got a chance to prove this point to the A's. Slip us the black spot; we ignore it.

This Series was decided in Game Four. The A's led with their ace, Dave Stewart. The Dodgers countered with a rookie who'd lasted two innings in Game One, failing, he admitted, from nerves: "I was going crazy out there," said Tim Belcher. Because of mounting injuries, the Los Angeles lineup was a collection of "Stuntmen"—spurned role players dedicated to earning some respect.

If any recent game has been mostly a meeting of minds and mythologies, it was Game Four. From the moment the Dodgers scored two mysterious runs on one tiny single in the first inning, the A's seemed mesmerized. Has their courage paralyzed our power?

When Howell—the exile, the avenger, the wrongly accused—took the mound, the feeling rose, and remains in retrospect, that he could not lose. Could the A's really bring themselves to deny him? After all, the year before, he was one of them. By the time Howell had defeated Canseco, McGwire and Dave Parker—about 700 pounds of muscle—there was hardly any need to play Game Five.

One by one, all the A's myths about themselves for 1988 had disintegrated. Canseco and McGwire (a combined 2 for 36), Stewart and Eckersley (both beaten) had all been disarmed. Merely excellent. But not possessed of magic or luck. At least not This Season.

In the final game, the head Stuntman, Mickey Hatcher, hit a home run in the first inning. Other such folk provided more stunts—Mike Davis a two-run homer and Rick Dempsey an RBI double. Gibson was never even needed.

In the end, it became clear whose year this was. Like Bob Gibson in 1967 or Reggie Jackson in 1977 or Willie Stargell in 1979 or George Brett in 1985, there was one character clearly blessed by the fates: Hershiser.

To cynics, fate is another name for the process of elimination by which sports creates one champion per year. A team is always left standing; one man usually carries its flag. So he's got a heck of a chance to look like Agamemnon.

Superstition has its proper place in sports. There are times when it's a wiser course than strategy. And Tommy Lasorda loves to believe in mysteries. That's why he left in Hershiser to face Canseco—the tying run—in the eighth inning. Talk about burning the Book! All managers know you never let a tired pitcher give away the last run of a big lead when you have a strong bullpen. However, Lasorda trusted his gut— and Hershiser's. Our magic's better than yours. Let it ride.

The count on Canseco went to 1–2. Hershiser shook off Dempsey once, twice. What was he thinking?

"I wanted to surprise Canseco," said Hershiser.

What the choirboy wanted to do was tempt fate, trust his luck, finish his roll. He wanted to throw the last pitch in the world that anyone would dare.

A fastball belt-high and inside.

Miss by inches and it's the pitch Canseco hits farthest. Hitters love to say your strength and your weakness are usually only a couple of inches apart.

Hershiser didn't hit Dempsey's glove. He hit the fly sitting on the glove. And Canseco's sickly pop-up fell like a dying dream.

After that, the A's were mush. Parker swung at what Hershiser mischievously called "a 55-foot curveball. So I threw him another one." Why not? His spell was at full virulence. The inning, and the A's last rally, ended as Parker took two preposterous swings at pitches that bounced before they reached him.

In defeat, the A's were philosophical and gracious. What else could they be? When you feel yourself in the grip of ancient scary powers, humility is easy. The Dodgers, immortal now for a winter, drank champagne, the wine of forgetfulness.

Next spring, the Season begins again. The mythology starts from zero. Because we have all agreed to say that it does. On opening day, the Dodgers will still wear a residual glow. The A's, as they receive their Series losers' rings, may hang their heads with just a hint of a hex still clinging to them.

But what the Dodgers and Athletics bring forward with them from this week in October will last them exactly one game. That's the half-life of a demigod. Then it will be 1989—the "next year" we all invoke. And, once again, we will say to each other that while baseball is just a game, we're certainly glad it's back, with all its strange, almost haunting power.

Managing (Life)

Stranger in Paradox

RETIREMENT

MIAMI, March 1983 — The clubhouse of the Country Club of Miami, the golf course that has become Earl Weaver's home, is an ugly, comic burned-out shell of a building. Though the fire occurred four years ago, what remains of the clubhouse looks as though smoke should still be curling up from its charred girders. Miami cynics murmur that Marvin the Torch held a kerosene party here; it makes a fine fable, the sort that raconteur Weaver loves to tell, especially when the truth —a spark in the laundry room—is so bland.

Whichever way you tell the tale, Weaver loves the result: as soon as that consarned clubhouse burned, he started getting serious about retiring. "Hell, yes, I'm glad it burned down. And I'm glad they don't have the money to rebuild it. Hope it stays just like it is," says Weaver, whose home adjoins the seventh fairway of the West Course. "It drives away all the phonies." In swanky, nouveau-riche Miami, who, except a truly serious golfer, would belong to a country club that looks like a Charles Addams cartoon!

"It sure brought down the dues—$600 a year," snorts Weaver, perhaps the only man in America who can play 500 holes of golf a month for $50. "I got my own private golf courses, two of 'em. Never crowded. Tee off anytime I want."

Weaver is the vice-president of the men's association of the club, a group whose avowed purpose is to keep the club solvent (to maintain the courses) but too poor to rebuild that clubhouse.

If you want to know what the best baseball manager of his generation claims he intends to do every day for the rest of his life, then meet him in the pro shop around noon almost any day. By then he's finished a morning tending tomatoes. The Earl of Bal'mer is ready for the serious business of enjoying himself, just as he's sworn to himself for thirty-five years that he would.

Outside the pro shop sits a white, orange and black golf cart with the word "Orioles" written in script across the front and "No. 4" stamped on the side. This vehicle, the fantasy-come-true of the fifty-two-year-old little boy who owns it, is equipped with a radio, an electric fan, a sun roof and two beer coolers. When the cart was presented to Weaver at "Thanks Earl" Day in Baltimore last September, the crowd of 41,127 may have wondered who in the world would have the chutzpah to play in such a wonderful-ridiculous contraption. Not to worry.

In a corner of the bare-bones pro shop, Weaver perches next to a computer. The men's association hasn't gotten around to painting the pro shop's walls or carpeting its floors, but they've requisitioned a computer to show every score shot by every member. These guys are serious.

For years, Weaver kinda wanted the Orioles to put a little computer in his office to replace all those clipboards of charts and stats on his wall. Now Weaver is delightedly punching in the code numbers of his partners for the day; he's scouting a five-dollar Nassau. It's a good thing for Billy Martin that Weaver never learned how to work these gizmos before he retired.

"Here, wanna see how bad I been playin?" Weaver asks.

On the screen are Weaver's last 20 scores, all in the 80s, except one

77. "My handicap's up from 6 to 10. If I get much worse, I'll have to come back," says Weaver, who's always joked that only two things could bring him back to managing: inflation eating up his money or bad golf eating up his pleasure.

One foe in Weaver's foursome is of particular concern to him—a Mr. Lucky LeChance [*sic*], with whom the diminutive legend has been in combat for decades.

"I used to have to give Lucky so many shots that I'd hide when I saw him coming," says Weaver. "I can't guess how much money I've lost to him."

The slim, stylish LeChance appears and recounts how, in recent months, he has battled and finally defeated Legionnaires' disease. "They packed me in ice to get my fever down," he says. "Twice they pronounced me dead. I guess I really am Lucky."

Weaver listens, then says, "When LeChance was in intensive care, we were all rooting for him to die. Him and that damn 19 handicap."

"Would you believe," says LeChance, "that Earl only has one more class left before he graduates from charm school?"

"It worked out all right," says Weaver. "He's playing better now than before he died. It cut down his swing. His handicap's down to 17 and now we're getting some of our money back from him."

"If Earl has ever lost any money on this golf course," says another of Weaver's partners and friends, Ernie Lantz, "then it must have fallen out of his pocket."

At the first tee, Weaver's fivesome becomes a small tornado of team wagers and individual side bets; someone should have brought the computer. As soon as the play begins, so does the agitating.

On the second hole, Weaver hits the shot that may have drawn him away from baseball—a long, powerful fade that nurses the wind and hard fairway until it rolls to rest on what, to the ecstatic Weaver, must seem like the horizon of the world. For a little man with a lot of pride, it's a kick for Weaver to know he can drive it with anybody this side of a real pro.

"Nicklaus and Koch? That's a 310 [yards]," crows Weaver, probably not exaggerating by more than the average golfer—about 50 yards.

As in all corners of his life, Weaver the golfer remains completely in character. He dresses like a pro and swings like a man who loves to study the technique and theory of sport. Once past an amusingly intense series of preswing waggles, Weaver's hack is basically that of a well-taught, dedicated amateur—quick, no quirks, aggressive. Around the greens, however, Weaver is a sight to warm an umpire's heart. He starts to choke, imprecating himself, as soon as any chip or putt stops more than two feet from the hole.

At the nineteenth hole, after all bets—which Weaver loves to keep track of in his head—have been computed, Weaver has clobbered LeChance and Lantz four different ways; and won all of eight dollars. A day when fifty dollars changes hands becomes part of the codger coterie's chronicles.

In baseball, Weaver found challenge, but also strain; wealth, but, in some seasons, frayed health; fame, but too little friendship. With the years, Weaver tired of the aloofness. More and more he craved what the CC of Miami could give him: a group of people who treated him with respect, but without awe; who gave him back as good as he dished out; who chose him for their companion for himself, not because he was the famous boss.

"We like it here because it's unpretentious; I've never found a country club that was so relaxed," says Lantz, a semiretired businessman as well as a former coach and major league scout. "Earl loves this circus. He and Lucky and a guy named Ben Horn are here every day. Earl can tell you every shot Horn ever made to beat him. They're like legends to each other. They start cussing each other on the first hole and never stop. You can hear them in the next fairway.

"I don't play with them that often," adds Lantz. "Golf is the worst waste of time in the world, if you have the talent for anything else. The more you play, the worse you get. In fact, it's worse than work. As Earl may discover." Lantz doubts this "daily circus" will hold Weaver past one summer.

Although he likes to keep it secret, Weaver is not in any significant sense retired. Nor does he intend to be.

Though the public doesn't know it yet, he has simply switched careers. Within a year or two, he plans to be more famous, more wealthy, more respected, more relaxed, more professionally secure and more of a national institution than ever.

For those who haven't noticed, Weaver has already constructed his retirement so that he will probably be on national TV much more often and get to say a hundred times more than he ever did as a manager. He's worked it so that he can be in the ballparks he loves about seventy-five times a year. And he'll make more money than he ever has in his life.

This season, Weaver's "retirement" income—from deferred payments for managing, from work as an Orioles' special consultant and from his NBC contract to do color on Monday night game-of-the-week telecasts—will be more than a quarter-million dollars. In past seasons, Weaver held himself to a $75,000 annual allowance.

If Weaver's master plan works, he'll manage to do all this in his spare time, working fewer than a hundred days a year, while leaving the rest of his days to argue with Horn.

Weaver's greatest concern this spring, and the single factor that will probably have the greatest bearing on whether he returns to managing in the next few years, is his new TV career. Weaver's reviews last fall, when he teamed with Jim Palmer on the A.L. playoffs, were mixed. He was knowledgeable, occasionally witty, but he was also reserved and almost dignified—an odd word to apply to a man famous for blowing his stack in public. He didn't seem much like Earl Weaver.

Weaver knows it and hopes that he gets more chances. He studied his playoff tapes over the winter and decided that he needs plenty of work. "I didn't get excited enough. I should have had more energy, so I could pass on more excitement to the people. They're playin' for the pennant and I said, 'What a wonderful throw. That might change the series,' " says Weaver mildly. "I should have jumped up and yelled, 'God damn, what a great throw! That's the turning point.'

"I took it very calm, but that's not me. I was worried about my grammar, and I didn't get involved enough in the game, so I didn't get excited enough. That's what I learned."

ABC hasn't given Weaver any offseason hints to its corporate evaluation of him or its plans for him. Despite several years of writing his own pregame radio shows as preparation for this, does Weaver feel like a rookie? "Yes," he says, nodding and adding, "I'll be all right if I do my homework."

Part of Weaver's homework includes scouting twenty-seven games this spring, driving to Fort Lauderdale, West Palm Beach and even Fort Myers. This doesn't sound too retired. As usual, Weaver has a quick, crusty answer: "I'm doin' it 'cause I'm gettin' paid. And I get eighteen cents a mile, too." Actually, Weaver wants a reason to get to the ballpark.

"I don't understand people who love the game and then disappear," says Hank Peters, the Orioles GM. "Some of them retire and don't even associate with baseball people after they've been around them their whole lives. I'm glad Earl obviously isn't doing that."

Last Saturday, Weaver, in a curly permanent hairdo, reappeared near the batting cage. The atmosphere was strained but pleasant.

"I heard about this," said coach Lee May of Weaver's hair. "You've grown."

"Got the stopwatch on me?" asked Al Bumbry.

"Nope," said scout Weaver. "I'll just write down 'fast.' "

At one point, Weaver and Altobelli held court fifteen feet apart—back to back. Neither greeted the other. Maybe they just didn't notice each other. To be sure, Weaver and Palmer didn't meet; they're not speaking. "Earl got annoyed," says Palmer, "because I told a reporter about how Scotty McGregor told him last year that he swore so much during games that lightning was going to strike him down. Scotty was making a point about some of Earl's behavior, and he sat at the other end of the dugout from Earl all last season.

"The next time I saw Earl," recalls Palmer, "he said, 'For sixteen years I got paid to talk to you. Now I don't have to, so I won't.' "

Palmer says he responded, "Don't you still get a consulting fee? You should consult me."

They haven't spoken since. "The game passed him by," says Palmer.

After thirty-five years in the dugout, sitting behind home plate among scouts is a mystery to Weaver; he might as well be watching cricket. Weaver often can't tell one pitch from another, asking the kid with the radar gun for help. "Was that a straight change?" he says. "I'm having trouble."

Fans wander up for autographs, reporters seek interviews and a congressman climbs over a railing and practically falls in Weaver's lap so he can have his picture taken with the former manager. The man pitching coach Ray Miller called "the most patient impatient man in the world" tolerates the aggravations.

Quickly Weaver outlines the plans he has for every week through the World Series: visits to St. Louis, Houston, Atlanta, Elmira, Baltimore, North Carolina to see his children, relatives, in-laws, friends, to scout or broadcast or play golf. "You wouldn't believe my schedule. And Marianne and I still haven't used up the cruise," he says, meaning the Caribbean cruise he got on "Thanks Earl" Day.

On Weaver's eighteenth hole of the day, his drive lands in a fairway trap. His next shot—a feeble dribbler—lodges under the lip of the trap. His third barely escapes and ends in the rough. Weaver's fourth shot is a dead shank under the only tree in sight.

Weaver is disgusted as he skulls the ball across the green into more weeds. His chip back stops in that hair-pulling six-foot range.

The little man, who has been called the first thoroughly modern manager, lines up his putt. In an age of free agents, Weaver commanded his teams without fines, virtually without rules, without phony friendships with his players, without recriminations or grudges. For fifteen years he built the best managing record in the game by sheer force of personality, quick wit and a sort of cosmic insubordination regarding conventional ideas about how to do his job.

"This is for seven," Weaver mutters as he lines up the putt. He misses. His quadruple bogey gives him yet another 85—10 shots worse than when he wasn't retired. Weaver smiles and shrugs.

This retirement is such a sweet gig—making money hand over fist, staying on the comfortable fringe of the limelight, while having a ball—that even quadruple bogeys can't bother him. In a couple of years, maybe he'll decide what he *really* wants to do when he grows up.

RETURN

BALTIMORE, May 15, 1985—When a significant pleasure is taken from us, the typical human reaction is to deny the loss by erasing the memory.

That, perhaps, is why Earl Weaver has seemed so far from our baseball thoughts for the last two and a half years. Once he was lost to us as an almost daily pleasure, we forgot his vividness, wit, energy and passion for the sport.

When he saw Al Bumbry heading to chapel services, did he really say, "Take your bat with you?" Was it commonplace for him to toss off lines like, "We're goin' so bad that back-to-back home runs means one today and one tomorrow?" Did he actually mutter, "I gave Mike Cuellar more chances than my first wife?"

Was he really intelligent and original; irritating and insulting, yet also charming; vain and volcanic, yet stubbornly patient and even compassionate? Was he a rich example of coping with the complexity of adult life, yet a poor model to hold up to a child? Was he always and altogether more interesting and profanely human on his dullest day than almost any other manager on his best?

Even the Baltimore Orioles were caught by psychological surprise when they learned of his sudden and shocking decision to return as their manager. Their separation from him in 1982 had been such a gradual and painful weaning that it seemed beyond the club's comprehension that such a piece of good luck could actually occur.

Yet in less than two days the news had begun to be digested. Weaver's return has already had two immediate effects.

First, it energized the team, which immediately went from a comatose five-game losing streak under Joe Altobelli to a three-game winning streak full of home runs, fielding acrobatics and rallies. Suddenly it became obvious to the Orioles that they had gradually forgotten how to care—that is, truly care in the head-first-slide, bear-down-every-second sense that had once been habitual.

"We needed a kick in the butt," said Storm Davis. "We didn't realize what Earl meant to us until he was gone," said Rick Dempsey, always an antagonist. "All his sarcasm was our spark. I don't think some of us will ever take his criticisms as personally as we used to. And I know nobody is going to loaf, because we're not going to let anybody take advantage of Earl."

Second, the team felt a fascination with reintroducing itself to Weaver at the personal level because, for sixteen men who had played for him previously, it offered the possibility of a final chapter to a long and unfinished story.

The best metaphoric image for Weaver has always been that of a crab; in recent years, a molting crab. Once he was secure in his crustiness. His managerial *modus operandi* was to pretend that he didn't care about anyone's feelings, that he didn't need friends, that to be successful he would always have to be perceived as a rotten guy.

He cultivated his irascibility, like a man planting burrs under his own saddle, even as he found himself outgrowing his lifelong persona. Twenty years in the minors had taught him how to be a rock, a leader, an invulnerable crab. And he was sick and tired of it. In particular, his drunk-driving charges humiliated him. An Orioles executive said, "Earl has killed more brain cells than most managers ever had." When Weaver slap-punched an umpire in 1982, it reconfirmed his own fears that he might snap from his self-imposed demands for intensity. He wanted to be feisty, but he didn't want to leave the game as a burned-out head case who punched umpires.

"Just once I want to see the sky turn to dusk without the stadium lights coming on," he once said in a dugout reverie so touching it made you want to cry for the tenderness trapped so long inside the crab. Weaver had created the prototype for a modern manager. As coach Ray Miller once said, "Earl doesn't care if your hair is down to your ass and you wear ten pounds of beads, but you better take pride in your work." Weaver's mask of insolence seemed to hide a longing to get away and turn inward—perhaps even rethink himself.

"I've always worked for one reason," said Weaver. "So I could retire." The philosopher's position. Even owner Edward Bennett Williams could not quite reach a high enough rung to grasp why a healthy man at the peak of his powers would want to spend the rest of his life playing golf, visiting relatives and having dinner every night with his wife.

Few men seem capable of growth past a certain middle age. Perhaps personality can calcify too. Weaver may yet prove an exception. With his passion for finding the simple line of "commonsense logic" that runs through events and through personalities (including his own), Weaver has always been a man in slow evolution. If anything, Weaver retired because his development seemed to have reached a cul-de-sac. He needed a sabbatical so that he could come back fresh but also, perhaps, so he could come back slightly different.

After all, the title of Weaver's autobiography was *It's What You Learn After You Know It All That Counts.*

One thing is certain: Weaver knew the animus that increasingly surrounded him during his last two Orioles seasons. In 1982 one of his own coaches said, "I may quit. Earl won't listen to anybody. He's carried away with himself. I've made a million suggestions and he hasn't taken one."

Said veteran Tippy Martinez, "He was a pain in the butt. I don't think anybody will miss him personally." Added Dempsey, "We won't have to put up with all his screwups and his second-guessing." Jim Palmer, a sort of surrogate son, bade him farewell with bitter public words like the ones that Mark Belanger and Paul Blair had used before.

The Weaver who reappeared in Memorial Stadium was a hybrid version of the Li'l Genius. He greeted old friends warmly. He almost cried at a news conference when he recalled his final game in 1982. He admitted his nervousness, even his uncertainty about whether he should have returned at all. He apologized to the team for being unprepared to manage the previous night. He begged indulgence of everyone until he got on the same page with everybody else.

In the very first inning of that first game, Weaver faced a decision. Storm Davis was wild. Four walks in an inning, one with the bases loaded. Milwaukee's lead was already 3–0, with the bases still jammed, and here came two more balls to the no. 9 hitter. Welcome back, Earl. This is exactly what you're paid to decide. How long do you wait? How far can you fall behind?

"My thoughts were 'I hope we don't get blown away.' I was nervous," said Weaver, a huge joke bottle of Rolaids on his desk. "Storm was close to his last batter. Maybe he was there. One more hit it's 5–0, top of the order up. And it's a long way back. I'm looking at him and he seems to have his stuff. Nobody's having good cuts against him . . .

"But I haven't seen a big league pitch up that close for two and a half years. Maybe anybody would look strong to me. You had to figure, 'This guy's throwin' good.' Or is he?"

Many in Weaver's office had never, not in fifteen years, heard any such concession of vulnerability in judgment. Seldom would he even admit that he had faced a difficult decision, much less admitted that he feared it.

Weaver left Davis in the game and watched as he allowed no runs and only two feeble hits the rest of the night as the Orioles stormed back to win, 9–3.

"I'm a fortunate person tonight," said Weaver. "I thanked the boys . . . It was something special for me."

In everything, the new Weaver seemed slightly altered, who knows with what results. He tolerated dumb questions. Asked what George Bamberger had said to him at home plate during his standing ovation, Weaver said, "He told me, 'Enjoy it. Enjoy it.' And I did."

Perhaps more surprising to old Weaver hands was something he didn't do. He did not curse. Least, not so you'd notice it. Maybe it was just first-day good behavior, or a carryover from broadcast booth inhibitions. Nonetheless, nobody ever enjoyed cussing more, or did it better, than Weaver. Already Weaver's oldest Orioles acquaintances say they may have to get reoriented. General Manager Hank Peters, asked if he expected to have the same prickly relationship with Weaver that had been so difficult for him in '81 and '82, said, "You know, Earl may be different this time around. He's a man who always surprises you."

The notion of a crab without its shell returning to combat is unsettling. The Weaver of '85 looks a little pudgy, a good deal older in the throat and a lot less pugnacious. On the other hand, Weaver now has several new forms of protection that he always lacked.

"I enjoyed every moment of my retirement," he said, recounting days on roller coasters and Dodg'em cars with grandchildren as well as nearly a thousand straight nights at home with his wife—nights when he usually did the cooking, just as he always grows his own vegetables and collects recipes and loves to shop for bargains on meat. "Now I'm back. I'm gonna manage a ball club and I'm gonna enjoy that, too."

It is a rare man who knows in his heart that, anyday, he can leave his lifework behind without gnawing regrets and a sense of loss. It's rarer still to know that you have the means and the temperament for retirement.

Weaver is also armed with knowledge. Only in retirement—with the ovations and the tears and the farewells—did the crab learn how well he was liked. Under his shell, Weaver always wondered how he would be treated when he wasn't the boss, the star, the hot commodity. He found out. His players liked him better once he could let his hair down and say a kind word. Even in his experience as an ABC commentator, where he was fired from a job for the first time in his life (because he was too reasonable, too unemotional, too kind), Weaver learned that he was still accepted by the friends who mattered to him.

It's impossible to say how a slightly aged, slightly altered and somewhat less manic Weaver may fare. What the Orioles want from him is fire. "He needed a break," said Dempsey. "He takes it very seriously. The pressures of the game can get to you, like they may have gotten to Earl a little his last couple of years. Now he's fresh and full of energy."

The old Weaver, one good enough to have a Hall of Fame plaque locked up, depended on his claws for results.

"Earl has always intimidated young players. Hell, I was scared to come back into the dugout after making a mistake for four years," Rich Dauer once said. "But when you get over the grilling Earl gives you, you're a better player than you ever thought you'd be." Added Mike Flanagan, "You knew he'd be waiting for you on that top step asking you 'Why?' . . . When you play for Earl, you don't 'do what your heart tells you.' You better be thinking out there."

"Players have to admit to themselves that what they did was not right," said Weaver, who claims never to have studied a word of Freud. "Then there can be improvement."

How essential are sarcasm and distance to Weaver as educator and motivator? If he curbs his tongue, even a little, or shows his heart, even a bit, will Weaver become just another weak manager, another Nice Joe who'll have to walk the plank for a bunch of overpaid jocks who need a swift kick? Hourly.

What Weaver and his team may not realize is that a milder Weaver may develop compensating virtues. It's true that Weaver drove his teams to victory. But he also took, and demanded, such a central role that he never allowed leadership qualities to blossom in his players or coaches. He tended to be immune to suggestion and bullheaded on personnel moves until it was too late.

On the greatest stages, and for the highest stakes, Weaver's teams often failed—in the '69 Series, where they lost to the undermanned Miracle Mets, in the '71 and '79 seventh Series games against the Pirates and in the last stages of the '80 and '82 pennant races. Some believed it was because Weaver's intensity became tension and infected his team. Strange as it seems, both Hank Bauer and Altobelli each managed the Orioles to as many world titles as Weaver: one.

The old Weaver felt such complete responsibility, and such tense insecurity, that even his superstitions gave away his state of mind. For instance, he believed that "every time I fail to smoke a cigarette between innings, the other team will score."

Casey Stengel once said, "The trick is growing up without growing old." To Earl Weaver, who once lived as though the only bad taste that mattered was the bad taste of defeat, there's always been growing up left to do.

Tigers, they say, can't change their stripes. But, in Baltimore they know that crabs come in different kinds. Lots of folks like the soft-shells better.

RETIREMENT, AGAIN

BALTIMORE, September 9, 1986 — Only one storybook ending to a customer.

The last time Earl Weaver said goodbye, it was done right. In a full Memorial Stadium on the last day of a historic pennant race with tears in every eye, including Weaver's. This time, Weaver's goodbye comes out all wrong.

This week, he sat in the Baltimore Orioles' dugout appearing as cocky and comic as ever. You laughed, and it wasn't until you reread his words that you knew this was no laughing matter.

"I put every damn thing I had inside of me into it this year," said Weaver, whose team has lost more games than it has won for the first time since he managed at Fitzgerald in 1957. "What new things would there be to teach in spring training next year? I've done everything I know how to do this year. I don't think this team is going to get much better at the fundamentals of baseball . . . we didn't do too many silly things this year. Everything was good. Except the record. To tell the truth, we didn't have that many bad years from our key players . . . There's not a hell of a lot to correct here."

That is the worst news the Orioles could hear. Weaver did everything but come out and say it: the Orioles just are not a particularly special baseball team anymore. In his view, they don't have much immediate prospect of getting much better. If they can play close to their form and still be in sixth place, why should he stick around and suffer with them indefinitely?

"It's all there in black-and-white," he said. "You can't deny it. How many have we won the last three years [85, 83 and now on pace for 79]? Two, three, four games over .500. That's no good year."

Of rumors that he might quit as early as this week, Weaver said, "That's false . . . as of this minute." Might he retire again? "Yeah, there's a good chance." Would he fib and say he had not made up his mind to quit when, in fact, he already had? "That's what I'm tryin' not to do [i.e., lie]."

Then Weaver told a story about a minor leaguer who retired "while he was going down the first-base line. By the time he got to the bag he had his hat and shirt off and he just kept right on goin'. Never played another game. I also had a guy climb over the center-field fence and never come back."

Perhaps saddest of all this season has been the sight of Weaver's confusion at the cause of events and his disappointment in his own baseball judgment of players such as Storm Davis and Mike Young. He thought he had a contender and he worked harder than he ever did in 1981 or 1982—seasons that were not his best. Out of a pitching staff infected with faint hearts and hard heads, he nursed a decent team ERA. The only thing he could not do was bat for his hitters. And that sank Weaver's dreams. "I can't get away with .500, to tell the truth." Not good enough for him.

"What I love about Earl is that he just hates to lose. That's never changed," said pitcher Mike Boddicker, one of the few current Orioles still carved from the savvy, play-hurt mold that was once an Orioles' norm. "He's mellowed a little. He's not out there screaming at the umpires as much. But nobody can go on a rampage like him. I don't think you can blame this on Earl. We just don't have the same mixture of people—real students of the game—that we had in '83," added Boddicker. "Nothing against the guys now. But you just miss people like Bumbry, Lowenstein, Palmer and Singleton."

Most of all, the Orioles will miss someone named Weaver. He was their link to twenty-five years of tradition, their hope for a rebirth of intelligent, unselfish play. When he leaves, won't the Orioles be just another team with plenty of supremely rich but only semiproductive stars overseen by an impatient owner and a general manager whose autonomy is constantly undercut?

While Weaver was away, every Orioles defeat was accompanied by a chorus: "It wouldn't have happened if Earl were still here."

"They won't be able to say that anymore," said Weaver. "It has happened with Weaver."

The little manager sat in his dugout a moment more, and that somber realization seemed to sink in deeper. Quickly, without explanation, Weaver hopped up and disappeared down the tunnel toward the clubhouse. "See ya, gentlemen," he said.

Sometime, somewhere.

Dick Howser

July 21, 1986 — By the batting cage at the All-Star Game, I felt somebody poke me in the ribs with a bat handle.

"Sorry, Dick, am I in your way?" I asked All-Star manager Dick
Howser.

"Just wanna talk for a second."

I thought, "What's he mad about? Have I criticized his team?"

"What's the problem?" I asked.

"No problem," Howser said. "Just wanted to say hello. How's it goin'?"

We talked a couple of minutes about the pitchers on his World Series
champion Kansas City Royals who had gone sour, and his team's recent
eleven-game losing streak, which had given him what he thought was
weeks of tension headaches.

"See ya next week in Baltimore," said Howser.

Howser has always been full of surprises.

Nobody thought he could win a division flag with a team as bad as the '84 Royals, or a world title with a club as full of holes as the '85 Royals—but he did both. What manager ever did more with less in consecutive seasons? Nobody ever thought the quiet, modest, serious, inconspicuous Howser would become one of the most popular and respected men within the game—although he still ducked the public spotlight almost completely.

And most of all, nobody ever thought that Howser would wake up one day at age forty-nine with a brain tumor as big as a golf ball.

On the night of the All-Star Game, people started noticing that Howser was forgetting the names of players and seemed confused. "Guys were asking me, 'What's wrong with your manager? He looks awful,' " said George Brett. "I'd say, 'The way we're playing, with that eleven-game losing streak, I think he's holding up pretty well.' "

By Thursday, Howser was in the hospital. Friday the diagnosis was in.

Dick Howser didn't make the trip to Baltimore this week.

On Tuesday in Kansas City at 11 A.M., he will begin four hours of surgery to remove a five-centimeter tumor from the left front of his brain. Doctors say he has a 90 percent chance of surviving the surgery. They will not know for another day whether the tumor is benign or malignant.

Seldom has the sport been more saddened or more united in one emotion than it has been the last four days. One of our worst habits is that we often take the best for granted while seldom overlooking the worst. Suddenly it's as if everybody has realized how special and unique Howser is.

"It's going to be a long twenty-four hours for a lot of us tomorrow," said Brett on Monday night. "Dick wasn't popular because he tried to be. He didn't try. He was popular because he was a nice guy. He always laid all his cards on the table . . . Everybody knows he'll accept this battle. He needs more courage now than he's ever had before."

As irony would have it, the coach whom Howser defended against Steinbrenner in 1980, Mike Ferraro, is the interim Royals manager. As a further twist, Ferraro is not only one of Howser's closest friends, but almost the only man in the game who might understand what Howser is enduring. Ferraro overcame kidney cancer in 1983.

"Dick has always been a great inspiration to me. We were utility men sitting on the end of the Yankee bench in 1968. Throughout the seventies he helped me when I was managing in the minors. He was my example of how it should be done," said Ferraro Monday. "Now I hope I can be an inpiration to him when he thinks about how I licked cancer."

As a team, the Royals have had an almost uniform reaction to Howser's misfortune. First, of course, they are rooting and praying for him.

"Here I thought I had a problem with being out of the lineup [with a shoulder injury]. How trivial does that sound right now?" Brett asked. "All the little problems that you let eat at you in this game or in your life are back in perspective for a while now.

"Here we have a man who's a friend to all of us and nobody knows his fate. It makes me think about the ridiculous things that I let upset me sometimes. You're so mad and frustrated if you go 1 for 20, you can feel suicidal. Or I can. You ask yourself, 'Am I washed up? Am I too old to play this game?'

"At a time like this, you say, 'What does all that mean?'

"We just want Dick to come back so that when people look at him they think nothing ever happened. Just so he has a normal life. Whether he comes back to managing, that's another slice of cake. We hope so, but that's not what we're thinking about now."

General Manager John Schuerholz, who insisted that Howser go to the hospital after the manager couldn't remember familiar names, is fiercely optimistic.

"We've gotten so many calls from people who have had brain tumors removed and resumed normal life," he said. "A Kansas City doctor who's back practicing medicine. A Seattle Seahawk assistant coach who's back coaching. Even the official scorer here in Baltimore, Neal Eskridge, who just went through the same thing and may be back out here this week at the park for the first time . . .

"This is another very stark, straightforward reminder that life is precious. The things we take for granted we should enjoy and appreciate."

Since 1958 baseball has always tended to take Dick Howser a bit for granted. That won't happen again. For now, as a long and worrisome couple of days begin, let's just leave it with what people all around the world are thinking and hoping.

Dick, see you next trip in.

June 17, 1987 — Dick Howser's life was much too short. There is nothing he or we could do about that. The reputation and the memories he left behind as his sliver of baseball history are, however, just right. What was within his power he handled as well as anyone could ask. He will be recalled, and for a long time, as a man who proved the difference between book and cover, between show and substance. With Howser, what you saw was much less than what you finally got.

Howser could not have been given much less in the way of raw material. As they say, he wasn't tall, but he didn't have muscles either. Yet he played shortstop for eight years in the major leagues and hit .248, which, nowadays, probably would have made him a million bucks. Then it got him a coachship.

Scrubbed and brushed, he was boyish and agreeable; but he couldn't pull off handsome or even mildly impressive. His voice wasn't deep, his glare wouldn't have pierced cream cheese and, though he was natively smart, he wasn't brilliant or bookish. He waved home runners and hit fungoes for ten seasons before the New York Yankees promoted him to manager. A boy wonder he wasn't.

In his first season, his team won 103 games and almost made it to the World Series. Then Howser did something that will be remembered much longer. George Steinbrenner told Howser to fire coach Mike Ferraro, one of Howser's friends, as a scapegoat gesture after the play-offs.

Quietly Howser said, "No."

Steinbrenner screamed, "Yes."

Howser told Steinbrenner to take the most glamorous job in baseball, the job he had worked twenty-two years to get, and shove it. Fire my friend, fire me.

At a news conference, Steinbrenner tried to gloss over Howser's dismissal, saying Howser had asked to leave and had not been pushed. Howser, a man with no power in his game or personal wealth, silently refused to back up the owner's version. He had too much integrity to lie and too much grace to get into a public argument. Howser's defiant silence in public may have been Steinbrenner's worst humiliation. Step on Dick Howser and they'd have to get him off you with a wrench.

Within baseball, that incident answered all the questions anybody ever had about Howser. It was a dugout Profile in Courage. You couldn't buy him. You couldn't intimidate him. His loyalty was absolute. No prize baseball had to offer could make him lie or betray a friend.

In a world of large, gifted, ambitious and often belligerent men, Howser quickly became one of the few who was universally respected, admired and warmly liked. One out of three wouldn't be bad. How many others could claim to be all three?

Howser's most remarkable trait was that when he spoke, people absolutely believed every word. Not that his words were profound or different from those a hundred other managers had said. They weren't. What distinguished Howser was that he said only what he truly thought. In 1985 his Royals trailed California by 7½ games at the All-Star break, but beat the Angels by one game. Then, in the playoffs, they trailed a superior Toronto team, three games to one. Howser called a meeting and said, "I still feel like we can get this thing done."

As second baseman Frank White recalled, "That was about all he said. He didn't yell. But he really believed it. And then we believed it."

No team of mediocre gifts ever did so much against odds so great as those Royals. They beat Toronto, then fell behind the significantly better St. Louis Cardinals, 2–0 and 3–1. They of course came back to be world champions, winning six sudden-death postseason games.

The clearest memory from that World Series is of Howser. In Game Two he had left a struggling starter, Charlie Leibrandt, on the mound and Dan Quisenberry, the most effective relief pitcher of the decade, in the bullpen until too late. Leibrandt lost the game.

The next day in St. Louis, there was no game. Just questions. Thousands of them from hundreds of reporters who were convinced that Howser had blundered badly. The first several times Howser explained his decision, I still thought he was dead wrong. Then I noticed my watch. Wave after wave of reporters descended on Howser. Every twenty minutes the same questions would recur. For two hours Howser did not move. He knew he would be blasted in every paper, on every radio and TV broadcast from coast to coast. He wasn't going to change the second-guessers' minds.

And he didn't care.

"I did not feel good at 3 A.M.," said Dick Howser. "I didn't feel any better at 5 A.M. And when the morning finally came, the sun was not shining and I did not say, 'It's another day.'

"Very few people in this country don't know what happened last night," continued the manager of the Kansas City Royals.

"Everybody's got an opinion. But only mine counts . . . Everybody is second-guessing me . . . but, you know, that's probably the way it should be. That's a big part of why people pay to get in the park—to second-guess the manager."

So he stood and loaded his own quotes into all the guns aimed at him. The loss of a World Series was going to be laid at his small feet.

When they told Howser last July that he had a malignant brain tumor,

221

he told the Royals to hold his job, please, because he'd be back for spring training.

Some people may think that Dick Howser failed because he could not manage the Royals this year, because he could not beat cancer, because he died Wednesday. Some others think that the day he reported to camp, dozens of pounds underweight and his uniform hanging on him like a sheet, he won. He stood in his big floppy golf hat with all the fresh scars underneath and answered the questions. He reported for duty, shoulders back, proud of what was left of himself. Two days later he retired. Too hot. Too hard.

Howser's private tragedy is simply that he did not live long enough to suit the family he dearly loved. We can't touch that or help it. The public Howser is our province; that part of him got to fulfill most, if not all, of its destiny. In another twenty years of managing he probably would have won more pennants. But he could not have proved anything new about himself. All the best was already on display.

Born-Again Sparky

DETROIT, April 28, 1984—The last five years here in the Motor City have been extremely painful for Sparky Anderson. That's how long it's been since baseball's best motor mouth could turn his eight-cylinder turbo tongue up to maximum revs and say everything that came into his wily, witty, white-haired head.

Being in first place affects the Detroit Tigers' manager the way laughing gas hits a schoolmarm: he gets to giggling and blabbering and has so much fun that nobody can find the "off" switch. Or would want to.

This morning, fresh from a nineteen-inning, near-six-hour defeat, Anderson was a chipper skipper with a ball club that looks as if it's about a heartbeat away from greatness. "I got a carload of cannons"

223

is Anderson's typically enthusiastic and immodest appraisal of his team.

At the moment, Anderson's Tigers have a 17–2 record, a 10-game lead over the world champion Baltimore Orioles and a lease on what looks like a long summer of kicks. "I told this team down in Lakeland [Florida], 'Boys, you are good. What'll happen, I don't know, but you are *good*,' " said a beaming Anderson. "There's nothing like being the frontrunner [again] . . . I tell 'em, 'Be the team that people want to see. Be glad that all the TV people and the magazines and newspapers are all over us. That's what you should want.' "

That's what Sparky wants, and is ecstatic to have once more after his bitter firing in Cincinnati in 1978 and his five years of disappointment here—disappointment fueled each season by his own exaggerated predictions about his young players. This is the fellow who at the '75 and '76 World Series would yell at a hundred writers, "Hey, guys, where ya goin'? I'm not finished talkin' yet."

At last Anderson is back on center stage, where baseball needs one of its major folklore personalities. "Ain't it funny how the same managers always seem to be so lucky?" said Anderson today, a biography of his spiritual predecessor, Casey Stengel, conspicuously on his desk. "Yeah, Casey sure was lucky . . . Some people can stand in front of trees and don't even know it's a forest. Other people know what they're looking at . . . but they're [called] lucky."

When his Tigers finished fifth, fourth and fourth in his first three full seasons here, Anderson's stock tumbled. Maybe, it was whispered, anybody could have managed Johnny Bench, Joe Morgan, Pete Rose and Tony Perez to all those victories.

When Anderson predicted that Kirk Gibson would be the next Mickey Mantle, eyes rolled. When ol' Sparky nominated four different American League managers for manager of the year last season on his visits to each of those gentlemen's home cities, it seemed that Anderson's compulsion for gab might be getting the best of him.

"I was givin' 'em all good PR in their own towns," says Anderson sheepishly. "What's so bad about that?"

Now, at least, Anderson's cheery comparisons of his eighties Tigers and his seventies Reds don't sound so farfetched.

"What team *ever* has had the quality players up the middle that we have now?" asked Anderson. "Go back to the old Yankees, anybody you want, and tell me who was better than Lance Parrish [catcher], Lou Whitaker [second base], Alan Trammell [shortstop] and Chet Lemon [center field]."

Anderson can take special pride in these Tigers because all of the club's central players have either been acquired, or blossomed, during his years. Parrish, Trammell, Whitaker and the Tigers' Big Two pitchers—Jack Morris and Dan Petry—are in their sixth season of listening to Anderson's inspirational speeches about how they should be in Cooperstown someday.

Outfielders Lemon and Harry Herndon were acquired in trades with Anderson's blessing. Gibson still has Anderson's provisional seal of approval. Rookie Barbaro Garbey—the Cuban boat-lift exile who is batting .455—has been called "the next Roberto Clemente" by you know who.

These are Sparky's hand-picked men, make no mistake. In fact, he won't let you make that mistake. Maybe he inherited most of the Reds, but *this is his team.*

"The manager's main responsibility is to mold the team's image. After you've been in a town a few years, that team better remind people of you."

That molding process has not been easy, painless or without controversy. When Anderson took charge of the Tigers in midseason of 1979, he was shocked by what he saw. "There were chicken bones all over the clubhouse floor and clothes and towels. All over the floor. I said, 'What the hell is this? Food on the floor? I can't live like this,' " recalled Anderson, who laid down the law that his players would no longer act as if they were raised in a barn.

"We went on the road and they all had on running shoes and Levi's. I said, 'This is Sunday. On Tuesday I better see everybody in slacks, shirt and jacket.' Mark Fidrych said, 'I don't even own one [a jacket],' I said, 'You do now.'

"They were laughing after a defeat. I told them, 'You are frauds.' I told them, 'You don't know how great the fans of Detroit are to put up with you guys in fifth place. In Cincinnati, I got fired for second place and 92 wins.' "

Anderson said he stood in the middle of his clubhouse and pointed his finger around him. " 'I could trade any of you and I wouldn't be missing a thing . . . If it takes me every day, I will wheel and deal until I get people in here that I want to be around.' I told 'em, 'I gotta walk the streets around here and it's getting unsafe.' "

Perhaps the nicest irony surrounding those years of Anderson lectures and imprecations is the team that the manager used to illustrate everything that he wanted his club to be—the Baltimore Orioles, the bunch he now has to beat.

"You don't see the Orioles screaming or yelling or giving high fives. They just beat you and say, 'See you tomorrow.' They're not out to show you up. When you beat them, they don't even act like they noticed it happened. Ever since I got here I've told them, 'Watch the Baltimore club, act like them. If you're good and act like them, then you'll be *real good.*' "

In the past the Tigers have given the impression that, under pressure, they didn't feel like the equals of the 1981–82 Milwaukee Brewers or the 1982–83 Orioles. They've come dangerously close to getting a reputation as a team that, thanks to its mediocre third through fifth starters, has a habit of collapsing in the final two months.

Despite potential pitching headaches, the Tigers are well on the way to surrounding themselves with the sort of charmed aura that carries clubs to special seasons. The Orioles had it last year; this month the Tigers have generated those vibrations with nearly every act.

On opening day, Morris won the first of five consecutive victories. In his next start, Morris pitched a no-hitter—the first by a Tiger since 1958.

The Tigers' first major free agent, Darrell Evans, announced himself with an Opening Day home run in Minnesota, then homered with his first swing in his first at bat in the Tigers' home opener.

When the Tigers met Chicago's LaMarr Hoyt—a pitcher with a fifteen-game winning streak—they greeted him with a leadoff homer. In Boston's home opener the Tigers scored eight runs before the poor Red Sox got to bat.

These days, Anderson is working on a book called *The Puzzle of Champions.* He thinks he's just about completed this Tiger jigsaw. "You wait for these kind of teams; it's like a dream," he bubbled. Asked what pieces his team lacks, he said quickly and candidly, "Three left-handed pitchers."

True, Anderson's Tigers may lack those two starters and a top-quality left-handed reliever. Come September, that hole in the puzzle may even set him up for another of his great-expectations falls.

But, for the moment, the baseball world can't wait to hear what George Anderson has to say next. "If you get up in the morning and you don't see yourself in the mirror, then you ain't there," he said today. "But if you do see yourself, then you're the greatest thing God ever made."

Welcome back, Sparky. Casey couldn't have said it better.

AFTER

LAKELAND, Florida, March 16, 1985 — "If Pete Rose can catch Ty Cobb in hits, then I can pass John McGraw in wins. If my health holds up, I'll get him about the year 2000," said Sparky Anderson, Detroit Tiger manager, shoulders back, pipe puffing.

Maybe the Soviets aren't thinking big enough. Maybe their agriculture keeps stinking out the joint because it's hung up on Five-Year Plans. Maybe the U.S.S.R. should hire Anderson as manager. Here's a man with a Fifteen-Year Plan.

Most folks sneak up on a goal, pretend it's not there till the thing's so close to hand they can't mess it up. Not Pete. Not Sparky. Ten years ago Rose told the world that Cobb's ghost better stop resting so easy 'cause 4,193 looked like a nice round number to him.

Now we can all circle 2000 A.D. on our calendars.

"I've got 1,342 [victories] now. McGraw had 2,840," said Anderson, smoking a huge pipe worthy of Sherlock Holmes. "I'm fifty-one. I have the lowest blood pressure on the team . . . The doctors say I have a perfect heart. I don't drink. I know how to get mad. My wife's a good listener. I'm about 70 percent deaf in my right ear . . . but otherwise they say I ought to last awhile.

"I'll get him."

Now, you might say that Anderson, caught up in the bliss of being the first manager to win a World Series in both leagues, has overlooked something. Or rather, someone.

The Baseball Encyclopedia says Cornelius McGillicuddy, Connie Mack to us, had 3,776 victories in 53 seasons. So, you might think, if Anderson leaves his body to science and the Tigers prop him in the dugout and say, "Ol' Spark sure has gotten quiet the last few years," he might have a shot at Mack's record.

Fear not, Anderson has this one finessed (to his satisfaction). "I don't really think Mack was a manager a lot of those years." The records committee won't buy that one, but it probably is true Mack wasn't calling every hit-and-run in 1950 when he was eighty-eight years old.

Everybody knows there's enough hot air in Sparky Anderson to stop an Ice Age in its tracks. Once Sparky makes up his mind, he never changes it. Unless somebody new enters the room.

Despite the cheerful waywardness of Anderson's monologues, there truly is a new Sparky on display this spring. Can this be the same man who, last October, looked haggard and ill in his moment of greatness?

When Anderson, whose father had died just months before, said he would retire after 1986, there were no jokes. Had the rest of Anderson finally caught up with his prematurely white hair?

Now, he says, "I feel like a newborn human being. Mentally and physically, this is the best I've ever felt. And it's only happened in the last few weeks since I came to camp."

What's happened?

The Tigers tease that Kirk Gibson knocked some sense into their manager's head. During a celebration last fall, the hyper Gibson conked Anderson so hard with a champagne bottle that blood ran down his head and he needed stitches. At a winter banquet the team presented Anderson with a Tiger-blue football helmet, inscribed, "In case we win again next year and Gibby's still around."

That blow didn't alter Anderson. But time did. People change. Sometimes outside, sometimes inside, sometimes both. They change so much that because we like comfort and familiarity, we often don't admit it. One of baseball's unsettling sources of power, one reason we follow its sagas for decades, is that we get to observe, safe in our seats, the way men change under pressure.

Few have metamorphosed as much as Anderson, who, in fifteen years as a manager, has gone from joyous and simple to embittered and driven and now, finally, to a point where he feels vindicated and almost reconciled.

You doubt it? Let baseball's reigning monologist, heir to Stengel and Weaver, tell his tale.

"I felt that when I was fired in Cincinnati [in 1978], it took all those accomplishments [four pennants] away from me. All I heard was how I had inherited a team of superstars and was just a 'push-button manager.'

"Now I have [the accomplishments] back. Was I bitter? Yeah. Well, I just say I didn't get bitter, I got better.

"I told my son, 'I'm going to show you how to turn defeat into victory.'

"The best thing about last winter on the banquet circuit was that I never heard one time that I was the manager of Cincinnati. I was always the manager of Detroit. That tie [with the Reds] was finally broken . . .

"It was a long [six-year] strain [in Detroit], though. I told 'em when I came I'd build a world champion in five [full] seasons, and I did it in five.

"That was the most luck I ever had in my life, like pullin' it outta heaven, 'cause if you say something and don't do it, they *will* remind you . . .

"By the end of last year I was tired, totally wore out. That's why my wife and I had long talks all winter . . . We're all confused about what we want to do [in life] . . .

"I decided I don't think you have to 'burn out.' It's just that last year I was so emotional, so wrapped up. My wife and I'd take walks in the morning and I'd tell her, 'We started off 35–5. I'll never have another chance like this. And if we blow it, I'll never live it down.'

"I put everything on my own back, even though it didn't have to be there. Losing, or the thought of losing, will never affect me like that again. I'll be laid-back now forever. Just watch. I'll never burn out. I don't have to prove anything anymore. They can say, 'He managed bad in '85.' But nobody can ever again say that I can't manage . . .

"I didn't know what an obsession it had become with me until a couple of weeks ago when I got down here. It lingered in me for three months in wintertime. I went to every banquet and I didn't have time to sit down and let it go.

"I'll never do that again, either. You burn out when you forget the big picture, take yourself too seriously. The game goes on without anybody. Babe Ruth's in a graveyard in Baltimore and we're still playin' today, aren't we.

"I'm learning to say no to people. We never took vacations, but the next five winters we're taking thirty days to go to Maui, the Greek islands, Australia, Rome, Jerusalem. I'll be perfect the rest of my life now . . . What you see here now is the final thing . . .

"I told the team, 'People will tell you that you've gotta repeat, you gotta do this and that. You don't gotta do nothin'. Be in the best shape you can be. Play with your hearts all season. That's all you gotta do. If that's fifth place, it's fifth. If we win again, that'll be wonderful."

As Anderson has been speaking, he's been sitting in his stark office here decorated only by a vast, frightening mural-size photo of an old and sinister Ty Cobb glaring out from behind sunglasses.

How odd to juxtapose the outwardly cherubic Anderson with this tribute to baseball's most driven, tormented and hated personality. Now, his day of vindication won, perhaps Anderson can turn Cobb's hard face to the wall and begin his long, laid-back pursuit of John McGraw.

Inside the Inside

All in the Stance

May 12, 1985 — For years, Rick Dempsey's wife, Joanni, has known better than to sit up quickly in bed in the middle of the night if she hears a swishing sound above her head. It's just her husband, Louisville Slugger in hand, continuing his eternal quest for the perfect batting stance.

Like almost everyone who's ever been infatuated with playing the game, Dempsey is convinced that his .239 career batting average has nothing to do with those cursed pitchers. If he could just comfortable at the plate, really feel relaxed and yet concentrate . . . If he just felt that he had all of home plate covered, that he could wait long enough to see what the pitch was, yet still be quick enough to smash it . . .

If he could just find the right way to crouch, then coil, then, finally, pull the trigger perfectly so his hips would clear and the bat would slash across the plate, delivering effortless power to the exact point his mind's eye had imagined . . .

Yes, it's all in the stance. Dempsey knows it. Don't we all?

For a ballplayer the search for a batting stance is a kind of search for athletic identity. Is anything in sports so undeniably a signature as the Stance?

Yeats has that haunting line "How can we know the dancer from the dance?" It's true in baseball, too. Once a man does something from childhood on, stands in front of countless mirrors, watches his shadow in the dust, even stands above his own bed in the dark, that thing becomes one with him.

When you must stand before thousands, perhaps millions, of eyes and perform, the way you stand—the tilt of your head, the cock of a wrist—is no accident but, rather, a kind of animal body language.

Ted Williams was clinical, almost dispassionate, his stance drained of quirks until only a sort of arrogant majesty remained. His passion for distinction so overrode his other traits that he was able to burn away the personal and leave only the coldly artistic.

To swing at a bad pitch, even if it might win a pennant, was a violation—in a broad sense—of his stance toward the world. On bad teams or good, isolated in a lineup of clowns or surrounded by Pesky, Doerr and Stephens, Williams still had to be dealt with on his own terms.

"Ted's stance was a thing of beauty," says California manager Gene Mauch. "He was so balanced, so commanding. And he changed on every pitch, depending on the count and the situation. When he wanted power, he got his feet closer together, took a longer stride. When he had two strikes, he'd choke up an inch on the bat and widen his stance so he could wait a split second longer to decide."

Once, in the 1946 All-Star Game, Williams even invented a stance for a new pitch—Rip Sewell's blooper. Williams ran up in the box so he could generate enough power to hit the pitch over the wall. Nobody else ever did it.

Just as a politician with style can lead or mislead millions simply by the conviction in his voice and the gesture of a hand, so a great hitter can give false clues to a whole generation.

"No one ever ruined as many hitters as Joe DiMaggio," continues Mauch. "He *looked* so wonderful with his wide stance and his hands high that, for years, we all thought you had to hold your hands that way. We couldn't imagine Joe's way was only his way, not the right way."

Like a golfer's tempo, a hitter's stance runs so close to the grain of his personality that the two must coincide for him to perform at his best.

Henry Aaron's inner calm, his desire to blend with his surroundings until it was time to strike, was reflected in his motionless, almost camouflaged stance. Willie Mays, left index finger off the bat, never really seemed to have a stance until the pitch was thrown. He was a creature of reaction and he hit that way, too. Mays seemed to scramble in the box, stride into one pitch, then open up on the next. Even when a home run left his bat, it sometimes seemed Mays had to regain his balance before he could sprint to first base.

When we see films of Babe Ruth and hear of his legendary excesses, can we imagine him having any different stance? Feet together so that he could stride his whole 250 pounds at the ball in one great lunge that would produce either a 500-foot blast or a whiff that would force the man into the ground. Could Ruth have gripped the bat anywhere but on the end—no one ever had before—or resist using a bigger club (48 ounces) than any man before or since? No, no more than he could have stopped eating those hot dogs and drinking those beers.

The closer you get to the game, pairing images from the batter's box with the human faces that match them, the more undeniable it becomes that a man's batting stance may give you a more honest reading of him than his face.

Frank Robinson stood on top of the plate in a posture of perpetual territorial defiance. Meet him off the field and he'll still crowd the plate on you.

Dave Winfield thinks mighty well of himself, likes to spread himself out, take up all the space that his six-foot-six frame permits. Naturally, he's the only man who's in danger of obliterating both the front and back lines of the batter's box.

His Yankee teammate Rickey Henderson loves to irritate people. He's the kid who snatches your glove, runs away and taunts you to chase him. In the box he has such an exaggerated crouch that pitchers are tempted to throw at *him* instead of the plate. Henderson wouldn't mind. Then he could steal second, and third, too.

Few hitters have been more of a chameleon than Carl Yastrzemski, who had a half-dozen barely similar incarnations. Not only did he hold his hands a foot above his head at one stage, but for a whole year he laid the bat forward (has anyone else ever tried *that?*) as though pointing the barrel at the left-field foul pole. Yaz's transformations weren't cosmetic. He remade himself from a fastball hitter into a breaking ball scourge late in his career. He also had high- and low-ball periods.

Interestingly, Yaz may also have done as much growing and changing as a person during his career as any player. He arrived in Boston remote, selfish and narrow in perspective; he left twenty-two years later communicative, unselfish and broad.

While Yastrzemski paid attention to his stances, he sometimes forgot to watch his mouth. "Pitchers loved to watch Yaz's stances and guess with him," recalls ex-Yankee pitcher Mel Stottlemyre, now a New York Mets coach. "I didn't. I read his lips."

"Yaz talked to himself silently at the plate. If I saw his lips saying, 'Be quick, be quick,' I'd throw him a change-up. If he was saying, 'Stay back, weight back,' I'd throw a fastball."

Of all hitters, none was more distinctive than Stan Musial, who almost turned his back on the pitcher, showing that no. 6 to his foe. Musial was always thought to be a quiet man whose stance seemed too stylish for him; meet him now in silvery old age and he can match clothes with anybody. It just took the Man a while to get his off-field game down.

Often cited as a player who hit and lived oppositely was Lee May. Off the field, he seemed utterly phlegmatic. At the plate, he waggled the bat constantly above his head as though about to have an adrenaline fit. May's silent treatment was an act, a defense mechanism. In the safety of the clubhouse, when he didn't think reporters were in sight, he immediately went into a jag of tall tales and high-pitched laughter.

When modern players talk about stances, they focus on the good, the bad and the ugly. Two ideal models come up often: Steve Garvey and Pete Rose.

Of all current players, Garvey seems to have most self-consciously carved a stance that is a perfect mixture of defensive inviolateness and the potential for attack. His whole posture says, "I've got every inch of this plate covered. You have nowhere left to throw it."

Garvey measures his distance from the plate, the relative position of his feet, and, basically, never changes. He always knows exactly where he is. What else would you expect from the Senator, who also must know his conservative bearings absolutely in politics and morals? His stance is uptight, yet admirable—a mirror of the man. "His weakness is the fastball on his fists," says catcher Bob Boone, "but he's so strong that he muscles that pitch over the shortstop's head time after time, even if you break his bat."

Rose's stance is as combative as his heart. He crouches and glares.

No one, it's said, can hit so many types of pitches in so many locations so hard. Rose has grooved his swing by monomaniacal practice to the point where he sees a pitch, identifies it, then applies the meat of the bat to that spot.

Says one catcher, "Pete's only weakness in his prime might have been the fastball down the middle. Since nobody ever tries to throw that pitch, he didn't bother to learn how to hit it. We got him out for a while throwing it down the pipe. Of course, he learned."

Rose's screwing his helmet onto his head, as though it were a grapefruit, is, in a sense, part of his stance, too, because it brings personality to bear on the battle with the pitcher. He's advertising his determination just as Thurman Munson's batting glove fidgets and neck twitches held menace.

As Reggie Jackson says, "How you walk *to* the plate can be important. You can tell which hitters own which pitchers just by how they go up there. In a game situation, I might go into that act even if I don't hit that pitcher too well. Hey, maybe he doesn't remember."

Tiny Joe Morgan's "chicken wing" move—flapping his elbow against his side—always looked like a little man's way of spurring himself on beyond the normal limits of his ability. That "wing" made Morgan look as threatening to a pitcher as a rattlesnake shaking its tail.

Perhaps the most exotic notion of the relationship between personality and stance belongs to Roy Smalley, Jr., son of the former National League shortstop, nephew of Mauch and maybe the best-read player in the game. Smalley is a switch-hitter who points out that the left half of the brain, which is more analytical, controls the right side of the body. And the right half of the brain, which is more intuitive and poetic, controls the left side.

"So I have different stances," says Smalley. "When I'm up righty, I'm more mechanical and precise. Left-handed, I improvise and guess more often." The '85 *Elias Baseball Analyst*, the game's stat bible, says, "Smalley's dominant switch-hitting side has alternated every year of his career." Strike up the "Twilight Zone" music and call Dr. Freud.

The lore of stances is almost endless, since no two are identical. In fact, perhaps only one successful team—the late-seventies Kansas City Royals—ever had what might be called a "team" stance. At one point, coach Charley Lau had eight hitters using his theories. All used variations of the stance that George Brett continues to make famous: fairly narrow, closed stance; stand far off the plate and stride in toward it; start with weight shifted to the back foot as the pitcher winds up, bat held so flat it's almost parallel to the ground.

Lau and Rod Carew may be the two major recent contributors to stance theories. Even a slugger like Mike Schmidt has bought the elaborate Lau notion that the baseball swing is just the golf swing in another plane.

Carew's contribution is the concept of multiple stances to combat different pitchers. Sir Rodney, who owns seven silver bats, holds the bat in his fingertips like a baton and has, he says, six positions for his feet. Cecil Cooper and Eddie Murray are his disciples. Each can inside-out one pitch to the opposite field, then change stances and pull the next pitch out of the park. Murray claims to have five stances—three lefty and two righty—plus a couple of others that are still in the stage of batting practice research and development.

"I want my hands to be quick and I want to see the ball well," says Murray. "If I don't see the ball well against a [certain] pitcher, I'll change stances. That changes my head position. Can't hurt . . . Why be stubborn?"

Few pastimes intrigue major league ballplayers more than mimicking others' stances. A player like Derrel Thomas can imitate the whole league.

Among the bizarre favorites are John Wockenfuss, Mike Fischlin and Mike Hargrove. Not since the days of Sammy White in the fifties has baseball seen as weird a stance as Wockenfuss's. White laid the bat back so far it looked as if he were trying to stab the catcher. Wock's trick is to screw his front foot around so far that it's actually pointing back at the catcher. "Helps me keep my front shoulder closed," he claims. Also, Wockenfuss "flutes" the bat handle with his fingertips constantly.

"How can you pitch to somebody who looks like that?" says Mike Flanagan of the Orioles. "He kills me. I start looking at his feet or his fingers and I throw the ball right down the middle."

Mauch says, "I hate to use Wockenfuss's name in the same sentence with Lou Gehrig's, but Gehrig used to 'flute' the bat handle that way, too."

A journeyman like Fischlin—what's he got to lose?—thinks nothing of batting with his hands so low that he looks as if he's trying to scratch his ankle with the knob. However, other players don't become All-Stars until they *stop* changing stances.

Dwight Evans had eight mediocre years until Boston coach Walt Hriniak got hold of him in '81 and told him, "Stop changing your stance every time you have a little slump. Stick to one method." Evans, with only himself, not his stance, to blame, became a star.

Most opponents wish Hargrove would get into *any* stance. Not since

Vic Power whirled his bat like a propellor in the fifties has anybody made such a show out of getting in position. One frigid night in Baltimore, Hargrove was adjusting his glove and helmet, measuring the plate, holding his hand up for "time" as the Orioles screamed, "Get in the box and hit." Finally Dempsey found a cure. One of his throws back to the mound "slipped" and drilled Hargrove right in the ear.

Catchers are always the stance experts. Nothing tells so much about a hitter's thinking as his feet. Boone calls stance study "a big part of my program. I couldn't tell you exactly how everyone in the league hits, but a bell goes off in my head if they've *changed*. I'll say, '[Steve] Balboni's different. What's he doing? Do we need a new book?' "

Some pitchers don't need a brainy catcher. "I can tell a hitter's weaknesses the first time I ever see him," says Gaylord Perry. "If he carries the bat high and wraps it back around his neck, well, then you know he can't hit the fastball in on his hands. It takes him too long to get the bat started and clear his hips out of the way.

"And if the hitter holds the bat low or lays it out away from him, then he can't hit the outside pitch with authority, especially the breaking ball. You can get him to pull the trigger too soon."

What if a hitter changes stances in mid-pitch? Do you drill him?

"I hope so," said Perry.

Stance reading has reached such a level that Flanagan says, "Now the hitters try to set you up. Chet Lemon will move way up in the box like he's looking for a curve so that you'll throw him a fastball.

"The worst guy is Al Cowens. He's got a thousand stances. I finally figured it out. He's looking for a fastball in *all* of them."

Some hitters even have a bunting stance. "Whenever Pepe Frias wanted to bunt for a hit," says Baltimore coach Ray Miller, "he'd stand in the back of the box and get a running start charging toward the pitch.

"So as soon as we saw his foot hit that back line, we'd throw a fastball up and in and he'd almost kill himself trying to flip backward out of the way. He looked like Charlie Brown when he gets undressed by that line drive in the comic strip.

"Pepe'd get back in the box, shake his head and ask Dempsey, 'How you guys *know*?' "

It is a pleasure to report that, with stances, it's never too late to find the right one, as Joanni Dempsey knows. It took fifteen years of married life, but her husband, Rick, *finally* found the right stance recently.

Let's see. Feet wider apart. Hands back and lower. Chin on the left shoulder. And swing as hard as you can.

What happens? Why, the ball goes over the fence, dummy.

Since his discovery, Dempsey has a dozen homers—five times his previous career rate.

At last Mrs. Dempsey can sit up in bed anytime she wants.

At least until Rick hits a slump.

One if by Fastball

August 27, 1987 — In his prime, Sandy Koufax found one hitter almost impossible to retire. Koufax and catcher Jeff Torborg held many confabs discussing selection of pitches to this nefarious fellow, who once hit two home runs in a game and built a .400 average against the Dodger southpaw. "We tried everything. Curves and fastballs. In, out, up, down," recalled Torborg, now a New York Yankees coach. "Nothing worked. Bob Uecker owned Sandy Koufax."

Uecker sits alone atop the bleachers in his beer commercials these days, while Koufax resides in the Hall of Fame, yet the greatest pitcher of the 1960s never figured out the humblest batter of his period. Welcome to baseball's central strategic mystery.

When we try to run baseball to earth, trace it to its lair, we seldom come closer to our game than when we talk about pitch selection. Interview major leaguers for years and you will always hit dead silence

241

at the same juncture. No, not on topics like a million-dollar contract or drug use or who hates whom in the clubhouse. Just ask, "How do you pitch this guy?" and suddenly you'll get a double-talk cover story that would do the CIA proud.

Pitch selection is Top Secret Classified Material. It's simply too important to discuss, at least in the active tense. What you throw and why and when—or, from a hitter's point of view, what you expect and when—is at the center of the daily test. Only the past tense evokes answers. Ask about players who have retired and the anecdotes and the laughter pour out.

"After he retired, I asked Hank Aaron what he looked for at bat— if there was any pattern to his thinking at all," said New York Mets manager Davey Johnson. "He said, 'I looked for the same pitch my whole career. A breaking ball. All the time.' He could tell I didn't believe that was possible. Everybody looks for the fastball, then reacts to the curve. Aaron said, 'I never worried about the fastball. They couldn't throw it past me. None of 'em.'"

Inside the mind, that's where the secrets are in this game of timing and deceit, anticipation and disinformation. And not just the minds of the pitcher and hitter. "The catchers are the key," said Tim McCarver, the only catcher to play in four decades. "The first player I knew who understood that was Ron Santo. He'd say, 'I hit off the catchers. They're out there every day. Spot their patterns.'"

"I actually hate it when a team changes catchers in the middle of a series," said Bob Boone of the California Angels. "It messes me up [as a hitter]. You're in a constant state of flux anyway, making adjustments, then readjusting to what they're doing. That's the difference between the majors and minors. In the minors, you can get five or six guys in a lineup out the same way every time. In the big leagues, it's a necessity that you be able to handle all the pitches [at bat]—if you're looking for the right one.

"So just when you feel like you're thinking along with the other catcher, they go and change on you."

How can we decipher what a catcher thinks when he's behind the plate? Why, like as not, watch him when he's at the plate—hitting. "You'd be surprised how many catchers call for what they can't hit themselves," said first baseman Keith Hernandez of the Mets. That's just the way the mind works. "I wouldn't say who does that, but let's say that Bo Diaz and Jody Davis are two who don't."

A few catchers, however, can't get out of their minds the pitch a batter has just missed. "For years the story on [catcher] Andy Etchebarren was that if you swung and missed, all you had to do was wait, because Etch would call it again. And soon," said Johnson, a former teammate in Baltimore.

Even top catchers have trouble being analytical and free of predictability. Johnny Bench, the best of all, loved to call fastballs, especially with a swift runner on first, because he was vain about not allowing a steal. "I knew no. 1 [fastball] always went down when Garry Templeton was on first base," said Hernandez.

The code of the dugout dictates that all catchers and managers swear that pitchers, ultimately, call every pitch, or at least take responsibility for it. Just listen to the rap. "It's the pitcher's livelihood. It's his game. He pays for it," said Manager Johnson. "He has to believe in what he's throwing, so he has the final say. If he doesn't want to throw a certain pitch, he won't throw it well."

In 1986 the Mets' new and famous catcher Gary Carter had many pitch selection differences with star Dwight Gooden. Finally Johnson told Carter to swallow his great experience for the sake of Gooden's great talent. "I told Gary, 'Dwight is the one pitcher who can make the wrong pitch right. He can add or subtract a yard to his curveball. He can run the fastball right in on the fists. Let him do it his way.'" So Carter stopped insisting.

Despite that myth, it's simply not true that most pitches are called by pitchers. The manager, coaches and advance scouts help form the team's "book" on each hitter. The notion that pitcher and catcher can be on the same wavelength on 119 out of 120 pitches is nonesense.

Many pitchers prefer to concentrate on throwing, not thinking, so they're delighted to be led. Want proof? Think of any Jim Palmer game. Now, that's what a game called by the pitcher looks like: hill conferences, dozens of shake-offs and a pitcher turning to reposition fielders between pitches.

"Palmer had great control in and out," recalled Johnson. "He divided the plate in half as well as anyone." Choosing between high and low is easier—and allows more margin of error—than trying to hit the proper side of a plate that's only seventeen inches wide. "Jim always moved fielders because he was so confident which half of the plate he'd be working on."

For every veteran in charge of his own selections, there are entire staffs that look toward the bench, and the manager, on every pitch or, at least, on every important pitch. "Roger Craig [San Francisco Giants manager] calls the most pitches now," Hernandez said. "I've tried to pick up his signs. Not yet."

The most famous recent signal-calling manager was Billy Martin. One of his Oakland players, Wayne Gross, once noted that Martin called pitches until the situation grew desperate—i.e., tie score, bases loaded, none out, ninth inning. Then no credit was to be gained. "The catcher would look in the dugout and Billy'd be over by the water cooler, head down, getting a drink," recalled Gross. "You were on your own."

Just as certain catchers call what they couldn't hit, some managers have the same reputation. In particular, both Earl Weaver and Gene Mauch had their great pride as players squelched by the existence of one pitch: the curve. "Almost every Mauch staff is known for curves," said McCarver.

"All Earl understood about the curveball is that he couldn't hit one," said Palmer. "So that's what he wanted you to throw."

That led to many battles. One of Weaver's coaches, Ray Miller, stood firm with the big league majority that believes the fastball is, and always has been, the best pitch—the bedrock of most repertoires. In the face of Weaver's fetish, and the sore arms it engendered, Miller went so far as to research every pitch thrown by every twenty-game winner in Orioles history. To his glee, he discovered that every one had thrown at least 60 percent fastballs in every twenty-win season.

To this, Weaver replied that although fastballs are satisfactory in mundane situations, pitches that swerve are still the best choice in a crisis.

Would that the game were as simple as guessing fastball or curve. In an age of sliders, forkballs, screwballs, change-ups, scuffballs and spitters, the permutations are endless. Modern baseball has gotten so studious that batters expect to see new patterns each time they face a rival. "The advance scouts always see you, especially if you've just had a bad series," said Hernandez. "So the first game of a series becomes a feeling-out process. You might take more pitches, see what they're thinking."

When a vital pitch fails, the second guess arrives as sure as the morning sun. That's how confidence can get destroyed. "Veteran pitchers can save young catchers," said Torborg. "I got a reputation as a smart catcher because Don Drysdale never shook me off. I appreciated it."

Players watched for years to see if the great Bob Gibson, who terrified both foe and friend, would ever shake off the green McCarver. What was with this kid? One day Johnson asked Gibson, with McCarver present, if he'd ever shaken off a McCarver sign. McCarver's chest swelled until Gibson said, "Yeah, I always shook off one sign . . . the pitchout. Timmy couldn't throw out anybody."

McCarver's signal-calling rep got so inflated that Steve Carlton insisted that he be his personal catcher. Good enough for Hoot, good enough for me.

Some parts of pitch selection are a permanent paradox. How could Tommy Hutton kill Tom Seaver, or Mark Belanger hit Nolan Ryan so well that Weaver batted him leadoff in big games? Other aspects are an impromptu seat-of-the-pants art. "Every game is different," said Boone. "You don't know what stuff your pitcher'll have. I expect my pitcher to be perfect. I don't start with low expectations or fears. I make him prove to me which pitches aren't at their best that night."

First-inning strategy, with the pitcher on a new mound, is much debated. Do you start simply with lots of power pitching? Do you establish one effective pitch, especially a curve, then add others, one by one? Boone tends to go for the whole package immediately, but many don't. Is that part of the reason pitchers allow more runs in the first inning than any other?

Once a hurler feels confident of three or even four pitches, the middle innings can be masterfully quick and riveting. "Then," said Mike Flanagan of the Orioles, "it's like a pool game when you plan three or four pitches ahead. One thing sets up another."

In particular, a wise pitcher studies the hitter's reaction to the previous pitch. Clubhouse meetings are all very nice, but if a hitter has decided to "sit on" the change-up—that is, wait for it all night in hopes that he can get just one to hit out of the park—then you'd better spot it early.

Time for a quiz: If a right-handed hitter swings late on your fastball on the outside corner and fouls it over the first-base dugout, what do you do? There's only one right answer, folks. The man either has a slow bat or is looking for a curve. "It's an unwritten rule," said Johnson, "that you throw the fastball again, but farther inside. Then he has even less chance to get the bat head out over the plate."

While pitchers (and fans) tend to think in terms of types of pitches, some hitters think primarily of location. That can mystify an entire league. "Zone hitters can be tough," said Johnson. "Ted Williams was one. It was late in my career before I learned how much I liked the ball down and in." So, in his first National League season, Johnson looked for nothing else until he had two strikes—and hit 43 home runs after having had more than 10 only once in his whole career.

While hitters must decide whether to focus on location, velocity or spin, pitchers must decide whether to attack a hitter's weakness or emphasize their own strength.

"Seaver and Gibson pitched me entirely different," said Johnson, to illustrate the point. "Seaver, a power pitcher, went away from his own strength and threw me breaking balls in the World Series and kept the ball away—going to my weakness. Gibby, on the other hand, was determined to prove he could get everybody out inside, because then he could get you out anywhere. You were defenseless. He came right after me, and I was an awful good inside hitter."

A compromise position exists between these two theories that tries to take into consideration the style of both the pitcher and the hitter. Catfish Hunter epitomized it. "I only wanted to know one thing," said the new Hall of Fame inductee, who was gopherball prone: " 'Where is his power?' I'd stay away from that area, but pitch my own way in all the other parts of the plate."

False information can also play a vital part in this guesswork world. "If you're going to hide your real pattern, then you sometimes have to run the risk of setting up a false pattern," said McCarver. "Billy Williams was a devastating breaking ball hitter. But with two outs and nobody on, you might throw him two curves in a row. Now, you might get shown something; you might get buried. But if you got away with it, it made everything else work better."

By the same token, one out-of-character pitch can shape a whole game-long battle between a pitcher and a key hitter. Said McCarver, "If you'll throw that curve on 3–2 for a strike in the first inning, when it'd be easier just to go with the fastball and stay away from the aggravation [of a walk], you might put an oh for four on that guy's ledger. All day he's going to think you have complete confidence in your curveball, even if you really don't."

One pitch selection is perhaps the most controversial of all: the old-time knockdown. "With Drysdale, you'd just give a quick thumbs-up sign [like hitching a ride]," recalled Torborg. If the batter happened to see the gesture, Drysdale couldn't have cared less. "Nobody ever defended his own hitters like Drysdale. His rule was two for one: you flip one, he'd flip two; hit one, he'd hit two."

Torborg shook his head, thinking back to those simpler days when pitch selection was a tad less sophisticated. "Drysdale wouldn't just drill you," said Torborg. "While you were lying in the dirt, he'd come right in to home plate, stand over you, pick up the ball and walk back to the mound."

Amazing how almost any pitch will suffice, if the hitter truly wishes he were back home, say, mowing the lawn.

Balance of Terror

July 12, 1987 — Maybe the home run boom of 1985, '86, '87 is not caused just by rabbit balls or weighlifting batters or a generation of crumb-bum pitchers. Perhaps it's also part of baseball's oldest battle of wits: the war between pitchers and hitters to figure out better ways to play the game. Maybe, just maybe, what we're seeing is a period when hitters have gotten one big theoretical jump ahead.

Let's pose another possibility, too. Perhaps the concomitant eruption of beanballs and brawls is not a measure of bad temper and low character. Maybe it's basically an inevitable by-product of the same trends in pitching and hitting that have brought us so many home runs. Our argument takes a while. Conclusions come at the end.

Baseball has always been a sport of cycles. Candy Cummings came up with a curveball, so John McGraw figured out the hit-and-run. We'll see your thick-handled bat with a spitball and raise you a chaw of

247

slippery elm. Almost as soon as Babe Ruth learned to hold the bat down at the knob, Carl Hubbell perfected the screwball. So what if Ernie Banks proved you could hit the long ball by whipping a thirty-two-ounce bat? Jim Bunning was busy working on his slider. When we thought nothing could be more dastardly than a scuffball, hitters figured out how to cork their bats. The pitchers formed a "union," exchanging information about hitters across team lines. So batters decided to study films of their swings and collaborate on theories about technique.

What's up in the eighties? Why do so many hitters seem so confident these days, so sure what they're trying to do meshes nicely with the weaknesses of the generation of pitchers they're facing?

Over the last twenty years, baseball has seen more and more pitchers who live by the sinker and slider, rather than the fastball and curve. It takes a great arm, and a young one, to throw directly overhand at more than ninety miles an hour or make a ball drop a foot. On the other hand, a less gifted pitcher, or an aging one who has started to drop down to three-quarter arm, can master a pitch that snaps six inches sideways or drops a bit at the end. It's an easier trick.

Also, since the days of Juan Marichal and Bob Gibson, it's been gospel to preach that "the low-outside corner is the way to the Hall of Fame" and "keep the ball down."

The vogue of "the high hard one" and the glamour of "getting in his kitchen"—i.e., throwing fastballs up and in—has waned. That's not to say Nolan Ryan never existed. We're just talking about trends, not laws.

Gradually the knees and the outside corner became the target of most "quality" pitches. Anything up or in that got hit was dismissed as a mistake, while any homer off a low or outside pitch was excused as "a pitcher's pitch" that somehow ended up traveling four hundred feet. Pitchers begged umpires to give them low or outside strikes, so that's what they got. The strike above the belt or in on the belt disappeared. Even the American League's switch to inside chest protectors for umpires—allowing a better view of low pitches—tended to move the strike zone low and away, where pitchers thought they wanted it.

Another factor contributed to this infatuation with sinkers, sliders, "cut fastballs," low change-ups and (the latest craze) split-finger fastballs. Fewer and fewer pitchers could throw a true big league fastball.

"I watched the College World Series this year and saw one guy with an honest fastball," said Dave Righetti of the Yankees with disgust to Ron Guidry. "They all want to throw forkballs. Mike Loynd comes out of college—twenty-two years old [and six foot four]—and all he throws on 2–0 is curves. They've forgotten to work on the fastball."

"It's all changed. You just don't see the real strong arms anymore," agreed Guidry. "[Greg] Swindell [of Cleveland] is one of the few young guys who really lets it loose."

When a Roger Clemens, Dwight Gooden or Bret Saberhagen arrives with real 95 mph heat, he blows the league away. No wonder Ryan, in his dotage, still comes as a shock to hitters' systems. He's not what he was, but he's more than they've ever seen.

The fastball has gone the way of Little League and the aluminum bat. For years now kids have grown up playing in leagues rather than cooking up kids' games. "No wonder nobody can throw hard. Mom comes in the station wagon and the game's over. We played from sunup to sundown. You develop arm strength as a kid and you do it by throwing the ball hard a zillion times," said Yankees coach Stump Merrill.

At the high school and college level, the aluminum bat is ubiquitous. Try jamming a hitter who has a light, unbreakable stick in his hands. It just doesn't work the way it did for a century. Experience teaches developing pitchers not to challenge hitters up and in.

During all this time, have hitters been fast asleep? No way. "They've all been listening to [the late] Charley Lau and [Boston coach] Walt Hriniak," said Righetti. "They stand off the plate, look for the outside pitch and dive in. They drive the ball to all fields. Every good hitter now is a low-ball hitter."

"Look at the big young guys like Mark McGwire, Jose Canseco or George Bell," said Guidry. "They lift weights. They want the ball down or away so they can extend their arms and generate power. They don't care whether they hit it over the center-field fence or to the opposite field."

"The only way to get them out is with good fastballs above the belt or in, so you tie them up," said Righetti. "You used to see four or five guys in every lineup who turned on the ball to pull it or put their foot in the bucket. Now, almost nobody. Everybody charges the plate."

Yankee slugger Don Mattingly, listening to this conversation, agrees completely. "Almost every good pitcher these days works inside first or up and in. You go in to set up the pitch away," he said. "But there aren't many pitchers around who can do it."

Pitchers see the problem, at last. The pendulum has swung—at them. A world of Mike Schmidts and Dale Murphys, Andre Dawsons and Jesse Barfields couldn't care less about pulling every pitch or waiting for the "high hanger" to clobber. They lust after the low sinker or the slider away—as long as it's not perfectly placed. That's when they can really unlimber. Lau started off teaching the purity of line-drive singles, but his disciples, from George Brett to Dave Winfield, quickly learned how to elevate those liners a few degrees and start driving Jaguars and Porsches.

Nowadays the place to aim is inside or up and the place to miss is up and in. If a hitter has to slip a vertebra getting out of the way of a pitch that only misses the plate by six inches, whose fault is that, say the pitchers. What business does he have diving into the plate, taking away the outside corner—the pitcher's half of the plate. It's no accident that every team Lau coached had a sudden increase in hit batters and brawls. His theories reversed generations of baseball territoriality. A price had to be paid.

Now, however, almost every team is a Lau team. And baseball finds itself in a strange, exciting, home run–filled, yet distinctly dangerous and barely explored new place.

Cheaters Always Prosper

Baseball is the very symbol, the outward and visible expression of the drive and push and rush and struggle of the raging, tearing, booming nineteenth century.
—MARK TWAIN

August 6, 1987—One day after a rain delay had left the diamond muddy, players from another team noticed that the Philadelphia Phillies' third-base coach was, inning after inning, standing with one foot in a deep puddle of water. They also noticed that their pitchers were getting killed.

Why would a man deliberately stick his foot in a shoelace-deep puddle? Between innings the suspicious players dug around in the mud—and unearthed a block of wood with a buzzer button. Next they tore up the underground wire connected to the box to see where it led. To the center-field scoreboard.

251

There they found a Phillies player with binoculars, stealing signs, then relaying them to Cupid Childs, the coach, who could feel the tip-off signal in the sole of his wet foot.

This happened in 1899, as related in a book called *Pitching in a Pinch*, written by Christy Mathewson. As Heywood Broun put it, writing in the *New York World* in 1923, "The tradition of professional baseball always has been agreeably free of chivalry. The rule is 'Do anything you can get away with.' "

In many ways, that was the American rule of the nineteenth and early twentieth centuries, a time of cartels and robber barons, Wall Street skulduggery, Elmer Gantry charlatanism and big-stick foreign policy. Avarice and a will to power posed as philosophy behind names like Social Darwinism and Manifest Destiny.

What goes around comes around, they say. So perhaps it is only fitting that in a decade that has given us Ivan Boesky and Jim Bakker, we should also see a full-scale revival of cheating in baseball. Why shouldn't scuffballs and corked bats be rampant in an age that glorifies leveraged buyouts? Under our public pieties, the subtext of the eighties often seems to be "Do anything you can get away with."

Ballplayers are a cross section of society—followers of the national mood. And they've heard the message: Make the umps catch you red-handed. And always maintain plausible deniability.

Recently American League president Bobby Brown suspended forty-two-year-old Joe Niekro for ten days for defacing baseballs—the first such suspension in five years and only the fourth since spitballs and the like were outlawed back in the 1920s. Niekro claimed the emery board and sandpaper that came out of his uniform when the umpire told him to empty his pockets were just there to trim his fingernails. A plausible denial, right? It's tough to find a manicurist between innings at ten o'clock at night.

Everywhere you look these days it's scuff this and cork that, grease here and saliva there. The National League's 1986 Cy Young Award winner, Mike Scott, is almost universally assumed, within dugouts, to be a creation of illegal scuffed pitches, plus a new forkball. Rick Rhoden and Tommy John are reasons 1 and 1A for the Yankees' presence in a pennant race; if they don't abrade the horsehide, then maybe the whole thing is just a UFO scare and nobody cheats.

Ask pitching coaches and veteran pitchers to guess how many hurlers cheat, at least occasionally, and estimates almost always range between one third and one half. The difference is that scofflaw behavior no longer seems to carry much stigma. As Cal Ripken, Sr., has noted, pitchers now cheat on any count, not just on a vital two-strike pitch with men on base.

Hitters are just as brazen. After Howard Johnson was accused by St. Louis manager Whitey Herzog of corking his bat, the Mets third baseman tweaked the Cardinals by leaving one of his bats in the St. Louis clubhouse when he left town; the club was sarcastically plugged everywhere with corks. Very funny. "He's going to get bleeping drilled for this," said one Cardinal reliever.

Many fans feel considerable ambivalence about the sport's laissez-faire attitude toward the rule book. Something in almost all of us loves an outlaw, a rascal, if only his daring and style are sufficiently maintained. That's not to say that most of our nature approves—just a part. A few generations ago that passion for rapscallions was not so well hidden. America was half-proud of its desperadoes and gangsters, even as it printed wanted posters and organized manhunts. To run the little man out of business like old John D. Rockefeller or rouse the rabble like William Jennings Bryan or rejoice in war like the young Teddy Roosevelt was not inconsistent with being a national hero.

In our time, sports is one of the preserves within a civilized society where scofflaw emotions can feel at home and not be run entirely off the turf. We love to hear the story of Earl Weaver visiting a struggling Ross Grimsley at the mound and saying to the much suspected left-hander, "If you know how to cheat, start now."

Let an old-timer give us what might be called the pure professional view of cheating in baseball. "I'd always have [grease] in at least two places, in case the umpires would ask me to wipe off one. I never wanted to be caught out there without anything. It wouldn't be professional," wrote three-hundred-game winner Gaylord Perry in his book *Me and the Spitter.*

That is the old voice of nineteenth-century baseball, full of rush and push, boom and drive, an age of energy and can-do certainty, not of conscience and ambivalence. It charmed us then and still seduces us today. It is a familiar voice, telling us that, if we only see things properly, dead wrong can be rationalized as perfectly all right.

The voice of Joe Niekro. And Oliver North.

It's Cricket

LONDON, July 3, 1984 — England took a 342-run lead into the final inning today at Lord's Cricket Ground.

And lost.

Talk about a bad bullpen.

It's a good thing George Steinbrenner doesn't own England.

England hasn't had many days worse than this, inflicted at the hands of her children of the Empire, since the Battle of Yorktown.

This gray day at Lord's was going to be one of the brightest in English cricket annals, as the hosts had a chance to even this best-of-five-match test series at one each against the mighty West Indians, who have been the best in the world since the mid-1970s. Bookies had England an 8-to-1 favorite.

All the English needed today in their cricket equivalent of the World

Series was to get ten outs—that's one inning's worth in cricket—before the visitors from the West Indies got 342 runs.

By dusk the West Indies had scored 344 runs.

And made one out.

That's right. Three hundred and forty-four runs and one man out. And that out (called a wicket) was made on a base-running blunder. Think England could use Nolan Ryan?

The West Indians didn't even have to send up their Babe Ruth, a gentleman named Viv Richards. The Prince of Antigua stayed in the on-deck circle for six hours and never got to bat. Now, that's a long rally.

"This is the worst humiliation of an English test [i.e., national] team in history," pronounced Brian Scovell of the London *Daily Mail*, taking in 107 years of cricket at a swallow.

"Only once has a team scored more runs in the last inning to win. The Australians scored 404 in 1948, but that pales in comparison to this," said Scovell, one of England's senior cricket authorities. "England got three wickets against the Australians. Today, just one—which is as incredible as it sounds. And in '48, that English team was badly injured. This team is fit."

Fit to be tied.

"It's a bit of a blow, isn't it," said England's twenty-seven-year-old captain, David Gower, with amazing understatement, even for a Leicestershireman.

In almost every way, this day and this place and this particular match were a suitable introduction to a Yank at his first cricket match. I came with an open mind but a suspicion that I would despise the world's slowest team sport. After all, where else does it take five days and thirty hours of play to reach, in many cases, a tie?

Who ever heard of starting play at 11 A.M., knocking off for a forty-minute "luncheon interval" at 1 P.M., then continuing until a twenty-minute "tea break" at 3:40 P.M. before finally finishing at 6 P.M.? A test match is like watching a tripleheader for five days in a row.

However, instead of coming away a mocker, I now suspect it's lucky for me that I don't live in England. There's a cricket nut trapped somewhere deep inside me; stop me before I become addicted again.

Why wouldn't I get the bug? Cricket is, in many ways, baseball raised to the nth degree. Almost every basic tendency or theme of baseball is mirrored or exaggerated in cricket. In some cases, like the ludicrous duration of matches, this is *reductio ad absurdum*. In other ways, however,

I am titillated by the thought that cricket might be a *heightened* form of baseball.

First of all, cricket has an instant visual and aesthetic similarity to baseball's. Lord's, built in 1814, looks like an Old World version of Wrigley Field. At least eight styles of stadium and grandstand construction have been used over its two-century history, with the result that the joint looks like many different sections of ballpark bleacher welded together into one circle.

The total size of the field itself and the distance between the wickets (66 feet) are almost identical to those of baseball. The bowler and wicketkeeper are the battery mates of cricket. The nine other players resemble baseball's lonely fielders, each with an impossible area to cover.

If anything, cricket's bowling is even more complex than baseball's pitching, just as cricket's batting is a more encyclopedic sort of acquired skill than hitting a baseball. We may have fastballs, curves and such, but cricket has more variety of pitches because the ball can be curved in the air, then spun or redirected again as it bounces. You haven't lived till you see a leg break—googly bowler, the cricket equivalent of a screwballer.

Bowlers and batsmen spend their lives analyzing one another's weaknesses and psyching out one another, just as hitters and pitchers do. Cricket also has its dangerous dusters and brushbacks, called "bouncers" and "beamers."

While it's true cricketers have the enormous advantage of being able to bat the ball in any direction, including straight backward, and they also may decide which batted balls to run out and which to eschew, their task at the wicket is more various than a baseball batter's.

A great cricketer like W. G. Grace (1848–1915) could unfailingly swat balls that were bounced at his legs and behind him, as well as those "off-stump" offerings he could wallop cross-bat style, as with a baseball swing. A baseball hitter has, essentially, one swing, while a cricketer must be a stroke maker in the same sense that a tennis player must attack balls with many types of swing.

The cricket batsman has many edges, but he also must wield a bat in the forty-ounce range; Gordon Greenidge, a five-foot-eight bundle of muscle, had to bat (not to mention run from wicket to wicket) for nearly six hours today in his amazing 209-run performance.

Late in his sixth hour, Greenidge spun on a bouncer at his head and, seemingly with the ball out of his vision, blasted an enormous "six" on the fly over the distant boundary for the equivalent of a home run. If Joe Morgan had bailed out on a knockdown pitch and, in the process, hit the ball 400 feet over the center-field fence—on purpose—it would have had the same impact.

The parallels between cricket and baseball would fill a long monograph. Both sports have ridiculously intricate and arbitrary rules that appeal to the legalistic mind. Both have tomes full of statistics going back to the nineteenth century and legions of devoted recordmongers and figure filberts.

Crickets even has an almost identical equivalent of the baseball card. An 1896 tobacco card of wicketkeeper Quaife Walter of Warwickshire could easily be an American tobacco card of Cap Anson for all anyone could tell. Don't kid yourself that the United States had "baseball cards" first; Australia had cricket cards in 1880.

Even the heartstring appeals of the two sports—the vocabulary of praise their fans use—sound like echoes. Cricket buffs sound so much like baseball fans that you think you're listening to a Stateside recording.

"Cricket is a minor art form that has a sort of pastoral beauty about it," said Scovell. "The conflict between bowler and batsman has an intellectual dimension and overtones of individual and group psychology which appeal to an educated sort of fan. Cricket is a sort of theoretical drama that is full of changing strategy. A team's fortunes can change completely in a very short time.

"Like bullfighting, cricket is a sport which seems boring or pointless at first but which has level upon level of understanding built into it. The more you know about cricket, the more you like it."

Did I hear Red Smith murmuring, "Baseball is only dull to dull minds"?

To be sure, the contrasts between cricket and baseball also are vivid. Each game reflects the nineteenth-century atmosphere in which it came to its current form. Cricket, with its origins in medieval times, prides itself on snobbish, aristocratic traditions, just as baseball sings endless songs of praise to itself for its democratic tendencies.

There's one tricky question about cricket—a sticky wicket, as it were. With time, would the English game come to seem like a more subtle, more leisurely, more elegant game than baseball?

Or would cricket simply seem to have the same virtues as baseball but in such an exaggerated form that they almost became vices?

After one day at Lord's it just wouldn't be cricket to say.

The Flame of Fame

No More Ruths,
Only One Reggie

May 19, 1986 — Reggie Jackson turned forty Sunday. Let's watch him while we can. Watch him swing for the moon and wear his uniform too tight—top button open to let all those muscles breathe. Watch him boast and brawl and take the heat for being Mr. October, Buck Tater Man and the Straw That Stirs the Drink. We may not see his like again for quite a while.

That's not to say we won't see others who will hit 537 home runs. We will. What's becoming increasingly scarce, however, is the star athlete who revels in his celebrity and eats it up—even though it may eat him up.

The country that has always loved its brave and risky extroverts—men such as Babe Ruth and Dizzy Dean, Muhammad Ali and Joe Namath, Dr. J and Riggo—is in danger of breeding a generation of timid, self-protective and boring heroes.

We have watched what has happened to the Jacksons and Pete Roses, smart and gifted, in the last fifteen years. We've read the biographies by Kareem Abdul-Jabbar and even Steve Garvey. And we've felt from afar the warping, wounding effects of a big persona in a public life.

As a nation, we've built ever larger stages for our jocks, offered them millions, plus fame that refuses to quit. And they're saying, "No thanks. Do what you've done to Reggie and the rest of 'em to somebody else."

On Sunday in Baltimore, Eddie Murray of the Orioles, who may one day surpass most of Jackson's achievements, drove in seven runs and hit the fourteenth grand slam of his career. Only one man has more than eighteen slams: Lou Gehrig with twenty-three. After the game, instead of discussing his pursuit of the Iron Horse, instead of enjoying his eleven RBI in two games, instead of playing the hero in exchange for his new $13 million contract, Murray said, "I've got nothing to say." Pressed for a reason, he elaborated, "Because I don't choose to."

Reggie Jackson says that Eddie Murray is the best player in baseball. But he's no old-fashioned hero.

When the klieg lights shine, Murray puts Murray the Man far ahead of Murray the Myth. If that means that the Orioles lack a team leader—which they do—and if it means that the public is given little more than a performance conducted behind a deliberately crafted mask, then Murray couldn't care less.

Like many others of his generation, he's decided that it's all or nothing. Let the press and public in, as Jackson has, and they'll take up residence in every room of your emotional home, going through the laundry and the linen.

How can we blame Murray any more than we can criticize the influx of clean-livers such as Cal Ripken, Jr., and Dale Murphy, or the monosyllabic Wade Boggs and Don Mattingly, who pick their spots to utter a ten-word sentence? Why shouldn't Dwight Gooden live in a total media blackout, except for a few guarded minutes after he pitches? What good did celebrity ever do Mark Fidrych?

Guys such as Keith Hernandez, beer in one hand and cigarette in the other, or Dave Parker or Mike Schmidt have let their egos show—taken the leash off their personalities—and what did it get them? They get booed in their home park, as Schmidt did, or, when it's tale-telling time in court, they're the high-profile ones who take the bust.

Might it not be safer just to be a grouch like Jim Rice or a recluse like Steve Carlton?

Plenty feel that way. They see John McEnroe, battered into hibernation at twenty-six by the 400 blows of maturing in public, while Ivan Lendl—the prototype of the introverted but physically superior athlete—inherits the tennis kingdom.

Jackson's manager, Gene Mauch of the Angels, said, "I wouldn't be Reggie Jackson for all the money in the world . . . I can't begin to comprehend the life he's led. No one can. It's unimaginable . . . His entire life is public."

"I'd be me for all the money in the world," Jackson said last week, but he added, "It's tough. I find I've become bigger than my career, if that's possible . . . The expectations of people are a tremendous burden . . . The average person has absolutely no idea what I go through. No way."

Jackson talks about the dwindling desire of stars to be heroes as well. "It gets easier as you get older. People tend to remember the best. But it bothered me a long time. At one time or another, I've come across as everything—a good guy, a bastard, humble, an egomaniac. I got called an egomaniac a lot more than I liked. I know I'm fallible, flawed, but I think I'm a nice man.

"What I've been, through it all, is human." And that's what we're losing now.

Luckily, we still have exceptions—stars who don't fear what Jackson once called "the magnitude of being me." You can't tell Magic Johnson not to smile or the Refrigerator not to snack.

What we're left with is a dilemma. Everybody likes virtue, humility, strong character and wisdom. But in the meantime, what are we going to do for red meat? In an earlier age, Americans didn't mind if a man was a glutton for food or bathtub gin, didn't mind if he broke a few laws and taboos, just as long as he held the bat down on the knob and hit sixty home runs, just as long as he visited the kids in hospitals and smiled for the camera like a big fat lusty moonrise.

We let an athlete be a hero then and looked the other way when he wasn't. Now we never blink, we seldom forgive, we tell all. One standard fits all. And we wonder why the stage is getting kind of empty.

Just hypothetically, let's say that one night in a bar, Babe Ruth had it up to here with some fan badgering him for an autograph. And let's say the Babe grabs this guy, squeezes him till he's blue in the face, then casually drops him on the floor like a bag of flour.

Back then America would have had a good laugh. And the guy who ended up with a couple of stitches would have showed that scar off

263

proudly for the rest of his life and said, "The Babe sure laid one on me that night."

Now it's see you in court, Reg.

And Eddie Murray decides he'll take the Fifth after his grand slams. It's probably progress.

But sometimes you wonder.

Carlton and Sutton: Opposite Equals

June 28, 1986—Someday a little boy is going to look in the Baseball Encyclopedia and see that two men, born four months apart, played in the major leagues together more than twenty years and had *career* records almost as identical as could be imagined.

That little boy is going to think that Steve Carlton and Don Sutton probably had something in common. Boy, is that boy gonna be wrong.

At the moment Carlton has 318 wins and Sutton 301. But eventually that gap may diminish or be erased. Carlton has 10 fewer losses and an edge in career ERA: 3.09 to 3.20. Overall, Carlton had better hitters behind him, Sutton better relievers.

Both are forty-one and have pitched an almost identical number of innings (about 4,900) and allowed almost the same number of hits (about 4,300). Carlton actually has been slightly easier to hit and has walked more than 400 more men. But Carlton has struck out about 600 more and given up fewer home runs.

Sutton has 57 shutouts, Carlton 55. Both have pitched for 5 division and 4 pennant winners. Sutton is 6–4 in postseason, Carlton 6–6. Both have been nearly indestructible. That's about how close they are.

When else in baseball history have two men been so statistically similar, yet so utterly opposite as pitchers, public figures and people?

On the mound, the six-foot-five, 210-pound Carlton was a classic left-handed intimidator. As Clint Hurdle once said, "When you call a pitcher Lefty and everybody in both leagues knows who you mean, he must be pretty good." Carlton threw the three basic pitches of his era and used them in predictable patterns: high fastball, vicious slider down and in to righty hitters and a sweeping curveball. For left-handers, he was a nightmare—"like drinking coffee with a fork," said Willie Stargell.

Some righty hitters—particularly Johnny Bench, who owned him— gave Carlton fits because he was incredibly stubborn and predictable. (After all, he did lose 223 games.) Carlton believed his pitches complemented each other, one setting up the next; some foreshadowing shouldn't really help the poor hitter much. Carlton, obsessed with dominating and controlling every situation, wanted a battle plan in which he could believe absolutely, just as, in his martial arts training regimen, he wanted to feel he was a step beyond everyone else.

Where Carlton was smooth and graceful, with the best and most liquid pick-off move since Warren Spahn, Sutton seemed stiff, too erect, slightly herky-jerky and mechanical. Not pretty, barely memorable. Nothing about Sutton, from his six-one, 190-pound build to his fastball, which rarely broke 90 mph, was too impressive.

His curveball had more variety—of speeds and swerves—than raw quality. Most important, he could throw it for strikes behind in the count as well as any pitcher of his time. What Sutton's fastball lacked in heat it made up for in life—his ball ran and nicked corners. Naturally, he was sneaky, too, outfoxing everybody and constantly jamming power hitters. Nobody had more gall or staying power with bad stuff. Sutton battled.

Some players think Sutton cheated—and was proud of it. Nothing tickled him more than being accused of scuffing and defacing the ball. Thanks to who knows what hidden tools, he could throw a full-speed fastball that, a few feet from the plate, would suddenly acquire sinker or screwball properties of its own volition. When Sutton won his 300th game, a bitter rival player said that he'd scuffed so many balls (which

266

had to be thrown out of play) that every CYO team in town could have a new supply.

While Sutton was perhaps the most consistent pitcher in history from one year to the next, Carlton had spectacular highs and lows. For 21 straight years, Sutton never worked less than 207 innings (except in strike-shortened 1981, when he was on a 240 pace). Sutton also lost more than 15 games only once. By contrast, Carlton led the league in defeats twice.

As most fans know, Carlton was the only man to win four Cy Young Awards and had six 20-win seasons. This properly established him in the public mind as a giant. "Carlton's the best pitcher in the world," said Pete Rose, "unless the Russians have got one I haven't seen."

Sutton, however, won 20 only once. Because of the sacred qualities attributed to the arbitrary number 20, it took Sutton a whole career to be considered a Hall of Fame candidate. If, for some reason, baseball worshipped the number 17, then the tally would favor Carlton, 8–7. Or, if 15, then Carlton would lead, 12–11. Carlton was better, but by far less than usually supposed.

Both pitchers fed their contrasting images. Carlton was probably the most arrogant, serious and reclusive player of his time. By contrast, no star was more prone to being silly, self-deprecating, and available than the sardonic Sutton. Carlton wanted to bully; Sutton preferred to sneak up behind.

When Sutton obliterated most of Sandy Koufax's team records with the Dodgers, he said, "Comparing me with Koufax is like comparing Earl Scheib with Michelangelo."

For years, Sutton was the Dodgers' resident dissident in the Lasorda Era. "I'm leery of Tommy. I believe in God, not the Big Dodger in the Sky," Sutton said when Lasorda appeared.

Sutton took himself no more seriously than he took others. As he bounced from the Dodgers to the Astros to the Brewers to the A's to the Angels—usually helping somebody in a pennant race—he quipped, "I'm the most loyal player money can buy."

While Sutton played Columbo, Carlton created an opposite media mystique—one of utter silence. At times it has almost seemed as if Sutton deliberately counterpointed himself to Carlton—to his advantage. After an early knockout this year, Angels boss Gene Mauch told Sutton to go home early to change his luck. Sutton called the press box and asked, "Anyone have any questions before I leave?"

Now Carlton and Sutton's paths may finally diverge.

With his $1.1 million contract and 5–16 record over the last two seasons, Carlton seems done. Just as all admired his skill in his prime, so few will miss or mention him after he's gone.

Sutton somehow keeps functioning—14–12, 15–10 and 6–5 (so far) the last three years. Good enough to stay employed. He wants to play in '87 and beyond. Then, he matter-of-factly says, he intends to stay in the game in some visible capacity forever.

"Yes, it's just a job, and I don't get my self-worth from it," he says. "But . . . it is irreplaceable."

Only a few years ago Don Sutton would have had a hard time being included on a list of the ten greatest pitchers of his own era within his own league. Where he ranked in history would not have been thought a serious question.

At the moment, Sutton needs just 18 more victories to move into sixth place in wins among all the pitchers of the twentieth century. The top five are Walter Johnson, Christy Mathewson, Grover Cleveland Alexander, Warren Spahn and Eddie Plank.

Carlton may have been the quiet one, but it was Sutton who was sneaking up on us all along.

Goodenough

THE PHENOM

NEW YORK, June 8, 1985 — High in the upper deck of Shea Stadium, over near the left-field foul pole, Dennis Scalzitti is running toward the railing with twenty-seven huge placards, each bearing the letter *K*.

"I bring twenty-seven," says Scalzitti, twenty-three, dressed in Hawaiian shorts and T shirt, plus leis in the colors of the New York Mets, "because someday Dwight Gooden is going to strike out all twenty-seven men he faces."

What happens, Scalzitti is asked, if a game goes extra innings and Gooden strikes out *more* than twenty-seven?

"I got a Magic Marker," says Scalzitti. "I'll take off my shirt and write on that."

The first batter of the game steps up. Strike one. Strike two.

"Jeez, he's got two strikes already," wails Scalzitti as he rummages through his stack of signs. "The K Korner," one says. "The Heat Is On," reads another. "Goodenough" and "Dr. K" and "The Doctor Is In" say others.

The huge Mets crowd begins its roar, asking Gooden, as it will all night, for one more strike so it can erupt. Scalzitti and his two friends, also in ludicrous Hawaiian garb, fumble with their signs, actually dropping one K over the railing into the field level seats, where fans fight over it as though Gooden had touched it.

Strike three. One batter, and already the flame of fame has been fanned again.

Dwight Gooden walks slowly and softly, speaks in a deep, quiet voice and always allows a second of pause—like the coil at the top of his windup—between the moment an idea lights his eyes and when it escapes his mouth.

He still carries with him a trace of rookie circumspectness, although he is in his second season and well on his way to being the most exciting and important player in baseball.

If he isn't already.

Whenever Gooden pitches, every fan carries those twenty-seven K's somewhere in his mind, as does every hitter. National League batting champion Tony Gwynn of the San Diego Padres, told that Gooden was working on a change-up to go with his fastball and curve, said that if he ever got one, Gooden would pitch a game someday where "nobody touches the ball."

This is preposterous, but Gooden inspires the outrageous. At twenty, he is still all golden with expectation.

Last year, as an unknown teenager up from A ball, Gooden had the greatest strikeout season in baseball history—276 in 218 innings, or 11.39 per 9 innings. This year, he's better.

Do you really have to mention that, at his current pace, he'd win about 25 games and strike out more than 300 men this season? And that, barring injury, otherwise sane humans expect him to do the same for as far as the eye can see?

Once you've said that his fastball is one of the best in the game and that his curve may be the best, isn't it almost overkill to mention that it's really his control that is unique?

That he broke Sandy Koufax's NL record for strikeouts in consecutive starts (with 32) last year isn't nearly as unfathomable as the fact that he didn't walk anybody in either game. He didn't go to three balls on a hitter in one of them, with 92 strikes on 120 pitches.

It's taken a year for baseball to get a line on Gooden, but now he's beginning to seem comprehensible. Looked at from a certain perspective, it almost seems Gooden has had every circumstance of life that might contribute to him being what he is.

Born and raised in Tampa, Florida, he was exposed to half the teams in baseball as a child during spring training. He saw major leaguers, not as mythic figures glimpsed from the bleachers of some big league stadium, but up close as human-sized folks on the tacky practice diamonds of Florida.

Gooden's father, Dan, was a baseball fan of the first order and the game was what he shared with his son. By the time Dwight went to school, Al Kaline was his hero. Not only did Gooden grow up in a family that prized the game and in a Sunbelt play-year-around town that hosted the grapefruit leaguers, but Tampa also started one of America's most successful youth leagues a couple of years after Gooden was born.

After Tampa's race riots in 1967, the Belmont Heights Little League, which has made four appearances in the Little League World Series, was formed. By the time Gooden was ready for a hot kids' league, it was waiting for him. The same coach, Billy Reed, who was instrumental at that level also guided Gooden at high-powered Hillsborough High, where a dozen scouts might attend a game. Nowhere could Gooden have met better coaching, better competition or a more baseball-saturated town than in Tampa in the 1970s and '80s.

Besides a tough work-ethic father, Gooden also had a strong mother, Ella Mae, who worked in a nursing home, and plenty of female relatives who gave the family's only male child constant attention.

Solid family, top coach, big town but simple values, Sunbelt season, spring training site. Gooden was blessed but never spoiled. Although he always was the special child—the one who was going to make the family's mark—the rod was not spared.

Did his parents worry about him heading to big bad New York City last year? "Oh, never," Gooden says. "Well, maybe a little at first. But once they came up and saw it, where I was living, how I was set, how people were taking care of me, they just loved it."

All that crosses Gooden's mind is that his parents would worry about him eating well, having friends, being comfortable. The idea that he might get into mischief, cause himself harm—or that his family might think he would—does not even come onto his radar screen.

Just when we think this is the limit, just when everything about the six-foot-three, 198-pound Gooden seems too good to believe, we find out we haven't reached the bottom of the pot yet. Gooden isn't just composed, intense and dedicated, he isn't just swift and mechanically sound, he's also old. Old for his age.

"Playing in the majors is a lot more fun than I thought it would be," said Gooden recently.

The money? The crowds? The steaks?

"What I like most is there's always something you can learn. As long as you're listening. The older players know a lotta ways to get people out.

"Like last night I didn't have my outstanding curveball. They were waiting for the fastball and got two runs. But [coach] Mel Stottlemyre told me that I had to keep showing them the curve, even if it wasn't for strikes. If nobody'd told me, I'd have thrown fastballs all night," said Gooden, who didn't allow a run after the first inning.

Last year, 47 of 50 runners stole successfully on him. Now he has a better pick-off move. He was told that someday—about the year 2000—he'd need a change-up. He's got it now. His hitting was weak. "My only goal this year," he says, "is to hit .250." He's become a good and tricky bunter, and last week Gooden had three hits in one game off Los Angeles' Fernando Valenzuela.

Other pitchers with a fraction of Gooden's ability, fame and accomplishments fall in love with themselves, gaze into the mirror of their public image and forget the central goal of games: self-improvement.

The surest proof that Gooden's still on this track is that he's already gotten over the K's.

Scalzitti and his band don't know it yet, but Gooden has already seen through the chimera of strikeouts and even of no-hitters. It took Nolan Ryan a dozen years to have this insight, and Sudden Sam McDowell never got it.

"Wins keep you around longer than strikeouts," says Gooden, who wasn't much impressed with his 17–9 record last year and thinks his current 9–3 mark (and a 1.72 ERA) should get even better. "If you can get an out on one pitch, take it. Let the strikeouts come on the outstanding pitches. Winning is the big thing. If you throw a lot of pitches [trying for strikeouts], before you know it, your arm's gone."

This sounds so simple, so obvious. Haven't Jim Palmer and Tom

Seaver said it for years? Yet for a twenty-year-old to believe it and act on it makes veteran players rub their temples in disbelief. Just as others pronounce Gooden an immortal, he senses his mortality and guards himself against the dangers of believing yourself invincible.

What about the K Korner? What about that game for the ages when (who knows) maybe he'd pitch a perfect game and strike out twenty? How can he resist that addictive rush of adulation?

Gooden shrugs. "Strikeouts just give the fans something to do."

Scalzitti is standing on a seat, jumping up and down, waving his arms, leading tens of thousands of people in chants and cheers. Although he says, "No drugs, no liquor, natural high," he looks as if he might take off from that perilous railing and try to fly.

"I work for an IBM dealership, sellin' typewriters. But I'm hopin' for the movies. This could be my break," says Scalzitti, who wears a headband that says "Divine Wind Kamikaze." "If the Mets go to the World Series, everybody in the whole world will know who we are.

"On the way to the game tonight, we smashed into a taxi cab. But the driver knew who we were, didn't even take our insurance policy number, just said, 'Get goin'. You're late for the game.'"

Already Scalzitti, just by remote association with Gooden, has gotten his picture on national TV many times, has been on the cover of a book, has been interviewed by New York TV stations and has to "give away about ten of these K signs to fans after each game."

He autographs the K's.

Already a self-appointed group of K Korner surrogates, led by a couple of Yonkers brothers named John and Steve Wieder, has taken up residence by the left-field foul pole. They hope that one night Scalzitti and friends will ram a taxi too hard and then they'll be able to horn in on the Gooden act and have their sniff of fame.

"This whole experience freaks me out," says Scalzitti. "So outrageous."

When the K Korner crowd got to meet Gooden, he told them that he appreciated what they were doing to get the crowd behind him. "Dwight was shy," Scalzitti says, surprised that a hero would be almost ashamed at the thought of having worshippers. "We said, 'Just put us in your book.' And he did."

The fame that Scalzitti has tasted Gooden must eat for breakfast, lunch and dinner. "It's been pretty tough," says Gooden of his celebrity. "If you jump for everything, it will just take up all your time.

"I can't be too much to the press. I'm not really outspoken. That's not my nature. But it's easier for me now."

Around the edges, Gooden shows the strain. Since last winter, he's missed some appointments, skipped some scheduled interviews. In spring training, many were shocked when a player so supposedly phlegmatic was ejected from a game by umpire Bob Davidson.

To relieve pressure, the Mets have established that Gooden will talk to the press only after he pitches. This is the most protective and restricted possible arrangement, one usually reserved for players hot in pursuit of some great record.

Contrast Gooden and those K Korner fans, who actually are a few years older than he is. They'd do almost anything for fame. He seems to know it's not worth having. They seem out of control. He's in control. They wear garish outfits. He wears jeans. They can't stop talking and self-promoting. He seldom talks about himself.

Between innings, Gooden sits motionless in the Mets dugout. Nine K's already hang from the upper-deck rail. He can't stop the flow of strikeouts that he no longer cherishes. From the K Korner, Gooden is barely a speck. Through binoculars, he comes into focus. While his teammates bat in a tight game, he never changes expression.

Only one muscle moves. Gooden's foot is tapping constantly.

Who's in there? What manner of man is growing slowly inside the husk of a famous but barely formed kid?

What will he do? What will be done to him? Who will he finally be? Wait and see.

THE JINX

March 30, 1986 — This spring in Florida, they are the Golden Arms, the Multimedia Millionaires, the Aces. They're Dwight Gooden, Bret Saberhagen and John Tudor: the three best pitchers in baseball.

They should have nightmares. In fact, they should be scared to death. Their careers, their wealth and their happiness may be in immediate danger.

If they don't think so (and they surely do not), they should contact Mark Fidrych, J. R. Richard, Vida Blue, Randy Jones, Frank Tanana, John Candelaria, Mike Norris, Steve Stone, LaMarr Hoyt, Mike Flanagan, Bert Blyleven, Pet Vuckovich, John Denny, Mike Boddicker or Rick Sutcliffe.

These are just some of the pitchers who, in the last decade, have come to spring training in the same situation as Gooden, Saberhagen and Tudor: as one of the game's three most celebrated starting pitchers at that moment.

Since 1976 they all either (1) won the Cy Young Award, (2) were the ace and postseason hero of a pennant winner or (3) set such incredible statistical marks at such a young age that the Hall of Fame looked like a logical expectation. Or all three.

What happened to every one of them? They met baseball catastrophe. And, in every case, their downfall began instantly—in the *next* season.

For the lucky ones, that only meant a slump or the lingering regret of unfulfilled promise.

But for more than half of the aces of the last decade, it's taken the form of a career-ending injury, a plunge to mediocrity or severe drug and alcohol abuse.

Their collapses have been so brutal we almost seem to deny how great these pitchers once were. Richard struck out 313 men in a season and was finished the next. At age twenty-one, Blue struck out 301 and Tanana 269; Fidrych had 24 complete games. All of them looked nearly as good as Gooden.

Pitchers always have been fragile of arm and psyche. But in the free agent era of big money, big pressure, big media and big temptation, the tendency toward an Icarus syndrome has risen radically. Get too close to the sun of total success and you burn.

Lest Gooden, Saberhagen and Tudor scoff, they should be warned that they have all shown symptoms of this trend. As Mets general manager Frank Cashen says, "We don't have pitching stars anymore. They're more like meteors." Looking at Gooden's off-season, when he missed appointments or was hours late, Cashen says, "Those are bad signs . . . He has incredible talent. But other people have had in-credible talent, too—yeah, like his—and . . ."

And blown it.

Our horror tales take five shapes. Causes of demise: playing hurt, freak injury, overwork, too much fame and distraction, drug or alcohol abuse.

• 1976: Maybe it started with the Bird. Fidrych, twenty-one, led the majors in ERA (2.34) and complete games (24) while winning 19. Next spring, injured. Three premature comebacks later, finished. Won 10 games the rest of his career. In the National League, Jones won the Cy Young (22 wins, 315 innings). Can't hurt your arm throwing that slop, the Padres thought. After 600 innings and 42 wins in '75–'76,

Jones's arm went dead in '77 (6–12). Finished as a winner at age twenty-seven.

• 1977: The Candy Man and the Top Tanana. At twenty-three, the six-foot-seven Candelaria led the majors in ERA (2.34) and went 20–5. What wouldn't he achieve? Too much fame got him. Only one 15-win season since. Tanana was sadder. At twenty, 269 innings. At twenty-two, 23 complete games. After leading the American League in ERA and shutouts in '77, he started slipping. By twenty-five, arm shot, he was a journeyman. At six-two, 185 pounds, he had Gooden-like physique, repertoire and control.

• 1979: J. R. Richard, six-eight, indestructible, struck out 313. Next year, a stroke. Career over. (Last summer he was named in the Pittsburgh trial as a cocaine user during this period.) Mike Flanagan, the AL Cy Young winner, won 23, was nicknamed Iron Mike and looked like a 250-game winner; too tough for his own good, he pitched hurt during 157 consecutive turns without missing a start. Hasn't won 17 since.

• 1980: Steve Stone won 25 games; next summer, retired. Too many curves trying to win a pennant. His arm resigned its commission. Norris won 22, threw a screwball and was one, too. In a dead heat, his arm and private life soured. Now awaiting a drug trial.

• 1981: Remember Steve McCatty? Led AL in wins and ERA. Big guy. Couldn't hurt him with a bazooka. Billy Martinized by too many complete games.

• 1982: Vuckovich—the Cy Young winner—pitched hurt in the pennant race; won *zero* the next two years.

• 1983: Hoyt won 24 and the Cy Young, was 13–18 in '84 and just got out of a rehab clinic this week for substance dependency. Denny, a late-career "Eureka!" guy (like Tudor), has had arm problems and was traded last winter.

• 1984: Sutcliffe was 16–1 for Cubs. Next season: injured and 8–8 because of premature returns. This month, disabled on his first pitch of the spring season. The best AL starter, Boddicker, the ERA and wins (20) champ, slumped to 12–17 last season. Probably too many innings and curves for a fragile build.

Could it be Jim Palmer was smart to nurse injuries, and Tom Seaver to insist on four days' rest and never have a 300-inning season?

Perhaps Gaylord Perry wasn't unlucky to play in obscurity or Steve Carlton to build a cocoon of silence. Was it a break Don Sutton won 20 only once and always played second banana? Perhaps Phil Niekro was lucky he never had one great arm-wrenching pitch and had to learn the knuckleball.

Maybe Gooden, Saberhagen and Tudor should be more wary.

In St. Petersburg, Florida, last week, Gooden was working on his new change-up. "After three years of practice, I can get it over for strikes every time," he glowed, dreaming of a record better than 24–4 and an ERA lower than 1.53. After one of the ten best statistical seasons in the 116-year history of baseball, Gooden wants to get better. Admirable. But nobody could hit Sudden Sam McDowell (better at twenty-two than ever again) until vanity prompted him to learn a change. Hitters prayed for it.

What drives the Mets crazy is Gooden's glut of endorsements. When you pay a twenty-one-year-old $1.32 million, you figure he should be home getting his sleep. Gooden endorses Diet Pepsi, Nike, Toys "R" Us, Spalding gloves, Kellogg's corn flakes and Polaroid. So far. Gooden's also collaborated on two biographies, appeared in a Bruce Springsteen video of "Glory Days" and applied to copyright his nickname, Dr. K.

Agent Jim Neader thinks Gooden can double his income with deals. "It's a nice feeling to see your name on a lot of things you always dreamed of," Gooden said. You can find Gooden at autograph-signing sessions ($5,000 for two hours). In radio and TV promos. Every reporter on earth wants interviews.

"Some people call it 'the Marketing of Dr. K,'" said a senior Mets official. "But you might also call it 'the Exploiting of Dwight Gooden.'"

"It's our duty to protect Gooden," said Cashen. "It's been written in blood—our blood, because we've been crucified for it—that he will only give interviews on the day after he pitches."

So wander into the Mets clubhouse and what is Gooden doing on the day before he's due to pitch? He's giving a radio interview. For twenty minutes the young pitcher seems unequipped to break away until, finally, practice begins.

The previous day, Gooden showed up three hours late to shoot a commercial. "He's a young man who's so nice that he cannot bring himself to say no to anybody," said the exasperated Cashen. "Finally his plate gets so full that he just has to have time for himself and he misses an appointment . . . Those are bad signs."

Gooden even missed the Man of the Year banquet in his honor in his hometown of Tampa, Florida.

"Dwight has worked harder this year than either of his other two springs," said Manager Davey Johnson. ". . . But it's true that you can crowd your mind to the point where you sour yourself. He doesn't seem to have much 'relax time.'"

Of his obligations, Gooden says he's now at his acceptable limit and is, basically, having a ball. Cashen runs his hands through his gray hair. "He's such a good kid, so unspoiled yet . . . But it's just a smorgasbord of vices and temptations waiting outside every clubhouse for these kids. You almost have to be superhuman to resist."

Ironically, other ballplayers see Gooden as the player who has been immune to distractions while Saberhagen has taken naturally to superstardom.

"Dwight is similar to me, a private person," said Tudor. "He's protected from the press. I've been jealous of that. He's done a great job of handling himself. I've never seen him talk trash about another player in the papers.

"Saberhagen seems to be much more open than we are. That really helped him in the World Series. It seemed like he took everything in stride. That's why he's a 'media darling' now."

When you win 20 games at the age of twenty-one, as Saberhagen did, then top it off by being Most Valuable Player of the World Series (including a seventh-game shutout), people tend to get curious about you. Especially when you do it while your wife is past due with your first child. From fatherhood to a visit to the White House to a world championship ring to a $925,000 contract, Saberhagen had a lifetime's worth of experiences in a matter of days.

Oddly, he hardly seems to notice it. Is he abnormally mature or just young and oblivious? The notion that staying on top might be tough sledding doesn't seem to register with him. "I'm just going to do everything the same as last year," he said last week. "Take it one step at a time. Can't do too much too fast. I just have a feeling of confidence. Every time you go out there you have to think you're going to win or you won't . . . If I give the best Bret Saberhagen can give, then I'll be happy with it."

Counting postseason, Saberhagen pitched 260 innings in '85—about 100 more than his previous high. Has that already taken a toll on the slim, six-one, 160-pound right-hander? And how many innings will he work from now on?

Saberhagen's great good luck may be that he does *not* play in media-mad New York. Even the Royals training camp in Fort Myers, Florida, is remote. "I think that once you start considering baseball a job, it's no longer fun and you don't do nearly as well," he said. "I don't know too many ballplayers who consider this a job."

Then Saberhagen obviously doesn't know Tudor, a man for whom the role of celebrity is as welcome as a dental appointment. Some might say that Tudor's fall from grace has already begun. After finishing the '85 regular season on a 20–1 streak, then winning three times more in the playoffs and World Series, Tudor completed his season in disarray.

Weeks of prickling relations with the press culminated in a Series scene where Tudor invited a reporter to slug it out. Then, in the biggest game of his life—the seventh—he suffered his earliest knockout of the year. In frustration, he punched an electric fan, slashed his pitching hand and ended up in the hospital for stitches. A week later, Tudor publicly apologized.

To make matters worse, Tudor's St. Louis Cardinals traded Joaquin Andujar over the winter, placing the responsibilities of staff ace on Tudor's shoulders for the first time.

Oddly, Tudor may have been fortunate to see his luck go bad *before* the offseason. He's had a winter to think, cope and plan for the future.

"I try not to worry about it, but it's still painful. People are still taking shots at me," he said of the nationwide bad press he received. "I can't worry about it, but that's not sayin' I like it."

Unlike Gooden and Saberhagen, Tudor refuses to think of himself as a great pitcher. "I don't consider myself a big star. What I did was a reflection of what the ballclub did. It helps you stay on top to think that way. If I can't throw strikes and let Ozzie [Smith] and Willie [McGee] catch 'em, then I'm beating myself.

"I may never get to that point again," he said of his 20–1 streak. "My control was as good as it's ever been, and it just stayed there. Even when I got out of rhythm at the end of one start. The streak just kept going; then, when you figured it was time for it to stop, it just didn't."

If experience is a teacher, Tudor has it. If Gooden or Saberhagen fail, it will be a new trauma. It's old stuff to the twice-traded, thirty-two-year-old Tudor. "When you lose two or three in a row, you doubt yourself. It compounds on you. You just have to hang on until you win, even if it's by luck, then it starts turning around . . .

"Last season was something you'll remember forever. Lotta fun, great team. But the seventh game is the one I'll remember the most," said Tudor on a rainy day in St. Petersburg. "It was the last game, so it's with you all winter. And it was so disastrous in many respects. You can have scars all over your body, but the one you feel is the fresh wound . . .

"I don't think there'll be any lasting damage. I always knew I could be beat. And I've gotten mad a hundred times before and taken a swing at something. If you don't ever get mad, you're not giving everything you've got . . . Just so long as you don't quit on yourself, you can look in the mirror. But if you do [quit], the mirror can look bad."

What Tudor, Saberhagen and Gooden face is a contemporary exacerbation of the pitcher's traditionally precarious lifestyle.

• More money can mean more chances to play with dangerous, expensive drugs.

• More media exposure means an exhausting succession of interview demands.

• A multimillion-buck contract means you need an agent to negotiate. However, that agent, who may make 10 percent off your contract, will probably get 25 percent of any big endorsement contract he lands. So, unless he's a saint, he may see you as the horse he can ride hard to his own millions.

• Teams that spend big need to win big to stay in the black. So there's more pressure than ever to pitch hurt and pitch often. Teams think, "Use him up now while you've got him."

• Big contracts make some players feel *more* responsible to their team and town. They end up millionaire martyrs.

And finally, pitching remains what it has always been: the single most unnatural, injury-prone act in all of American sports. In the dugouts they say, "Your career just hangs by your cords."

For decades we've heard the graybeards of sport say, "The hardest thing isn't getting to the top. It's staying there."

Who dreamed that the hardest task could become so much harder.

THE PITS

NORFOLK, Virginia, May 12, 1987 — Dwight Gooden's comeback Tuesday was a scene that perfectly combined the sad, the hopeful and the ridiculous. Of all our stumbling modern baseball heroes, from Denny McLain to Willie Wilson to Keith Hernandez, none seems so sorrowful or so worthy of our best wishes for full recovery as Gooden.

None of our other publicly humiliated idols came to fame so young. Gooden was a national celebrity as a teenager, at nineteen. At twenty, he had one of the ten best pitching seasons in history. At twenty-one, he was a disappointment. And by twenty-two he was in a drug rehabilitation clinic.

No one in baseball ever came to glory more prepared on the field but less prepared off it. Shy and roughly educated, Gooden always looked like a gentle deer frozen in the headlights of his own parade. He arrived at the nadir of the New York tabloid war triggered by sleazemonger Rupert Murdoch. Gooden's private life became an open innuendo. He couldn't miss an appointment, misreport an injury or even have a bad-mannered girlfriend without being back-page news. Discovery of his out-of-wedlock child and the scandal over his fistfight with Tampa police were flogged for months.

No player ever picked a worse time to acquire a drug problem. Gooden was in the wrong vice at the wrong time. A year after Commissioner Peter Ueberroth said baseball had beaten its cocaine problem, Gooden—the most famous and popular young player in the sport—made him look like a liar.

If this were 1982, when coke was a fashionable indulgence, a "recreational drug" connected with the ritzy, Gooden's month in rehab might have found its way into sports-page "transactions" as a mere visit to the disabled list with a slow-to-heal groin-muscle pull. Lots of stars have taken the cure for liquor or drugs without the public hearing a word. But Gooden slipped in an era of knee-jerk conservatism when Just Say No had supplanted Do Your Own Thing—one simplistic silliness replacing another.

Perhaps no player has ever suffered so great a punishment of shame in relation to so commonplace a crime. Even the Smithers Clinic, where Gooden was treated for twenty-eight days, claims he never was addicted to cocaine. Gooden himself requested the drug test that came back positive. Presumably, and it's all guesswork at this point, Gooden felt his life slipping in a destructive direction and asked for the test as a kind of cry for help. Surely it will complete his break from young peers on the Tampa streets who tempted him.

"Socrates admitted to those who recognized in his face some inclination to vice that that was in truth his natural propensity, but that he had corrected it by discipline," wrote the philosopher Montaigne. The natural propensity to vice, even in the most gifted and decent people, is so common that Gooden should not waste a single night's sleep over discovering it in himself. Rather, he should focus, as so many have, on putting that normal inclination on the leash of self-discipline.

As though Gooden's misfortunes were not bad enough, the circus that now surrounds him is in danger of stinking worse than anything he has done.

The Stadium Club restaurant behind home plate in the Tidewater

Tides' ballpark was full here as Gooden pitched three shutout innings in his first get-back-in-shape effort. However, the restaurant's owner, Spike White, had mixed feelings about the boom business. "If Gooden had a torn rotator cuff and had come back here in the regular course of rehabilitation, would the stands be full?" White wondered. "Isn't that shame on us? Isn't this what they mean [in defining pornography] by prurient interest?"

More than one hundred members of the national media gathered, despite the Mets' insistence that Gooden would not talk directly to anybody about anything. After Gooden threw his 39 pitches, the reporters were herded into a batting cage—a sort of outdoor lobster tank—where a Mets official, without consulting any notes, attempted to paraphrase his long postgame conversation with Gooden. Then, for a second wave of reporters, the Mets man did his number again, quoting Gooden on many of the same subjects but using substantially different phrases. Talk about getting what you deserve.

Despite all that's depressing about Gooden's last six weeks, there's also much that seems encouraging. Norfolk may not be Peoria, but Gooden certainly played well here. The fans loved him, welcomed him back without a hint of a single boo and even cheered when he struck out. The Tides are the Mets' AAA affiliate, and Gooden was a big star performing in a smallish town. But it would be nice to think that a twenty-two-year-old with so much to give and so much to bear will be greeted this way everywhere.

George McClelland, sports columnist for the local *Virginian Pilot*, said, "This country has been built on the second chance. Even George Washington got a second chance after his army got smashed. Just because Gooden's a rich athlete, I don't see why he shouldn't get that second chance."

In some ways, Gooden has gotten terrible breaks. He's had to grow up in the center of the largest public spotlight in sports history. He's been handed millions of dollars amid a society fraught with temptations. Like many a young man, he thought the fast lane looked like it might be worth a try. When he showed up for spring training in 1986 with a satin jacket with an embroidered dragon on the back and a wet, curly Billy Dee Williams hairstyle, the handwriting was on the wall. It was just a matter of time till he'd tried on the whole lifestyle to see how it fit.

Perhaps Gooden's one piece of good luck, and it may prove to be a large one, is that all of this has hit him so suddenly and so hard. If the last few months haven't served as shock therapy, nothing could. If Gooden doesn't see how much he has to lose, how far he can fall, and how quickly, then he isn't just young. He's foolish.

Denny McLain, the last man to win 30 games, cultivated his vices—gambling, mobster friends—over a longer period. He'd been in the majors eight seasons before the crash of exposure. McLain could never lose his tastes or get rid of his wrong friends once they were an ingrained pattern in his adult life. He's in prison now—a huge, tragic joke. And an example.

Gooden is in his formative years, his changing years. He should still be able to make himself into something like the person he wants to be. Fortunately for him, the American principle of a clean-slate second chance seems to be locked firmly in the public mind in the case of appealing young twenty-two-year-old pitchers nicknamed Dr. K.

THE RETURN

NEW YORK, May 27, 1988—A year ago he was deep in the minor leagues, at Lynchburg and Tidewater, working his way back to Shea Stadium. Then he was still trying to digest a month in a drug rehabilitation center that turned his life upside down.

Now the numbers say he is the old Dwight Gooden. That's what some of his New York Mets teammates say, too. "It feels like nothing ever happened," says Keith Hernandez. That 8–1 record, the most wins in the National League, and those three shutouts are enough to make you begin believing the fantasy. Come on, Dr. K, pitch a no-hitter. Strike out twenty. Win thirty.

But that's just bleacher prattle—an image from a past that's not going to return. And Gooden knows it. At the old age of twenty-three, Gooden is a rather different pitcher, and a far different person, from the K kid who, in Manager Davey Johnson's words, "was great at nineteen and unbelievable at twenty. Doing things nobody had ever done at that age."

Gooden has returned with his old smile intact, his silliness and gentleness. But perhaps he has the beginnings of some wisdom, too, although, after all he's endured, it's too early to know where his metamorphosis will end.

"A man can be elated and enriched and ennobled by going through hell," says Dr. Allan Lans of the Smithers Institute for Drug and Alcohol Rehabilitation, who has been Gooden's counselor through his ordeal. "Dwight has become strengthened by all of this. It has something of 'Whatever does not destroy me makes me stronger' about it. This whole thing really does feel like the return of a prodigal son."

This evening, a Shea crowd of 45,315 cheered Gooden as he battled the San Francisco Giants' aging ace, Rick Reuschel, in a scruffy duel with a truckload of men left on base. On the mound, that's the new Gooden—a competitor more than an overpowering force of youth. Sometimes Gooden says he wants to scream at people not to compare him to the Gooden of 1985 who went 24–4 with a 1.53 ERA. Then he catches himself making the same comparisons. "I don't understand how I did what I did in '85," he has said. "Sometimes I get chills thinking about that season."

When he struck out eleven Phillies last month, he laughed and said, "You know, I didn't think I could do this anymore."

The truth is, he doesn't do it much anymore. This year, he's given up 10 hits in a game more often (4 times) than he's fanned 10. In his career, he'd allowed 10 hits only 3 times before 1988. Gooden's curveball still stands hitters on their ears. However, when his curve isn't knee-high, it's hittable. And his fastball can be put in play. Whoever thought Dr. K would need luck?

He's had it all spring. Tons of runs. But not this time. Two years ago, he might have been torn apart internally by a game like this Giants 5–2 victory. As he entered the seventh with a 2–1 lead, Gooden's tank hit empty. Five of the next six Giants got hits. Once the pressure of astronomical expectations and the desire to justify his large salary might have tormented Gooden.

Not anymore. "This is the toughest kind of loss to take," he said, quickly, quietly, calmly. "I had great stuff, hit my locations, but their hits just fell in. You'd rather get hit hard . . . But it evens out. You can get spoiled and start expecting a lot . . . I was wondering myself how far I could go . . . but it's over now . . . All good things come to an end."

Thankfully, most bad ones do, too. Compared to last year, everything is roses to Gooden. He keeps remembering that. It's all how you see it; not long ago, he saw it all backward. No one sympathizes more than Johnson.

"Getting to the top is the easy part," says the manager. "Then the pressure arrives to stay there or improve. You know you can't give any more. And you have to relax just to give what you gave before. But you can't. Not even when you tell yourself to relax. That's when it's got you."

You might even take your escapes and your releases where you find them.

"Certain personalities can blossom in a media nightmare. It's like an elixir to Ali, Rose, Reggie Jackson. They even love the controversy," says Johnson. "But to people who are more private . . . the microscope and all the attention can be smothering, suffocating. The celebrity status you get here can change you and make you do strange things."

Last year, many Mets did lots of strange things, including Johnson. Is stress-related neurosis contagious? The team's response has been to follow Lans's therapeutic advice, even to the point of bringing him on flights as a counselor at large. "I don't believe Freud advised taking showers with patients," says Lans, laughing at his meet-'em-where-they-live method.

Lans's view of Gooden is simple and sympathetic. He agrees with General Manager Frank Cashen, who says, "We stole Dwight's youth."

"A kid finds ways to try on different [styles]. How many of us go through a phase as the hipster or the revolutionary?" says Lans. "When you don't get to do any of that . . ."

It can feel like jail?

"It damn near got him in jail."

If the Mets were going to take Gooden's youth, they decided at least to return his joy, if they could. "Dwight's reached the point where he feels, 'Whether I ever [go 24–4] again, it's not important to me. I'm going to enjoy baseball,' " says Johnson. "He's decided to have fun and not set goals."

There we have it. A big league boss telling his star not to set goals. "Now I'm a person first," says Gooden, "and a pitcher second." If the Mets return to the postseason this year—and they seem quite serious about it—it will be a grave blow to the theory of competition living as applied to baseball.

"It's wonderful to compete and have that drive to excel," says Johnson. "But when it starts going over into an obsession, when that's all you do to justify yourself, then you have to ask what you're doing with your success. Then competition is just a form of greed. There's a time to let go."

To a degree, the Mets' team attitude seems to have been reborn along with Gooden's. If the year of scandal, injury and embarrassment that rent the Mets in '87 wouldn't chasten you, what would? "Sometimes," says Johnson, "you can't even identify the animal that's eating you."

Dwight Gooden's struggle to find peace within himself, and in his microscopically examined and colossally celebrated life, is a constant process. "Is Dwight 'happier' now?" asks Lans. "It's not a steady state. It's ups and downs."

Through those ups and downs, Doc Gooden and the good doctor have worked up an image to remember. "You may be in orbit," says Lans. "But you have to remember the launching pad."

4,192

September 7, 1985 — When the symbolic, the statistical and the historic intersect in sports, the larger world pauses in its rounds to pay attention and pass its judgment.

Now in our national on-deck circle: Pete Rose.

Pay attention, America. The middle-aged boy who epitomizes effort, enthusiasm and the willed refusal to grow up is about to have his greatest day.

Rose has 4,189 career base hits. Just three more hits and the Cincinnati Reds' player/manager will pass Ty Cobb as the lifetime hit leader among all those who have played professional baseball in the last 116 years.

Only one record-breaking moment in baseball history—perhaps in any American sport—has been so long awaited or has engendered so much debate. Eleven years ago Hank Aaron hit his 715th home run (on the way to 755) to break Babe Ruth's career record. That homer countdown fixed the nation's attention and spurred countless debates about Aaron's worthiness to supplant such a near-mythic figure in so symbolic an athletic category.

Rose's hit total is outrageously improbable, far beyond the dreams, let alone the deeds, of other men. When Cobb died in the summer of 1961, at age seventy-four, it is scarcely conceivable that the incendiary old Georgia Peach could have guessed that the man who'd someday supplant him was already a pro player.

Deep in the Florida State League, twenty-year-old Peter Edward Rose was already sliding face first into bases, sprinting to first after walks and earning the nickname—at first given sarcastically—of Charlie Hustle.

As was the case in 1974 with Aaron and Ruth, the linking of Rose's and Cobb's names carries a weight of connotation that goes beyond sport. The mild, modest, intelligent, well-mannered Aaron was the antithesis of the soft-hearted, sentimental, sensual, fat and loutish Ruth, whose every trait and gesture was larger than fiction. Aaron and Ruth counterpointed, but seldom illuminated, each other. For Aaron, a black, the chase after the beloved Ruth was often a bitter experience, besmirched by racism and denigration of his achievements.

If Ruth meant raw appetite and Aaron its opposite—a kind of athletic aestheticism—then Rose has come to be seen as a mirror image of Cobb; mirrored in the sense that the features seem familiar and similar, yet somehow reversed.

Both were pure distillations of personality types. Now, across generations, they embody such basic human qualities that their apposition seems to demand a moral response.

Both worked fanatically and played fiercely. Both courted fame and grasped the spotlight. Both amassed fortunes and were shrewd businessmen. Neither concealed his vast pride nor claimed a balanced personality. Neither hid that his drive came almost entirely from his relationship with his father.

Yet there the two part company.

Cobb, whether mastering the bunt or filing his spikes like blades in the dugout while his foes watched, worked with a demonic, tight-lipped energy. His sport was really warfare where cheating was the rule, violence acceptable and psychological intimidation essential.

By all accounts, Cobb was the best and most hated player of his age. No flattering personal portrait, if one existed, has survived. "I feel like a coiled spring with a dangerous flaw," Cobb supposedly said.

No one has ever claimed Rose was baseball's best player. An ordinary runner, fielder, thrower and power hitter, Rose was only exceptional as a switch-hitter, a distinction he earned as much by diligence as by talent. Rose found labor a rough joy. He never claimed virtue for his work ethic because he never said he wasn't having fun.

If Cobb was swift and gifted, Rose is doggedness incarnate. No player was ever so durable. In twenty-six professional seasons, he has, essentially, never been injured—or at least has not admitted it. All the sport's endurance records—games, at bats—long have been his.

Cobb may have batted .367 to Rose's .306, but Rose dragged himself to the plate more than 2,200 more times.

In the last four years, as Rose has at times embarrassed himself— batting .271, .245, .286 and, this season, .265 in his unabashed marathon tracking of Cobb—so some have forgotten how fine a hitter he once was. From 1965 through 1980 Rose *averaged* more than 200 hits per season. The best lead-off man of his period, and perhaps in history, Rose both scored 100 runs and got 200 hits 10 times.

Where Cobb was a warrior, Rose was a gamesman. Where Cobb was vicious and mean, Rose was fierce and clean. Either might break your leg, but Rose would do it by accident. The best that could be said of Cobb was that he asked no quarter. Cobb *had* to win; Rose merely played to win. At the height of a famous World Series game, Rose said to Boston catcher Carlton Fisk, "Isn't this a great game?"

Even Rose has never claimed his stature in his era matched Cobb's; Rose is too much a fan, too much a sportsman, to claim an iota more than his due. But Rose is also too much a competitor to accept *less* than his due. And he will let anyone, including Cobb's ghost, know that baseball is not an individual sport but a team game.

That's where Rose shines. Cobb had better stats; Rose had better teams. Cobb isolated himself, divided others. Rose immersed himself in the team and united every club around him. No player ever approached Rose's ability to meld his own glory-seeking with the team's goals. How Rose walked this invisible line, knowing and following every clubhouse rule of proper pecking-order behavior, was a feat in itself.

No veteran ever gave advice or cash more freely to rookies than Rose. No star ever took such care in sharing praise so precisely. Once Rose gave every coach on his team a free truck as a postseason gift. No reason. Just felt like it.

This made Rose the most popular, admired and emulated of modern players within the game. A winner.

In fact, Pete Rose was the first historian to note that Pete Rose had actually played in more winning baseball games than any player ever. No one had ever thought of such a category. So Rose invented it.

In twenty-four seasons, Cobb played on three first-place teams. Rose had been to seven playoffs and six World Series. Two seasons after the Philadelphia Phillies bought him at auction as a $3.2 million free agent, Rose led them to their first world title in ninety-seven years. "If I can do that, I can do anything," said Rose with typical disarming immodesty.

Neither man has left behind much doubt about his emotional mainspring.

Cobb's coiled-spring nature took its basic flaw from his macabre boyhood. Well born, he fell in love with being a ballplayer against his stern father's wishes. While off seeking his fortune in the disreputable world of pro sport, Cobb learned that his father had been shot to death while climbing in his mother's bedroom window. By his mother.

Cobb's baseball quest became a fixation as he tried to vindicate both his own choice and his father's memory.

Rose and his dad were inseparable, connected by sports. A local Cincinnati star athlete, Rose's father could have wished nothing sweeter than that his boy make the majors with the Reds. Rose's father also died young, but not until Pete had been National League rookie of the year.

Like Cobb, Rose proudly dedicated all his deeds to his father's memory. But there the parallel ended. Cobb felt he could never please, so he could never take pleasure. Rose knew he had pleased, so his work became a joy.

Few clearer paradigms of sickness and health have appeared in America's national pastime. Perhaps that is why Rose—Cobb's inferior as a player—is seldom begrudged the record he will soon hold.

Rose, who may be the best baseball *fan* of his time, has given due thought to the issue and decided that he himself is the proper person to hold one of baseball's most central career records. As Rose's final great playing moment approaches, more and more Americans have come to agree with him.

Who knows how long Rose's new hit record will stand? After all, his new son—Ty Rose—is not quite a year old.

☐ ☐ ☐

September 9, 1985 — Ever notice how those who stand for nothing are anxious to prove that no one else stands for anything either? Those blighted by lack of love or principles or dreams say such things don't exist or aren't what they seem.

On Saturday in Chicago, from bars and taxis to the press box and bleachers, wise guys were letting Pete Rose have it. They figured Charlie Hustle went hitless because he'd gone in the tank.

What will our cynical age say now? Can it explain away the Day Rose Tied Cobb? On Sunday, Rose put aside every selfish and even sensible consideration just so he could play the game right.

When all the smart money said, "Don't play," he played. When he should not have hit, he hit. When, down to the very last inning, he could have played it safe with a sacrifice bunt, Manager Pete Rose told batter Pete Rose to swing away and try his darndest to spoil his own greatest moment.

At least to one man, baseball remains a game, yet hasn't become a toy. In a season full of drug scandal and labor bluff, Rose showed that somebody still knows what the threadbare phrases "integrity of the sport" and "best interests of the game" really mean. Maybe a quarter-century of sweat teaches you more about what's right than all the books Rose never read in the college he never attended.

Everybody from Cincinnati Reds owner Marge Schott to Baseball Commissioner Peter Ueberroth thought Rose would not play in Wrigley Field on Sunday; or, if he did, that he'd only pinch-hit. That way, Rose would return here for the home stand that started tonight needing either three or two hits to break Ty Cobb's career record. Boy, could he and the Reds milk that baby.

Tonight, sit it out. Tuesday and Wednesday, get one hit a night, then stop. Try for No. 4,192 Thursday, then maybe have a Thanks, Pete night Friday. A minimum of 80,000 extra ticket sales (over $1 million with parking and concessions) could be at stake.

Talk about megabucks and maximum exposure.

That's entertainment.

But it's not baseball.

And Rose knows it.

On Sunday, Cubs left-hander Steve Trout said he'd hurt himself in a bicycle fall. Some believe this. Would the Cubs scratch him just to prime the gate? "I better never find out that Trout doesn't have a bike," Schott said.

With a right-hander, not a lefty, starting, Rose and his principles were on the spot. During his whole career, Rose has sworn that despite all his personal goals and self-promotion, he's never put himself ahead of his team. Now he's the team's manager to boot.

Told about Trout and his bicycle by a Cubs coach, Rose snapped, "Maybe you should buy him a tricycle."

Quips aside, he was stunned.

His wife and son had gone home to Cincinnati. Owner Schott had made her wishes clear: break the record in your hometown, where you've played eighteen of your twenty-three years. Even Ueberroth stayed in New York, certain Rose would never cross up the smart money. After all, why should Rose play? Tony Perez, hitting .343, was available. As Schott said, "No one would blame Pete for sitting one out." Doesn't twenty-six years of sliding on your face earn you the right to have your crowning moment before your family and friends? Sunday's game wasn't even on TV in Cincinnati.

Within minutes, Rose put himself in the lineup. By the fifth inning, he had two hits, a Ty with Cobb and a big problem.

"Doggie [Perez] kept walking by me looking at me with his big old eyes, saying, 'What are you doing? What are you going to do?' I said, 'I'm trying to get a base hit.' Davey [Concepcion] said, 'You better get your batting gloves and go upstairs and watch it on TV.' I said, 'You can't do that.' "

Some might say Rose is just too simple to appreciate a moral dilemma. Not so. "I was real confused," he admits. "I was in sort of a situation where I didn't want to disappoint everybody. I had thirty thousand yelling here and one lady back in Cincinnati, every time I got a hit, kicking her dog."

His final test, one perhaps only he appreciates perfectly, came in the ninth inning. A pure baseball situation. Tie score. Sun going down. Game certain to be stopped by darkness at the end of the inning. Men on first and second. None out. Dave Parker on deck.

Joe Fan says, "Sacrifice."

A Hall of Famer knows that means an intentional walk to Parker, leaving the clutch hitting to lesser men. Rose knew in his gut that the Reds, eight games out of first place, had a *slightly* better percentage chance for victory if he swung away. Just the tiniest edge.

So, for a sliver of advantage in a pennant race that his team has only the most remote prayer of winning, Rose hit away. Sure, he struck out after a hard-swing foul ball.

No cop-out bunt for Rose.

During the rest of his life, he probably will listen to a thousand wise guys who'll say he struck out on purpose Sunday.

You think not? For seven years, he has been nagged about his criticism of the pitch Gene Garber threw to end his forty-four-game hitting streak in 1978. And Rose was dead right, by his own purist lights, then as he is now. Garber didn't "play the game right." He threw a submarine change-up to end a game when he had a twelve-run lead—something he'd never have done except for Rose's streak. Garber played with the record foremost in mind—so he could be the guy who ended the streak—not according to the context of the game itself.

Neither the criticism Rose got then, nor some of the praise he'll get now, ever really affects him. He's in touch with his game and with himself.

Hit no. 4,192 will be a testament to baseball skill. But no. 4,191 meant more. It was proof of something rarer—a moral sense.

CINCINNATI, September 11, 1985 — For the second time in his adult life, and the first time on a baseball field, Pete Rose cried tonight.

"I cried when my father died," said Rose. "And tonight."

"I was standing on first base, all alone," he said, recalling the seven-minute standing ovation he received after his first-inning single broke Ty Cobb's all-time career hit record of 4,191. "I'm a tough son of a bitch, but I just could not handle it. I had nobody to talk to, nobody to throw a ball to. They even took the base.

"I've never had feelings like that before," said Rose, who also had a walk, a triple, a spectacular game-ending defensive play and both runs scored in a 2–0 Cincinnati Reds' victory. "I looked up in the sky and started thinking about my father. I thought I saw him there. And right behind him was Ty Cobb.

"Regardless of what you think," said Rose, turning in an instant from sentimental to sly, "Ty *is* up there."

Confetti snowed upon the outfield, fireworks sent their sparks showering on Riverfront Stadium and flashbulbs burst like lightning bugs at 8:01 P.M. as Rose became baseball's Hit King.

On the fifty-seventh anniversary of Cobb's final game.

After twenty-three seasons, 3,476 games and 13,768 at bats, Rose finally got what he calls "the big knock."

The Ty-breaker, which both Rose and baseball historians have awaited for at least five years, came off the San Diego Padres' Eric Show. After taking a fastball high, fouling a fastball back, then skipping away from a breaking ball near his feet, the Reds' player-manager attacked a slider, erupting from his left-handed hitting crouch.

The ball streaked high over the shortstop's head on what has become Rose's patented hit since he reached age forty: a hard opposite-field single to left-center. The historic hit was clean, hard and convincing—worthy of generations of television replays.

As soon as the record-setting hit landed, all of Rose's teammates engulfed him around first base. The ball and base were preserved for posterity. Several Padres joined the congratulations, including one, Bobby Brown, who ran from the dugout to get in the act.

Rose, who had gone 0 for 6 since tying Cobb Sunday in Chicago, stood at first base, taking deep breaths, while the grounds crew cleaned the outfield turf. Reds owner Marge Schott hugged Rose and got in a plug for her car dealership by having a red convertible—a gift to Rose—driven all over the field.

After five minutes of applause, Pete Rose, Jr., age fifteen and dressed in a Reds uniform, ran out on the field and gave his father a long hug.

From his seventh-inning triple, which landed a foot fair in the left-field corner, to his diving, somersaulting grab of Steve Garvey's grounder to end the game (Rose threw to first while still prone), Rose admitted that this whole game "was like someone wrote the script. It was just like I was playing the part tonight."

President Reagan wrote in a part for himself, calling Rose to offer congratulations for breaking "one of the most enduring records in sports history.

"I've rooted for you for a long time," said Reagan, a former Chicago Cubs radio broadcaster. "Come to think of it, I used to root for the fella that once held that record [Cobb].

"We ought to do this [talk] more often," added Reagan. "Those of us who are in the middle of our careers need to share tips on how to stay ahead of those younger folks that are comin' up on us from behind."

Although it took Rose 442 more games and 2,339 more at bats than Cobb to break the record, Rose has played one fewer season than Cobb's twenty-four. "I've been more durable," said Rose. "Cobb missed five hundred games, thank God."

Told that Cobb's last at bat, as a pinch-hitter, came September 11, 1928, Rose wondered why Cobb hadn't played anymore that season. "He went home early," Rose was told. Aware of the gun-toting Cobb's temper, Rose said, "No one was going to tell him not to, either, was they?"

Again tonight, Rose chatted with fans, teammates, umpires, writers, TV crews, grounds crewmen and all the other denizens of his baseball subculture whom he knows by first name and treats as old buddies. His spirits were ebullient, his energy endless, his smile craggy and sincere. As always, his competitiveness was as obvious as his sportsmanship.

"I had fun again tonight," said Rose. "I was tight on Tuesday because I hate to inconvenience people and I felt like I was holding everybody up waiting for this. Criminy, a lot of you writers wanted to be in New York covering the Cards and Mets."

Few seminal events in any sport have as little to do with athletic ability and as much to do with the triumph of basic human qualities as this night of Rose's ultimate triumph. Before the game, Rose was asked if he could explain his almost superhuman energy, his ability to sleep five hours or less a night, yet outwork men half his age, give interviews round the clock and, it seems, cram the existences of several men into one life.

"I can only think of one thing," said Rose, a mischievous grin growing.

Then, like Superman pulling off his suit coat to reveal the *S* underneath, Rose ripped off his snap-open jacket to show a Wheaties T shirt beneath.

That's Rose. Quicker-witted than those around him. Funny. But always looking for an edge, a buck or a plug.

"A lot of people will remember me for tonight," said Rose, as known for his honesty as his hustle. "There are a lot of things you can remember me for, not all of them good. You can remember me for a divorce . . . for a paternity suit. I know what I've accomplished. I really can't worry about it."

Purists have nagged for years that Rose cannot approach Cobb as a player. Their arguments have, as this night neared, evaporated. If the proper player does not hold this record, then, as Rose showed again tonight, the right man does.

Too Good for His Own Good

December 15, 1985 — Heaven protect us from achieving a greatness that the world decides we do not deserve.

Better that we do evil, then repent. For that we'd probably be forgiven.

For Christmas, let us hope that, next baseball season, neither Brett Butler nor Kirby Puckett hits safely in 57 consecutive games. Please don't let it befall Steve Balboni or Tom Brunansky that either should hit 62 home runs.

Mortal men can be crushed by immortal deeds.

Wasn't that the moral of Roger Maris's career?

Right to the end, Maris never caught a break. When he died Saturday of cancer at the age of fifty-one, that ridiculous asterisk was still beside his name in the record book of the public mind.

No baseball player in history ever has had his accomplishments so denigrated or received such criticism for the sin of having performed too well.

When I was thirteen years old in 1961, I hated Roger Maris. Why? Because I was supposed to hate him. Every baseball fan did. And no fan is more serious or certain than a thirteen-year-old. My finger was on the baseball pulse then as it never again will be. I knew for certain how to feel about this Mr. Roger Maris.

Memory says that during one Sunday doubleheader in Washington, Maris hit two home runs and Mickey Mantle hit three. Whether the record book would say such a five-homer day ever happened I neither know nor care. What matters is that I remember cheering all of Mantle's homers and booing Maris as though he were the incarnation of some evil principle. It's a safe bet most of the crowd did the same.

Maris, you see, made a horrible mistake for which, by most accounts, he paid bitterly the rest of his life. He hit too many home runs. He could have atoned for 59. Sixty-one, never.

That figurative asterisk—a separate category created for records set in 162-game, rather than 154-game, seasons—was his scarlet punctuation mark.

"The fun was gone after the '61 season," Maris said, twenty years after the fact. "It was the aftermath that was so hard to explain. There wasn't a ballpark I had relief in. They booed me at home, and they booed me on the road. It wears on you."

"Maybe I wouldn't do it all over again if I had the chance," he said on other occasions. "I think it wasn't worth the aggravation.

". . . Going after the record"—Babe Ruth's sacred 60—"started off as such a dream . . . It would have been a hell of a lot more fun if I had never hit those 61 homers . . ."

In 1960 Maris hit 39 home runs; he was a young star on the rise. In 1961, under the adrenaline thrall of his pursuit of Ruth, he had 142 RBI. In 1962 he drove in 100 runs, but he was already a battered man, at twenty-seven. His career never left another statistical ripple.

Maris, whose hair fell out during the Ruth chase, never returned to a Yankees old-timers' day until 1978. He accepted one public speaking engagement in nineteen years. When TV asked to buy the rights to make a movie of his life, he refused, terrified that it would start the circus anew. In retirement, his goal was simple: to achieve a perfect anonymity. Twice in recent years I casually introduced myself to him (as a reporter) at baseball functions. He looked at me as if I'd pulled a loaded gun on him.

To imagine what happened to Maris requires an act of imaginative re-creation. Maris not only broke the most famous record in the sport at that time. He broke it playing in Ruth's town for Ruth's team, and even playing Ruth's own position (right field). Not only did Maris usurp the crown of a dead king, he stole that crown from the rightful heir —Mantle, the man who played next to him in the Yankees' outfield and who batted next to him in the Yankees' order.

Mantle was handsome, glamorous and properly anointed as the greatest power-hitting switch-batter in history. His home runs were "Ruthian"—the highest compliment.

Maris was in all ways pronounced deficient. With his flattop haircut, he looked more Hessian than handsome. At twenty-six, the introverted, proud young man from Fargo, North Dakota, did not have a fraction of the charm, sophistication or patience to deal with becoming one of the most famous and controversial figures in America.

It might help our sleep to believe Maris was a reclusive oddball figure, uniquely ill suited to fame. For years he was portrayed as an antisocial grouch. With time, a contrary profile emerged. Now, as eulogies roll in, he's painted as a family man, a loyal friend, a modest down-to-earth guy proud of his unselfishness as an all-around ballplayer.

Unfortunately, we have to look back no further than the last game of the most recent season to get a chill. Perhaps Maris's experience, on a smaller scale, is far more frequent than we like to think. This year, John Tudor of St. Louis played the Maris role. On June 1 his career record was 52–50.

Thereafter, until the final game of the World Series, he was 23–2.

Tudor—a rigid, proud man in the Maris mold—found himself a center of national attention. He loathed the experience. Curt with the press and abrupt in public, he seemed like a man holding on for dear life to maintain his magical form on the field. Many (including me) tended to nag Tudor for his gracelessness in the spotlight, and others took off the gloves and ripped him.

By the Series' seventh game, Tudor had feuded with the media ("What do you need to get a press credential, a driver's license?") and even made a veiled threat to punch a reporter who asked why he didn't seem to be enjoying himself.

When Tudor was knocked out of the season's culminating game, he punched an electric fan in the dugout, sending himself to the hospital. When this was announced in the press box, it brought laughter. "Well, the shit finally hit the fan," yelled one reporter. And the laughter escated to the point where a few people actually cheered.

Within two weeks, Tudor had issued a generalized public apology, although, between the lines, he still seemed perplexed, uncertain just what he'd done wrong or what he could have done differently.

With a quarter-century of perspective, it's easy to see the injustices —the small-minded asterisks—of another generation. Perhaps—human nature having so many dark unswept corners —it's more difficult to see our own.

Changing Times

The Worst Damn
Team in Baseball

BALTIMORE, January 31, 1985—Draw a line across the page and mark the end of an era in baseball.

The Baltimore Orioles could be great again someday, even someday soon. But they will never be the same.

The Orioles, as we have known them for the last quarter-century—placid, excellent, hermetic, slow to change, tasteful and conservative —are gone.

The advent of baseball's dubious modern times at last is complete. The Orioles, the game's last successful across-the-board tories, now are of a piece with the temper of their times.

Draw up a profile of a modern major league franchise—free-spending, impatient, controversial, willing to hurt feelings and take wild risks—and the Orioles, once the antithesis of the type, now come close to matching it.

Out of desperately felt necessity, the Orioles have just about mastered the new dance steps. The Orioles, perhaps even owner Edward Bennett Williams, preferred the waltz tempo that accompanied so many Baltimore victories from '64 to '84. But times change; everybody's had to learn to rock.

Make a list of characteristics of a wild-and-woolly eighties ball club, and the Orioles suddenly have the same traits.

• Multimillion-dollar free-agent players, some vastly overpaid and signed despite obvious risks.

Outfielders Fred Lynn and Lee Lacy and pitcher Don Aase have new contracts worth $12 million. Lynn's deal ($6.8 million for five years) is twice the going rate for a player at his statistical level; it's a staggering gotta-win-now contract. Lacy will be thirty-six in April, and Aase is coming back from tendon transplant surgery.

• A warped salary structure.

Lynn makes far more than Eddie Murray or Cal Ripken, Jr., while Aase makes more than pitchers Mike Boddicker and Storm Davis combined.

• The release of old beloved faces to save money to buy free agents.

Jim Palmer ran out of a Memorial Stadium press conference in tears after his sudden midseason pink slip. Ken Singleton and Al Bumbry, told late last season that their tenure was ending, still think they should be Orioles. Williams calls these decisions "a hard wrench" on the emotions. They also are decisions that tug at the fabric of the quasi-family feeling that has long bound the Orioles.

• A team decision to get out of an old park by using leverage on city and state governments to build a modern park.

• A brilliant, high-powered owner who looks over everyone's shoulder and has wide control in many areas. Since Earl Weaver retired as the team's manager, Williams has increasingly taken such team personnel decisions as free agent signings into his own hands.

• A manager (Joe Altobelli) whose job may be in jeopardy after a fifth-place finish and who has a famous newly hired coach (Frank Robinson) who could turn out to be a manager-in-waiting.

To add to speculation, Williams says, "If I had to bet, I'd say that Earl Weaver will get tired of this self-imposed leisure and miss the game so much, now that his ABC-TV contract has not been renewed, that he'll be back managing in the next couple of years." Williams and Weaver have a gentlemen's agreement that Weaver will offer his services first to the Orioles.

• A farm system that has not been providing quality players as fast as old players depart. The Orioles decided to spend millions on free agents because they didn't think their prospects looked surefire.

• A new electronic TV scoreboard. A video screen roughly as big as the left-field scoreboard will be added in right field this season. It'll have advertisements.

Because the Orioles, who've won far more games than any other team in baseball the past twenty-five seasons, have attracted a traditionalist following both inside and outside Baltimore, it's likely that this trend toward modernization will get mixed reviews.

It's probably closer to the truth, however, to say that the Orioles simply had little choice. They held the line as long as possible, even winning a world title the old-fashioned way in '83 with home-grown talent, no major free agents and a controversy-free team with a special blend of brains, camaraderie and an imprecise "chemistry."

Ever since Williams bought the team in '79, there's been a sense he was in a seat-of-the-pants waiting game. How long until Weaver retired? How long until the over-thirty players that were at the heart of the '79 Series team went over the hill? How long until the farm system ran dry, making huge free-agent contracts mandatory rather than optional?

How long until increased attendance and network TV money made it possible to offer a free agent—such as Lynn—an inflated contract without throwing the whole payroll out of whack?

How long until Baltimore came around to wanting a new stadium as much as Williams wanted one?

Finally, how long could Williams—who has had more than one operation for cancer—afford to play along with this charming conceit of chemistry and team play and Orioles magic when he knew he had the bucks to buy talent as well?

In 1984 all the questions were answered.

The oldsters went over the hill. Some youngsters, such as center fielder John Shelby, flopped when given a chance. And the money was there for a quick fix. So the Orioles, with Williams leading the way, entered their new world.

"We were not in panic," Williams says firmly. "We had meetings in September and felt we had no alternative except to release four players.

"It was a hard wrench to give up on Kenny and Al, but we concluded that their days were over with us. We anguished over how we could fill those four holes and decided we couldn't do it from within."

Just as Wrigley Field in Chicago seems fated to have lights before long, so the Orioles and Memorial Stadium could be headed toward a parting of the ways. They say it's progress. Like free agents and $6.8 million contracts to .270 hitters with 80 RBI. Like instant-replay scoreboards and cylindrical Astroturf ballparks. Like showing the old guys the exit instead of carrying them an extra year.

It's the new baseball age. Worry and hurry. Spend and offend. Win this year because the future is a mystery. Perhaps, in time, we'll see that the Orioles haven't bought the whole nine yards. Maybe they've found a way to accommodate old values and new methods. For the time being, it's enough to mark the passing of a style of running a baseball team that was exemplary in almost every respect for twenty-five years.

BALTIMORE, September 9, 1986 — For the Orioles, in their time of distress, the two Cal Ripkens, father and son, have become twin touchstones. They symbolize what the best organization in baseball used to be. And they show the Orioles where they want to return—back to their roots and their strengths.

Like those "Ed-die, Ed-die" chants that once built here in Memorial Stadium, another grass-roots ground swell is gaining impetus. This murmur goes, "Cal, Cal, Cal Senior for manager."

Baltimore Orioles baseball means something in this town, stands for certain values and ways of conducting business. It's not just the 68–72 record that galls this town. It's the shabby way the collapse has been mishandled.

A hard edge appeared in the firing of Ken Singleton, Al Bumbry, Jim Palmer and Rich Dauer. Too little grace, too many bad feelings. Not one stayed in the organization. The very mention of Joe Altobelli's name brings cringes of pain from lifelong Orioles middle-management folk who consider the cruelty of his firing an organization disgrace. A good servant was stripped of his due and dignity. This week, Altobelli said, "I was fired by someone who doesn't know baseball [owner Edward Bennett Williams]. I was not fired by the baseball people."

As an organization, the Orioles are fed up with Williams. Talk about a collision of world views.

Williams represents the best of America's liberal urban professional fast lane. He's smart, pragmatic and slick. The Orioles, particularly the Ripkens, are rural, conservative, blue-collar lovers of the slow lane who have degrees in hard knocks.

To the Orioles, Fast Eddie seems too sharp by half, too fascinated with power, too impatient for success and too enraged when he's thwarted. EBW is into politics, power-brokering, real estate and Perry Mason: competition living. Great stuff, no doubt, but alien, almost frightening to the Orioles. Their guiding idea is stubborn, uncomplicated merit—the game played properly.

To Williams, the Orioles Way can seem like a glorification of rustic mediocrity, a celebration of a baseball era that is gone and not coming back. Williams is a man who lives to see the future and get there first. Yet he owns a team of ancestor worshippers.

The sainted Organization got its way when Altobelli was hired and oversaw a world title. But since the collapse of '84, Williams has had his way almost entirely. Now the Orioles consider their boss an illustration of the bromide: "A little [baseball] learning is a dangerous thing."

In the wake of Manager Earl Weaver's upcoming re-retirement, the team and front office have closed ranks in quiet defiance of Williams. And Ripken Sr. has become their symbol. It's not mutiny. It's cold anger as all the old Orioles who remain—Weaver, Hank Peters, Eddie Murray, Rick Dempsey, Scott McGregor, Mike Flanagan, Mike Boddicker and the Ripkens—have formed a grim united front.

Ripken Sr., the fifty-year-old coach, is the perfect emblem of what Williams does not grasp about the team he owns. The elder Ripken is methodical, clichéd, a media disaster. He has no "image," no marketing punch. He has no major league managing experience, no obvious gifts as a motivator, no fancy theories about the game, no glitz or glamour. He won't even utter one sentence in his own behalf. And he has a frightening temper.

Ripken has liability written all over him. That's all the more reason why the Orioles are behind him and pushing hard. Imagine, if you will, Williams being held squirming to the floor as his whole club tries to shove the elder Ripken down his protesting throat.

Weaver has already quit. Murray has let it be known that he'll drop his trade request only if Ripken is picked. Flanagan's contract is up, and now he says he may be leaving. Ripken's son, while saying all the right political words, has also let the grapevine know that if his father gets the brush, then, when he hits the free-agent market after '87, he'll feel no more loyalty to the Orioles than they showed his dad.

The Orioles are testing Williams.

They feel that he has undermined and exhausted Peters, the team's general manager. That he has found no place for former stars. That he humiliated Altobelli. That he has spent for free agents while scrimping on the farm system. That he has imported other teams' problem players while giving up on career-long Orioles such as Sammy Stewart and Dennis Martinez. Now home-growns such as Storm Davis, Mike Young and Floyd Rayford are trade bait. Finally, the team senses that the tension that pervades the franchise, eroding morale and performance, is largely Williams's creation.

"I've felt more pressure than ever before. The environment around here isn't conducive to relaxing and playing," says McGregor. "Everybody is stretched to the max. There's no room for error. If you have an off year, you must be dogging it. When there's too much pressure put on players, it just chokes off their natural ability."

The last straw came recently when Williams publicly criticized Murray, suggested that Ripken move to third base, held out the idea of Alan Wiggins returning from the minors and called a clubhouse meeting to try his oratorical powers on the employees.

Rayford's stomach, Davis's heart, Weaver's diminished fire and every other Orioles flaw have been duly castigated. Now it's time for Williams to prove that he can take it as well as dish it out—eat some crow for the sake of proving himself to his Orioles.

Usual Williams style would be to hire a brand name such as Frank Robinson. Recently, the feeling here was that Robinson would be a decent compromise choice. That feeling has changed. These aren't normal times. Compromise isn't in the wind. Capitulation is.

Big Rip is not Ed Williams's kind of guy. Everybody knows it. That is why he should make Ripken his manager. As a kind of contrition, a way of saying, "We're all in this together. I'm not just the owner, I'm an Oriole, too."

What Williams has done in recent years, he has done from the best motives—to help the team win. He has reached deep into his own pocket for that reason. Williams is no petty imitation George Steinbrenner on an ego trip; he is a smart man caught in difficult baseball times when it is excruciatingly tough to figure out how to maintain a top team. It's possible that no course of action would have kept the Orioles at their 1966-to-1983 level.

But Williams has also made mistakes, hurt feelings and been a bully. He needs to make amends, show confidence in his team and remove the heavy hand he has kept on his team's neck.

Williams should hand the Orioles over to Ripken and back to Peters, as well as to the rest of a competent organization. And then get the heck out of their way.

BALTIMORE, September 20, 1987—All is quiet now. The pain is over. Everything that possibly could be done was tried. But the malady—old age and the evil work of time—was incurable. Finally, after nearly four years of worsening illness, and much anguish for the nearest kin, the patient succumbed.

No tears for the Baltimore Orioles, please. A moment of silence'll suffice. This time, bad news is good news.

The old Orioles are no longer with us in this baseball world. At last we can pronounce them deceased, remember them with fondness, relax and proceed with new work. Never again will this team be measured against old standards or be called disappointing. When a bad team plays badly, it is not letting anybody down. It is just being itself.

As recently as July, when the Orioles won eleven in a row, there were false signs of the old life. Hopes, long flogged to shreds, were raised. One last chorus of "We're not really this bad" was heard.

But they are, and, surely, no one is left who doubts it.

No team in thirty years—not since the Washington Senators of Dean Stone and Connie Grob (career 7.83)—has had a team ERA as high as the Orioles' mark of 5.06. When the Toronto Blue Jays hit 10 home runs in one game last week—a major league record with room to spare—that was the line at the bottom of the page. Someday soon, the Orioles will allow their 221st home run of the year and they will have another all-time record. Only 13 to go. On, Dinger Dixon; on, Boom Boom Bell; on Need-a-New-Ball Niedenfuer and Big Mac McGregor. With 15 games left, you beauties are a lock.

This team is so miserable that no self-delusion remains possible. What a perfect week to schedule organizational meetings to spend four days analyzing everybody and everything. Presumably, no one has suggested a "fix" or even a solution. At this point, only process and patience hold out any hope at all.

MINNEAPOLIS, April 27, 1988 — This might have been a gloriously ridiculous moment in baseball history, this night when the Baltimore Orioles began a new season with their 20th consecutive defeat. Humm, you Bird babes. Lose on a walk, a balk and a throwing error—perfecto mundo. Way to tie that all-time American League record. Hey, why not go for 24 and the twentieth-century record.

Innocent, goofy and harmless. That's how it ought to be now, making the best of the worst. Evoking tales of the thirties Brownies, the forties Pirates, the fifties Senators and the sixties Mets. Bad isn't sad in baseball, it's just unique, eccentric, endearing and inevitable. Somebody has to be at the bottom. Joe Garagiola and Bob Uecker have made fortunes milking their gaffes. Baseball has always had its clown princes and beloved buffoons. But that's not how it felt here in the Metrodome tonight.

These Woes, these Zer-Os, make themselves, and everybody who comes in contact with their magnificent losing streak, feel depressed.

The Orioles, you see, are mostly nice people—soft-spoken, unpretentious. They want to do the right thing. So they feel guilty. Enormously guilty. About everything. This is all an incredibly big deal to them. They're suffering. And they can't help but want you to know it; that's all the dignity they have left.

It wouldn't be so bad if they didn't care. But most do. Larry Sheets rubbed Eddie Murray's shoulders in the clubhouse, moments after a ninth-inning rally fell short, rubbed them as you would a favorite brother's so he wouldn't cry. But it was Sheets who seemed near tears. "It's just not to be right now," murmured Sheets.

"I admire these players," said Frank Robinson this evening. "Nobody's really gone off the deep end. All except one game, there's been a real effort. I can't ask 'em to play any harder."

This evening's battery, Scott McGregor and Terry Kennedy, feel guilty about the million-dollar salaries that they're not earning. "This is my fourth chance to be the stopper," said McGregor, before getting shelled again, blowing a 3–0 first-inning lead.

The Ripken brothers feel guilty that their father got fired. Cal has his name; Billy now wears his number. Mike Boddicker and Murray, two old-school old Orioles from the glory days, say they want to get out of town by trade. But they really feel the guilt, too. They're trying to jump ship after being Orioles their whole careers.

Manager Robinson even feels guilty about letting down the team's supporters. Of one stay-on-the-air-until-they-win radio disc jockey who's getting famous off the losing streak, Robinson said, "We're gonna kill the poor guy." Of the Birds fans, he says, "You would think people would act worse, that they'd really be down on you, and they haven't been. We really appreciate that. The fans have been so great, you start to feel bad for them."

"The fans watch us to get pleasure or relax or get rid of frustrations," said General Manager Roland Hemond, who tried to change the team's luck by roaming all over the park, never sitting in the same section two innings in a row. "When you play like this, you feel like you aren't providing them with what they're entitled to."

All the new Birds, nineteen of them in the last two seasons, move into an atmosphere poisoned by memories of firings and lost faith, unfulfilled promise and high anxiety. Many players feel guilty about making owner Ed Williams, who has had six cancer surgeries, endure their blundering. "I suffer for Ed," says Hemond. Everybody here is into suffering, depression, guilt. Believe it.

A secret admirer sent Ken Gerhart flowers before this game. Players draped his locker with them. "They're sending us roses," said Jim Dwyer, "like this was a funeral parlor."

Nearby, Cal Ripken, Jr., spotted a new reporter on the death-watch scene, one more media type who can't go home to his family until the Orioles release him with a victory. "Join the hostages," said Ripken.

That's as close to humor as the Orioles generally come. They are not so much self-deprecating as self-flagellating. This isn't a team with a jinx on it. Don't call an exorcist. What the Orioles need is a team shrink. They're in the grip of a group depressive psychosis—or something with an equally gaudy name. Just as a good team can play above its head almost indefinitely in a pennant race, so the Orioles seem capable of finding ways to lose as long as they have a goal in sight.

But what is their goal?

What is all this about? How much do they have to punish themselves? How much is enough to make up for the wrongs they imagine that they have done? Five losses in a row, or even ten, is about baseball— i.e., who's injured, who's in a slump. Twenty in a row is about something else.

"Nobody likes to be the joke of the league," said Robinson, "but we accept it." In the manager's desk drawer was a lapel pin, given to him for luck. "It's been lovely," the pin read, "but I have to scream now."

MINNEAPOLIS, April 28, 1988—This could be the day. Please, let this be the day. It is written on every Orioles face on every pitch. They have the World Series look. Drawn, worried, faces so seriously, studiously intent that the idea of a smile or a word of idle infield chatter is unthinkable. You need binoculars to see the truth in the Baltimore Orioles' faces, but it is there, plain as twenty-one losses in a row.

Maybe, a couple of weeks ago, there were Orioles who didn't care, Orioles who were mad or sad or distracted by the firing of Manager Cal Ripken, Sr. But now, not a chance in the world. Not when they broke the American League record for consecutive defeats Thursday. Not now when they are just two losses shy of the twentieth-century mark set by the '61 Phillies. Especially not now when they do not have a single victory all year. In the last 120 seasons, baseball has had countless slumps. But this is The Slump because of that "0" in the win column. "Weaver's Heroes to Robinson's Zeroes," said the cruel upper-deck banner.

All twenty-four Baltimore players are in the same foxhole, under fire. Every day, they are in the national spotlight, followed by more cameras and pencils than some pennant winners. They are jokes, clowns, symbols of ineptitude and failure in the clutch. Objects of pity. The President calls to sympathize. If a man in Duluth falls down the basement steps, his wife will probably tell him he's ready to play for the Orioles.

Suddenly, in the fifth inning Thursday, Cal Ripken, Jr., smiled a crooked grin and clenched his fist. What had happened? On a team where no one—absolutely no one—will visit a pitcher on the mound when he is in trouble, where no sound breaks the infield silence for innings at a time, why would the Zeroes' best man be chuckling?

The binoculars turn; the realization is simple. Kirby Puckett of the Twins is on second base, yammering at Ripken. "I told Cal I saw his wife outside the park yesterday. She must be six feet tall. I asked him, 'Is your wife getting taller or am I getting even shorter?' " said the five-foot-eight Puckett. "He said he thought she was still growing."

That is how the game should be, three weeks into a long season. But, as Puckett moved on, the silence returned. The Orioles were, once more, in the grip of the Thing That Ate Baltimore.

"It's like World Series pressure," said Ripken, the team's only hot hitter. "That's the only way to describe it. That's the way it is."

For a couple of hours Thursday in the Metrodome, the Orioles had, if not hope, then some tingling of anticipation. A 1–0 lead, then a mere 2–1 deficit as late as the sixth inning showed distant promise. Better than those nine runs the Royals scored in the first inning in Kansas City last week. Maybe, as Larry Sheets said, "Somebody will give us one—a walk, a couple of errors in a tight spot. That's what we need." Baseball's beggars receive as few gifts as the poor of the real world.

First Kent Hrbek dialed the upper deck for his fourth home run in three days; of course, he had none when the Baltimore Welcome Wagon arrived in town. Then a long fly ball, the kind Frank Robinson would have caught on cruise control twenty years ago, thudded against the bottom of the right-field Baggie with Keith Hughes in sluggish and misdirected pursuit. Two more Twins scored.

"It would've been a great catch," said Hughes, "but it was catchable."

"My runs, my responsibility," Mike Boddicker said. That, too, is how it is in the World Series; if you've got class, you never pass the buck on a national stage.

Let no one say Tom Kelly and his Minnesotans have no sense of pity. Or perhaps a sense of humor. The Twins' starter was Allan Anderson, who had a 10.95 ERA with the Twins last season and was in Class AAA last week. He was followed by Mike Mason, who walked every batter he faced, and Mark Portugal, 1–10 in the minors last season.

In the seventh, the Twins gave it their all. Anderson walked two. Mason walked two more. Up stepped the heart, or at least the wallet, of the order. Fred Lynn struck out chasing pitches over his head. Ripken took a borderline two-strike pitch. Daryl Cousins called it a ball. Have one more hack, Cal. So Portugal hung one—a real gopher ball. And Ripken missed hitting a grand slam to Canada by a fraction of an inch. Instead, just a roof-scraping fly out.

"Almost got it. Had a good swing," said Ripken. But Ripken also had to wonder if, in this Twilight Zone, any player could really know his own emotional state. "When you press to do well, you squeeze the bat tighter, you're not as quick . . . Support is great. [Team] morale is great. But when you're up there alone, it's just you. Maybe we need to be a little selfish, each do his own job and not worry about 'us.' "

Though the Orioles cheer for each other outwardly, each feels isolated. Glances are seldom exchanged. Byplay has died. "You're in your own little void out there," said Sheets.

Exacerbating enormous pressure is confidence that has almost evaporated. "We got a bunch of old guys who are over the hill, or going over it, and a bunch of young guys who just can't play baseball," said Oriole coach Terry Crowley before the game. "We're trying. We just don't have any talent."

The Orioles, those twenty-four sorrowful little voids, head to Chicago next. Charms will be invoked, like General Manager Roland Hemond's "lucky suit." Some might look for a silver lining to this slump of slumps. A few might blather about adversity building character.

Maybe. But not this level of adversity. "I feel for 'em," said Puckett. "Bet ya, a million to one, they come out of it." Then, more quietly, he added, "The whole thing's getting out of hand."

The Orioles have known that for some time. "Usually, in a losing streak, there are lessons to take out of it. We're so far beyond that point it's not funny," said third base coach John Hart. "There's not a positive thing about this, nothing to be gained or learned.

"We just want it to end."

BALTIMORE, May 2, 1988 — The huge words etched on the façade of Baltimore's Memorial Stadium say, "Time Will Not Dim the Glory of Their Deeds." That patriotic rhetoric refers to those who died in battle, but, in a more modest sense, the words apply to the Baltimore Orioles who, from 1960 through 1985, had only two losing years.

It was a long run of true excellence—625 games over .500, or an average of 25 more wins than losses every year for a quarter of a century. Except for the Yankees, who held it together for more than forty years, it was a streak that would bear comparison with almost any.

Those days were finally, and almost formally, laid to rest in a wild and silly wake last night on Thirty-third Street as a sellout crowd of defiantly optimistic Oriole fans celebrated their club and its amazing won-lost record: 1–23.

Or, as the bleacher sign had it, 139–23.

Have so many ever cheered so much for a team so bad? From the moment Morganna the Kissing Bandit bussed Cal Ripken on his demurely proffered cheek, the order of the night was foolishness. Roars of World Series force rolled over the meaningless game as though the crowd had decided, for one night, to suspend reality and re-create a scene—complete with nostalgic chants of O-R-I-O-L-E-S—from many a pennant race past. Yes, it was weird—as strange as a Fantastic Fan promotion arranged by a team to celebrate its own lousiness. Anything for a buck? However, it was also a night of lovely innocence. Hey, let's go see those poor lugs and give 'em a boost.

In a sense, this night was a burial: for the false hopes of the past four seasons. Then every shortfall finish was greeted with more big bucks paid to more fading stars from other towns. This afternoon, in a symbolic statement of the club's decision—finally—to rebuild slowly and from the bottom, the Orioles released Scott McGregor, eating the $1.97 million left on his contract to give a younger pitcher a chance.

Once McGregor was the emblem of the Orioles intelligence and their almost "magical" ability to surpass their apparent skills. With a fastball that Billy Martin said couldn't black his eye, McGregor won the two showcase games of his Oriole generation—the '79 American League pennant clincher and last '83 World Series victory.

Then, in the days when every Orioles virtue shone in the sun, McGregor was seen as poised and unselfish; he once signed for $200,000 less than the team offered to help "sign the other guys." As he and the team aged, his flaws, like every Oriole flaw, came into the glare of criticism. McGregor did not change nearly so much as the Orioles world around him changed, drawing him down with it. The little left-hander was never much on physical conditioning and his composure didn't go very far once the defense behind him deteriorated; his margin of error, never much, evaporated, and with it his confidence. Once more, he stood for his whole team.

The Orioles could hardly believe the forgiveness, the promise of a fresh start, that was extended to them here in one of baseball's strangest nights.

"I'm quite confused. Usually, when a team plays like this, nobody goes to the park. Nobody could care less," said Billy Ripken. "I'm quite bewildered by 47,000 [pregame] tickets [sold]."

General Manager Roland Hemond, who'd make Norman Vincent Peale seem manic-depressive by comparison, gave the official cheerful, and perhaps correct, version of this spectacle. "Now I can understand why players have always been so proud to be Orioles and why so many move to Baltimore to live. I knew the reputation of people in this area, but this is beyond anything I'd imagined. It's a display of the genuineness of these people. This is America at its best."

For one night, when so many of their staunchest fans wanted so badly to be given any sliver of hope for the future, the Orioles had the good sense to play even better than their best.

New Rites of Spring

March 1985 — For traditionalists, spring training is becoming almost alien. "We used to go to the racetrack after practice in my day," says two-time batting champion Mickey Vernon, an instructor for the New York Yankees. "Four of us would chip in fifty cents each to go to the two-dollar window.

"Yesterday I asked a player how he did at the track. He said, 'My horse won.' I said, 'How much did he pay?' The player said, 'No, coach. I didn't *bet* on the horse, I *own* it.' "

Nearby on the Yankees' practice field, another coach, Roy White, pointed to Exhibit A in his own consternation at these strange new times in the Grapefruit League. With an expression of suppressed disgust, White stared at the compact, thigh-high machine beside him in the batter's on-deck circle, whirring and awaiting commands like an electric parody of man's best friend.

"I never thought it would come to this," says White, who played more games in pinstripes than anyone except Mantle, Gehrig, Berra and Ruth. "The thing is called a Ponza Hammer. They gave it to me to start spring training and said, 'It can shoot fungoes better than you can hit them. Flies, grounders, foul pops.' I said, 'Yeah, sure.'

"One day I had a sore shoulder, so I gave in and tried it. You know, the day of the fungo bat may be over. I always thought I'd be one of the last to go to gadgets, but I use it every day now.

"The big change in spring training is the new machinery. It's everywhere you look."

Will the fungo gun make it to Yankee Stadium this year? "We're not at that stage yet," White said with a laugh. "I hope the fans would boo it off the field."

In recent years, especially in the last decade, spring training has been significantly transformed. It isn't just that players, who once bunked in leaky dorms or rented furnished garages for their families, now own $250,000 condos on the beach.

From the training room to the weight room, from the clubhouse to the dugout, from the field back to the room where a player sleeps at night, almost everything has been altered.

In one sense, baseball has barely changed. Pick-off plays and cutoffs, rundowns and double-play pivots are taught and practiced, just as they have been since the first Florida training camp opened in St. Petersburg in Babe Ruth's time. But step outside the white lines, and the game can seem unfamiliar.

Machines and money, modernity and medicine, even the martial arts and meditation, have made the difference.

Once pitchers ran sprints until they wept. Now some, such as Steve Carlton and John Denny, study karate and do ballistic stretching. In fact, the most famous conditioning coach in the game, Gus Hoefling of the Philadelphia Phillies, says, "Running's a thing of the past.

"It doesn't 'loosen you up.' It very quickly tightens you up. It doesn't make you stronger. After a certain point, it's more likely to weaken the heel, knee and back. I don't advocate running for ballplayers. For eight years I've tried to get it out of baseball."

Once players warmed up with simple calisthenics. Now many do ballistic stretching or aerobic dance. Gaze into the outfield on a morning in Florida or Arizona and you might think you're looking at a wrestling tournament or tryouts for the ballet.

Baseball's highest-paid player, Mike Schmidt, begins his day by grappling in the dirt behind the Phillies' bullpen with Hoefling, a 230-pound martial arts expert who looks as if he is trying to bend Schmidt's legs back over his head until they snap off.

"Stretching is the most neglected part of conditioning," Hoefling said. "You need strength to create motion, but flexibility is even more important than strength because it permits motion.

"Ballistic stretching means forcing muscles to go farther than a man can get them to go by himself. It's painful and it's dangerous if you don't know what you're doing.

"Running full speed into a wall would also be a kind of ballistic stretch," says Hoefling, who loves to say such shocking things as, "The perfect form of exercise is electrocution because then you get involuntary contractions that snap ligaments and tendons." Whether you think Hoefling is a guru or just gruesome, he's baseball's most influential conditioning innovator.

The muscle maharishis argue like prize professional beauties. None can prove his theory and each loves to dwell on the injuries of other men's pupils. Hoefling, again, is an example. He doesn't think much of Dr. Gideon Ariel's theories on Computerized Biochemical Analysis. Same with kinesiologist Mike Marshall. Of small-weight workouts, emphasizing repetitions, which some teams, such as the Orioles, emphasize, he says, "Doing a lot of reps is insane."

Since it's easier to build biceps than brains, almost every team is into muscle management, although even Hoefling concedes, "We're in the Dark Ages of conditioning the human body. We all do different things."

Once upon a time, you spit on a cut and rubbed a bruise. Now, if you don't feel perfect, a battery of trainers, doctors and masseurs try to decide whether you need diathermy, deep heat, whirlpool, ice, massage, ultrasound, acupuncture, cortisone, hypnotism or an L.A. shrink.

A trainer for the Yankees, asked if there is any piece of equipment he might wish to possess but did not have the money in his budget to buy, says, "No."

Once, if you bounced your curves, they sent you to a coach who glared at you and growled, "Babe Ruth's dead. Throw strikes." Now they send you to a clean-cut kid with a videotape machine who does a slow-motion analysis of your mechanics. Past tapes are on file. George Brett is still studying tapes of himself in '80, wondering how he hit .390.

Once, if you couldn't hang tough against left-handed pitchers, they questioned your manhood. Now they send you to a computer wizard who tells you that you're swinging at too many first-pitch breaking balls. Want to know what player in the majors has managed to get the ball airborne in the highest percentage of his career at bats against sink-erballer Dan Quisenberry? Andre Thornton, nine for 11. Teams keep or buy such info. Come on, gang, how can we prepare for a new season if we don't know these things?

All these newfangled methods go down particularly hard in baseball. Other sports, blinded by science, infatuated with the age, can't wait for the latest gizmo, the newest miracle cure or trendy diet. But baseball? From Honus Wagner through Willie Mays, ballplayers "dieted" on steak and potatoes with a six-pack of beer. Now the fad is scallops, brown rice and Perrier water. "Look at what it's done for Martina Navratilova," says Butch Wynegar, thus becoming the first Yankees catcher named Butch to have a 145-pound woman as his idea of a model physique. At least for himself.

"The idea that you need lots of protein, especially in beef, for muscle and strength has been disproven," he says. "Low fat, high carbohydrate and very little protein."

Well, what's for lunch, Butch? "Pasta but with no meat. I just put lots of Butter Buds on it. Except I'm having trouble finding my [low-fat] Butter Buds down here in Florida."

Yeah, the Babe probably had that problem, too.

In fact, if the 1927 Yankees walked into the clubhouse of their 1985 counterparts, they'd probably trash the joint. "Hey," they'd yell at club-house man Pete Sheehy, who was there then and still is now. "Where are the mountains of cold cuts? Where's the lasagna for Lazzeri?"

And what could Sheehy say? Just what he said last week, his lip a little curled: " 'Scuse me, I gotta go get the tray of raw carrots and celery."

Once, just a decade ago, a batting champ who needed knee surgery might be out a year. Now Don Mattingly misses two weeks and has no scar from arthroscopic surgery. Mattingly pedals a fancy new Cybex variable-resistance stationary exercise bicycle in the Yankees' camp and hardly seems to know the bullet he's dodged.

Once a pitcher with a ruptured Achilles' tendon might be finished. Now the Orioles' Mike Flanagan gets a costly new cast and leg brace every week, wears electrodes to make his leg muscles "fire" to prevent atrophy and expects to be back by midseason.

"I've talked to people who had this injury years ago and I'm so far ahead of [their] schedule I can't believe it," he says.

Once no ballplayer would touch a barbell. Now stars spend the spring debating whether to do isometrics or Nautilus, repetitions or mass weights. Wanna hear a fierce argument? Just ask two players whose strength coach is best.

Fred Lynn worked with weights in the late seventies, built himself up to the point where he hit 39 homers, then, suddenly, fell apart as he had one lower-body injury after another. "I didn't know as much about weight work then as I do now. Nobody seemed to," says Lynn.

But in baseball, old hands always ask the same question. Who needs to hit a ball harder than Jimmie Foxx or throw one faster than Walter Johnson? Wind sprints and batting practice were good enough for them. Who'd dare change something as tried and proven as the rituals of spring training? Who'd doubt that the best way to learn to hit, pitch or field was to go out and hit, pitch or field until you were tired and then quit?

Weightlifting, bah. Aerobic dance, my foot. Ballistic stretching, sure, if you want to break your neck. Computer, shmooter. Think Cobb ate carrots? Spit on a spike wound, never baby a sprain, keep your pitching arm out of a draft and always pound that beer.

Sound like the precepts of the nineteenth century? Try ten years ago. In fact, for some extremely successful teams, such as the Baltimore Orioles and Detroit Tigers, who have won the last two World Series, the old ways still are assumed to be best.

And they could be right.

"You don't see too much new machinery or weightlifting equipment around here," says pitcher Jack Morris of the Tigers. "What I do, I go out and do on my own."

"Spring training never changes here," pitcher Scott McGregor of the Orioles says. "Don't fix what's not broke.

"We're glad to see other teams trying something different every year. They just mess themselves up."

Baltimore's pitching coach, Ray Miller, says, "The Yankees sound like they're trying to play in the NFL. Baseball's not nearly as much a sport of muscle as it is a game of conditioned reflex and mental alertness.

"You see teams with these 'complexes' with six fields where they're taking BP on every field. We've never had that luxury, so we've spent our time on the little field working on base running, signs, relays, cutoffs, bunt plays, bunt defenses and all the other boring fundamentals. Those things never change. And we think they win more games."

What does the future hold?

"In all the science fiction movies, you see these humanoid robots from the future," Miller says. "Someday I figure us coaches will just be robots like that. They'll put us back in our lockers at night, all slumped over. Then, in the morning, the manager will just come in, flip a switch on our chests and we'll come to life again."

Miller sees White aiming his fungo gun toward the Yankees' outfielders and says, "You think somebody's not working on it?"

New Lights of Wrigley

CHICAGO, August 8, 1988 — As evening fell and the house lights came up, the old brick walls turned a deeper shade of red. The ivy on those bricks became, if anything, an even more lush hue of green. As the sun set, a firm sweet summer wind arrived, snapping the flags on the roof to attention and blowing the heat and humidity of a stifling day out toward Lake Michigan.

Everything about Wrigley Field, from the Cubs' white home uniforms to the baby-blue togs of the Philadelphia Phillies, became sharper, crisper, just a little bit more beautiful than it has been for the past seventy-two years. Like a painting that gains depth and strength as a master makes his final strokes to emphasize contrast, the most praised ballpark in the National League got better Monday night.

It will take this tradition-loving city some time—perhaps a long, grudging time—to learn what the rest of baseball has known for generations. All things being equal, baseball is a tad better at night. More dramatic, more vivid, cooler, more accessible to far more people. That, to put it simply, is why twenty-five of twenty-six major league teams play most of their games at night. The parallel to theater is accurate; you can't charge as much for a matinee. As the day dies, the night and baseball seem to arrive in tandem, one leading the other along, the purples of sundown announcing the lineups. No other American sport uses the changing sky so effectively as a visual overture.

Many here have embraced the six compact, unobtrusive light standards above this historic yard. For the vast majority of fans, facing out toward the field, the lights are behind and above them—effectively out of their vision. Perhaps the greatest shock about the new Wrigley is that the lights blend in so well that you hardly notice them. From foul pole to foul pole, above the bleachers, nothing has changed.

"Let There Be Lights," were the words emblazoned on thousands of T-shirts. When a ninety-one-year-old fan threw the switch to the power, there were far more cheers than boos. Were dissenters just boycotting? Or have Cubs fans already accepted progress as their fate?

For the most part, this was a festive and silly evening—a final what-the-hell resolution to a long and tangled debate. How often do you get a symphony orchestra playing in the on-deck circle and 537 media members interviewing each other? (Did someone whisper "The Democratic Convention?") Even Count Dracula was happy. Standing at the corner of Clark and Addison in full black cape and red fangs, the famous ghoul told the passing crowd solemnly, "Zee people of zee night welcome you."

No more fuzzy cable reception in the castle coffin. The Count can even get out to Bat Night.

Many people in these parts, however, were not amused. They feel, with a sincerity that cannot be questioned, that both they and Wrigley Field have been robbed, wronged, diminished. A huge billboard near O'Hare Airport shows a lighted Wrigley Field with the words, "No. I asked for a Bud Lite."

Since 1916, Wrigley Field has been the place to play hookey, whether you were fifteen or fifty. Invent a dead aunt and disappear for a very long lunch. And how can we forget the Bleacher Creatures? Isn't it a fan's inalienable right to get a third-degree sunburn, drink beer until he can't stand up and throw bolts at visiting outfielders?

Wrigley Field has, in many minds, become a symbol of all that the modern world endangers—every rare animal, old building or as-yet-uncolorized movie.

For that reason, the debate about lights for Wrigley has been conducted at a scream for the last six years. The team, now owned by the *Chicago Tribune*, has threatened to build a new park and abandon Wrigley entirely unless lights were added. The *Trib* has a tough bottom-line-first image in this town; many think it was not bluffing and that these accursed newfangled lights have actually saved Wrigley.

Angry baseball owners, fearful of lost TV revenue, have voted that the Cubs would lose any future World Series home dates unless they got lit up in a hurry. For instance, if the Cubs had won the National League pennant this year, but did not have lights, they'd have held their home Series games in St. Louis. That's playing hardball.

On the other hand, citizens' groups near Wrigley Field have threatened every imaginable lawsuit and claimed an amazing range of hardships from noise and light pollution to the lack of parking spaces. The last has not been heard from them.

Just as the question of night games on the North Side has been ambiguous for decades, this game ended with a double-edged conclusion. In the bottom of the fourth inning, with the Cubs leading, 3–1, an enormous lightning bolt lit the sky behind the left-field bleachers and, a minute later, torrential rain began.

The Cubs could decree, "Let there be lights," but some other force had decided, "Let there be rain."

Was this a heavenly vote against lights? After all, this game could have been played to conclusion in sunlight. Or was it a celestial endorsement of Astroturf and domes?

Probably it was a thunderstorm.

In the long view, lights for Wrigley Field is the best available solution for the Cubs and their fans. Now the park itself, which is a hundred times more valuable than the issue of lights, should be immune to the wrecking ball for decades. Also, the Cubs have shown the good sense, so far, to limit night games to eight this season and eighteen per season through 2002.

"We think we'll have the best of both now. We'll have games for the people who've had trouble getting out to the park during the day," Cubs general manager Jim Frey said. "And with sixty-three games in the day, we'll keep the identity and traditions and beauty of the ballpark."

For Cubs fans, this whole experience of joining in the moral debauchery of late-twentieth-century living may even have a shocking conclusion. They may discover—like millions who've felt their hearts quicken at the first glimpse of brilliant stanchions in the distance—that night baseball has joys and beauties that are uniquely its own.

Bigger and Better

May 1986 — Once, and not so long ago, baseball was the game that could be played by the person of less than superhuman gifts. Big league lore is full of fat sluggers, flat-footed pitchers, shrimpy shortstops and swaybacked catchers. Babe Herman played right field with his forehead and, at first base, Dick Stuart was "Dr. Strangeglove." While speed and grace weren't essential, neither was special size or strength. Whitey Ford was a tidy five feet ten. Warren Spahn weighed 172 pounds, and even Willie Mays, that colossus, was five feet ten and a half, 170 pounds—just a natural middleweight if he'd trained himself to prizefighting shape. You had to have something on a ball field, to be sure, but you could overcome the lack of almost any one thing.

Those days are ending, if they're not already over. The major leaguer of the late eighties is a different breed of cat from the ballplayer of just a dozen years ago.

Today's everyday regular cuts like a halfback, leaps like a basketball star and runs like a trackman. He's into weight work and serious diet and could run the majority of NFL players into a puddle of sweat. Check out "This Week in Baseball" for the acrobatic plays that have become commonplace. The next Eddie Stanky better try to be a jockey.

"Sleek, trimmed down but still powerful" is the way Toronto general manager Pat Gillick describes the players, his Blue Jays. "I've been looking for the superior athlete with a great arm and speed for twenty years. But then, I've always been with Astroturf teams since 1966."

"We're raising a society of giants, especially in sports," said John Schuerholz, general manager of the Kansas City Royals. "We're redoubling all the biological effects of a healthy society with our new training techniques and diets . . . They're not necessarily better baseball players, but the star player today is a better athlete and a better ballplayer, too." We'll take the chance that [the great athlete] can learn the rest."

Sorry to be the one to bring good news, but baseball's better than it's ever been, especially for those who don't remember Joe DiMaggio or Babe Ruth firsthand but count baseball time from Willie Mays and Mickey Mantle. Ten years of free agency have had one enormously dramatic side effect that nobody anticipated. Young players, especially in the mid- and late eighties, have gotten more chances to break in, to play and to become integral parts of their teams than ever before in baseball history. To find anything remotely comparable, we have to go back to the early 1950s, when Roberto Clemente, Hank Aaron, Willie Mays, Frank and Brooks Robinson—a fabulous generation—arrived between 1951 and 1956.

Today we may have even more great players because they start from a base of such raw physical superiority. The magnitude of the phenomenon is so big that baseball hasn't even noticed it—a classic case of not seeing the forest for the trees. Just look at the 1986 World Series: Roger Clemens, Dwight Gooden, Ron Darling, Sid Fernandez, Oil Can Boyd, Roger McDowell and Calvin Schiraldi—the cores of the teams' pitching staffs—have all been in the majors three full years or less. Bruce Hurst and Bobby Ojeda are ancient. They have four full seasons under their belts.

Other Series starters in the same three-years-or-less category: Marty Barrett, Wally Backman, Len Dykstra, Spike Owen, Rafael Santana, Kevin Mitchell. Old-timers like Wade Boggs and Darryl Strawberry are eligible for pensions. They've been around all of four years.

Look at recent batting champions Don Mattingly and Tony Gwynn, or RBI leader Joe Carter. The same: three years or less. Or just mention the megaphenoms of '86—Pete Incaviglia, Jose Canseco, Wally Joyner, Danny Tartabull, Cory Snyder and the next true mind-bender, Eric Davis.

Baseball's never seen a time like this. In a sport where stars last for twenty seasons, such dominance by the most youthful demographic sliver is unheard of. In fact, you haven't heard of it because nobody's noticed. Why? Because it's impossible. So why look for it?

Now we have Glenn, Alvin, Eric and Storm Davis, Tony and Sid Fernandez, Julio and John Franco, Juan Samuel, Mel Hall, Teddy Higuera, Dennis Rasmussen, Tom Browning, Bret Saberhagen, Frank Viola, Todd Worrell, Orel Hershiser and Charlie Kerfeld.

Yep, you got it. Not one had played a full season on Opening Day just four years ago. And there are dozens more, like Phil Bradley, Mariano Duncan, Shawon Dunston, Mark Eichhorn and Mike Pagliarulo. Striking out 200 men, like Floyd Youmans, or scoring 100 runs, like Oddibe McDowell, or stealing 50 bases, like John Cangelosi, or batting .300, like Scott Fletcher, or driving in 100 runs, like Jim Presley, barely gets you mentioned.

Oops, forgot nearly half of the AL's ERA leaders: Danny Jackson, Kirk McCaskill, Jimmy Key and Mark Gubicza. Oh, okay, throw in AL strikeout champion Mark Langston.

Baseball has always been extraordinarily lucky. Dumb lucky. And it's happened again. All these outstanding young players are arriving at a time when we have a superstar vacuum. The people who defined the game from the late sixties through the early eighties—just listen to the names, we'll be telling them to our grandchildren: Pete Rose, Reggie Jackson, Steve Carlton, Tom Seaver, Jim Palmer, Don Sutton, Phil Niekro, Rod Carew —have all either retired or should.

Let's step back now and ask the big thumb-sucking questions. Why was the Rose-Seaver-Jackson generation—including recent retirees like Carl Yastrzemski, Johnny Bench, Willie Stargell and Jim Palmer—so strong? Why is the generation behind them, the guys in the twenty-eight-to-thirty-eight-year-old category, so weak? (And, brother, it is weak. After you get past Eddie Murray, Gary Carter, Dale Murphy, Mike Schmidt, George Brett and Jim Rice, the Cooperstown candidates dwindle fast.) And why the glut of talent now?

Let's try this simplification on for size. American kids born in the forties grew up on the golden baseball of the 1950s—Ted Williams, Willie Mays, Warren Spahn and all that mythic good stuff. So they became baseballers.

American children born in the fifties developed their tastes and made their career choices in the very period when the NFL was blossoming and football began to challenge baseball as the nation's favorite sport; also, the NBA came of age. The result: Walter Payton and Julius Erving didn't ask for baseball gloves for Christmas.

And finally, kids born in the sixties matured in the seventies —in the post-Vietnam era, when the violence of football made it less popular and the lucrative, pastoral pleasures of baseball were once again in vogue. Push the line of arbitrary demarcation back a little and we see Rickey Henderson (born 1958) and Tim Raines (1959) as forerunners of this breed of coulda-been-anything jocks who picked baseball.

Okay, so it's hopelessly broad-brush and maybe you couldn't really prove it. But it feels nice.

It's also possible that free agency had another long-term effect that paved the way for new blood. All that free-agent money tended to encourage established major leaguers to rest on their laurels, rest their injuries and lose their hunger. Dozens of Disco Dan Fords essentially retired the day they hit the jackpot. They were deadwood ready to be replaced. And owners are still paying them tens of millions of dollars in alimony.

What we see is a combination of two patterns. We're getting rid of the players who've been around so long that we're sick of looking at them and hearing about them, no matter how interesting they've been for twenty years. And we're getting dozens of new players of comparable skill, whom we barely know. We haven't even been able to give them nicknames yet. We crave the details of these new life stories. We want to know which ones, like Gooden, almost before we can herald them, will find ways to start going downhill.

On top of all other factors, the modern ballplayer is simply bigger and more gifted than his predecessor.

Baseball is still divided into new-wave teams—e.g., the St. Louis Cardinals, who are in love with speed and defense—and other more tradition-minded organizations that revere the home run and the heady finesse player who could only thrive playing on natural-grass fields. "Clubs like the Orioles and Angels really should not be able to win on Astroturf," said Toronto's Gillick. "They don't have the lateral movement to cut off the alleys or take the extra base on offense. Turf teams have an [inherent] advantage. It's easier for the pure athlete to adjust to the grass game than it is for the bulkier power-oriented player to adjust to our turf."

"What drives me crazy," said Kansas City's Schuerholz, "is thinking of all those fifty-sixth men suited up on big NCAA football teams who are wonderful athletes but are never going to play a down. They get on weights, bulk up, and we lose 'em forever. There are so many potential ballplayers who are attracted by the hoopla of college football. It's tough to convince a kid to turn down a chance to run on the field in front of beautiful cheerleaders with sixty thousand people screaming and growling. If the teenager has a choice between the Notre Dame Golden Dome and a bus ride in Kingsport, Tennessee, we lose, even though we know that he has a vastly better chance for a far longer and richer career in baseball."

"It's more difficult to attract the top black athlete. The more immediate gratification is not in baseball. It's not the shortest route, though the ultimate payoff is much higher. We go where the talent is and where it's motivated to play baseball—Latin America," says Gillick.

"Of the 175 players we have under contract, 25 are from the Dominican Republic," said Oakland general manager Sandy Alderson. "Other clubs, like Toronto, Houston and Pittsburgh, also think that the raw talent is in Latin America." In 1985, nine players from one small town—San Pedro de Macoris, in the Dominican Republic—appeared in the playoffs.

Most modern team-builders would echo Alderson when he said, "We scout tools, not previous [baseball] performance." Yet a minority still despises the trend.

"I hate Astroturf," said Texas general manager Tom Grieve, a former big leaguer. He hates the bizarre brand of baseball it engenders, complete with chop hits, ground balls that scoot to the wall for triples and Texas League bloops that take thirty-foot-high hops to become stand-up doubles. The excellent athlete who is basically converted to baseball never catches up with the subtle skills—built over a lifetime—that traditionalists feel are essential to the sport.

"I really think we knew how to play the game better in the old days," said Grieve. "I look at my own kids, and the only time they play is in an organized league. Don't you learn more about something if you do it because you love it? Now it's just another kind of piano practice. I look at the six- and seven-year-olds with all the fathers barking at them—and they've got to be miniature nervous wrecks."

Grieve even resists the ubiquitous trend toward drafting and signing the "best available athlete," a phrase borrowed from football.

"I liked Mike Ditka's approach in the NFL," said Grieve. "When he coached at Dallas, they believed their computer could measure everything. But Ditka always fought the computer and said, 'I want the guys who can play the game.' And when he got to Chicago, he went for the Mike Singletarys who weren't the right shape but they had heart and an intuition for the game."

On two points everybody agrees.

First, "the whole physical culture process has been improved—nutrition, work habits, year-round training," said Harry Dalton, general manager of the Milwaukee Brewers. "Even in the mid-seventies your players still had off-season jobs. Nobody worked all winter to improve his body. Now, when a $300,000-to-$600,000 season at the end of your career is worth ten times as much as the early seasons of your career, you see the thirty-two-to-thirty-three-year-old player working like a demon so he can last until he's thirty-nine . . . Do you know that Bobby Doerr retired at thirty-three? Nobody will ever do that again."

Second, "weight training can transform players of all types. It has made Jose Canseco," said Oakland's Alderson. "He added thirty-five to forty pounds, and that extra bat speed put him over the top." A decade ago, weights were suspect; twenty years ago, anathema.

Bulk, however, means debate. The game's most controversial trend is the 1980s infatuation with huge pitchers. Walter Johnson, the Big Train, who was six feet one, would be considered a shrimp today. The average height now is a fraction under six-three and growing. As Milwaukee's Dalton said, "We've switched to the thinking that the guy six-four is four inches more impressive-looking out there. He's more likely to have the exceptional fastball. When you come up with one, it's worth all the tribulation."

"There are less minor leagues today, so we can't use the Branch Rickey theory of signing everybody, throwing 'em up against a wall and seeing what sticks. We have to be more selective initially," said Oakland's Alderson. "So we want the big pitcher—at least six-two, and six-five is no problem. The off-speed stuff can be taught."

Teams such as the Twins, Yankees, Mariners, Red Sox, Brewers, Rangers, Braves, Cubs, Phillies, Reds, Astros, Expos, Pirates and Giants have gone so size-crazy that they look as if they're prepping for a ten-man tag team wrestling show. At six-two, 210 pounds, Nolan Ryan was only the ninth-biggest pitcher on the Astros' forty-man preseason roster in 1986. Go back a dozen years, and on the combined roster staffs of the Dodgers, Giants, Cardinals, Mets and Cubs—a total of ninety-nine pitchers—there were only three men listed as six foot four. The human race hasn't evolved that fast.

What's fascinating is that the teams with the consistently best pitching of recent years—i.e., the Dodgers, Mets, Blue Jays and Royals —not only reject this Big Pitcher theory but think it's dead backward. "We have done a study of the size of winning pitchers, and we've concluded that we want to go against the trend. We don't like big pitchers. For starters, anybody higher than six-four you can have," said Schuerholz. "We think that six-one, 180 pounds, to six-four, 205, is ideal." The Royals' top low-minors prospect, Scott Bankhead, is five-nine.

"We don't knock the ninety-mile-an-hour fastball, but we also want to know if he can throw strikes, change speeds and throw three or four pitches," said Peters of Baltimore. "The bigger the pitcher, the less likely he can do those other three things . . . You wouldn't take a second look at Bret Saberhagen if you judged by physique [six-one, 160]."

"It's hard to keep a big pitcher compact. They have a tendency to fly open and not have a consistent delivery," said Gillick of Toronto. "The pitcher who's five-eleven to six-two is the best."

"Maybe we'll change our whole philosophy," said Grieve, laughing, when told how successful the teams are that disagree with him.

Amid all this flux and fulmination, it's nice to know that one position on the roster hasn't changed. We may have giant pitchers and semi-late-inning "setup men" in the bullpen and back-flipping shortstops and Mr. Olympus outfielders who could throw the javelin in 1988 in Seoul. But nobody has found a way to make a catcher who doesn't look like a refugee from a glue factory.

Farewell, Old School

May 1986 — Most baseball managers of fifteen years ago couldn't get a job today. Of all the game's recent changes, none is more visible than this radical transformation in managers—from their outward style to game strategies to basic personality types and backgrounds.

"If Earl Weaver came along today, nobody would hire him. Never even give him a chance," said Oakland's general manager Sandy Alderson. "And that's wrong. That shows you how much things have changed and also how much debate there is over whether we're going in the right direction."

Look at the skippers of the early seventies and we see autocrats and disciplinarians—hot-tempered and poorly educated men who lived by intuition; strong, silent types who would freeze up on camera and malaprop artists who mangled the language. Any one of those qualities would be a liability now. Two might be fatal.

Looking at the managers of the late eighties, we see gung-ho, positive-thinking, slick-talking motivators and psychologically acute ego strokers who never miss a public relations opportunity. We also find well-rounded and well-educated men who may even have advanced degrees in law, literature or mathematics.

Instead of a tobacco-chewing midget who cusses a blue streak, we're more likely to encounter a computer-literate innovator who keeps a computer beside him in the dugout, has a satellite dish on his roof and keeps instructional TV monitors all over his clubhouse. We may even find a gentleman so mild-mannered that he'd rather be fired than argue with an umpire.

First, for perspective, let's look back. Here they are, a diverse gang from 1971:

Silent, milk-sipping Danny Murtaugh in his rocking chair. Leo Durocher the martinet. Square-jawed men of military stamp who would never take a course in sensitivity training: Ralph (the Major) Houk, Gil Hodges, Red Schoendienst, Walter Alston, Ted Williams, Bill Rigney and Alvin Dark. Violent-tempered former players who demanded that you do it their way: Weaver, Billy Martin, Gene Mauch, Dave Bristol, Harry Walker and Frank Lucchesi. Plus the assorted inoffensive musical-chairs lifers from the good-ol'-boy network: Charlie Fox, Lum Harris, Preston Gomez, Eddie Kasko, Bob Lemon and Lefty Phillips.

Now check the current crop, especially those who have arrived recently or have already held one managing job in the eighties and probably will resurface soon:

Tony LaRussa (White Sox), who is licensed to practice law. Davey Johnson (Mets), a self-made millionaire in real estate who has a degree in math and grasps every esoteric twist in Professor Ernshaw Cook's classic incomprehensible tome, *Percentage Baseball*. Steve Boros (Padres), who discusses Faulkner and uses a stop watch on most everybody. Bobby Valentine (Rangers), who communicates so genially with his players that one president of another club said, "He's just their buddy. How can he be their leader?"

Everywhere we look, we see gab artists who love to tell their players how wonderful they are and how great it is to be playing a doubleheader on this beautiful 103-degree day on artificial turf in St. Louis.

Tommy Lasorda, Sparky Anderson, Whitey Herzog, Chuck Tanner and Pete Rose—all sometime managers of the year—have been cut from the same inspirational motor-mouth mold.

Not only are their office doors open, but if you walk too close, they may drag you in, ask about your family, work the slice out of your golf game and make sure you know exactly how you fit into their cosmic scheme of things. To them, you're a truly valuable human being, even if you haven't played in two weeks, and don't you ever forget it . . . or (they all have hidden tempers) they'll invite you into their office again and break every bone in your inner ear. It's the school of managing Weaver loves to call "all that happy horseshit."

The eighties have also seen the emergence of a group of mild-mannered, personable, quick-thinking, organization-man nice guys who "communicate" well, "treat each player as an individual" and know how to manage the media as well as their players. Dick Howser (Royals) personifies the type, and Ray Miller (Twins), Hal Lanier (Astros), John Felske (Phillies), Lou Piniella (Yankees), Jim Leyland (Pirates), Jimy Williams (Blue Jays), Rene Lachemann (ex-Mariners) and Jeff Torborg (ex-Indians) also qualify. These guys usually have hidden depth, emotional sincerity—or maybe they used to be the owner's clubhouse informant.

It's no wonder that, in such an era, Dick Williams and Billy Martin have a hard time staying employed. Their role now is to follow one of these failed new-wave sweethearts and serve as a total shock treatment.

"You can't scare 'em anymore with 'We'll bury you in the minors forever,' " said New York Mets general manager Frank Cashen. "The gruff old codger is history. 'Communicate' is now the number one skill on my checklist for a manager."

"The players are independent contractors . . . more comfortable, educated," said Toronto executive Pat Gillick. "You can still be firm, but a guy who sees things as black or white can't survive. You need to be sincere and honest, but also a motivator. Maybe con the guys a little. The manager today needs to be more well rounded—not more intelligent, but better educated. It used to be street smarts. Today they have college degrees or broad interests."

"You'd like a guy with an organization background in player development, scouting and coaching. Also, someone who's PR-oriented and is a little bit of a psychologist," said General Manager Tom Grieve of the Rangers. "There's a lot more today than getting some tobacco spitter who beats the players down. You've got to bring a lot more to the party. We want somebody who accentuates the positive."

Milwaukee's Harry Dalton sees a tendency toward younger, untried people. "The musical-chairs game of rehiring the same managers is gone."

Once the monosyllabic Dutch uncle type, such as Joe Altobelli, Danny Ozark or Don Zimmer, could corner a player on a cross-country flight for a meandering heart-to-heart. Now—lights, camera, action—that's not enough. Those guys get publicly mocked.

"The good manager always had to be part psychologist and father confessor. But now he has to be able to draw together his thoughts and emotions and convey them to the world in a split second, often right after he's lost a tough game," said John Schuerholz, general manager of the world champion Kansas City Royals.

"We're more of a media society now, and the manager is the one who presents your organization to the public. We're the number one fishbowl industry in the country. The manager has a huge responsibility as spokesman. Some old-style managers haven't been able to withstand the crunch of that," continued Schuerholz. "It's no accident that the most successful managers—Herzog, Weaver, Lasorda, Anderson, Howser—often speak to the team by what they say on TV and in the papers. You don't need team meetings to set your club's tone.

"Maybe Casey Stengel was ahead of his time. He spoke Martian, but he made his point."

Ol' Case would never have understood Sabermetrics—the new pseudo-science of baseball stats. Today he might have to pass a test on *The Elias Baseball Analyst* or *The Bill James Baseball Abstract*. Want controversy? Start here.

Valentine, and several other managers including Johnson, have computers in their dugouts that spit out esoteric numbers. Any pitcher versus any hitter. The probability of a certain pitch being thrown or hit on a certain count. A player's career figures in specific circumstances—say, with men in scoring position with two out in the late innings of a close game (honest). Performance day versus night, home versus away, on grass versus on artificial turf, month-by-month or versus left- and right-handed pitching—it's all there. And much more.

Of course, you might expect this of Valentine. He's the guy who has done away with the advance scout who reports on upcoming opponents. Instead, Valentine tapes every game in creation off his satellite dish and condenses the previous seven games of every team the Rangers are about to play. Watch a game in half an hour or study the previous twenty-five at bats of any particular hitter. Valentine has three television monitors in the clubhouse and three more in the team TV room. They're on from 3 P.M. until after the game.

"A scouting report is just words," Grieve said. "It doesn't give you a picture. If a young pitcher sees Eddie Murray repeatedly chase a par-

336

ticular pitch in certain situations, it makes an impression. He says, 'I bet I can get him out with sliders down and in.' "

Although Valentine may be the extreme case, everybody is stat-crazy these days. Schuerholz photocopied and marked up 100 pages of the 430-page Elias Analyst for Howser. Nobody's laughing. They're world champs.

"The older GMs and managers are slow to go to the new stat theories," said Dalton, who built winners in Baltimore, California and Milwaukee. "We still play eyeball baseball. There are so many variables. All the facts in those books don't tell you whether the grounds crew [left a pebble out of place] or whether Jim Gantner's baby was sick last night and he didn't sleep. We tend to think more about that.

"We're seeing a disagreement between generations—the computer-literate and us old fuds—in which each side has a tendency to believe too firmly in its own view while being too jaundiced toward the other," said Dalton. "I still want to know about the impending divorce or the pulled muscle, not that some guy is one for seven off left-handers in the day at home on grass. But facts are facts, and when the [statistical] base is large enough, you can use it."

The computer wave may already have begun to recede, leaving behind some newly chastened skeptics. "We were known early for being computerized," said Alderson, "but we dumped it at the tactical [dug-out] level while keeping it at the strategic [front office] level.

"We found that [statistical] stuff began to override all the other managerial tools—intuition, human relationships, recent trends and hot streaks. We began to have doubts about a computer in a foxhole setting . . . I was a marine lieutenant in Vietnam and there's a heat-of-battle mentality. You don't want your players thinking that the manager has more faith in the machine than he has in them."

"Weaver isolated the important stats fifteen years ago," growled the Mets' Cashen. "Every hitter versus every pitcher; hitters versus left- and right-handed pitching; and recent streaks to see who's hot and who's cold. The first guy to keep those stats with sophistication—on index cards—was Bob Brown in the Orioles' front office. When you go much beyond what Earl always used you're just confusing yourself."

Four seasons at the helm has sobered Alderson in Oakland. "If I had to face that [new manager] situation again, I'd be much less concerned about hiring a so-called retread than I would have been. There's a value in having proved you can do it, and it's hard to measure leadership with credentials and diplomas.

"Managers aren't fired because they're incompetent. They're fired because leadership situations change. [Former A's manager] Martin is the quintessential example. He may be perfect for some situations, then, two years later, on the same team, he may be just what you don't need."

"Now it's recognized that there are very few managers for all seasons. You need to have the manager for where your team is now," said Cashen. "After a disciplinarian has gotten the team so tight it can't move, you need a paternal type, an antidote . . . I always thought the best in the business for adapting to managing in almost any situation was Weaver . . . head and shoulders the best."

But, these days, could he—or Stengel or Durocher or Alston—even get a shot at the job?

Franchise Player

May 1986 — If you're in a major league ballpark this summer and see a middle-aged man in a conservative business suit wandering aimlessly among the corridors and ramps of the maze, bumping into people, mumbling to himself and perhaps pulling out what remains of his hair, be especially kind to him.

Ignore him when he babbles, "Damn all agents and their multiyear contracts with trade-veto clauses and attendance bonuses . . . Oh no, forgot to call the cocaine rehab center . . . Wonder if anybody's got a left-handed reliever they'll trade me . . . Did I forget to protect somebody on our forty-man roster? . . . What time's my plane to Tallahassee for that AA game? . . . What we really need is a new multimedia marketing strategy . . . Let's see, I got to be in court tomorrow to testify in our cleanup hitter's trial . . . Maybe I can schedule the meeting with the salary arbitrator for lunch, right after I listen to all the scouts and decide who we should draft . . . Anything else? Hmmmmmm, almost forgot. Guess I better fire the manager."

Take this poor sad creature by the arm and lead him gently to the team's front office. Knock on the door and tell the secretary, "Here's the boss."

These days, your reward for twenty or thirty years of perfect service in baseball, for being the brightest and best in your industry, is that they make you general manager of a big league team.

Then watch you slowly go crazy.

Two years ago at the World Series, Hank Peters of the Baltimore Orioles—at that moment the reigning executive of the year in baseball—collapsed at a party and was rushed to the hospital. Diagnosis: total exhaustion. Peters took some time off, lost a few pounds, then jumped right back into a job that, if you tried to do it all correctly, would be too complex for a man with the brain of Einstein, the body of Schwarzenegger and the enthusiasm of Pete Rose.

Being a baseball general manager in 1976 was difficult. In 1986 it's completely impossible. Every day, you just pick out what you'll neglect first.

In the last ten years, the responsibilities that fall to a baseball boss have exploded. The modern player has changed significantly, the modern manager rather radically, but the contemporary general manager has changed utterly.

Free agency, with the hundred complexities it brought along, was the huge earthquake. But salary arbitration, drug addiction and rehabilitation, big-time marketing and the burgeoning possibilities for millions of dollars in cable and local television money are also recent arrivals.

That doesn't touch all the traditional roles. Make trades. Hire and fire managers and all the other personnel at every level of the organization. Supervise scouts. Oversee the whole minor league operation, from whom you draft to whom you cut to whom you protect from raids by other teams. Consult with the manager and owner on how the team on the field should be constructed and play the game.

"You have a lot of plates spinning on the tops of a lot of sticks," said John Schuerholz, general manager of the world champion Kansas City Royals, "and some of them are going to fall and crack." If you don't fall and crack first.

Pat Gillick of the Toronto Blue Jays, as smart a young general manager as you'll find, said that to run a team these days, you'd "need a three-headed monster. Many times I've wished I could clone myself.

"One [person] would do player contracts, salary arbitration, negotiations [for TV contracts, etc.] and marketing. Another one would deal with drugs and alcoholism, psychological and financial problems all the way down through the system, as well as rehabilitation programs. And another one would work with player development in the minors, personnel moves at the major league level and making trades."

Actually, even that probably wouldn't be enough. What you'd need would be three people with contrasting personalities, training and experience.

Do you need a man with the legal and business training, plus patient, pragmatic charm to be a contract negotiator, marketer and chief executive officer of a business with a $15 million payroll? As General Manager Tom Grieve of the Texas Rangers pointed out, "The days of offering a player a contract and saying, 'Take it or leave it,' are gone forever. One of my assistants made seventeen phone calls, two of them over an hour each, to a player's agent, and that player—Steve Buechele—had only two months in the majors and wasn't even eligible for salary arbitration. Can you imagine the groundwork that goes into a star's contract with incentive clauses, deferred payments, bonuses, insurance policies, annuities and trade-veto clauses?"

What sort of wise philosopher will counsel nineteen-year-old minor-leaguers on saving money or help a twenty-nine-year-old superstar kick drugs? "That rising tide of abuse seems to be ebbing considerably," said Milwaukee's Harry Dalton. "That's great, if true, but it's still out there."

"We have spent a lot of time on drug programs for the last four years," said Toronto's Gillick, "and we aren't going to stop."

Would either the legal eagle or the parish priest type feel comfortable in the role of wheeler-dealer trader? As Trader Jack McKeon, San Diego Padres' general manager, said, spitting out the tip of his big cigar, "A lot of these new guys forget that your whole marketing strategy is the damn team you put out on the field. If somebody doesn't get you some good players, who's gonna come see 'em?"

Trades were always tough to make. Now they're like figuring out a checkmate in three-dimensional chess. Agreeing on whom to deal for whom isn't the problem. It's wading through the morass of agents, lawyers and contract provisos. "Tough, but not impossible," said Schuerholz of the modern trade. Beyond this, somebody in an organization has to make countless crucial personnel decisions that require a lifetime of eyeballing ballplayers. Dalton of the Brewers wonders where that next generation of ballpark gypsies will come from. "Your working day is pulled away from making the nine innings that night as good as they can be," he said. "You have agents calling to discuss their players' future and you're not spending that time on the phone with your top scouts, talking about who should be moved up through the system or who needs to learn another pitch or who you might be able to steal in a trade. You're not out seeing your AAA club with your own eyes. Dealing with the people in uniform is the great fun of the sport—what attracted us to it."

"There are only a couple left, the last of a breed, who do everything from the CEO role to negotiating TV contracts to negotiating with players' agents to making trades and drafting players. That's almost a lost art now," said the Mets' Frank Cashen, one of that endangered species.

"Most teams have specialists to help out in whatever area their top man is not an expert," said Dalton, who knows how little that relieves the pressure.

Relaxed, charming, somewhat roguish personalities such as Dalton, Cashen and Dallas Green of the Cubs may be a dying breed. A more orderly, make-every-minute-count type of personality could replace them.

"Not long ago, a person was considered good if he'd been in the game thirty years. That was enough," said Grieve. "Now you might want someone, like me, to grow into the job. Sandy Alderson [A's], Mike Port [Angels], Hawk Harrelson [White Sox], Andy MacPhail [Twins], Bobby Cox [Braves], John Schuerholz, Pat Gillick, Murray Cook [Expos], Joe Klein [Indians], Dick Balderson [Mariners], and Dal Maxvill [Cardinals] are more or less in that category."

"Baseball is an industry of increasing specialization. You have to analyze what a GM is. Only a handful of clubs have one person who does basically everything, or at least oversees it—Cashen, Dalton, Green, Peters and myself," said Schuerholz. "Most clubs make a clear delineation between baseball and business . . . Baseball had some GMs who got spun around in their chairs when players started bringing in pros to do their negotiating."

On the business versus baseball breakdown, Alderson of Oakland thought he was "the front-runner of a new trend" toward legal/negotiation expertise. "But now, a few years later, I don't see any other guys like myself. The trend is the other way. More with baseball backgrounds—like Harrelson, Grieve, Maxvill and Cox."

What baseball has discovered, to its surprise, is that the most difficult and important sort of expertise to find is deep lifelong knowledge of the game itself. Sophisticated as a $10 million player contract or a $20 million TV deal or an integrated marketing strategy may be, it's not as mysterious a subject as which rookie league pitcher will someday be Tom Seaver.

And coming up with a Roger Clemens or Cal Ripken is more important than the rest put together.

"Now you don't just have to find stars, you have to keep them," said Gillick. "You have to make sure you have a backup in your system for the player who may become a free agent. We have a flow chart here. You may have to make a personnel decision in the minors, or a trade, a couple of years ahead of time because you know that you've already decided not to bid top dollar to keep a certain player."

With all the responsibilities, it's easy for a general manager to lose a grasp on the chemistry or personality of his own team.

"If you don't make the effort, a GM can be totally out of touch with his players," said Peters. "[Former Reds and Indians executive] Gabe Paul said he never went in a clubhouse. That won't work now. Sometimes I go in there just to be seen, just to exchange a pleasant word. With agents doing the talking now, if you wanted to, you could go an entire career as a GM and never speak to a player."

So, on top of everything else, don't forget to stay at the park until ten or eleven o'clock at night so you can chat up those players after a tough loss. No wonder Peters' wife, Dottie, comes to every home game and sits next to her husband. When else is she going to see him?

When Peter Ueberroth became baseball commissioner two years ago, his first practical task was to locate "the competence in the game"— find out who made it tick, understood the mechanisms. That didn't take long. The general managers impressed him more than the owners, players, managers and union leaders all put together. When he wanted advice or a critique, he listened to them. "The GMs tend to have the long-term interests of the game at heart more than any other one group," he said.

"Ueberroth consults GMs on problems. He wants to take advantage of their expertise and create more visibility," said Oakland's Alderson. "A lot of GMs have felt rather alienated, like they [ran] the teams, but weren't consulted on basic issues. We represent the game."

Now more than ever.

The End

High and Lo

BALTIMORE, May 17, 1984—The better they are, the harder they fall.

The greater the skill, the tighter the link to the game. The brighter the fame, the deeper the addiction. The longer the career, the tougher the break. The smarter and more sensitive the nature, the deeper the wound. The greater the glory, the harder to believe that it must really end.

That's why Jim Palmer, a man who has used every conceivable method of control to maintain order in his paradoxical, whirligig life, broke into tears this morning at a press conference where the Baltimore Orioles announced his release.

That's why Palmer, who has always put such a premium on appearing perfect and almost above human blemish, bolted from a podium,

347

dashed down a hallway and drove away from Memorial Stadium and the awful truth it held.

That kernel of fact, which he could no longer escape, was that the Orioles—his team and his baseball family for twenty years—had told him he was finished. Pink slip. Hit the road.

Today, dressed like a civilian and surrounded by coffee and danish, Palmer found himself in a jam he couldn't pitch, talk or smile his way out of. It was a sadder sight than any shelling he ever took on a mound.

"Well, I really don't want to be here," Palmer said to the media assembled in Memorial Stadium. "I thought I'd start with a joke because I know it's the only way I'll keep from crying. I was going to say, 'This is a heck of a way to get out of going to Rochester [for the Orioles' exhibition game].' "

Palmer's eyes were full of tears. His cover-boy face seemed ready to crumble into a half-dozen different expressions: childlike hurt, befuddlement, nostalgia for the long Oriole years, anger at the indignity of his release, disbelief that, despite all his gifts, it was beyond his power to hurl one more pitch in Baltimore.

Palmer had already heard General Manager Hank Peters say, "These are not happy days . . . Today is a very painful experience to me personally . . . Jim Palmer is the greatest pitcher this team ever had and probably ever will have."

As he stood in shadows in a hallway watching the whole scene, Palmer's face finally seemed to register the full reality of his professional calamity.

Once on the podium, Palmer almost seemed ambushed by the subterranean strength of the emotions which, under normal conditions, he so systematically masters with grooming, manners, logic, talent and glamour.

"There's no way that I can get through this," said Palmer, explaining that an orderly farewell statement was beyond him. "I'll just take questions."

He made it through only one.

"What are you going to do, Jim?"

The devil could not have asked it better if he had been playing for a soul.

"I don't know . . . come back in ten minutes with clearer eyes," he quipped. "Boy, this is difficult," added Palmer, who used to tease Steve Stone about crying at his retirement announcement. "Bear with me . . . I hope you've got a lot of tape [in the television cameras]."

Not much was needed.

"I still think I can pitch," Palmer said firmly. And that seemed to hit a button. Perhaps he had heard, and mocked, so many other players for not knowing when they were finished. Maybe the fact that he might never pitch again welled up in him. Maybe his anger at, in effect, being fired after winning 268 games did a dance along his spine.

Palmer stopped. "I'm going to leave," he said, head bowed. "Thank you very much."

Then, just as he did so often when Earl Weaver came to the mound to relieve him, Palmer jogged down off the podium just as he loped off the mound. In seconds, Palmer was out of the park, leaving a charged and sorrowful silence behind him.

"This is a very difficult day in his life. I think it all just hit him this morning," said Peters. "When somebody says, 'Hey, this is it,' it hits you hard. It's difficult to wake up in the morning and realize you don't have a ball game to go to anymore."

"The Orioles have dealt with Jim in a compassionate way," said Palmer's agent, Ron Shapiro. "They told him that if he retired his whole [1984] contract [for more than $500,000] would be paid in full anyway. They said they'd try to make a trade to any team he named, if that's what he wanted. This was gradual, not like an ax dropping on him, that is until today when he walked into [the ballpark]. He almost didn't come into the [interview] room.

"I told him that this macho business of hiding your feelings, pretending you don't have emotions . . . that's a dangerous thing . . . I thought he needed to be human, show people the depth of his feelings. But it was still painful to me to see it come out because it means the end of something."

The Orioles had the courtesy to say that Palmer was "requesting" his release; everybody knows it was jump or be pushed. The team would not even keep him for the rest of the year as a mop-up thrower and emergency starter because they think Bill Swaggerty (now up from Rochester) can do the lowly job better.

According to Shapiro, Palmer may pitch elsewhere this year. "I'll see what calls are on my desk when I get back to my office," he said.

Palmer would prefer to pitch for a contending American League team close to Baltimore that plays in a large grass park with a strong bullpen and a clear need for a fifth starter. Unfortunately, only one team perfectly suits all these conditions: the Orioles. And they're paying off a half-million-dollar contract just to clear the decks.

Or Palmer may become a regular ABC-TV commentator. "It's clear the network would like him to continue with them," Shapiro said.

Or Palmer might retire and have a day at Memorial Stadium. That's what Peters says he is rooting for: a clean finish like the one Brooks Robinson had.

Over the years, many a player has had to have the uniform torn off him. Few guessed that Palmer—so detached, so urbane, so well-connected in the TV/show biz/commercial world—would share the withdrawal pangs of a thousand Paul Blairs and Mike Cuellars.

At times, Palmer has been a prima donna and a pain in the neck to his employers and his teammates. He has been infuriating, paradoxical and self-centered. He has also been funny, honest, charming and anxious as a puppy to do the good and decent thing.

Teammates have seen that warm heart—the loyalty to friends, the generosity of emotion with little people, the love for game and team. Beneath the perfect face and form, a vulnerable but secluded man has always been peeking out.

This morning, when Jim Palmer broke down and fled from the sorrow of seeing his Oriole career come to an end, he may have shown as much of what is best in him as when he performed in perfect isolation on his stately hill.

□ □ □

BALTIMORE, May 14, 1985—John Lowenstein stood in the Baltimore clubhouse Monday in his jeans of many pockets, his moccasins and T shirt with the tail casually out. As the Orioles trickled in from batting practice, there was Lowenstein with a devilish grin on his face, except it was even more open than usual. After the worst has happened, you don't need to keep up the façade anymore.

When you're released after eighteen years of pro baseball, it's usually too much for a strong man to bear. Mark Belanger and Mike Cuellar cursed the manager. Jim Palmer ran off a podium in tears. Al Bumbry swore he could still play and switched leagues. Benny Ayala even went back to the minors.

What almost nobody does is what Lowenstein did. Take it in stride. Call it quits with good grace. Lead the laughter at your own wake.

"Gone," said Tippy Martinez, the way you'd say, "Going, going, gone."

"Still right here, pal," said Lowenstein, grabbing Martinez's hand.

350

"Who'm I going to dinner with now?" asked Martinez plaintively.

"I'm not going to rush off," said Lowenstein, throwing an arm around huge Larry Sheets, the rookie whose emergence made him expendable. "Thanks for all the help," murmured Sheets.

"Pleasure," said Mike Boddicker, leaving it at one word.

"Gonna live here all year or move back to Las Vegas?" Rick Dempsey asked.

"Home's here," said Lowenstein.

"Good," said Dempsey. "You got my number."

"He's about the only guy I ever saw that the game didn't get to," mused Martinez. "I wish I had his attitude. Once I gave up a home run and said to him, 'Jeez, what should I do?'

"Lo said, 'Ask for a new ball.' "

"I've known him since Reno in '68. We were teammates," said coach Ray Miller. "It was real nice of him to let me share some of his world. And lemme tell you, he's got a great world."

What's so great about it?

"Brother Lo's world is spontaneous, intelligent, humorous . . . He can just sit and amuse himself by thinking . . . He's taken good care of his money and his life. He'll go on to better things."

Usually managers don't mourn too long about releasing players who are batting .077 and the previous season hit .114 with men in scoring position. Yet Joe Altobelli was almost beside himself talking about Lowenstein. "Nothing but man. He understood everything . . . A manager's player. He'd give you 100 percent when he wasn't 100 percent [healthy] . . . Don't know if he had a brilliant mind, but it's close . . .

"When [Fred] Lynn hit that home run Saturday, he was the first guy off the bench to home plate . . . He's as much an Oriole as anyone who's ever been an Oriole. We all read the writing on the wall, but with somebody like that, you don't wanna read it till the last day."

Altobelli looked out at the field, punched his knee angrily and growled hoarsely, "It's too bad these bodies have to wear out."

At thirty-eight, Lowenstein wore out from hard and honorable use.

Before he came to Baltimore for the $20,000 waiver price in 1979, he'd been a .238 journeyman with no power. Earl Weaver made Lowenstein a project. "The man's a genius at finding situations where an average player—like me—can look like a star because a lot of subtle factors are working in your favor," Lowenstein once said.

For five years, Lowenstein was perfect for the Orioles. From '79 through '81, he batted 582 times, with 21 homers and 81 RBI, 30 steals and 84 walks. The next two years, he was better—a part-time superstar.

In 632 at bats, he had 121 runs, 39 homers, 126 RBI and a .301 average, with 103 walks.

In 38 postseason at bats, he slugged .500 with 9 RBI. In the '83 World Series, he jumped above the fence to steal a Phillies' home run. And in the '83 pennant race, he hit game-winning grand slams off Goose Gossage and Aurelio Lopez within eleven days.

"The only time I ever said, 'No comment,' was after the homer off Goose,'" Lowenstein said. "He can throw a ball *through* you if he doesn't like what he reads in the papers."

Lowenstein's gift was that he knew how to care a lot and yet be devil-may-care. "Baseball's a serious, difficult craft," he said. "It's also a lotta fun sometimes."

One thing he never mastered was bunting. After bollixing a sacrifice, he snarled, "Evaluate my bunting? Well, I bunt better than a billion Chinese. Those guys can't bunt at all."

Once he got knocked cold. As he was being carried off the field on a stretcher, he woke up, listened to the sympathetic applause, played possum, then, just before reaching the dugout, sat up suddenly and threw both arms above his head in a "Rocky" salute.

This man who ran rapids, shot the white water and backpacked in the mountains in the off-season was once a marine. He played like it between the white lines. However, off the field, he is a reader and a lazy meanderer, an amusing talker and a man with a college degree in anthropology.

Normally, baseball breaks out in hives when it sees a player with long, permed hair and a mustache, a man who speaks in an enigmatic, clipped deadpan or is sardonic and tart. If that fellow hails from Wolf Point, Montana, spends the off-season in Las Vegas with his former-dancer wife and wears sunglasses indoors, he might get shunned.

However, in Baltimore, he was, in General Manager Hank Peters's words, "a key to our chemistry. We don't want a team with everybody cut from the same bolt of cloth."

When cakes came into the locker room, the Orioles would chant, "Lo . . . Lo . . ." until Lowenstein took a bat and, samurai style, demolished the gift. When a black cat once entered the dugout during a vital game, Lowenstein reversed the hex by slamming a bat near the cat's tail, sending it, like a voodoo rocket, across the infield in front of the other team's startled pitcher.

In a game that often asks, as its price of admission, a large chunk of a man's dignity, Lowenstein managed to leave the game with his still whole. He was cut from a different cloth, yet never hid his colors.

Never Can Say
Goodbye

September 28, 1986—Pete Rose approached Don Zimmer in March and asked, "What's it look like?" The Chicago Cubs coach knew exactly what the Cincinnati Reds player-manager meant. In fact, Zimmer knew it was the most serious professional question Rose could possibly ask an old, old friend.

Rose and Zimmer grew up in the same neighborhood, went to the same Western Hills High in Cincinnati. As a boy, Rose idolized Zimmer, who was ten years older and already a Brooklyn Dodger playing in the World Series. They've been buddies much of their lives. Old-school throwbacks. Tight-lipped tough guys. Zimmer has a metal plate in his head from the beanings he endured rather than quit the game. Rose can say he lived for the game, but everybody in baseball knows Zimmer was willing to die for it.

"What am I going to say to him?" recalls Zimmer. " 'Pete, you can't hit anymore'? He's the greatest hitter ever lived. I hit .235. I'm gonna tell him to retire?" Zimmer spits in the dust by the batting cage, looks away, thinks. "But there had to be some doubt for him to ask me."

By April, Zimmer had made up his mind about the role of a true friend. He told Rose point-blank: "Pete, go to the general manager. Tell him you want to retire on May 15. There won't be an empty seat or a dry eye in the place." Rose didn't take the advice. He's hitting .219 now. Though he has benched himself the last five weeks, Rose still says he might play again in 1987.

"You know, they booed Pete Rose in Cincinnati this season," says Zimmer. "It depresses the hell out of me just to stand here and think about it. I'm a baseball man, and that hurts me. Why would you ever wanna put yourself in that situation, if you'd done the things that man has done, that they'd boo you in your own hometown at the end?

"But you can't blame Pete. Not a bit. How many can walk away at the right time? I've been in the game thirty-five years. I can name 'em on one hand."

And Don Zimmer starts to name all the players he has ever personally known who retired before they had to quit, before they had the uniform torn off them. He names all the men who left with their dignity intact. Zimmer can remember only three. "You know," he says, "it just seems to be gettin' worse."

The last taste of glory must be the sweetest. Or else the thought of lost glory must be the bitterest. Why else would men as great and rich as Rose, Steve Carlton, Reggie Jackson and Tom Seaver pay such a price in pride to play a game for such desperate odds?

Why else would Tony Perez, Graig Nettles, Hal McRae, Phil and Joe Niekro—all grandfathers, or old enough to be—still cling to the game even though they long ago reached the last symbolic milestones available to them?

When have so many of baseball's best men clutched at barren endings to their careers with such stubborn fierceness—playing for no other apparent reason than an inability to stop? Life may begin at forty, but baseball careers should end there, history suggests.

Perhaps thoughts of Jack Nicklaus or Willie Shoemaker—men who do not have to play a 162-game schedule—run in their heads. Maybe their decisions have been swayed by the way the public tolerated, then finally embraced, Rose as he staggered after Ty Cobb for four mundane years (.271, .245, .286, .264).

Possibly they remember Gaylord Perry, Rod Carew, Carl Yastrzemski, Al Oliver, Willie Stargell and the way they hung on until they were shouldered out the clubhouse door by their own teams or shunned by every other club. Or they may play for a simpler reason: greed. Orioles coach Frank Robinson rubs his fingers and thumb together in the universal gesture for cash: "They've gotten used to the really big money and they can't walk away from it."

This is not the standard-issue crop of over thirty-five players who seem to lose it every season. That's just nature. What's different now is the slew of future Hall of Famers who are past forty, some way past forty, who will not go away. They have their 3,000th hit, 500th homer or 300th win, yet they refuse to set a retirement date. When nagged or booed, or begged to quit, they bristle as if the very question were an insult.

Only the details give a true picture. The year after he broke Ty Cobb's hit record, Rose is reduced to saying, "What I don't like is people who know nothing about the game to try to diagram my life for me." Cincinnati papers have even run polls with fans voting for Rose to quit. Carlton won his 300th three years ago. The last two years, he has been 9–20. He has taken his $1.1 million salary to three teams this summer and has even deigned to speak to the media. Many say he needs the cash. Seaver won his 300th last season; now he's 7–13. Yes, he's with the Red Sox now. But he was willing to hang on with the White Sox until midseason, hoping to land in an East Coast pennant race. Jackson seems to have a perfect final October stage set for him with the Angels. Yet he says he's determined to play in '87 despite his unproductive season. Phil Niekro, forty-seven, won his 300th last season with a final-day shutout. He could have called it quits with 16–8 and 16–12 seasons. Now he's 11–11 with Cleveland and has allowed more than 345 runners in 211 innings. Tony Perez finally retired, at forty-four, last weekend after six years as a part-time player with three clubs. At the end, Big Doggie didn't scare anybody. Nettles (most homers by an American League third baseman) is forty-two and batting .217 for San Diego.

Of all the dogged old-timers, only one is still performing at exactly the same level he has for twenty-one years—Don Sutton, forty-one, whose is 15–10 for California and is maintaining almost exactly the same statistical profile and ratios he has for the last ten years. Will he be different?

"They don't know when to walk away. Or some know, but they just can't walk away from the cheers, the recognition, the challenge, the money—especially the money these days," says Robinson.

"When you're making $600,000 or $800,000 for one more year— well, in the old days, players weren't as worried about doing with 'less of' after they retired. But they weren't used to doing with 'more of' like the guys now." Good taste dies hard.

"We holler all the time about how great boxers like Ali and Leonard should retire before they get hurt," says Robinson, who retired 57 hits short of 3,000 rather than embarrass himself for a statistic. "Well, you can get hurt out here, too." Hurt in the heart, he means.

Back in 1975 Robinson sluggesd over .500 as a part-time player-manager. But in 1976 he suddenly faded. After just 67 at bats, he knew the worst, benched himself and never played again. "What I'd done [586 homers], I just didn't want to drag it down. People want to look at you when you're fifty or sixty and say, 'I bet he could still go out there and do it.' They still say that about Sandy Koufax, and he's been retired for twenty years.

"But when you stay too long, you answer the question. There's no such thing as that debate. They know you couldn't do it. And that makes you a little bit smaller."

Nothing makes baseball lifers sadder than witnessing that diminishing greatness in their friends; the best athletes respect fine craftsmanship as much as any virtue and hate to see it tarnished by self-deception. Joe DiMaggio, who got out pronto after one .263 season, said he knew it was time to quit "when I told my body what to do and it said, 'Who, me?' "

Nothing brings out the sentimental, even the maudlin, in ballplayers like talk about aging. "It's a mere moment in a man's life between an all-star game and an old-timers' game," said announcer Vin Scully. At his retirement press conference in 1981, Steve Stone said, "I guess this is one of the few times when you get to see your own last rites."

A more astringent perspective exists, however, one that dispenses tartly with the view of sport as an arena uniquely suited to grandiose personal myth-making. People with such a perspective snort when you call Reggie Jackson "Mr. October" and prefer to point out that he's going bald and never could handle the fastball in his wheelhouse, anyway. Earl Weaver is one such debunking realist. He never thought he was "the Little Genius." And he doesn't think it's so terrible that he came back at age fifty-five, for $1 million worth of contract, and failed.

"If we finish last, then we finish last," he says. "I'll at least have experienced it all. If you stay in this game long enough, everything will happen to you." Which, obviously, is why many want to get out, and stay out, before it does. "One good thing," says Weaver. "The memory of this'll help me stay retired. All I'd have to do is think about this crap and I'll never come back."

The great lure—perhaps even for Weaver—is a corny final hurrah. Sutton, Seaver, Jackson and Nolan Ryan (pitching against doctor's orders these days with a potential career-ending shoulder tear) all see it shimmering in front of them as their teams enter the playoffs.

"We all remember Catfish Hunter," says Yankees coach Stump Merrill. "Everybody said he was finished, but he came back and won a dozen games, then won the last game of the ['78] World Series."

The isolated few, such as Koufax and Ted Williams, who go out on a 27–9 season at thirty or leave with a .645 slugging average at forty-two, are such a poetic befuddlement to their peers as to redouble their place in lore.

"A couple have amazed me," says Zimmer. "Richie Ashburn was my roommate on the expansion Mets. Hit .306, played center field, could still run. But he knew, I guess, that it was over. Just retired, even though everybody assumed he'd be back. He was always a classy man, but that was impressive.

"Ron Santo signed a two-year contract at $100,000 per when that was big money. Santo told me, 'I can't do the job anymore. I'm quitting. I can't play well enough to draw my money.' I won a bet on that from a friend who said Santo'd never turn down the $100,000. But I knew Santo.

"Wish Willie Mays had done the same thing. Greatest player of my generation, but I'm sorry anybody saw his last two years. You'd never have believed it."

Sometimes a middle perspective is a suitable place to end. Roy White played fifteen years for the New York Yankees. He was good, but never anywhere near great. After one poor season, the Yankees said goodbye. He'd played on two world champions and he didn't want to bounce from team to team. He wanted to start and end as a Yankee. But he couldn't quit. So he headed to Japan and played three more years—decompressing, getting the game out of his blood, building his nest egg for the long decades ahead.

"Some guys say they keep playing to reach a record, like 300 wins. But that's not really it," White says. "The life is so great that you just don't want to give it up. It's that simple. There's nothing else that gives you the same excitement and challenge as building your skills for years, then going into a pressure situation and hitting a home run, or getting the key hit in a pennant race.

"I'm in harness racing now—and one of the reasons is that, when one of our horses wins, it's just like being in a game."

White isn't a party to all the pity that's spent on aging stars. He's a little sorry that Willie Mays didn't retire a couple of years sooner. But that's about it. He doesn't think that a fine deed, once done, can ever be undone or really damaged. "When you see the lifetime stats go down, like Mickey Mantle ending up hitting .298 instead of .300, that doesn't seem right."

For the rest of it, he understands why a man would sacrifice some dignity so he could play to the last game, the last hit, the last hope—yes, the last dollar, too. As time goes by, White almost wonders if he did the right thing by taking the high road. He never wore anything except the Pinstripes; but would a few more ragtag years as an Indian or Astro have been so bad?

"My only regret," he says, "is that I didn't reach 2,000 hits. Not too many did that. It would be something to be proud of."

Perhaps no one can tell another man where his own pride ought to reside.

Afterword

The Grip of the Game

April 15, 1987 — Friends have decided to give our new son every variety of baseball paraphernalia known to the baby industry. He has a tiny warmup jacket (in case it's blustery as he crawls in from the bullpen). He has his choice of uniforms. If anybody tried to throw an almost weightless Styrofoam ball past him, he has an almost weightless Styrofoam bat with which to hit it. That is, unless he wants to catch it with his equally weightless glove. Needless to say, he has hats and even a batting helmet with an earflap.

As you can see, there's an excellent chance that Russell Boswell, assuming he has a shred of independence in his nature, will grow up to hate baseball. This would, no doubt, be a fitting piece of poetic justice for his father, who has prolonged his own infancy well beyond the normal limit with the aid of this particular game. However, it would be a shame for the little boy.

Baseball was meant, and still is meant, to be irresponsible, anti-adult, silly, lyric, inexplicable, slightly rebellious and generally disreputable. The ballpark is the place you go to play hooky. When you get there, you scream, yell insults at grown millionaires, knock people aside chasing foul balls and eat nachos until your stomach is so full that you have to switch to ice cream sandwiches.

Edwin Pope, who writes a sports column for the *Miami Herald*, recalls that when he took his six-year-old boy to his first pro game, the lad said, "Where do I throw the peanut shells, dad?" To which Pope, with great delight, said, "On the floor, son."

That's baseball. Peanut shells on the floor. As much noise as you can make. And who knows what sort of person might sit next to you and yell what outrageous thing. Once, a quarter-century ago, I heard a man in RFK Stadium vow that he would swallow an entire sports section if Frank Howard ("Hondo, my hero—you big bum," he yelled over and over for two hours) hit a home run. Howard did, and the man spent the rest of the game slowly tearing the paper into strips and eating them.

They call baseball the summer game, which, to a child, means vacation and laziness and multifarious mischief. When you're indoctrinated from the cradle that baseball is officially acceptable, what chance have you got? My plan is to start piano lessons early and forbid the throwing of any ball within a hundred yards of home. That should set Russell on the noble track of showing his old man that he'll do just what he wants to do.

In *Ball Four*, Jim Bouton said he'd spent his life gripping a baseball and only after he retired did he come to realize it'd been the other way around. Baseball has more grips than Eddie Murray has stances and, whichever way you turn, the game grabs you in a different place. However, one of its most basic but least-mentioned holds is that it's obviously a bunch of foolishness from first to last. The more we belabor serious "issues" in the game, the more the small child in us wants to laugh and run down an upper-deck aisle, imperiling soft drink vendors. For summer fun in my formative years, two friends and I would climb to the top row of RFK with a hand-cranked siren and wind it up to such a crescendo that the crowd (usually 3,751) snickered and the rent-a-cops came running to apprehend us.

As well as being many other things, baseball is a wonderful waste of time, a raspberry in the face of authority. The same long division that plagues the grade schooler becomes a joy when it is his hero's batting average that's being computed. Arithmetic in pursuit of grades can be done hurriedly on the bus to school. Math for the sake of a batting title must be completed before breakfast and double-checked.

One promise of Opening Day is that every day for the next seven months the possibility of reckless, feckless escape is as close as the TV button, the radio switch, the morning newspaper, the weekly *Sporting News* or a trip to the park. There's baseball, waiting to burn our time as though we'd never age and tempt us to care deeply about a thing so obviously trivial that, minutes after the last pitch, we're laughing in our beer and knocking the manager.

Even our baseball sorrow is a delicious fakery. Ah, those poor Red Sox fans. To break good china in a true rage, like one loyal Boston fan I know, then have to answer the phone and know it's a friend calling to mock your misery—yes, that's the carefree, wait-till-next-year, better-to-have-loved-and-lost bonding that baseball fans share.

It is with some sorrow that we note the advent of respectability in the game. When men like Peter Ueberroth and A. Bartlett Giamatti set up shop atop a sport, as a suitable career stop between this presidency and that, it causes anxiety; why can't we have lovable Happy Chandler or befuddled Bowie Kuhn? These days, lawyers run Rotisserie League teams and "sabermetricians" cross swords with 500-page tomes, debating the exegesis of comically obscure stats. How can the game be dragged back to the state of ramshackle disrepute where it belongs, thrives and merits the love of children?

Much of the spirit of baseball lies with anarchic men like Bill Veeck, who would send a midget up to bat, give away a wheelbarrow of money, blow up a scoreboard or say that Kuhn was stiff-necked because he never got over being named after a racetrack.

The great men of baseball, though we don't say it too often, tend to eat hot dogs until they are hospitalized or discuss traffic violations with police while kicking the cruiser door. When we scratch the surface of our Ruths, Roses, Weavers and Jacksons, we find appetite and laughter and a wayward nonchalance that would be self-destructive in the lives of most of us.

In short, baseball is brave and scatterdash enough to fascinate a child and fit comfortably among such favorite pursuits as (let's see if I remember) climbing a condemned water tower or exploring a haunted old (Revolutionary War) fort. Those of us who are guilty of scrubbing baseball behind the ears and making it appear a mite more upstanding than it ever could be should apologize and promise not to sin again. For at least a day.